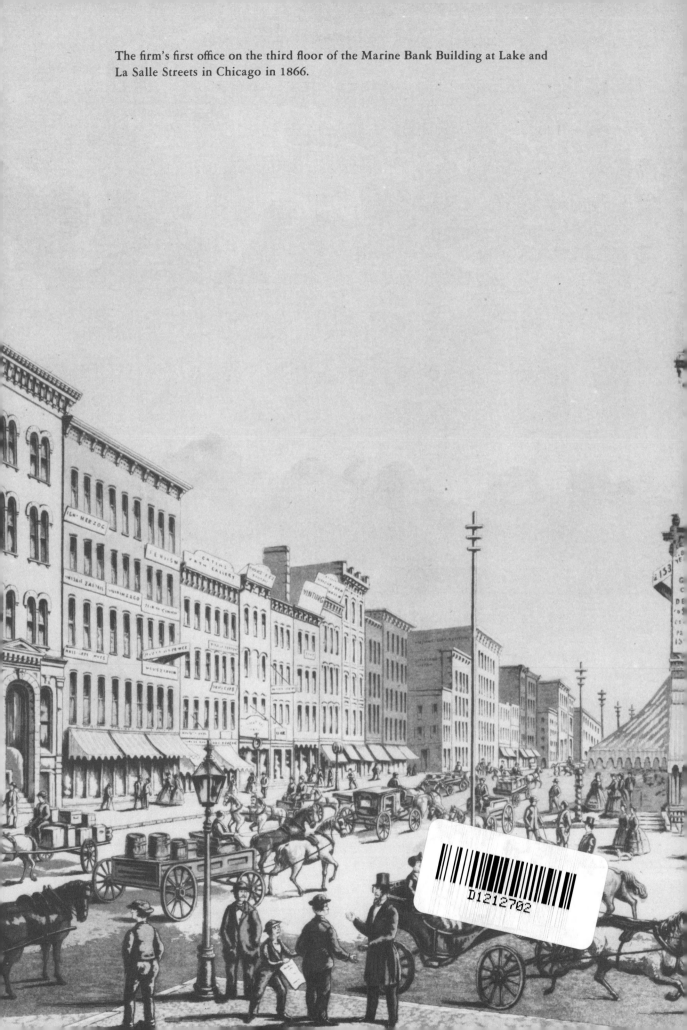

The firm's first office on the third floor of the Marine Bank Building at Lake and La Salle Streets in Chicago in 1866.

*Traditions
and Challenges*

TRADITIONS AND CHALLENGES

The Story of Sidley & Austin

HERMAN KOGAN

CHICAGO 1983

Library of Congress Catalogue Card Number 83-050886
ISBN 0-9612594-0-X

Designed by Mobium Corporation for Design and
Communication, Chicago, Illinois

Printed and bound at R. R. Donnelley & Sons Company,
Crawfordsville, Indiana

Contents

Preface   *vii*

I   *Williams & Thompson*
Founding of the Firm and early Practice
             1866–1871 *1*

II   *Williams & Thompson*
        1871–1882   *21*

III   *Williams & Thompson*
        1882–1889   *36*

IV   *Williams, Holt & Wheeler*
        1889–1899   *53*

V   *Holt, Wheeler & Sidley*
        1900–1913   *67*

Holt, Cutting & Sidley
        1913–1919

VI   *Cutting, Moore & Sidley*
        1919–1930   *91*

VII   *Cutting, Moore & Sidley*
        1931–1936   *119*

Sidley, McPherson, Austin & Burgess
        1937–1944   *v*

VIII   *Sidley, Austin, Burgess & Harper*
                     1944–1949   165

            Sidley, Austin, Burgess & Smith
                     1950–1956

IX   *Firm Matters*
            Sidley, Austin, Burgess & Smith
                     1957–1967   188

            Sidley & Austin
                     1967–1972

X   *Client Matters*
            Sidley, Austin, Burgess & Smith
                     1957–1967   206

            Sidley & Austin
                     1967–1972

XI   *Carney, Crowell and Leibman*
                     1945–1951   237

XII   *Crowell and Leibman*
                     1951–1962   250

            Leibman, Williams, Bennett and Baird
                     1962–1964

            Leibman, Williams, Bennett, Baird
            and Minow
                     1965–1972

XIII   *Mergers and Internal Development*
                     1972–1983   267

XIV   *Client Matters*
                     1972–1983   287

XV   *Service to the Profession and the Public*   324

XVI   *Sidley & Austin Today*   337

Appendixes

I	Firm Names	347
II	Partners	349
III	Counsel	399
IV	Associates	403
V	Law Schools	407
VI	Former Partners	409
VII	Legal Assistants	421
VIII	Staff	423

Acknowledgments 427

Bibliography 431

Index 439

Preface

IN RESEARCHING and writing this narrative about one of the great law firms in the United States, I have sought to fill the role of reporter rather than legal scholar, chronicler rather than august historian. My central aim, as enunciated when I embarked early in 1978 on this assignment, has been to produce an interesting and readable book about Sidley & Austin, citing its accomplishments, problems, crises, and growth and the people and events that figured significantly in its long life.

Whether that intention has been achieved is, of course, for readers to decide. As for me, after over half a century in journalism during which I reported and wrote about lawyers of every kind in and out of courtrooms —and was endlessly fascinated by their strengths and frailties, motivations, techniques, and varying philosophies—I have been educated and often exhilarated.

From the start of this project until his death this year, Edwin C. Austin was a constant and valued source of inspiration and instruction. The assistance given by him and his fellow-members on the firm's History Committee, William H. Avery and Newton N. Minow, was of immense importance. And the cooperation I received from other Sidley & Austin partners, present and past, other legal and non-legal personnel, and from colleagues in their profession not only furnished masses of essential data but brought enlightenment and understanding about the development of a large law firm. Access to the firm's historical files was freely afforded. Many of its lawyers took time from vital duties to write accounts of matters in which they were involved and to grant communicative and frank interviews that were extremely helpful in recreating important and interesting cases and the personalities and accomplishments of attorneys who were markedly influential in facilitating the firm's expansion over the decades in the range of clients and services.

Of inestimable value was the manuscript of the firm's history from 1866 to 1966 by the late Robert Diller. Edward J. Kernan, the firm's administrative director, supplied data and printed materials related to many aspects of office management and personnel. Julie DeBoer, chief librarian, assisted generously with copies of briefs, judicial decisions, and other pertinent legal documents. And much gratitude must be extended to Karen L. Bjurstrom, whose ability to translate hundreds of pages of my scrawling and scribbling into coherent and legible copy and to help immeasurably in other important ways evoked my awe and admiration. A full listing of others who helped appears in the Acknowledgements section toward the end of this volume.

All greatly appreciated aid and assistance notwithstanding, responsibility for all that follows is my own.

HERMAN KOGAN

Chicago 1983

William P. Sidley

Edwin C. Austin

Williams & Thompson
Founding of the Firm and early
Practice
1866–1871

I

CHICAGO, 1866: It bristles with energy and exults in the material progress it has achieved in its brief lifetime. This stripling that in the next year will mark the 30th anniversary of official incorporation as a city has challenged and even surpassed older midwestern rivals in trade and commerce, in economic expansion, and rate of population growth.

The tremendous surge of productivity and prosperity engendered in the recent Civil War years has hardly abated. During that conflict, the city's strategic location as the nation's prime railroad center served it well; with rail and water traffic untouched by warfare, vast and varied supplies and foodstuffs were rushed to Union forces in the field and to eastern cities for export to other lands. In a single year, 1862, shipments of grain harvested on northern prairies by reapers from Cyrus Hall McCormick's riverside plants soared from sixteen million bushels to sixty-five million, and pork production tripled (900,000 hogs packed in three months), thereby wresting from Cincinnati the sobriquet of "Porkopolis." Factories, many of them newly built, turned out everything from steel plows to saddles, harnesses, boots, metal and wood products of all kinds. Investments in real estate burgeoned, fortunes were made, and by mid-1864 the city had seven national banks. In the same year Eber R. Ward, who had come from Detroit in 1857 to establish the North Chicago Rolling Mill Company for the rerolling of old iron rails, produced the first steel rails fabricated in the United States.

Now, Boosters and Boomers abound, and, although demobilization has

1

brought some unemployment and hardship, they hail the present and foresee a more abundant future. And they are quick to cite statistics and examples: In 1840, the infant city had a population of 5,000, this year it is nearly 265,000. Thousands of miles of rail stretch out through the Northwest and elsewhere, a distant cry from the opening in 1848 of William B. Ogden's pioneering ten-mile Galena and Chicago Union ("The Best of Everything" its cocky slogan), which was absorbed this very year into the larger Chicago and North Western Railway. The Union Station is going up on Canal Street between Jackson and Van Buren Streets, the first stone depot in town, with three stories and a mansard roof and a trio of towers, all at a cost of $300,000. At LaSalle and Washington Streets stands the year-old Chamber of Commerce, which houses the Board of Trade and faces the Cook County Courthouse, with its clanging tower bell. The Union Stockyards—officially the Union Stock Yard and Transit Company of Chicago—with its 345 acres centering around Halsted and 39th Streets, capitalized at $1 million by nine railroads and major meat packers, has been open since the previous Christmas Day with pens sufficient to receive and house 75,000 hogs, 20,000 cattle, and 20,000 sheep a day. Thirteen thousand vessels this year will traverse Lake Michigan and the smelly Chicago River, bringing iron ore from the upper Great Lakes region and lumber from northern Wisconsin and Michigan, the latter for the hasty erection of workers' homes or to be sent on timber trains to farmers for fencing and barns.

Scant mention is made of such areas as Conley's Patch or Hardscrabble Row or other dismal stretches of workingmen's shacks and ramshackle cottages on the far South and West Sides. But praises resound for various distinctive elements: elegant private residences, such as a brewer's $200,000 West Side mansion, and others slightly less expensive on Near North Side streets and along tree-lined South Wabash Avenue or Michigan Avenue's Terrace Row and along the lake shore southward to the new suburb of Hyde Park; and Uranus H. Crosby's magnificent $600,000 year-old Opera House on Washington Street off State, comprising not only a splendid auditorium but an art gallery and studios, offices and the city's best restaurant, Kinsley's; and blocks of stores, the finest of them the five-story edifice on Lake Street, "the street of merchants," of Marshall Field, Levi Z. Leiter, and Potter Palmer which will, in this buoyant year, have dry goods sales exceeding $7 million. And more and more and more that stir the compiler of *Chicago As It Is: A Strangers' and*

Tourists' Guide to The City of Chicago to hyperbole: "To visit Chicago is like entering a new world. . . . Nowhere on the face of the globe have the energy, the enterprise and the genius of man accomplished greater wonders than in the city of Chicago, the Granary of the World, the Garden City of the American Continent."

Nor are all compliments homegrown. James Parton, a well-known historian and biographer, visits and will soon offer plaudits in the esteemed *Atlantic Monthly* for diverse attributes: "hotels of great magnitude and public buildings that would be creditable to any city" and some sixty book stores and public schools ("large, handsome and convenient") and many breweries ("Blessed are the people of Chicago and blessed are the strangers in their midst in the articles of malt liquor") and cultural quality ("It is more common to see good engravings and tolerable paintings in the residences of Chicago than in New York").

The circumstances that produced lush times for Chicago during the Civil War also escalated its reputation as one of the wickedest cities in the land, and that dubious renown persists. Amid the many thousands who migrated from eastern cities and Europe to do honest labor were inevitable scoundrels and riffraff ready to exploit the disruptive times: thieves and gunmen, gamblers, confidence game operators, army deserters, thugs, pimps, and prostitutes. "We are beset on every side by a gang of desperate villains!" cried the *Chicago Journal* during the worst of this influx, when desperadoes robbed in daylight and angry, hot-tempered ruffians of every kind engaged in gunfights along the stretch of Randolph Street between Clark and State Streets known as Hairtrigger Block. Now, the *Chicago Tribune*, bemoaning the hordes of prostitutes and "war widows"—women claiming to have lost their husbands on the battlefields—charges, "One woman in every thirty-seven of our entire population is an adulteress!" And the *Chicago Times*, touting its daily front-page column, "Nymphs Du Pave," filled with anecdotes about madams and their establishments' blandishments and incessant stories about the city's evils, piously editorializes: "It is only by bringing immorality and crime to the public gaze that society may know of their existence and take the proper methods to insure against them."

Many of the gambling dens and brothels that thrive within a few blocks of the central business district and on its outer rim have the protection of members of the Common Council—"bummers," the newspapers call them—and carry on unimpeded by venal members of a police force that is

3

Courthouse Square, 1866

inadequate, inefficient, and woefully disorganized. In the mayor's chair is John B. Rice, a former actor and theater manager who reaped wealth from earlier real estate investments and then entered politics as a leader of the Union Party, on whose ticket he was elected the previous year to the first of two two-year terms. Still given to histrionics, Rice dotes on any opportunity to make public appearances and orate at dedications, whether recently of the towering monument to Stephen A. Douglas off the lake shore at 35th Street or the huge intake crib two miles out in the lake at Chicago Avenue whose pumps will, within a year, send purified water coursing through a tunnel into the city's 154 miles of piping. On all occasions large or small Rice is ready with lofty praise: "Hail Chicago, metropolis of the great West, vast in its resources, fortunate in her citizens!"

Among those citizens are some 500 members of the legal community. Some have been well-educated in eastern schools or in the University of Chicago's law department, which had opened in 1859 with twelve students in the Larmon Building at Clark and Washington Streets. Many others have had no formal legal education but were admitted to practice by passing a rudimentary examination after having worked and read law in the offices of licensed attorneys. And there are a significant number of

4

unlicensed shysters operating mainly in the shabby police courts or before inept justices of the peace in an armory at Adams and Franklin Streets. Men of repute engage primarily in general litigation and real estate matters, those of greatest stature represent railroads. Others specialize in divorces which, in this time of social turbulence, have risen to 300 in a single year. Most practice alone, but there are partnerships, mainly of two men—one the "office member," the other the "court member." Most of the city's six courts are clustered in the central part of the city. The Circuit and Superior Courts, with Erastus S. Williams presiding in the first and Joseph E. Gary newly elected to the second, are in the Cook County Courthouse and so are the County and Recorder's Courts, the latter established in the early 1850s to try all crimes except murder and treason and civil suits involving more than $100. Periodic sessions of the United States District Court for Northern Illinois are held in the building at Dearborn and Monroe Streets that also houses the Post Office and Customs House.

This is a city that has already accomplished much and teems with promise of bounties to come, a place filled with hustlers and entrepreneurs and men of imagination and ideas and ambition, and with inevitable problems—legal, social, economic, and political—evolving from its rapid development and continuing expansion. And in this city at this time Norman Williams and John Leverett Thompson carry out a pact made in their adolescence to practice law as partners.

2

Like many lawyers then in Chicago, Williams and Thompson had come from New England states and their compact had been made when they were freshmen at the venerable Kimball Union Academy in Meriden, New Hampshire.

Williams, born on February 1, 1835, in Montreal while his parents were visiting there, came from a family resident in Vermont since pre–Revolutionary days. His grandfather, Jesse, had served as a Probate Court judge in Hartford and his father, Norman, was for years a leading attorney in Woodstock. After attending the Woodstock public school, young Williams was sent, at thirteen, to the preparatory school in Meriden and then went to the University of Vermont in Burlington, from which he graduated in 1855. He took several courses at Albany Law School, considered one of the best in the East, and returned to Woodstock to do office work, without salary, and carry on his studies in the offices of Tracy, Converse and Barrett.

Early in 1858, Williams was admitted to the Vermont bar, but that autumn he left for Chicago, where he was soon licensed to practice. For two years he did so alone, developing a reputation for dealing well with matters affecting business men, and in 1860 he formed a partnership with two other former Easterners, Francis H. Kales and William H. King, the latter a man who would subsequently achieve standing for legal and civic accomplishments that, in the characteristic phrasing of A. T. Andreas, the era's stellar historian, would gain for him "an honorable name and a pecuniary competence."

In that same year, Thompson came to Chicago. Born in Plymouth, New Hampshire, on February 2, 1835—precisely four hours later than Williams—he, too, belonged to a family that included lawyers. His father, William, had a solid clientele in Plymouth and nearby towns, and his grandfather, Thomas, had practiced in Salisbury, New Hampshire—in his office Daniel Webster had briefly read law before embarking on his political career—and later served as speaker of the state's House of Representatives and its United States senator.

Young Thompson's education after attending Kimball Union Academy was broader than Williams'. There were two years of general studies at Dartmouth and Williams colleges, then, after a stint in the law offices of F. H. Dewey in Worcester, Massachusetts, and brief attendance at a law school in Poughkeepsie, New York, two years at Harvard Law School, from which he was graduated in 1858. Admitted promptly to the Massachusetts bar, Thompson delayed starting practice and went instead to Europe, where for the next two years he engaged in the study of civil law and kindred subjects in universities in Berlin, Munich, and Paris.

Upon his arrival in Chicago, Thompson continued his training in the offices of a major firm headed by Jonathan Young Scammon, Ezra B. McCagg, and Samuel W. Fuller. Scammon was a pioneer member of the city's legal establishment who had originated, in 1839, the first of his four annual volumes of reports of Illinois Supreme Court decisions. He later assisted William B. Ogden in organizing his Chicago and Galena Union Railroad and was now influential in banking, real estate, and insurance circles.

Scammon and his partners took an avuncular interest in Thompson and he learned quickly and well. He was advancing in the firm when the Civil War broke out. Among the earliest to answer President Lincoln's call for volunteers, he enlisted as a private in the First Illinois Light Artillery. When McCagg told him, "Thompson, you are too good a man to enlist as a private," Thompson replied, "If I am a good man I shall be a good private." A few months later and before he could take part in combat, Thompson fell ill and had to resign, but after convalescing in his family home back east he re-entered the Army with a first-lieutenant's commission in the First Rhode Island Cavalry. Thereafter, he had an active wartime career, leading his regiment in innumerable battles from Second Bull Run and Fredericksburg to Chancellorsville and Gettysburg, where his regiment captured a portion of the rear guard of General Robert E. Lee's forces.

Mustered out late in 1865 as a brigadier general in the First New Hampshire Cavalry, he returned to Scammon, McCagg and Fuller, where, among several newcomers, the slain President's son, Robert Todd Lincoln, was undergoing legal tutelage. Thompson won admission to the bar and set out on his own the next spring, numbering among his clients Scammon, for whom he won a case in the Illinois Supreme Court that dealt with the number of days' notice of publication required in a condemnation proceeding.

Late in that summer, General Philip H. Sheridan, under whom Thompson had served in battles in the Shenandoah Valley, wrote to him with an offer of a commission as a field officer in the regular army. But Thompson chose to remain a civilian, for by this time he and Williams— who had not served in the war but had been active in securing arms for the first black regiment recruited in Chicago—had renewed their schoolboy friendship and were ready to fulfill their long-remembered covenant and to start a firm that, through good times and bad, setbacks and triumphs, and with innumerable developments and changes in the nature of and ever-developing, ever-changing areas of the law, would have enduring continuity.

3

On October 1, 1866, the partners were ready to receive clients in a three-room set of offices on the third floor of the Marine Bank Building, a four-story structure at Lake and La Salle Streets that was owned by

Norman Williams

John Leverett Thompson

Jonathan Young Scammon

Scammon, the bank's president since its founding fifteen years earlier. Williams occupied one outer room, Thompson the other, and the room in between served as their library. For the next five years this arrangement continued, except that when Charles E. Towne, a recent Harvard Law School graduate, came in 1867 to work as an unpaid clerk after passing his bar examination, he was given a desk in the center room and was also permitted to have clients on his own. In this period, no additional clerks were taken on nor any employees save for a succession of errand-and-office boys whose weekly pay was three dollars. Williams and Thompson shared such office duties as making entries in the daily journal and fee ledger, the latter showing at the end of 1866 a total of $2,357.15 from twenty-five clients.

Their first client was Corydon Beckwith, a Vermonter who since coming to Chicago in 1853 had acquired considerable fame as a skilled lawyer in and out of court and was now general counsel for the Chicago, Alton and St. Louis Railroad, one of ten centered in the city. McCagg also gave business to the new firm, as did Scammon, the latter for personal matters and a modicum of representation in enterprises in which he held major interests, including the Marine Bank itself, insurance companies, and the *Chicago Republican*, a daily newspaper he had started publishing the preceding year.

The firm's practice in its first five years was concerned in the main with matters that ranged from suits to collect money owed on promissory notes or accounts—and usually settled out of court—and protests against tax assessments to insurance claims and drafting wills and codicils. There was a great deal of real estate work involving mortgages and deeds and requiring examination of abstracts of title to properties and rendering opinions on the validity of titles. Among other early clients were Samuel Walker, a supercharged real estate magnate nicknamed "Napoleon" by the local newspapers and responsible for many developments including a Near West Side tract called "Little Kentucky" because its residents came from that state; Albert A. Sprague, a former classmate of the partners at Kimball Union Academy, and now a wholesale grocer and later founder of Sprague, Warner & Company; Chicago and North Western Railway Company; M. C. Bissell, a Joliet landowner described by Thompson as "worrisome, garrulous"; and the city's most fashionable draper and tailor, Edward Ely, equally as bothersome as Bissell and given to dispatching notes urging the partners to put other business aside so that whatever matter concerned him could be handled speedily and without undue delays.

In addition, three other clients had special importance in this period and later and helped to enhance the firm's standing in the business and legal community: George M. Pullman, Western Union Telegraph Company, and Mrs. Walter Newberry.

4

George Pullman had gained a large measure of renown locally and even nationally after coming to Chicago in 1855. Originally a cabinet maker in upstate New York, he had become a contractor and had supervised the removal of buildings to permit the widening of the Erie Canal. Because most of Chicago was set on a vast drained marsh, it wallowed in mud after every rainfall and in various places around town pranksters placed crude signs reading "This Way to China" or "No Bottom Here." Drawing upon his experience with the Erie Canal project, Pullman devised a plan in 1857 to raise an entire mud-mired block of buildings on Lake Street. He hired 500 men to place some 6,000 jackscrews beneath the structures and raise each four feet by turning every screw simultaneously at a given signal, after which a new, solid foundation was installed. He did likewise with the Tremont House, one of the city's premier hotels, lifting it eight feet without, according to a contemporary account, "disturbing a guest or cracking a cup."

Then Pullman, aggressive and ambitious, embarked on a new career— and his most productive and lucrative.

At the time, Theodore T. Woodruff of Springfield, Massachusetts, was among a number of makers of sleeping cars and several of his were in use on the night runs of New York Central and Pennsylvania trains. On a visit to Albion, New York, in the summer of 1858, Pullman was told by Benjamin C. Field, an old friend active in railroad building and state politics, that he had obtained from Woodruff patent rights to sleeping cars used on western railroads and wanted a partner to help develop the franchise. For the next two years, Pullman devoted his efforts to the venture. He and Field contracted with the Chicago, Alton and St. Louis to remodel three of its day coaches in its Bloomington yards at a cost of $2,000. The innovative feature was an upper berth hinged to the side of the car and supported by two jointed arms by which it could be pulled down from the ceiling.

But although passengers reacted favorably, profits were minimal and Pullman was not able to persuade other railroads to emulate the Chicago, Alton and St. Louis. He and Field also knew that if they wanted to manufacture their own sleeping cars instead of continuing to convert coaches much capital would be needed. So Pullman suspended operations and joined the thousands heading for the Colorado gold fields. He was twenty-nine and eager for riches that newspapers and magazines enthusiastically reported as being available to those willing to work hard. Pullman stayed out west for three years, operating a store in Central City, a quartz mining mill and a wagon train for miners heading to the fields, amassing $20,000 and paying visits to Chicago periodically to invest in a shirt factory and the city's Third National Bank and to keep track of developments in sleeping cars.

When he returned to Chicago for good, Pullman was ready to concentrate wholly on the sleeping car business. In the interim there had occurred an extensive expansion of railway lines in all directions and he envisaged a future in which there would be an increase in long-distance travel and a need for what he could offer.

After converting several more coaches for Chicago, Alton and St. Louis, Pullman and Field determined to make their very own sleeping car. In the winter of 1864, their carpenters, draftsmen, and fitters started its construction in a railroad shed near the Union Station. Completed the following spring, it was luxurious and gaudy and cost $20,000, five times the cost of any such existing car. It had, in addition to upper berths, lower berths that could be made by unhinging the back of a seat and the seat cushion

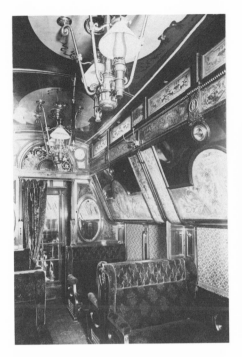

Section of an early Pullman
sleeping car

George M. Pullman

extended to meet that of the opposite seat. Pullman called it "Pioneer"
and it received national attention when it was attached that April to
Abraham Lincoln's funeral train in Chicago on its slow, dolorous final leg
to Springfield for the use of Mrs. Lincoln. Because "Pioneer" was higher
and wider than any other railroad cars in service, platforms and bridges
along the route had to be altered to make room for it, but within weeks
"Pioneer" was added to the retinue of cars on the Chicago, Alton and St.
Louis' run from Chicago to St. Louis. In the months that followed, more
cars were under construction in various railway yards and by mid-1866,
buoyed by publicity and investors' funds, Pullman held contracts with
every railroad extending from Chicago to build sleeping cars. At the end of
that year, forty such cars were running on seven lines and another dozen
were in the making.

Pullman realized that to expand further and keep pace with the ever-
growing railroad lines throughout the country he would require greater
amounts of capital. Among those who had invested in the project that
produced "Pioneer" was John Crerar, a transplanted New Yorker who
had prospered since 1862 as president of Crerar, Adams and Company, a

manufacturer of railroad supplies and contractors' materials. As a director of Chicago, Alton and St. Louis, he had come to know Pullman well. Crerar was also a close friend of Norman Williams, and when Pullman—having amicably dissolved his partnership with Field—decided to incorporate his enterprise, Crerar suggested to him that Williams draw up the corporate charter. This was duly done and approved February 22, 1867, by the state legislature. Pullman, Crerar, and Williams were named as incorporators of the firm—designated as Pullman's Palace Car Company—with its capital stock set at $100,000, divided into shares of $100 each. Fees recorded in the law firm's journal came to $1,000, part of it as an initial retainer and the greater portion—$800—for "services procuring the charter and disbursements."

With an infusion of money from new investors, among them Marshall Field, the city's prime merchant, Pullman broadened his operations rapidly in the next few years. He bought out smaller sleeping-car companies and formed an alliance with a strong rival, Central Transportation Company, in which Andrew Carnegie held a major interest. Then he contracted with virtually every one of the nation's railroads to furnish sleeping cars and, later, his elaborately furnished parlor cars and diners. By the time he established the "model town" of Pullman in 1880 some fifteen miles south of Chicago, with 3,600 acres designed to provide manufacturing plants for the Pullman Car Works and a number of subsidiaries and homes for employees, he was on his way to gaining a virtual monopoly on the nation's sleeping car business and had his in-house corps of attorneys headed by Alfred Ennis. Williams and Thompson played a small role in the town's affairs by facilitating the establishment of a free library there, but in future years their successors would serve the company in a variety of significant ways.

5

Just as John Crerar had been instrumental in effecting representation of Pullman by Williams and Thompson, the influence of another prominent Chicagoan helped them to acquire another major client in those fledgling years.

That man was John Dean Caton, for many decades one of the luminaries of the local and state bar. In 1833 as a newcomer from upstate New York, Caton had been the first full-time practicing lawyer in what was then still a village with 200 inhabitants. As such he had instituted the first civil suit in the Cook County Circuit Court and had also been engaged to prosecute a thief in that court's first recorded criminal case—an action in which he was successful and was paid a ten-dollar fee. After Chicago's official incorporation as a town at the end of that year, he was named its corporation counsel, later served as a justice of the peace and an alderman, and from 1842 until his retirement in 1864 sat on the Illinois Supreme Court bench, the last nine of those years as its Chief Justice.

Caton was also an astute and wealthy business man. In the years since Samuel Finley Breese Morse's initial practical demonstration of his electro-magnetic telegraph and dot-and-dash code in 1844 by tapping out from the United States Supreme Court chamber, "What hath God wrought!" along his Washington-to-Baltimore line, the telegraph industry had burgeoned. Companies large and small sprang up in various parts of the country, and in Chicago one of the biggest of several was Illinois and Mississippi, organized by Caton in 1849. Within three years, Caton was its president and chief stockholder. When Western Union Telegraph Company, established by Morse's business associates with headquarters in New York, set up district offices in Chicago in 1856, it strung its wires on Caton's company's poles, an amicable arrangement made possible because each firm's lines served different territories. Year by year, Western Union absorbed competing lines; by 1866, its original capital investment had increased an incredible 11,000 percent. In 1867, Illinois and Mississippi was acquired by it in a transaction noted by the *Chicago Legal News* as one in which Caton and his fellow stockholders "were enabled to make most advantageous terms for the disposition of their interests." This purchase not only brought great profit to Caton but gave Western Union a monopoly in the city, prompting the *Tribune* to call for government ownership of all telegraph lines.

In that same year, on December 11, Norman Williams married Caton's older daughter, Caroline. He and Thompson had taken no part in the transfer of Illinois and Mississippi to Western Union, but within two years the influence of his father-in-law was felt. In 1869 Western Union, larger in national scope than ever, joined the firm's ranks of clients when it shifted the headquarters of its central division from Cleveland to Chicago, with General Anson Stager, chief of the Union forces' telegraph system during the Civil War, as superintendent.

Later there would be expanded representation of Western Union amid

15

Family group on John Dean Caton's front porch 1885: *Left to right:* Mrs. Arthur Caton, Mrs. Norman Williams, Norman Williams, Judge Caton, Arthur Caton, Mrs. John Dean Caton, Mr. and Mrs. Charles Towne.

strife and predatory competition, but now most of the legal work entailed claims for damages sought because of purported errors in transmission of telegrams or for tardy or no delivery. The partners dealt with these matters in Chicago and nearby cities, but in other parts of the Middle West and as far as Texas local attorneys were selected by them. Such arrangements required large amounts of correspondence and conveyance of data and information to help in disposing of such suits. Not only was this experience of general value to the partners but such contact with lawyers elsewhere and in the main Western Union offices in New York added to Williams' and Thompson's reputations as efficient, hard-working, and knowledgeable.

6

One of Chicago's wealthiest citizens when Williams and Thompson began their partnership was Walter L. Newberry, who had amassed his large fortune primarily by extensive purchases—and subsequent reselling at huge profits in boom times—of land in and around the city after coming from Detroit in 1833. Besides such lucrative investments (he also owned tracts in Michigan and Wisconsin) he was in the commission business, had banking interests, and early in its lifetime had been president of William B. Ogden's pioneering Galena and Chicago Union Railroad. His activity in civic affairs had been persistent, from fostering the founding in 1841 of the Young Men's Library Association—forerunner of the city's first free public library—to service as city comptroller, member of the boards of health and education, and president of the Chicago Historical Society. And the Newberry mansion at Rush and Ohio Streets, where he lived with his wife, Julia, and daughters, Julia Rosa and Mary Louisa, had long been one of the community's showplaces, filled with fine books and art works and expensive furnishings.

But by 1868, for all his riches and stature among the city's business and social elite, Newberry was grievously sick. While his wife and teen-aged daughters were vacationing in France, he underwent a physical examination in which his doctor determined that he was afflicted with tuberculosis and could not live for more than two months. Preparing to join his family, he called on an old friend, Mark S. Skinner, a prominent lawyer who earlier had been the city attorney and a judge in Cook County Court of Common Pleas, to draw up his will.

Newberry directed that his estate, whose worth was estimated at nearly $3 million and consisted in great part of real estate, be held in trust for his widow and daughters, with the remainder to go to the latters' heirs. Skinner expressed the possibility that the daughters, when and if they wed, might not have any heirs and suggested that an alternative inheritor be a library. To this, Newberry, although certain that his pretty daughters would surely marry and have families, agreed. Skinner entered a contingent provision in the will that "in the case of the death of my said daughters without leaving lawful issue, then immediately after the decease of my wife, if she survives my said daughters," Newberry's trustees and executors, Skinner and Eliphalet W. Blatchford, a manufacturer of lead and linseed oil, were to divide the estate into two equal shares, one to be distributed to designated sons and daughters of his brothers and sisters and the other for the creation, supplying, and maintenance of "a free public library to be located in that part of Chicago known as the 'North Division'."

Early that November, Newberry set sail for France. Feverish and wracked with pain, he spent most of his time in his stateroom, and on the

17

morning of November 6, 400 miles out from Le Havre, he died. The ship's captain placed his body in a cask of rum that was part of the cargo and in due time, after cask and corpse were dispatched to Chicago, Newberry was buried in Graceland Cemetery.

Mrs. Newberry had need of legal advice in connection with her husband's will and, at Skinner's suggestion, she retained the Williams & Thompson firm. Thompson assumed the task of counseling her on what action to take—whether to accept the lifetime income of about $10,000 annually accruing to her from the established trust or renounce the will and claim her dower right to the extensive properties and also a one-third share of the estate under existing statute. Thompson proposed the second of these, a move the trustees unsuccessfully challenged, for purposes of clarification, in Superior Court. Early in 1869, the lower court's ruling was affirmed by the Illinois Supreme Court. Subsequently, there would be prolonged and complex litigation stemming from Mrs. Newberry's action before final disposition of her husband's estate could be made in accord with the will's contingent provision for establishment of a library.*

7

The firm was gaining in repute and bore good prospects for the future when, on the Sunday evening of October 8, 1871, the disaster forever to be known as The Great Fire befell the city.

It started in the hay-filled stable behind the Patrick O'Leary family's cottage on De Koven Street on the Near West Side and, propelled by self-generating "devil winds," rushed swiftly and devastatingly to the north and east throughout that night and all the next day. Structure after structure was devoured, 17,500 in all with a value of $200 million, and ultimately 100,000 of the city's 300,000 people were homeless and 120 known dead, with 300 more bodies unrecovered.

Sometime between two and three o'clock on the morning of October 9, the Marine Bank Building fell to the flames. Williams was spending the weekend at the Caton country home in Ottawa, and Thompson had been recruited by General Sheridan to help direct dynamiting of empty or half-smoldering buildings to prevent the fire's spread. But their law clerk,

*See Chapter III.

Famous—and inaccurate—Currier & Ives print of the Chicago Fire of 1871. The artist showed the flames blowing in the wrong direction.

Ruins of the Marine Bank Building after the Great Fire.

Charles Towne, had dashed to the offices when he learned of the fire in time to salvage the ledger, the daily journal, several abstracts, and a desk blotting pad. Before he could return, the building was scourged by fire and all else was destroyed—the library insured for $2,500, desks, office equipment, clients' records, files of correspondence, the docket book and briefs, and other documents.

Williams was back in the city the day after the fire had burned itself out and recorded in the journal that while all activities had of course been suspended during the twenty-nine hours in which the fire raged, it was time, on October 10, to resume the practice of law.

Williams & Thompson II
1871–1882

THE POST–FIRE decade was one of intense and important enterprise and growth for Williams & Thompson.

From the day after the devastation until the next summer, the firm maintained an office in a private residence at Wabash Avenue and Eleventh Street that, like the partners', lay outside the fire's southern border. The house belonged to Edward S. Isham, another bright and busy young lawyer originally from Vermont in 1858 and one of Williams' best friends. Earlier that day Isham had rented the residence to Western Union Telegraph Company, which sublet space at once to the two partners. Isham then took his family to Europe for a brief vacation with the money paid him by Western Union. When he returned in February he formed a law firm with Robert Todd Lincoln, the late President's son and another of Williams' close friends. Isham and Lincoln established their offices in a building on Congress Street owned by Scammon, and in June Williams and Thompson did likewise.

In the year following The Great Fire there was frenzied construction in the burned-out district, and one of the splendid structures was Cyrus McCormick's Reaper Block on the northeast corner of Washington and Clark Streets. Nine stories high—the city's tallest—and fronted by stout pillars, it was designed by John Van Osdel, the pioneer architect whose earlier buildings since his arrival in 1837 from Baltimore included the neo-Grecian residence for William B. Ogden and his family at Rush and Ontario Streets, the Tremont House in 1850, the first city hall in 1848 and its successor in 1858, and the first Palmer House in 1869 and the

Reaper Block, site of firm's
offices from 1873 to 1889

second in 1871. The Reaper Block was ready for occupancy in May 1873, and on the 20th of that month Williams and Thompson moved into four gas-lit rooms on the third floor. And there, after adding another room in 1876, they would remain for the next sixteen years. Gradually they organized in one of the rooms a reasonably adequate library whose valued cornerstone was the Illinois Supreme Court Reports, and they also, as did other lawyers, importuned friends in their native states—Thompson in New Hampshire and Williams in Vermont—to contribute books to the library of the Chicago Law Institute, whose several hundred legal volumes and general reference books gathered since its establishment in 1857 by legislative act had been destroyed in The Great Fire.

For a time, Towne was still the sole clerk, but shortly after the move to the Reaper Block an Ottawa lawyer, Charles F. Butler, was hired at a monthly salary of $166.66, a princely sum compared to the going rates in local law offices of from $40 to $60 a month. Butler was well-known to Judge Caton and skilled in jury trials, two apparent reasons for the high rate of compensation; he did not remain long, however, for he suffered from tuberculosis and, after a convalescent stay in Colorado proved futile, he returned to Chicago in 1875 and died late that summer. Caton may

22

have been responsible for the firm's employment of his son, Arthur, as an unpaid clerk in 1874 after reading law in the office the previous year. Young Caton was joined by George A. Talley, an expert in real estate law who would stay on until 1883. Caton and Towne both left in 1876, the latter after marrying Mrs. Williams' younger sister, Laura. While Caton and Towne were with the firm, they were permitted to have their own clients, using one of the rooms as their office. Both carried on separate practices in ensuing years but neither attained much distinction.

One newcomer who was hired in this decade and stayed to be a major member of the firm was Charles S. Holt, a young Chicago-born scholar with an interest in the classics and the Young Men's Christian Association. A graduate of Williams College, he came to work in 1876 for a year without pay and then went to Harvard Law School. Williams was especially impressed with Holt, a devout Presbyterian who did not smoke or drink and spoke with clarity and crispness. In 1878 he wrote to Holt offering him a clerkship at sixty dollars a month, noting that this amount was considerably more than he or Thompson had made in the first years of their careers and stressed the benefits to be derived: "Our idea is that your *great* compensation is the *opportunity* offered you. We propose that you shall take charge of the docket, keep the run of all affairs and be the executive man of the office. . . . Our wish is that you feel satisfied in your position and in all things connected with your work, ready to enter upon your duties with a high ambition to convert all means at hand to success. After all, we feel that the salary will be of less value than the opening for you. I feel a deep interest in your future. I want to see you succeed in conducting with skill and care a lucrative business and I am satisfied that your chances to secure this end are greater in entering an established office than in undertaking to build a business by yourself. It looks so to me through my 20 year glasses . . . ." That September, Holt accepted the offer and started four decades of service with the firm.

2

In the havoc wrought by The Great Fire, the firm engaged in a great amount of work for clients old and new.

One of many insurance concerns ruined was Mutual Security Company, a pre-fire client whose many stockholders included some of the city's prominent business and civic leaders. Early in 1872, it declared bankruptcy, requiring the immediate filing of some three dozen suits against individuals owing money to it, and later the defense—successfully handled by Thompson—of forty suits instituted against the stockholders by policyholders. The firm also represented dozens of other fire, life, and accident insurance companies in various actions; among these was Equitable Life Assurance Society of the United States, which became a client in 1875 and is one now.

In the city's rapid resurgence from the tragedy, construction of new buildings required mortgages, and the firm was employed by eastern insurance companies and local lenders to draw them up. Such New York lenders as Equitable Trust Company and Mercantile Trust Company sought counsel on provisions in trust deeds and opinions on titles to property, the latter requiring examination of abstracts, a complex task in which Talley excelled. The firm gained clients from among real estate developers and investors for whom they facilitated land purchases and sales, drew up leases and dealt with party wall agreements and disputes, condemnations and tax assessments. In the wake of the nation-wide financial panic of 1873, occasioned by unrestrained speculation in railroads and the fall of Jay Cooke's banking house in New York, came more clients. They were banks that foreclosed on real estate mortgages. They were creditors of small, hapless railroads in Illinois and Indiana, which were unable to make payments on loans or for locomotives that had to be repossessed and leased to solvent lines. And they were receivers for banks that went under, for various reasons, in the bleak 1873–77 depression.

New clients untroubled by these kinds of woes were added. The Young Men's Christian Association started its long affiliation with the firm in 1874—one that continues—upon construction and dedication of the third Farwell Hall on ground donated by the merchant, John V. Farwell, two earlier ones since the organization's birth in 1858 having been destroyed by fire. Among other clients were Hetty Green, called by newspapers "the world's richest woman," in a small mortgage matter; the Chicago Historical Society; Augustin Daly, the New York theatrical producer, in a conflict with a traveling theatrical troupe; Marshall Field, in real estate projects; the Second Presbyterian Church, of which Williams, Thompson, Holt, and Crerar were members and whose bonds the firm prepared to finance construction of a new edifice at 20th Street and Wabash Avenue after its predecessor on the Near West Side went down in The Great Fire. For a few months in 1872, Williams served Mrs. Mary Lincoln by

Two famous clients
of the 1870s:
Mary Todd Lincoln
and Marshall Field

counseling her on various problems and by passing on to her letters from her son, Robert, vacationing in Europe with his family, while she was staying with friends in Waukesha, Wisconsin.

Pre-eminent among new clients then and in the future was a company that had been formed in Cleveland early in 1869 by Elisha Gray, an Oberlin College physics professor and inventor, and Enos Barton, a telegrapher during the Civil War and later for Western Union in Rochester, New York. In a small plant and with an investment of only $5,000, they began to manufacture telegraphic and electrical equipment, and they prospered. Anson Stager, then head of the Western Union offices in Cleveland, was impressed with their progress and offered to become a partner with an additional $2,500 if they would join him in Chicago, where he was about to become general superintendent of Western Union's

Elisha Gray (*left*)
Enos Barton

new central division. By the end of the year, Gray and Barton were situated with a staff of a dozen workers, in a plant on South Water Street. Miraculously unscathed in The Great Fire, the firm steadily expanded operations in ensuing months to the extent that it was deemed advisable to meet larger capital requirements of a large-scale business by incorporating.

Impressed with how effectively Williams and Thompson were operating in their representation of Western Union, Stager recommended that they prepare and file papers of incorporation. On March 4, 1872, the firm previously known as Gray and Barton became Western Electric Manufacturing Company, with a capitalization of $150,000. One of the heaviest purchasers of stock in the initial offering was Western Union, for which it now became a principal supplier of telegraphic equipment, and for the rest of the decade and far beyond Western Electric would play a pivotal role in the rush of events in the rapidly growing communications industry, with Williams & Thompson—and successors—representing it in assorted matters.

3

One such event that kept Williams and Thompson occupied was the so-called "telegraph wars" instituted by Jay Gould, one of the nation's most daring financial buccaneers.

Dubbed by critical editorialists "The Mephistopheles of Wall Street," this heavily-bearded, diminutive speculator, had, with two equally rapacious associates, Daniel Drew and James "Jubilee Jim" Fisk, outmaneuvered Cornelius Vanderbilt for control of the Erie Railroad by dumping 50,000 shares of fraudulent Erie stock on the market in 1867. Then they bribed enough members of the New York legislature to secure passage of a bill legalizing the issue of the line's stock and banning a merger of the Erie with Vanderbilt's New York Central. In 1869, Gould and Fisk conspired to corner the nation's gold market by urging Abel Corbin to induce President Ulysses S. Grant, his brother-in-law, to prevent the government from selling gold. Grant refused, but Gould and Fisk spread rumors along Wall Street that he would oppose the sale, thereby hiking the price of their own holdings greatly. When Grant directed Secretary of the Treasury George S. Boutwell to order the sale of $4 million in gold, panic prevailed as prices plunged and brought ruin to many thousands on September

24, a day that came to be called "Black Friday." Gould was denounced throughout the country. There followed litigation over the sale of the fraudulent Erie stock. William Tweed, the political boss who was a central figure in the bribery, was sent to jail, and in 1872 Gould was ousted from his control of the Erie Railroad.

But, richer by at least $25 million, Gould was far from finished. In 1874, Gould, having acquired control of the Union Pacific and Kansas Pacific Railroads, was ready for the first of his onslaughts against Western Union.

Williams and Thompson were soon engaged in aiding their client fight off the attacks. Their work for Western Union had meanwhile broadened beyond such earlier rudimentary duties as defending against complaints of late delivery of telegrams. They were now contesting the right of grand juries to subpoena telegrams and gained their first experience with utility regulation by successfully resisting efforts by some members of the Illinois General Assembly to pass legislation requiring the installation of telegraph offices in every railroad station in Illinois. But in Jay Gould and his machinations they and their client faced the strongest challenge yet.

Gould began by gaining control of Atlantic and Pacific Telegraph Company. He forbade his railroads to deal with Western Union, strung wires on Western Union poles in sundry localities, set up parallel lines and even sent gangs into the hinterlands to cut down Western Union lines. For the next three years Williams and Thompson, working with lawyers in a dozen cities mainly in the Midwest, secured injunctions against such nefarious acts. But their legal victories could not overcome Gould's other tactics. He and fellow-speculators "shorted" Western Union stock, and his newspaper, the *New York World*, which he had owned since 1873, assailed Western Union and such of its major directors and shareholders as William H. Vanderbilt and John Jacob Astor for operating "a dangerous monopoly." So drastically did he affect Western Union's business that profits fell $2 million in a single year, and in 1877 Gould compelled Western Union to buy his company for a reputed $10 million. But the wars were not over. In 1879, Gould resumed his assault and maintained it by the same set of tactics in the field and on Wall Street and with formation of American Union Telegraph Company. He supplemented these activities with attacks in the *World* on Western Union's credit, forced the price of its stock down by assorted market manipulations, and gradually brought Vanderbilt and the other directors to the point of surrender. In March 1881, all three companies were amalgamated into Western Union—with Jay Gould in full control, settling in offices in the $2.2 million, bomb-proof Western Union building in New York and planning new and daring schemes in other fields.

4

During the years in which the "telegraph wars" were waged, Williams and Thompson became deeply involved in the beginnings of an industry that would have greater and more lasting significance locally, nationally, and internationally.

Early in 1876, Alexander Graham Bell, working with his assistant, Thomas A. Watson, in a Boston garret, climaxed three years of experiments on a harmonic telegraph, by which several messages could be sent at the same time over a single wire. These tests led him to develop a different device—a rudimentary telephone, which transmitted sounds and muffled speech and for which he received a patent that March 7. Three days later, testing a new transmitter on which to send a message to Watson in an adjoining room, Bell spilled acid from a battery on his clothes and called out, "Mr. Watson, come here! I want you!" Watson ran into the room shouting, "Mr. Bell, I heard every word you said—distinctly!" The first working telephone had been created.

Reaction to this invention after Bell exhibited it at the Centennial Exposition in Philadelphia that July ranged from interest among scientists to skeptical comment about "an electrical toy." After innumerable other

Alexander Graham Bell in 1876

demonstrations, Bell's prospective father-in-law and financial backer, Gardiner G. Hubbard, offered to sell all rights to Western Union for $100,000 but its president, William C. Orton, turned down the bid because he felt that Bell's invention had no future practical use.

More demonstrations followed, including calls to cities as far away as 140 miles from Boston and before Queen Victoria in England ("A Professor Bell," she noted in her journal, "explained the whole process which is the most extraordinary"), and on July 9, 1877, a few days before Bell's marriage to Hubbard's daughter, Mabel, Hubbard and Thomas Sanders, his co-sponsor of Bell's experiments, formed Bell Telephone Company.

A month earlier, Hubbard had gone to Chicago, bringing with him six of Bell's telephones. He gave four to Anson Stager and two to Leroy B. Firman, general manager of American District Telegraph Company, which had been organized in 1875 by Williams & Thompson—with Williams as president and with Williams, Thompson, Stager, Firman, and John B. Drake, a rich hotel owner, among its stockholders—to provide telegraphic service for summoning firemen, policemen, doctors, carriage drivers, and messenger boys. Hubbard supervised several demonstrations, notably one in which Charles Summers, ADT's electrician, and his two daughters, Maud and Flora, sang hymns from their home in Highwood to Stager's Western Union office, a distance of twenty-six miles.

Unlike his superiors in New York, Stager was enthusiastic about prospects for the new-fangled invention. Indeed, a one-block line had been in use since late in 1876 from his office to the offices of Williams and Thompson in what was believed to be, according to later accounts by Charles Holt, the city's first practical test of a telephone, made in Western Electric Manufacturing Company's plant with a transmitter developed by Thomas Edison and a receiver by Elisha Gray, who had filed a patent for his battery telephone four hours after Bell. While Hubbard was reporting to Sanders that negotiations were still pending for licensing of a local franchise from their company, Stager was exercising his powers of persuasion on Western Union to enter the field. It did so toward the end of the year by organizing American Speaking Telephone Company nationally and in Chicago its affiliate was American District Telegraph Company, which began to install Gray-Edison telephones made by Western Electric Manufacturing Company.

It was apparent that to furnish more efficient service to subscribers

Boy telephone operators of the 1880s

central exchanges would have to be established so that telephones in one part of the community could be connected to others in a different sector. The Bell firm's first commercial exchange opened in New Haven, Connecticut, on January 28, 1878, and its representatives in Chicago, led by Horace Eldred, planned one there. But before they could do so, American District Telegraph Company opened its exchange, the city's first, on the following June 18 in the Mercantile Building on La Salle Street between Madison and Washington Streets. Eight days later, Bell Telephone Company of Illinois opened its Chicago Telephonic Exchange directly across the street with notices warning that it held the only patents under which telephones could be manufactured and used and that legal action would be taken against "parties using any speaking Telephones other than the Bell Telephone."

Warnings notwithstanding, Western Union's local affiliate steadily outstripped its rival in ensuing months, so much so that some of Bell's New York officers considered outright sale of the Chicago business. That drastic proposal was fought by Hubbard and Theodore N. Vail, a former Western Union and Railway Mail Service executive whom Hubbard had hired at $3,500 a year to be the parent company's general manager. Vail dispatched copies of Bell's original patent to all company representatives in cities where franchises were held urging them to withstand Western

Union competition. In September 1878, a patent infringement suit was filed against Peter A. Dowd, manager of a Western Union subsidiary in Massachusetts, in the United States District Court in Boston. To offset Western Union's harassment on Wall Street by gobbling up blocks of its stock, the Bell company, at the start of the new year, combined with its New England subsidiary to form National Bell Telephone Company as a nationwide licensing company in order to speed up establishment of telephone service throughout the country.

The taking of evidence in the Dowd case began the following May. By September there were some 600 pages of data and documentation to support the Bell claims of patent infringement. George Gifford, a prominent patent attorney serving as Western Union's chief counsel, became convinced that there was no chance for victory and proposed a settlement, a course of action favored by William H. Vanderbilt, who was trying to fight off Jay Gould's campaign to win command of Western Union. On November 10, an agreement was reached in which Western Union acknowledged the validity of the Bell patents and left the telephone business, surrendering all its acquired patents, claims, and facilities that included 56,000 telephones in fifty-five cities and receiving in return 20 percent of telephone rental revenues for the remaining seventeen years of the lifetime of the Bell patent. To carry on the consolidation of the National Bell and Western Union properties, American Bell Telephone Company was formed the following March 20.

The settlement constituted a major triumph for the Bell interests, for it removed its most formidable foe, and the victory was signalized by a rise in its stock on the day after entry of the consent decree to $1,000 a share, a boon that represented a 2,000 percent appreciation over the preceding eight months. Of added interest was the fact that the Dowd suit was the first of some 600 instituted over Bell's patent; not until 1888 would the United States Supreme Court, in a 4-3 decision, sustain Bell's patent rights in every particular.

In Chicago, the immediate effect of the Dowd settlement was to negate a patent infringement suit brought by Williams and Thompson early in 1879 against the Bell company on behalf of Western Union's local affiliate. Competition between American District Telegraph Company and the Bell subsidiary continued for nearly a year, with an intensification of efforts by both companies to improve services and expand the ranks of subscribers.

But a merger was inevitable. On January 12, 1881, ADT stockholders held a special meeting and passed a resolution to consolidate with the recently-formed Bell subsidiary, Union Telephone Company of Illinois, and form a new Chicago Telephone Company. Two days later, the corporation charter of the company, drawn by Williams and Thompson, was issued, its capitalization set at $500,000, with 5,000 shares at $100 par value. Chief among the stockholders, in addition to Williams and Thompson, were Stager, John Crerar, and Robert Lincoln. For the first five days, Williams served as president, then Stager replaced him and held the office until his death in 1885 while Williams was a vice-president, director, and member of the important executive committee. Toward the close of 1881—specifically, on December 23—the new company was licensed by American Bell, and the way was clear for sustained expansion of the ranks of subscribers from the 3,000 then using the services of the competing local companies.

There were other vital developments. A month earlier, on November 26, Western Electric Company was organized by Williams and Thompson to succeed to the properties and business of Western Electric Manufacturing Company, and the partners also undertook complex negotiations for the acquisition by Western Electric of two smaller firms that had been fashioning telephones and essential equipment for the Bell interests, Gilliland Electric Company of Indianapolis and the Charles A. Williams, Jr., firm of Boston, in whose early workshop Bell and Watson had started their experiments.

Western Electric had by now become the country's foremost manufacturer of telephones and apparatus and various kinds of electrical devices, a fact well-known to Vail, who had grown increasingly aware that for greater efficiency and reduction of needless expense a centralized manufacturing operation was essential. He promptly responded to the proposal of Enos Barton that Western Electric was a logical choice. After considerable discussion and negotiation, American Bell purchased a controlling interest in Western Electric, and on the following February 6 a contract was formalized by which Western Electric became American Bell's manufacturing unit as sole licensee to make equipment under the Bell patents and devote itself fully to that endeavor for all Bell subsidiaries. It was an agreement that would be mutually beneficial and have long-range results —and problems.

It was now fifteen years since Williams and Thompson had started their firm, and the labors for major and minor clients had solidified their stature.

Indeed, early in the period after The Great Fire, notice was taken of their qualities by an astute observer, Franc Bangs Wilkie, the *Chicago Times'* editorialist, in *Sketches and Notices of the Chicago Bar*. He characterized Williams as a sound practitioner, "A young man who promises well for the future." About Thompson, whom he had occasion to observe in courtrooms, Wilkie was more voluble: "He takes a creditable position. He is well posted in the law, is very industrious and attentive, very cautious and, if he has a noticeable fault, it is that he is inclined to give more attention to what may be presented by an opponent than to his own resources for offense or defense. He has a large amount of force and character and has a business that includes some of the best men of Chicago."

Williams did not often appear in court but rendered service to clients as a legal adviser and was strengthening his reputation as a cogent business lawyer. Thompson sought, whenever possible, to discourage litigation but when he did go to court he was always scrupulously prepared ("It is better to try to do things than spend your time making excuses for not doing them" was one of his oft-repeated maxims). Normally even-tempered, he would grow exceedingly irate and his face would turn a mahogany color whenever he came upon statements by publicity-seeking attorneys in newspaper columns commenting on their cases, a practice he denounced as "bofunkum."

Both men were active in social and civic affairs. Williams had been one of the organizers of the Chicago Club in 1869 and, with Edward Isham, Robert Lincoln, and Henry Bishop, now met regularly there for lunch at a round table they jestingly labeled "the millionaire's table," an appellation given authenticity when they were joined there by Marshall Field, George Pullman, John Crerar, and others of wealth and prestige. In 1894–95 Williams would serve as the club's seventh president, and his portrait now hangs to the right of the entrance to its main lounge. In the year that his firm incorporated Chicago Telephone Company, Williams, because of an early interest in telegraphy and his firm's representation of Western Electric, was named a United States Commissioner to the Paris Electrical Exposition.

Thompson was now a member of the Republican-oriented and reform-minded Union League Club, organized the previous year. He had also participated in local politics. From 1876 to 1878 he served as alderman from the Third Ward in the "Reform Council" that was elected after the reign of Mayor Harvey Doolittle Colvin in which scandals prevailed that ranged from a shortage of $135,000 in the city treasurer's accounts to widespread gambling under control of Michael Cassius "King Mike" McDonald. The mayor—characterized by a contemporary journalist as "a puissant chief among bons vivants and a connoisseur par excellence in moral bric-a-brac"—had been a steady patron of McDonald's lavish four-story gaming house, "The Store," at Clark and Monroe Streets.

A few years earlier, Thompson had been enlisted to help undo what many leading citizens considered flagrant action by the state legislators in passing, on April 16, 1869, the Lake Front Act. Two provisions of that act were especially irksome. One granted title to the Illinois Central Railroad to lands submerged beneath Lake Michigan for a mile east of the road's right-of-way and for a mile south of Randolph Street, the road's northern terminus. The other ceded to Chicago the right to transfer title to the road of a stretch of land, mostly under water, for three blocks between its trestle and Michigan Avenue. (The railroad, by Chicago's Common Council ordinance in 1852, had been properly granted rights to lay down trackage along a portion of the lake front from Randolph to Twelfth Streets.) The first of the provisions aroused criticism because it was felt that the road's ownership of the submerged lands would hamper the city's intention of constructing and expanding a harbor in that area. The second did provide that the road—in conjunction with the Michigan Central and Chicago, Burlington and Quincy roads, whose trains ran along its tracks—would pay the city $800,000 to be placed in a park fund. But Governor John M. Palmer considered this far too low and asserted that $2.6 million would be a fairer amount. Inveighing against "reckless and shameful" legislators who voted for passage of the act and citing other provisions of the legislation he considered irregular—especially the granting of the submerged land east of the shore—he vetoed the Lake Front Act, along with seventy-one others passed in the session.

When the legislature passed the bill over the governor's veto, various newspapers and a civic committee led by Jonathan Scammon vowed to fight what they denounced as the "Lake Front Steal." Upon election of a new legislature and ratification of a new constitution in 1870 that, among other things, prohibited the granting of charters to private corporations, they continued their attack. Thompson acceded to Scammon's request to act as the civic committee's counsel in obtaining repeal of the Lake Front Act. He immersed himself in research into federal governmental action that had given Illinois ownership of the land above and below the shore of Lake Michigan upon assumption of statehood in 1818 and that had ceded sections of the lake front to the Illinois Central. He made innumerable trips to Springfield and testified frequently before committees examining the claims of Scammon's group and others opposed to the legislation of 1869, and on April 15, 1873, the new legislature repealed the Lake Front Act. But the issue was far from settled. The railroad maintained that the new legislature had no right to cancel contractual obligations incurred by its predecessor and legal action was planned that would be intricate and prolonged and extend well into the next decade and beyond.*

*See Chapter III.

III   *Williams & Thompson*
1882–1889

MUCH OF the firm's work in the aftermath of establishment of Western Electric Company as the exclusive manufacturing component of American Bell involved other matters in the swiftly expanding telephone field.

As American Bell's representative in the Middle West, Williams & Thompson effected the organization of regional telephone companies—the Western in Iowa, the Midland in Ohio, the Central in Indiana and sections of Illinois outside Chicago—and on June 25, 1882, consolidated these into Central Union Telephone Company, licensed by the parent company. Throughout the decade, various problems that occupied much of the firm's time ranged from efforts to prevent the cutting of overhead wires as decreed by ordinances passed by the City Council to opposition to the raising of licensing fees. In the latter instance, after innumerable discussions and meetings, in addition to action to secure court injunctions, the company-city conflict was temporarily brought to a halt in 1889 by passage of an ordinance that bound both parties to an arrangement by which the city would receive annually 3 percent of the company's gross earnings, free service, sets for the police and fire alarm systems at five dollars each, and the right to tax telephones if authorized by law.

In subsequent months, various bills were introduced in the state legislature to fix monthly rates for telephone users, but all died in committee; in one such instance, Norman Williams was especially articulate and persuasive in expressing the company's position to George S. Baker, co-author of a bill seeking such regulation, and copies of his letter to Baker were sent to each member of the House of Representatives, a move generally acknowledged to be a key element in the fate of this and the other bills. These were, of course, initial skirmishes in this area, and there would be scores of other similar contests with legislatures and regulatory commissions in years to come.

As work and duties for Chicago Telephone Company accumulated, the firm's representation of Western Union continued to taper off, especially as Jay Gould strengthened his control. Virtually the only tasks performed for Western Union throughout the 1880s and briefly into the next decade involved instituting action against scoundrels who tapped Western Union wires to get quotations from the floor of the Board of Trade or results of sports contests and horse races which they then transmitted to "ticker companies" for distribution to various parts of the city. Such action was not always successful, especially when cases were tried before juries inclined to sympathize with defendants against huge national corporations. This was true even after passage of a statute in 1895 making wire-tapping a criminal offense, and in a letter to George H. Fearons, Western Union's general attorney, commenting on an adverse decision, Charles Holt expressed anger and indignation: "The result is more than disappointing; it is positively maddening . . . We ought to have secured a conviction, and the verdict is simply one of the many disheartening evidences that trial by jury is often only another name for miscarriage of justice."

2

In a decade marked by heightened formation of scores of corporations large and small throughout the nation, Williams & Thompson continued to be active in the local sector.

In 1882, the firm incorporated Western Edison Light Company, one of four large companies to emerge then in the wake of the ever-widening application of Thomas Edison's incandescent lamps as a major source of illumination in public and private buildings; with a capitalization of $500,000, its stockholders included Anson Stager and Robert Lincoln. It did a thriving business until 1887, when its franchise was acquired by Chicago Edison Company, which also was incorporated by Williams & Thompson. The latter company, however, was not represented by the partners as it began the sale of electricity produced in central generating plants. But its prime competitor, Chicago Arc Light and Power Company, was a client after it was incorporated later that year and bought up small arc-light companies scattered throughout the Chicago area. Although the latter prospered as a supplier of electrical power, it was overshadowed by Chicago Edison Company, which furnished, from a central station, electricity for some of the city's foremost buildings, including the Grand Opera House and the composing room of the *Chicago Tribune*. By 1893, Chicago Edison Company's capitalization had risen from $500,000 to $3 million, and Chicago Arc Light and Power Company, which had enjoyed a satisfying if less spectacular surge of prosperity, was absorbed in a transaction worked out by the president of Chicago Edison Company, young Samuel Insull. A year earlier, Insull had given up a $36,000-a-year vice-presidency of Thomas Edison's General Electric Company to take a third of that salary in Chicago because he was confident that his future would be better served as an executive with a company that supplied electricity than with one that manufactured electrical equipment.

A new railroad client in this period was the Atchison, Topeka and Santa Fe. Its energetic president, William Barstow Strong, decreed that the time had come for the line, whose eastern terminus was Kansas City, to extend eastward to Chicago. The heads of other railroads with tracks already connecting the two cities sought to dissuade him, but Strong was adamant in his desire. In 1883, he sent surveyors from Kansas City to Chicago to gather information on bridges, traffic, and independent lines on the route along which his chief engineer, Albert Alonzo Robinson, proposed the tracks he laid.

Once the decision was made and approved by his directors, Strong hired Williams & Thompson to deal with myriad matters, ranging from filing of condemnation suits and examination of many dozens of abstracts of title to dissolving injunctions secured by landowners who opposed having the railroad cross their lands. By December 1886, the railroad set up construction offices in Kansas City and Chicago. The subsequent accomplishment was remarkable in railroad annals. Within nine months, some 350 miles of new railroad line were built, 100 were rebuilt, and five large bridges were constructed across major rivers along the route. Williams & Thompson had handled the acquisition of terminal facilities in Chicago through purchasing or leasing various short rights of way which, when put together, gave the railroad access to the Dearborn Street Station; over $3.3 million was spent on such acquisitions. After construction was completed and the initial service began on a part-time basis the following January and with regular, steady runs on May 1, the firm continued its representation—primarily in defending personal injury suits —until 1893, when George R. Peck, the road's general solicitor, transferred his offices to Chicago.

Incorporation of quite a different kind of enterprise involved the Chicago Auditorium Association and the Auditorium Hotel Company, instigated by Ferdinand Wythe Peck, a wealthy realtor and member of a pioneer Chicago family. A devotee of the arts, principally orchestral music and opera, Peck had long dreamed of establishing a combined theater-hotel-office building, with the theater to be financially supported by revenues from hotel residents and office occupants. After presenting his idea to the influential Commercial Club and receiving from many of its members a solid response and, more importantly, expressions of interest in investing in the venture, Peck sought out Williams & Thompson to prepare papers of incorporation. This done, he hired two of the stellar architects in what was then deemed Chicago's "golden era" of architecture, Louis Henri Sullivan and Dankmar Adler, and counseled them to create a structure that would represent "the future and not the corrupted past." The result—completed two years after President Grover Cleveland laid the cornerstone in 1887—was a Sullivan-Adler masterpiece, combining the individualistic artistic design theories of the first and the acoustical genius of the second. Extending along Congress Street from Michigan Avenue to Wabash Avenue, the Auditorium theater and adjoining structures captured the nation's attention after its formal dedication on the night of December 8, 1889, at which President Benjamin Harrison spoke and Adelina Patti, the operatic diva, sang "Home Sweet Home" before an assemblage of the city's foremost citizenry. (In subsequent years, because of financial difficulties, Peck's creation fell on hard times. Much later, the hotel and offices were transformed into the progressive Roosevelt University after World War II, and the splendid and unique theater, after years of disuse and near-decay, was restored in the 1960s to much of its earlier glory.)

3

Amid these assorted matters were two others whose resolution in the courts had steadfast and abiding consequences culturally and educationally.

The provision in Walter Newberry's 1868 will as to the disposition of his estate spurred protracted litigation after the elder of his two daughters, Julia Rosa, succumbed to a lingering fever in Rome in the spring of 1876. Inasmuch as neither she nor her sister, Mary Louisa, who had died two years earlier while vacationing in a French village, had ever married, a cluster of Newberry's nephews and nieces and grand-nephews filed suit in Circuit Court to compel instant distribution of the estate—half to them and half for the establishment of the free public library. The relatives alleged that Mrs. Newberry, who had survived the daughters, had no further claim to any part of the existing estate because in renouncing her husband's will earlier and electing to take her dower rights she was, in effect, "dead as to the will."

The suit was against the estate's trustees, Eliphalet W. Blatchford and William H. Bradley, clerk of the United States District Court of Northern Illinois, who had replaced an ailing Mark Skinner. In their defense, Edward Isham and Robert Lincoln, aided by Thompson, responded that the earlier action by Mrs. Newberry did not accelerate the time of distribution, that the will's phrase, "surviving descendants," denoted those alive at the actual death of Mrs. Newberry, and that meanwhile the estate should remain in trust. In July 1877, Judge Erastus S. Williams ruled for the plaintiffs and ordered the immediate distribution of the estate. But the decision was appealed and the following June the Illinois Supreme Court reversed Judge Williams, stressing this essential point: "The period of distribution appointed by the will has not yet arrived and will not, until the death of Mrs. Newberry, and to determine otherwise would seem to us to be, in this particular, making a will for the testator instead of expounding the one which he himself made."

In the next five years there were repeated efforts—all unsuccessful—by the plaintiffs, in one of which, James McCartney, the state's attorney general, joined the defendants to represent the public's interest. Not until April 1883, did the legal contest cease; the high court once again ruled against the plaintiffs—this time on a petition for a rehearing—and directed that the estate remain in trust until Mrs. Newberry's death. And it was another two years and more, in December 1885, when Mrs. Newberry died, before Blatchford and Bradley were free, at last, to make the distribution specified in Newberry's will. Interestingly—and gratify-ingly—the value of Newberry's real estate holdings was now more than twice what it had been at the time of his death, so that after payment of taxes $2.15 million was available as a permanent endowment for the library.

Within two years, Newberry Library was formally in existence in the first of three temporary locations it would occupy on La Salle Street until completion in 1893 of its imposing Romanesque building on Walton Street on the site of Mahlon Ogden's home, one of the few on the Near North Side that had miraculously escaped the raging flames of The Great Fire. Its librarian, William Frederick Poole, was an imposing figure in the field, a founder of the American Library Association (in later decades a client of the firm established by Williams and Thompson) and the American Historical Association, deviser of the indispensable *Index to Periodical Literature,* and renowned as an organizer of new libraries, including one in the United States Naval Academy and another in Cincinnati. Since 1874, Poole had been head of Chicago's free public library, guiding its growth since its origin a year earlier in a rusting water tank at the rear of a lot at La Salle and Adams Streets into one of the largest circulating libraries in the land.*

Poole took to his task with characteristic vigor, and by the time Newberry Library was settled in its permanent home its future course had been well-set as a major reference and research institution specializing in the humanities. Among the first acquisitions by Poole was an Italian count's collection of rare books relating to Italian music history and opera manuscripts and a Cincinnati bibliophile's 2,500 volumes that included, among varied treasures, three Shakespeare folios, eighty-eight rare Bibles, and ten editions of Homer, nine of Dante, and eight of Horace. By the time Poole died in 1894, the library possessed over 120,000 books and 44,000 pamphlets, and in subsequent decades and with funds from Newberry's bequest and many others, various gifts, and grants, Poole's successors multiplied these holdings many, many times over and broadened and expanded the library's services and resources for scholars and students not only in the Chicago area but from many parts of the world. (The firm has continued to represent the library and through the decades several of its partners have served on Newberry's board of trustees.)

Another distinguished institution of research and learning resulted from the firm's successful defense against challenges to the will of John Crerar.

*Most of the 7,000 volumes in the ''tank-library'' came from Great Britain, the donors headed by Queen Victoria and including Benjamin Disraeli, Dante Gabriel Rossetti, and John Stuart Mill.

John Crerar

That document, a lengthy and detailed one, was drawn up by Williams & Thompson on August 5, 1886, while Crerar was living in the august Grand Pacific Hotel. Crerar, then fifty-nine years old, had prospered not only as the head of Crerar, Adams and Company but from railroad, banking, and steel company investments, and was widely respected for his various philanthropies. He had never married, telling those who sought to learn why, "I am in love with all." He was a familiar figure at various social events and a man of piety as a pillar of the Second Presbyterian Church and staunch adherent and a vice-president of the Young Men's Christian Association.

In his will, Crerar bequeathed a considerable amount of money to religious, educational, and charitable causes and institutions—$900,000 in all. Another $100,000 was designated for a "colossal statue of Abraham Lincoln," which was created by Augustus St. Gaudens, exhibited in several cities, and eventually placed in Grant Park not far from the Lake Michigan shore. Half a million dollars was bestowed on friends who had shown kindness to his mother, Agnes, in her New York home, to cousins on his mother's side, to business partners, and to close friends in Chicago. Like Walter Newberry, Crerar made provision for a free public library to be erected and endowed it with an amount estimated at $2.5 million. He designated Williams to be its president and named to its board of directors such local notables as Marshall Field, Eliphalet Blatchford,

Robert Lincoln, and George Armour. Crerar also made interesting stipulations about this institution to be called the John Crerar Library:

"I desire the building to be tasteful, substantial and fireproof, and that a sufficient fund be reserved over and above the cost of its construction to provide, maintain and support a library for all time. I desire that the books and periodicals be selected with a view to create and sustain a healthy moral and Christian sentiment in the community and that all nastiness and immorality be excluded. I do not mean by this that there shall not be anything but hymn books and sermons, but I mean that dirty French novels and all skeptical trash and works of questionable moral tone shall never be found in this library. I want its atmosphere that of Christian refinement, and its aim and object the building up of character, and I rest content that the friends I have named will carry out my wishes in those particulars."

Williams and Huntington W. Jackson, another prominent attorney, were named the will's executors and the estate's trustees. They anticipated no problems that might stem from the numerous and varied bequests, but they reckoned without an array of Crerar relatives who had not been mentioned in the will. These were men and women related to Crerar's father, John, who had died four brief months after the birth of the future financier-philanthropist. In all the years since coming from New York to make his fortune in Chicago, Crerar had not known of their existence nor, presumably, had they known of him nor of his accumulation of wealth.

Early in 1889, Crerar suffered a stroke and was moved from his rooms in the Grand Pacific Hotel to the Williams residence on South Calumet Avenue, and there he died on the evening of that October 19. Because of his prominence and reputation, stories of his death and career and a vast memorial meeting in Central Music Hall were carried in newspapers all over the country. Soon after Crerar's burial in Brooklyn's Greenwood Cemetery beside the grave of his mother (his plain headstone bore the inscription, "A just man and one that feared God"), a Donald Crerar, a first cousin on Crerar's father's side, filed suit in the Cook County Circuit Court in his behalf and that of others bearing his surname. This attack on the validity of the will specifically challenged the gifts to the Second Presbyterian Church, the Chicago Bible Society, the Literary Club, the Lincoln statue, and the library as improperly and ambiguously drawn. The bequests to cousins on Crerar's mother's side were dismissed with the statement that "all of the cousins to whom such legacies were given have accepted the same and have released all claims to the estate." The complainants, the suit alleged, were entitled "as next of kin and heirs at law, to share in all property owned by Mr. Crerar at the time of his death and not legally devised by him."

Williams led the battle in the courts and in 1893 was victorious when the Illinois Supreme Court upheld lower court rulings against the plaintiffs. As president-designate, Williams then pressed forward to carry out the plans specified by Crerar seven years earlier. The library was officially chartered on October 12, 1894, and the first meeting of its directors was held the following month in the Prairie Avenue mansion of Marshall Field. Among the decisions taken there was to make of the library a center for books concentrating mainly in what were then called the "useful arts" and later "technology," the physical and natural sciences, philosophy, sociology, and, in small part, the fine arts. This was prompted by the fact that the city's other two major libraries concentrated on other areas of knowledge—the Chicago Public Library as a general repository of what its directors characterized as "wholesomely entertaining and generally instructive books, especially such as are desired by the citizens for general home use" and the Newberry devoted primarily to the humanities. Williams headed a special committee to refine further the precise nature of the library and by year's end prepared a memorandum stressing, among other matters, the need for establishing the library as one that would not duplicate others in the city and would become a reference library of major significance. He proposed that initially the library obtain "pioneer works in science, technology and medicine," emphasizing, "I do not sympathize with the suggestion that only the newest and latest publications be selected. Such a library would have neither a beginning nor an end. The student, every student, requires and demands a knowledge of the history of the subject he pursues, and should have at hand the means of investigation from the beginnings."

The library's initial quarters were on the sixth floor of the Wabash and Washington corner of the Marshall Field Building, most of which was occupied by the flourishing department store. In a small office was ensconced the first librarian, Clement Walker Andrews, a man of scientific attainments who had done graduate work in analytic chemistry at Harvard. For seventeen years, Andrews had been a professor of chemistry at the Massachusetts Institute of Technology, where he had organized and expanded its library. With an assistant and a secretary, he set about to build the new library's collection, basing his accessions on books he had acquired for the MIT library. Andrews not only heeded Williams' admonition about "pioneer works" but also sought out current periodicals dealing with technological and scientific subjects. For two years, he and a small staff worked at the tasks of amassing a good collection with funds allotted by the directors and acquiring more space on the sixth floor, solid oaken chairs and tables and adequate lighting and all other essential accoutrements for a first-rate library, and by the end of 1896 some 11,000 adequately catalogued volumes and 1,300 periodicals were on the shelves. Official opening date for the public was April 1, 1897; in accord with the directors' wishes, there were no ceremonies but notices in newspapers and distribution of formal invitations to academicians and educators and other librarians drew, in the first three days, close to 2,000 visitors.

Andrews remained the Crerar librarian until 1928, two years before he died. During this period, the number of books, pamphlets, and periodicals increased—volumes alone totaled over half a million—and both staff and users expanded greatly. In 1912, the directors, having wisely managed the original endowment so that a building fund of over $1.3 million was available, approved the purchase of a site and erection of a new home at Randolph Street and Michigan Avenue, across the street from the central branch of the Chicago Public Library. In an imposing fifteen-story structure—ten of whose floors would ultimately be occupied by various divisions of the library—the new John Crerar Library opened its doors on May 28, 1920. And as the years progressed under Andrews and his successors, its reputation burgeoned, its international fame enhanced by innumerable research resources, including one of the world's largest collections of published materials covering the biomedical sciences and all fields of clinical medicine and scientific journals in more than fifty languages. There it remained until 1962 when it moved its vast and valuable array of materials to a $2 million glass-and-steel structure on the Near South Side campus of the Illinois Institute of Technology, where it continued to serve not only scholars and researchers from all parts of the world but IIT students as well.*

*In May 1981, the University of Chicago concluded negotiations with the trustees of the library to bring its collections to a new library scheduled for completion on the university's Midway campus by 1984.

Charles S. Holt

4

In many matters one of the partners' most valued aides was Charles Holt. On July 1, 1882, at twenty-seven and four years after he had come to work as a clerk, he was named a partner. He continued to perform assigned tasks with dispatch, sharpening his writing and speaking skills and making impressive and articulate appearances in courtrooms. A man of peppery disposition, he relaxed from his office duties by continuing to devote considerable time to working with men and boys served by the Young Men's Christian Association, conducting Bible classes and officiating at sports events in the YMCA's various gymnasiums.

In that year, too, another young man who would serve the firm and one of its principal clients well was hired as a five-dollar-a-week office boy while he was a student at the Union College of Law at Clark and Washington Streets.* He was Arthur D. Wheeler, who, after graduating

*This school was created in 1873 by combining the law department of the original University of Chicago, then nearing the end of its second decade, with the new law department of Evanston's Northwestern University and remained the city's foremost law school until after the turn of the century.

Arthur D. Wheeler

from Lake Forest College the previous year, had impressed Holt with his work as a copyist. On January 1, 1887, when he was only twenty-six years old and shortly before marrying Holt's sister, he, too, was named a partner, and for most of the time he specialized in matters involving Chicago Telephone Company, later serving as its president from June 1889 to May 1890 and for a longer period from May 1903 to May 1908.*

As in the previous decade, others worked for the firm, mostly without pay while studying law, for short periods before going elsewhere to practice or assume teaching posts at law schools. One was William G. Beale, who left in 1881 upon being admitted to the bar and joined Isham and Lincoln, who made him a partner four years later and changed the firm's name to Isham, Lincoln & Beale in 1889. Such was the nature of employment of these temporary student-clerks or full-fledged clerks impatient for advancement that for a time in 1887 only one full-time clerk was in the firm's employ. He was Russell Whitman, who would subsequently establish a distinguished practice of his own and served impressively as president of the Chicago Bar Association in 1925.

*See Chapter V.

Besides the law students and clerks there was the expansion of a staff of lay employees in this decade. Having equipped itself with a novel device, the typewriter, for $100 the firm advertised for a stenographer-typist and in October 1885, Editha Phelps, daughter of a clergyman in Marquette, Michigan, dispatched her application: "I am a first class stenographer and typewriter of two years experience. . . . Am not a professional book-keeper, though I have no doubt I could do what book-keeping is required. Salary about $50 per month." The firm's first female employee, she turned out to be a decided asset, except that although she enjoyed working for Williams and Thompson, she disliked Holt and Wheeler for what she maintained were their demanding ways and curtness; she may also have riled Holt and Wheeler with her rather outspoken liberal views and a tendency to challenge established authority. In any event, she remained with the firm for ten years, then resigned to go to work at the newly established John Crerar Library, first as an order clerk and for the next twenty years in other diverse capacities.

An office boy hired the same year as Miss Phelps was Edward J. Witt, who proved bright and adept at acquiring knowledge of a kind that helped him advance to the post of bookkeeper and cashier, jobs which he filled until 1892 when he left to study medicine and to practice in St. Joseph, Michigan. Another office boy who showed promise beyond performance of routine tasks was John E. Duggan, a kinetic youngster whom Williams tutored in Latin sufficiently for the firm to enroll him in Lake Forest Academy, with all expenses and tuition paid. Disappointingly, Duggan lost interest in his studies in his senior year, left the school, got married, and dropped out of sight.

Employment of such people as Editha Phelps, Edward Witt, and John Duggan was followed, after their departures, by other stenographer-typists, bookkeepers, cashiers, and office boys in what was developing into a solid corps of lay workers and one that would grow as the firm's needs expanded in ensuing years.

5

In this decade, there was renewal of the long-standing dispute involving the 1869 Lake Front Act and its repeal by the state legislature four years later.

48

The Illinois Central Railroad had long maintained that the repeal was unconstitutional and invalid because it impaired the obligation of the contract between the railroad and the state. It was argued that the act was a present grant, that title vested immediately, and that the act's provision which called for the railroad to pay the state 7 percent of its gross receipts from the land's use and occupation was adequate consideration. Early in 1883, the railroad began to construct wharves and piers in the disputed area of submerged land, and Illinois Attorney General James McCartney filed an information in Cook County Circuit Court whose prime aim was to clear the cloud on the title of the state to the submerged lands and determine the right of the legislature to nullify the Lake Front Act.

Once again, Thompson was deeply involved in behalf of the state's claim and as president of the foremost reform organization, the Citizens Association. Ezra B. McCagg, his earlier mentor when he first arrived in Chicago, joined him, and Melville W. Fuller, a leader among the city's attorneys and five years away from appointment to the United States Supreme Court, represented Chicago. Subsequently the case was removed to the United States Circuit Court for the Northern District of Illinois for hearing by Justice John M. Harlan of the United States Supreme Court and District Court Judge Henry W. Blodgett.

By the time the hearings got under way, McCartney had been succeeded as the state's attorney general by George Hunt, and Thompson worked closely with him in presenting the state's case. The United States had entered the legal fray with the local district attorney, W. G. Ewing, to argue for its rights against the company's claims, and the railroad's lawyers were comprised of the learned and impressive trio of Benjamin F. Ayer, John N. Jewett, and former United States Senator Lyman Trumbull.

The sessions were long and protracted, with considerable testimony and presentation of documents by both sides. Thompson attacked the railroad for erecting the wharves and piers while no final adjudication of the complex matter had been made and asked that the railroad be enjoined from filling with earth any sections of the submerged portions of Lake Michigan "and to quit possession of all lands, waters and made-ground taken and held by it without right." Each of the plaintiffs united in contending that the Lake Front Act of 1869 was "inoperative and void," with Thompson offering added evidence that the act had been passed without the sufficient number of prescribed readings.

The railroad attorneys maintained, among many things, that by terms

49

of the original charter granted the Illinois Central in February 1851, the repealing act of 1873 was void and, indeed, violated the constitution. They also emphasized that in the four years between passage of the 1869 act and the repeal the railroad had spent $500,000 in various physical improvements in the section of submerged land "upon the faith that the provisions of the said act would be respected by the state and the city."

The case dragged on for several years. At one point the railroad sought to negotiate a sale of a portion of land ceded to the city years before but gave up that effort after the *Chicago Journal* reported that eight key members of the City Council were demanding a payment of $25,000 for a favorable vote on a proposed ordinance. The *Chicago Tribune* derided the report sarcastically: "Aldermen, even in Chicago, are cheaper, much cheaper than eight for $25,000."

On February 23, 1888, Justice Harlan and Judge Blodgett were ready with their judgment. In a highly-detailed document, they ruled against the railroad on every count, the decision in many respects reflecting the legal arguments and even the language contained in Thompson's brief. "Upon a careful consideration of all that has been said upon this important and difficult question," read a significant section of the decision, "the court is of the opinion, as respects the submerged lands constituting the bed of the lake, and expressly granted by the act of 1869, the repealing act of 1873 did not infringe any legal rights of the company, and was a valid exercise of legislative power." (The decision was appealed by the Illinois Central, first in 1892 and then in 1910 on a petition for rehearing; on both occasions, the United States Supreme Court affirmed the Harlan-Blodgett ruling, re-emphasizing that the state was owner in fee of the submerged lands constituting the Lake Michigan bed and that the 1873 repealing act was "valid and effective for the purpose of restoring to the state the same control, dominion and ownership of said lands that it had prior to the passage of the act of April 16, 1869.")

6

Sadly, Thompson was never to learn of the ruling by Justice Harlan and Judge Blodgett in behalf of the cause for which he had fought so arduously.

Early in 1888 he was constantly at work in the offices of the Wabash Railway Company's receiver, taking testimony in connection with the firm's representation of bondholders in the equity receivership of that line. He often passed up regular meals and worked far into the night, applying himself with characteristic industry to the complex task. He insisted he felt no ill effects from irregular eating and lack of sleep, but on the morning of January 29 he suffered a severe stroke while dressing for breakfast in his home at 1637 Indiana Avenue. Physicians were able to restore him to partial consciousness, although his entire left side was paralyzed. They and his wife, Laura, and two children, Leverett and Susan, held hope that recovery was possible. On the next evening, there was such encouraging improvement in his condition that he held an hour's bedside conversation with Williams about pending legal matters. During the night, however, he suffered a relapse and was pronounced dead the following morning, two days short of his fifty-third birthday.

Tributes to him were radiant and profuse. The Union League Club—to whose presidency he had been elected a week before his death—held a special meeting at which a memorial statement was read stressing his military career and legal acumen ("prudent in counsel, clear in statement and forcible in argument") and his association for two decades "with societies or bodies having the good interests of the community in view" and his assistance, "often with great self-sacrifice, in efforts for reform in municipal and state administration." Of the man and his legal practice, Judge Richard S. Tuthill, at this meeting, spoke with special pertinence: "He represented great corporate interests. His firm was one of the leading law firms of the city, and had important corporate interests always in its charge, but no man, no lawyer, no judge and no citizen ever heard it said, I am convinced, that that firm would for one moment consider a proposition of gaining their ends by any except honorable methods. I do not believe there was enough property or money in the world to have seduced General Thompson to do a dishonorable or unmanly thing." Charles Holt recalled Thompson's calmness and tolerance in dealing with others, his modesty, patience and extreme conscientiousness: "He only took a case and followed it through with interest and heart when in his soul he believed he was serving the cause of right." And words, too, from Justice Harlan, even then preparing to put the finishing touches to the ruling on the Lake Front Act: "He was an honest man, who hated devious ways and questionable methods. Let me say of him that no one ever stood before me, in a court of justice, in whose integrity of mind and heart I had more confidence."

Fellow-members of the Chicago Bar Association were united in stressing Thompson's diligence as a lawyer and his courtroom demeanor. Illinois Supreme Court Justice Benjamin D. Magruder expressed the sentiments of many: "He had the rare faculty of being spirited and zealous in the defense of his client's rights and at the same time courteous and gentlemanly in the treatment of his opponent. Undisturbed by the fear of defeat, he inspired those who sought his professional aid with the spirit of his own calm trustfulness. This power to allay the anxieties of those who ask for counsel is not the manifestation of self-importance or self-conceit. It is the product of careful investigation into the principles of the law, accompanied by a conscientious effort to apply those principles, and a manly self-reliance in predicting the results of their application."

Williams, Holt & Wheeler
1889–1899

F OR WELL OVER a year after Thompson's death, the firm kept its original name. Then, on May 1, 1889, it became Williams, Holt & Wheeler, a change reflecting the assumption of greater responsibilities by the younger partners, especially during Williams' increasing absences from Chicago because of various illnesses—principally a recurring kidney ailment—from which he sought relief by stays, sometimes for as long as five months, at health spas in Germany and elsewhere.

On that same day, the firm moved from the Reaper Block to the year-old Tacoma Building, a $500,000 thirteen-story structure on the northeast corner of La Salle and Madison Streets that housed 156 suites for lawyers, real estate operators, and insurance agencies, had electric lighting, steam heat and modern plumbing, and cable-operated elevators. The Tacoma had been designed by William Holabird and Martin Roche along principles established five years earlier by their former employer, William Le Baron Jenney, forever renowned as "the father of the skyscraper" because his fireproof Home Insurance Building at La Salle and Monroe Streets embodied his then-revolutionary concept of a self-supporting steel skeleton whose beam and girders were bolted together to form a solid framework for its masonry.

For the next thirty-one years the firm remained in the Tacoma, initially renting four rooms on the tenth floor, subsequently adding five more on that floor and two on the floor above by the end of that long stay. Most of the furniture in the new offices was transferred from the Reaper Block quarters, but for Williams, Jenney, a good friend, designed a solid, handsome, mahogany desk.

Tacoma Building, site of the firm's
offices 1889-1920

2

In autumn of 1889 there occurred an event whose effects would be long-lasting and vastly beneficial. This was the affiliation with the firm of William P. Sidley.

Born in Chicago on January 30, 1868, Sidley was the eldest in a family of six boys and a girl. He attended grade school on the South Side and later the South Division High School, where a close friend and fellow student and, like Sidley, an attorney of distinction and accomplishment in later years, was Lessing Rosenthal, whose father, Julius, had been one of the city's pioneer lawyers. After his sophomore year, young Sidley dropped out of school to work in the vast wholesale dry goods house at Madison and Market Streets owned by Marshall Field and Levi Z. Leiter. He did this, he said later, to gain business experience, but that career was cut short after he had been there for close to two years because his father, William, having visited Williams College on a trip to Massachusetts, insisted that young Sidley resume his studies with a view toward attending that school. Early in 1885, Sidley left his job and for six months studied so diligently that he was able to cover the last two years of high school and also to master Greek sufficiently to enable him to pass the college's rigid entrance examinations. By the time he graduated from Williams in 1889, he had decided on a career as a lawyer and enrolled in the Union College of Law. Moreover, through the influence of his father's employer, Edson G. Keith, the city's foremost wholesaler of hats, caps, furs, and men's wear (and a Williams & Thompson client in the 1870s), he secured unpaid employment with Williams, Holt & Wheeler, performing rudimentary duties but also serving as a notary public, as entries for that November in the firm's journal indicate: "To notarial seal for Wm. P. Sidley, $2.00" and "To Secretary of State's fee issuing license to Wm. P. Sidley to act as Notary, $1.00." Upon his graduation in 1891 from the Union College of Law with an LL.B. degree Sidley felt he needed more education, so he entered Harvard Law School, where he gained an M.A. degree. He returned to the law firm on August 1, 1892, as a clerk to resume an association that would endure for sixty-six years more, a period in which he would take a notable and vital role in leading and building the firm and directing its course of action and growth, its philosophy and policies, and the nature and success of its practice.

Sidley's first years as a clerk were marked by customary industry in carrying out duties capably and efficiently. Then came a rather dramatic opportunity for him to make a strong impression on his superiors.

On February 11, 1895, a claim was presented to Illinois Steel Company, one of the firm's clients,* in behalf of a Nick Halic alleging that Halic, a Croatian-born worker in the South Chicago plant, had suffered critical physical and mental injuries three years earlier when a wheelbarrow laden with iron bars had overturned on him while he was trundling it down a runway that had defective planks. When an early inquiry failed to disclose records or other evidence that so serious an accident had then occurred, E. Parmalee Prentice, the steel company's general counsel, rejected the offer of a settlement and continued the investigation into the charges.

After a suit for $25,000 in damages was filed by attorneys for Halic in Superior Court of Milwaukee County—presumably to avoid the bar of the

---

*The company, formed in 1889 through consolidation of another client, Joliet Steel Company, with North Chicago Rolling Mill Company and Union Iron and Steel Company, was the foremost steel producer in the area and also owned ore lands, coal mines, timber tracts, quarries, and small railroad lines.

statute of limitations—Prentice secured a hearing before a federal commissioner in Chicago and demanded that the man claiming to be the injured worker be produced. His suspicions were intensified when the supposed Halic, through an interpreter, testified erratically yet was able to give detailed information about the accident, even to the width and the thickness of the runway planks. Accompanying the complainant was a George Haralovic, who bore a marked resemblance to him.

Subsequent investigation spurred by Prentice disclosed a conspiracy to bilk the steel company. It was learned that a Niko Halic—whose real surname was Haralovic—had been hurt at the plant in 1892 but only in a minor way and had returned to his mountain village of Gric in Croatia, then part of the Austro-Hungarian empire. The man posing as Niko actually was his cousin and George Haralovic's brother, Dane, who had come to the United States a year after the slight accident and had been living with George in his South Chicago home until the hearing, after which he, too, had returned to the village in which the Haralovic clan lived.

Resolved to take action against the brothers and any others involved in the fraud, Prentice corresponded with a lawyer in Vienna who was able to locate Niko Haralovic and obtain statements from him and other relatives about Dane Haralovic's true identity and the time of his departure from his village for the United States. But it was necessary to get more testimony and documents for use as evidence in the case against the devisers of the conspiracy and for that purpose an American lawyer would have to go to Croatia.

Sidley was chosen to carry out this assignment, and he would fulfill it, beset with difficulties and travail, in a manner that imbedded the "Croatian Episode" forever in the firm's annals.

On January 28, 1896, he set sail on the *Fuerst Bismarck* for the Adriatic seaport city of Trieste, where he meant to establish his base of operations. Although the voyage was not without its visual pleasures, what with stops at various Mediterranean ports, the day of his arrival in Trieste two weeks later was, as he afterward recalled, "the most discouraging I ever experienced." Neither the Austrian lawyer nor another in Croatia whom Prentice had hired had troubled to furnish an interpreter to assist in taking depositions from residents of Gric who were willing to tell what they knew about Dane Haralovic. Moreover, the American consul in Trieste, J. Edward Nettles, who was expected to act as the commissioner for the taking of testimony, was seriously ill, knew of no one at the time who could serve as interpreter and expressed doubts that Sidley would be able to find anyone to write out the depositions in English if he were still confined to his bed on the day set for the examination.

All that day, Sidley pondered the grim possibility that after traveling some 3,000 miles he had no assurance that the important data he had been directed to obtain would be forthcoming. But on the following morning he found at his hotel Joseph Nemarnich, a clerk, who volunteered not only to serve as a guide into the Croatian interior but appeared to have sufficient serviceable English language skills. The pair went by train to Jaska, the town in which the Croatian lawyer, Gustav Gaj, resided, arriving there after a slow twelve-hour ride.

Because Gaj spoke hardly any English, he and Sidley communicated in German, of which Sidley had some knowledge, and with occasional Latin phrases. The lawyer informed Sidley that Gric was some twenty-six miles away, reachable only by way of narrow mountain roads. So the next morning Sidley, Gaj, and Nemarnich headed off in a horse-drawn wagon for their destination in snowy, bitterly cold weather marked, too, by fierce winds. The route was a circuitous one, in some places skirting the edges of mountain precipices. But the slow, difficult trip proved worthwhile. In a village at the end of the road, Sidley met an important witness, Peter Kekic, its burgomaster, who recalled delivering to Dane Haralovic on June 23, 1893, the passport he used in coming to the United States. After interviewing several other witnesses and arranging for them to come to the consular office for the taking of formal depositions, Sidley and his companions returned to Gaj's home and the next day were back in Trieste.

New complications arose. Nemarnich's English, it was soon apparent, was inadequate for any acceptable translation of testimony, so it became necessary to employ an English-German interpreter—found by the invalid consul—who could translate Sidley's questions into German for Gaj to transmit to witnesses in Croatian and then reverse the process when answers were given. This involved procedure started early on the morning of February 20 and continued for 34½ hours, with time out for meals and intermittent naps and the consul's frequent rest periods brought about by coughing spells. In that period, what with translations and re-translations and the need for Sidley and the consul to clarify the interpreter's English and the other delays, depositions were taken from only five witnesses.

But what they had to tell and what was laboriously written down by the consul filled seventy-five foolscap pages. And the testimony that emerged was crucial to the case. It dealt with Niko's employment at the South Chicago plant in 1892, his minor injury and return to Croatia after giving George Haralovic power of attorney, the bogus claimant's physical history and his departure for the United States and eventual return in the fall of 1895 with boasts of how the steel company was to be defrauded. The depositions, together with photographs of Niko and Dane Haralovic and data about the passport laws of Croatia, were dispatched the next afternoon to Prentice by Sidley in the midst of another wind-whipped snow storm.

Sidley was far from finished. He was determined to track down Dane Haralovic and get a confession from him. On March 2, he set out once more for Gaj's home, carrying with him a pocket English-German lexicon for use in conversing at length with Gaj and in translating whatever statement in Croatian Dane might make, if and when he was found. He persuaded Gaj to join him in his quest and the next morning the two went again by wagon into the mountain area. Because the road ended a mile from Haralovic's village, Sidley and Gaj were compelled to plod through drifted snow and heavy mud, over boulders and brushwood and on the rocky bed of a mountain brook before reaching their destination.

Accompanied by Niko Haralovic and a flock of villagers, Sidley and Gaj surprised Dane in his shabby dwelling at the end of a street. With Gaj interpreting from Sidley's German, Dane sullenly acceded to Sidley's request to see his passport, a crucial piece of evidence. With as great a show of unconcern as he could muster, Sidley offered Dane a crown (twenty cents in American money) for it. Dane refused to give it up, but when Sidley raised his offer to two florins (eighty cents), Dane handed it over. He denied any knowledge of the conspiracy against the steel company and mumbled evasive replies about his trips to and from the United States. But when Niko and others in the cabin to whom he had disclosed details of the plot shouted at him to tell the truth, he admitted his part but refused to talk about other conspirators or sign any statement. He did, however, agree to go to Jaska the next month to testify along with additional witnesses.

Before this could occur, there were new vexations. The consular agent in Fiume, who was scheduled to take down Dane's testimony, was actually unable to write English intelligibly although he could speak it fairly well. And Gaj abruptly informed Sidley that he was withdrawing from his representation of the steel company because Sidley had rejected what he considered his excessive charges.

Sidley acted promptly. He got the American consul in Budapest to agree to act as the hearing commissioner, if needed, and he persuaded Gaj to accept a lower fee, a reconciliation celebrated with an elaborate turkey dinner in Gaj's home. And in Zagreb, the Croatian capital, he located a retired sea captain, Levin Koller, who spoke not only English and Croatian well but German, Italian, French, and Hungarian. Then the trio went to Gric to confront Dane and bring him to Jaska.

When Koller angrily denounced Dane for his complicity in the conspiracy and praised Sidley for not turning him over to the Croatian authorities, Dane blurted out a full confession, making a trip to Jaska unnecessary. For six hours he talked on and on, his testimony recorded in Croatian by Gaj and later translated into English by Koller. In addition to what he had told earlier, he gave details of conferences with attorneys in Chicago, of being coached by his brother, George, on what to say about the allegedly debilitating accident of 1892, of his flight from Chicago to Cleveland and then to Croatia. Upon his return to Gaj's town, Sidley promptly sent off the confession to Prentice.

A final trip to Gric was made by Sidley and Gaj early in April to arrange for Dane to return to the United States, if necessary, to testify in the Milwaukee trial. But it soon developed that the testimony would not be needed. While in Vienna awaiting instructions, Sidley learned from Prentice that the conspiracy had collapsed. The suit in Milwaukee was dismissed—largely because of the depositions taken in Trieste, Dane's confession, and other evidence transmitted by Sidley. George Haralovic was indicted for perjury and attachment proceedings were instituted against property he owned in Whiting, Indiana. He was never brought to trial, however. After the indictment was returned, he fled the country and evidently took refuge in Croatia, where lack of an extradition treaty with the United States assured him immunity from further punitive action.

In six weeks Sidley was back in Chicago, after stopovers in Italy and Switzerland and on the French Riviera. His standing in the firm was considerably enhanced because of his success in carrying out his mission despite language problems and assorted complications. It followed quite logically that he was a good choice to be named a partner, and this was done on the first day of 1897, four weeks and a day short of his twenty-ninth birthday.

In the 1890s, Illinois Steel Company remained one of the firm's principal clients until its absorption toward the end of the decade by the new Federal Steel Company, a $200 million combine put together by J. Pierpont Morgan to vie for business and profits with the industry's titan, Carnegie Steel Company. Besides the attempted swindle by George Haralovic and his fellow-plotters, the firm also handled other varied matters for the steelmaker. One was an early case in administrative law, stemming from the refusal of an official of an Illinois Steel rail line to testify before the Interstate Commerce Commission, the nation's first regulatory commission that had been created in 1887. Prentice and Holt took the case all the way to the Supreme Court which held, in 1894, that Congress had the constitutional right to authorize a court to enforce a commission order to testify on pain of being held in contempt; the lawyers' slight consolation was that three of the justices dissented and a fourth took no part in the decision.

The firm played no role in the formation of Federal Steel.* But Williams did have occasion to counsel the mighty Morgan on another matter. In 1896, Morgan wrote to Williams to inquire about the soundness and "moral respectability" of General Electric Railway Company, which had recently been incorporated with the purported intention of constructing a streetcar line that would encompass the city's southwest side and extend into the central business district. An ordinance granting the company an assortment of special privileges had been introduced by one of the rulers of the city's tumultuous First Ward, Alderman John "Bathhouse John" Coughlin, and passed by the City Council over the veto of Mayor George Swift. It was a typical "shakedown ordinance," designed to force existing traction companies to purchase—for a reputed $75,000 —the franchise granted the new company, and it evoked angry outcries from reform groups and newspapers, the *Tribune* assailing "this infamous steal" and the *Daily News* editorializing, "This council is a remorselessly venal one. Cannot the Augean stable be cleansed of men who laugh the public to scorn?"

Williams reflected these reactions in his reply to Morgan. He cast

*In 1901, upon the birth of the United States Steel Corporation with a capitalization of over $1 billion, Federal Steel was one of many companies incorporated into that mammoth combine.

doubts on the validity of the bond issue planned to finance the construction of General Electric Railway's line—if ever—and cited various irregularities in the ordinance and its amendments. "In general," he wrote, "it is not too much to say that this ordinance was one of three or four which in general public estimation have a bad preeminence in the history of municipal corruption and scandal. . . . It was commonly understood at the time that the whole scheme was organized by a gang of aldermen in their own interest and the franchise granted in effect to themselves for purposes of sale." And he concluded: "You doubtless know better than we who will control the future management of the Company, if the proposed arrangements are consummated. Perhaps the question contained in your letter calls for an answer at least as specific as this: that judged by its past history we should regard it as doubtful whether a firm of your standing could identify itself with the enterprise without injury to your reputation."

The advice was sound. The plans of General Electric Railway Company, challenged by legal action taken by Chicago City Railway Company and Western Indiana Railroad Company, whose territories it had intended to invade, went awry, and the financial bounties envisaged by the city council's boodlers came to naught.

In this decade, as in earlier years, the firm incorporated another enduring Chicago institution.

One of the stellar attractions at the World's Columbian Exposition of 1893 was an impressive collection of stuffed birds and animals, precious gems and ores, botanical specimens, and, especially notable, a splendid array of North American Indian apparel, artifacts, and assorted anthropological items. The latter had been gathered over the years by Edward E. Ayer, a wealthy Chicago lumberman, and he was among a number of leading citizens who hoped that this collection might be preserved permanently when the fair came to an end. Among others with a similar idea was Judge Sidney C. Eastman, a prominent member of the Union League Club, who wrote a letter for the "Voice of the People" columns of the *Tribune* soliciting support from the citizenry. By the time the fair closed its gates for the last time, the interest of a group of leading Chicagoans, including Williams, had been aroused, and the firm drew up papers of incorporation for the Columbian Museum of Chicago.

A charter was granted that September 16 and a special Union League Club committee embarked on a campaign to secure funds with which to endow the museum. Ayer was chairman of this committee and one of the

Field Columbian Museum

first men he visited was Marshall Field. He shrewdly emphasized that a substantial contribution would do much to perpetuate Field's name as a benefactor of students, teachers, and all who wanted to learn more about natural history. After some thought, Field offered to give $1 million if $500,000 would be pledged by other business leaders. George Pullman, upon learning of Field's proposal, gave $100,000, and Levi Z. Leiter—once Field's partner in their department stores but now unfriendly because of business disagreements—tendered a similar amount with the proviso that the museum not bear Field's name. When Cyrus McCormick learned of this testy condition imposed by Leiter, he raised $85,000 in less than an hour, while other friends of Field added $15,000—and Leiter's subscription was cancelled.

By the following June 25, the collections were installed in the imposing fireproof structure in Jackson Park that had been the fair's Palace of Fine Arts, and the name affixed to it was Field Columbian Museum, altered in 1905 to Field Museum of Natural History. In the years before his death in

1906, Field contributed an additional $400,000 and in his will bequeathed $8 million, half for an endowment and half that was spent on a splendid white Georgia marble building designed by Daniel H. Burnham and completed by mid-1920 on the lake front at 14th Street facing the length of Grant Park. There it has stood ever since—undergoing further name changes to Chicago Natural History Museum and back again to Field Museum of Natural History—with constantly expanding holdings and exhibits on archeology, zoology, botany, and geology and firmly established as a world-famous scientific institution.

Foremost among the firm's clients in this decade, and for some years to come, was Chicago Telephone Company. Since incorporating this company in 1881, the firm had assumed duties of greater scope and variety attendant on the increase in the number of subscribers from 3,022 in 1882 to 35,347 at this decade's end. Such work dealt with acquisition of real estate, interpretation of local ordinances, personal property tax assessments, contracts and litigation stemming from personal injuries, and property damages. Central Union, a phone company outside Chicago, required legal aid in dealing with tax authorities, cities, and state legislatures in Ohio and Indiana. Along with the swift rise in the telephone companies' fortunes and problems was the expansion of Western Electric, necessitating assistance in acquiring real estate, tax assessments, contracts with customers and suppliers, and employee relations. The firm also looked to the contractual arrangements between the Chicago Telephone Company and American Bell, whose patent licensee the local company was, and with American Telephone and Telegraph Company, established as an American Bell subsidiary in 1885 solely to build and operate long-distance lines but destined by the end of the century to become the parent company of the Bell System.

Two-thirds of the firm's fees in the decade came from representation of the telephone companies, Illinois Steel Company, several railroads, and Crane Company, for whom Holt won a long-drawn-out case in the United States Supreme Court involving charges that the company had allegedly supplied defective pipe for a natural gas pipe line. In addition to Williams' successful culmination of the John Crerar estate contest, the firm represented the executors of the wills of John Dean Caton, who died in the summer of 1895, and F. F. Spencer, one of the founders of the wholesale hardware company of Hibbard, Spencer, Bartlett & Company, but neither, unlike the Crerar and, earlier, the Newberry estates, involved disputes or extended litigation.

As in previous years there was a fairly steady influx of law clerks—twelve in all during the decade—who remained for varying lengths of time.

One who went on to gain distinction as a legal educator was Henry M. Bates, who departed in 1892 to practice with John Harlan, twice an unsuccessful reform candidate for mayor and the son of one United States Supreme Court justice and father of another. In 1903, Bates joined the faculty of University of Michigan Law School and seven years later was named its dean, serving until his retirement in 1939 after developing the school into one of the country's best. In later years, Bates would recall his association with Williams, Holt & Wheeler as "one of the most fortunate and productive events in my life" and express gratitude for "the precepts and examples of accuracy and thoroughness in work, of fidelity, loyalty and high sense of honor" set for him at the firm.

Another was Charles Cheney Hyde, who came to the firm in 1898, stayed three years and then started a twenty-four-year career of teaching international law at Northwestern University Law School and later, still practicing his specialty, for two decades more on the Columbia University Law School faculty. A prolific writer, he produced in 1922 the authoritative two-volume work, *International Law Chiefly As Interpreted by the United States*.

Others included John Leverett Thompson's son, Leverett, who was with the firm from 1895 to 1897 and then became a prominent investment broker; Frederick S. Nave, whom Holt considered a man with "perhaps the most massive intelligence of all" in this period and who, after leaving toward the end of the decade for Arizona because of ill health, served in that state as United States district attorney and associate justice of the Arizona Supreme Court and president of the Arizona Bar Association; Henry C. Hall, who later was one of the city's top-ranked insurance lawyers as general counsel for Marsh & McLennan; and George Chipman, whom Holt would always remember not only for his ability as a lawyer but because when he was asked, after his first year with the firm, how he liked being there replied, "I like it fine, and the best part of it is that you are not expected to lie for the office."

As an unpaid clerk, Norman Hapgood stayed for a year after graduating with honors from Harvard Law School in 1893. A man with a strong literary bent, he found his assigned duties dull; although he stood high in his law school class, he had already had doubts about pursuing a legal career, writing of this later, "I was undoubtedly giving more time and undoubtedly more thought to what was then the *fin-de-siecle* literary thinking and practicing than I was to the rules for conveying real estate or the requirements for bills of exchange." He made his feelings known to Williams, a close family friend, and Williams helped him secure a job as a five-dollar-a-week reporter on the *Evening Post*. This was the start of a long and productive career for Hapgood, mainly in New York and Washington, as a journalist, magazine editor—successively of *Collier's*, *Harper's Weekly*, and *Hearst's International Magazine*—publicist, and reformer. He campaigned vigorously for passage of a pure food and drug act, although as editor of *Collier's* he had declined to serialize Upton Sinclair's *The Jungle*, a searing novel about conditions in Chicago's Union Stockyards, because he thought it too sensational. He assailed political corruption and the depredations of the Ku Klux Klan and other bigoted organizations. He involved himself frequently in politics, as an occasional consultant to President Woodrow Wilson and adviser and publicity man for New York's Governor Alfred E. Smith. He wrote many books, ranging from biographies of Smith, Daniel Webster, Abraham Lincoln, and George Washington to volumes about playwrights and the theater, and in his memoir, *The Changing Years*, he recalled his brief time with Williams, Holt & Wheeler as one in which he was well-treated but that was for him "without a spark of passion."

5

During these years, Williams' health continued to deteriorate and his trips not only to European spas but to resorts in California, Florida, and Arizona grew more frequent. Each summer, increasingly in the last half of the decade, was spent with his wife and children at their home in Little Boar's Head at Rye Beach, New Hampshire. He devoted time, of course, to his law practice but increasingly was compelled to rely on Holt and Wheeler and Sidley to follow through on complex matters. By 1898, he was in such bad condition that he had to give up the chairmanship of the John Crerar Library board, presiding for the last time at its quarterly meeting April 9. He was ill most of that summer at Little Boar's Head and in the months that followed made sporadic visits to Chicago. He returned for good in the spring of 1899 to his seaside home and there, on June 19, he succumbed to his long and lingering illness.

Typical of tributes paid him was that of Eliphalet Blatchford at the annual meeting of the Crerar library board on the following January 18. He delineated the various estimates made by fellow-lawyers and civic leaders upon learning of Williams' death: "One of the best lawyers in the city" and "The leading business lawyer in Chicago" and "A lawyer of high attainments and success" and "A citizen deeply interested in the welfare of the community, in its philanthropies and charities, a man who had the soul of honor, and a Christian gentleman." He enumerated Williams' activities as "guardian and adviser of large estates" and emphasized that he "acted in many other responsible positions where good judgment, integrity and honor were essentials." His role in establishing the John Crerar Library after winning the legal battle over Crerar's will was duly noted, as was his setting up of a free public library named for his father in Woodstock, Vermont, in cooperation with his brother, Dr. Edward H. Williams. And finally: "One, the genial light of whose countenance, the beauty of whose character, and the warmth of whose friendship will ever dwell with us."

The founders were gone now, but they had left a notable legacy of accomplishment and had set standards for the future. Men of rectitude and scrupulous devotion to their profession, they had built a firm whose reputation and place in the legal community were of the highest. Both had been steadily involved in labors in and out of their practice that had proved beneficial to their city in diverse ways, and upon their firm they had bestowed a staunch tradition of unstinting service to clients and a spirit that would serve as a model for all who came after them.

AT THE START of the new century, the name of the firm was Holt, Wheeler & Sidley, and for the next dozen years its principal clients and revenue-producers were the telephone companies of the Bell System in the Midwest and their equipment supplier, Western Electric.

Each partner spent most of his time with specific elements of that practice. From 1903 to 1908, Wheeler was president of Chicago Telephone Company, then its chairman until his death in 1912. Holt concentrated on all matters pertaining to that company and Central Union Telephone Company, which continued, as the "sick man" of the Bell System, to have varied woes—from low earnings to tax problems—in Ohio, Indiana, and parts of Illinois outside Cook County. Sidley's prime concern was Western Electric. In 1907, when the German and Russian governments adopted new policies requiring reorganization of Western Electric's subsidiaries in Berlin and St. Petersburg within a specified time of twenty days, he was dispatched post-haste to those cities and successfully reincorporated the company's interests with scant time to spare before passage of each government's deadline; a year later, he was appointed Western Electric's general counsel and elected vice-president. For the next quarter-century, while continuing as an active member of the law firm, Sidley would be concerned with a great number of varied duties for the constantly growing company that ranged from the acquisition of land in Cicero for erection of additional facilities of the giant Hawthorne Works and securing patents for scores of new telephonic products developed by

67

William P. Sidley in 1900

the company's scientists and technical experts to negotiations with unions and assumption of a half-interest, paralleling that of American Telephone and Telegraph Company, in the creation in 1925 of Bell Telephone Laboratories, which would over the years develop into one of the world's foremost industrial research complexes.

Wheeler's presidency of Chicago Telephone Company was beset with conflict and a battle for survival. Since expiration of the first of some 2,500 Bell patents in the mid-1890s, scores of independent companies—some fly-by-night, others substantial—had come into being in the Chicago area, many promising alternative and cheaper, if less efficient, service. Forty such firms, inveighing against what they denounced as the "Bell monopoly," formed the Telephone Protective Association. The Illinois Manufacturers' Association not only incorporated Manufacturers' Telephone Company and prepared to seek a franchise from the City Council but sued to restrain Chicago Telephone Company from increasing its annual business line rate from $125 to $175. Judge Murray F. Tuley's decision in Cook County Circuit Court in favor of the plaintiff was upheld in 1906 by the

Illinois Supreme Court, necessitating refunds of $106,377 to those charged the higher rate. In addition, the high court ruled in another suit brought by the city that the company was compelled to charge suburbs the rates that prevailed when these territories were annexed to the city in 1889 and in subsequent years.

Faced with intensifying competition and prospects of further refunds, Chicago Telephone Company countered by proposing a new ordinance. A council committee was named by Mayor Edward F. Dunne to study its proposal and that of Manufacturers' Telephone Company. While this was in progress, Angus S. Hibbard, Chicago Telephone Company's vice-president and general manager, and Wheeler arranged for publication of a widely-distributed pamphlet explaining the fallacies in its primary foe's claims. The company's 5,500 employees, in two busy weeks, secured signatures of 250,000 citizens on petitions advocating extension of Chicago Telephone Company's franchise that was due to expire in 1909.

In April 1907, the committee made its recommendations: Rejection of the Manufacturers' Telephone Company proposal because its rates would be no lower than those of Chicago Telephone Company and acceptance of the latter's ordinance as drawn by Assistant Corporation Counsel Maclay Hoyne after conferences with Wheeler. In a seventeen-hour session on November 7, climaxing months of rancorous protests from the most virulent and irate independents and charges—all unfounded—by them of cash payments to key aldermen for favorable votes, the ordinance was passed, giving Chicago Telephone Company another lease on life for twenty years beyond the 1909 expiration date. Adopted by the company's board of directors two weeks later, it became effective that December 2.

Among many requirements in the new ordinance were lower annual rates ($125 for business lines, $72 for single line residences, $56 for two-party lines), compensation to the city of 3 percent of yearly gross receipts, free service on incoming calls to police and fire stations and to the city hall, service for other city departments and the school board at a 25 percent reduction, and extensive rebuilding and modernizing of the telephone company's plant within eighteen months. To finance the latter, two steps were taken. The capital stock of the company was increased from $20 million to $30 million and the company's property was mortgaged to the First Trust and Savings Bank with authorization of the issuance of $50 million in bonds. Holt, Wheeler & Sidley represented the company in that financing late in 1908 which, with its representation two years later of

69

Western Electric in a $15 million bond issue, marked the firm's initial experience in large-scale public financing.

In the difficult 1903–08 period, Wheeler worked closely with Hibbard, each man complementing the other in respective skills needed to overcome difficulties and crises. In these years the number of telephones in the city rose from 60,395 to 156,079, with three-quarters of that increase, for all the competition from independents, constituting Chicago Telephone Company's gain. In May 1908, Wheeler was named chairman of the board and served four years while the law firm continued as the telephone company's legal counsel. His successor as president was Bernard E. Sunny, a telephone company official in earlier years, who had been persuaded by President Vail of the parent AT&T to leave his post as a vice-president of General Electric Company and return to assume the presidency.

Meanwhile, a fundamental change in the structure of the Bell System and, indeed, in the history of the nation's telephone industry was in the making in AT&T's New York headquarters.

In the aftermath of the 1903–08 challenges in Chicago and elsewhere, AT&T, under direction of Vail and with the financial backing of J. Pierpont Morgan, began to buy up scores of independent companies willing or forced, by the rigors of competition, to sell. Within three years, so many such independents were accumulated that they were shaped along state and regional lines; in the Midwest, the five companies affiliated with AT&T—Chicago Telephone Company, Central Union Telephone Company, Cleveland Telephone Company, Michigan State Telephone Company, and Wisconsin Telephone Company—constituted the parent company's Central Group in an organizational setup that was not a consolidation but was designed to insure adoption of unified interests and procedures and progress.

Vail's next step—a crucial one—was to follow the British example by establishing a combined telephone and telegraph service to give the public a cooperative service hitherto unknown. To do so he sought to consolidate with Western Union Telegraph Company and in November 1909, this was effected by the purchase of 300,000 shares of Western Union stock, amounting to 30 percent of that company and giving AT&T working control. Now, telegrams could be sent by telephone on local and long-distance lines, among other boons. But such service was available only on Bell System lines, thereby evoking new outcries against monopoly.

Protests reached a climax in 1912. Acting on complaints from Clarence

Chicago Telephone Company officials and 1908 service wagon

Mackay, head of Postal Telegraph Company, and a combine of independent telephone firms, United States Attorney General George H. Wickersham advised AT&T that planned acquisition of more independents in the Midwest would violate the Sherman Anti-Trust Act of 1890; and at the same time the Interstate Commerce Commission, whose jurisdiction over the telephone business had begun in 1910, touched off an inquiry into alleged monopolistic practices by AT&T.

Faced with possible protracted and expensive anti-trust litigation, Vail chose to compromise. This took the form of what came to be known as the Kingsbury Commitment. On December 19, 1913, Nathan C. Kingsbury, an AT&T vice-president, and James McReynolds, Wickersham's successor soon to be named by President Woodrow Wilson to the United States Supreme Court, agreed to dissolve the combined wire service operation and, most importantly, to dispose of Western Union stock holdings, to refrain from buying any more competing companies without approval of the Interstate Commerce Commission and to grant long-distance connections with independents wherever they supplied standard trunk lines to Bell System switchboards. President Wilson acclaimed the Kingsbury Commitment as a deed of business statesmanship. Independents welcomed the concession relating to access to Bell's long-distance lines. AT&T, for whom the action meant a loss of nearly $8 million in the sale of Western Union stock, had given up all hopes of maintaining a monopoly in the telecommunications industry, but it and its subsidiary companies were ready to proceed with technological developments and broadening services.

2

There were, of course, other matters handled by the firm in these years.

One involved the estate of Sidney A. Kent, a wealthy investor in gas and electric companies and a contributor to the endowment fund establishing the new University of Chicago when that institution, with the gifted and innovative Yale University scholar, William Rainey Harper, as president, came into being in 1892. Kent's will, drafted in the mid-1890s by Norman Williams, named The Northern Trust Company as executor and trustee and set up a trust for Kent family members. It was admitted to probate in 1901 and the problems stemming from it—among them, state inheritance taxes, mortgage foreclosures, personal injury claims, and administrative proceedings in three states—were complex and prolonged and would occupy the firm for years to come. The firm also represented Delia Field, widow of Marshall Field, in the settlement of the $120 million estate of the merchant prince after he died early in 1906 of pneumonia.

Activity in the relatively new field of corporate law increased, with acquisition of such new clients as American Bicycle Company, American Linseed Company, and American Piano Company, each of which had been formed through consolidation of small companies. For these clients and for such others as Borden's Condensed Milk Company, the firm dealt with issues ranging from increases or decreases in capital stock or in the ranks of directors to the securing of affidavits in anti-trust cases and the acquiring of additional properties.

This was also the "progressive era" of Theodore Roosevelt after he succeeded to the Presidency on September 14, 1901, following the death of William McKinley from an assassin's bullet. An avowed trust-buster, Roosevelt assailed massive industrial and business combinations. In one of his first moves he directed Attorney General Philander C. Knox to file suit for dissolution of Northern Securities Company, J. P. Morgan's railroad holding company ("We do not wish to destroy corporations," he told audiences on a speaking tour of New England and the Midwest, "but we do wish to make them subserve the public good"), and this action was upheld in a 5-4 decision by the United States Supreme Court in 1904. In other areas, laws were passed encompassing food and drug products, the meat packing industry, workmen's compensation, child labor, freight and passenger rates for railroads, and hours for working men and women. These and more were all harbingers of a future in which governmental regulations would proliferate and require innumerable hours, days, weeks, months, and even years of hearings before federal and state commissions of varying kinds and, in many cases, prolonged litigation in the courts of the land.

3

Significant changes were occurring in the firm's ranks.

For the most part, the pattern of the past prevailed. Clerks continued to come and go at a relatively rapid pace because of roseate employment opportunities elsewhere and Holt's conservative view about advancing them to full membership. But there were exceptions to this trend.

Two who stayed on to become partners were J. Dwight Dickerson and Donald F. McPherson. Dickerson was hired in 1908 after graduating with high honors from University of Chicago Law School. McPherson, a nephew of Mrs. Holt, came a year later upon graduation from Northwestern University Law School; within four years he would be named a partner, the first to attain that status from a clerkship since Sidley's similar ascension sixteen years earlier.

Paul V. Harper, the ebullient son of the late William Rainey Harper, joined as a clerk at the start of 1913 upon graduation from the law school of the University of Chicago, where he had received his undergraduate degree in 1908. He had spent some of the five intervening years traveling in Europe, where he attended Germany's Bonn University. In 1912, while in his senior year in law school, he served as a tutor to young Philip K. Wrigley on a world tour. This resulted from discussions the youth's father, William Wrigley, Jr., the chewing gum magnate, had often had in earlier years with his friend, President Harper, about the advisability of interrupting schooling for such a trip. The elder Harper, for all his erudition and interest in scholastic training, thought the idea a good one. Consequently, when Philip finished his freshman year at Chicago Latin School, Paul Harper accompanied him and his parents on a six-month tour of world ports, during which the bright law student held classes in various subjects for young Wrigley—and laid the foundation for a long and lasting personal and lawyer-client relationship with the Wrigley family. That the instruction proved rewarding became evident by the ease with which Philip passed not only the entrance examinations for Phillips Academy at Andover, Massachusetts, that year but also those for entry to Yale University later. (Philip Wrigley never did attend any university. Instead, he prevailed on his father after graduating in 1914 to permit him to work on the installation of a company branch and factory in Australia. During 1916–17 Paul Harper arranged for Philip to be enrolled as a special student at the University of Chicago to take chemistry classes and laboratory work in chemistry, a knowledge of which was essential in making chewing gum.) Harper remained with the firm until the end of 1915, when he left to form a partnership with William D. Bangs and John Mechem. That firm dissolved in 1917 when America entered World War I, in which Harper served as a captain of field artillery. For a number of post-war years Harper was an executive with a St. Louis business corporation, then returned in 1925 to the law firm where he had first clerked and resumed an association that would prove mutually meaningful for nearly twenty-five more years.

4

On an oppressively hot August day in 1912, Arthur Wheeler was stricken with a fatal heart attack in his Lake Forest home after attending an all-day meeting of the American Bar Association in Milwaukee. This led to an event of major importance, for as a result, Charles S. Cutting, since 1900 the highly respected presiding judge of the Probate Court of Cook County, became a partner in the firm.

Cutting's earlier years, after his birth in High Springs, Vermont, in 1854, had been spent in Minnesota and Oregon. After attending Willamette University in Salem, Oregon, without graduating, he was briefly assistant editor of the *Times* in Cedar Rapids, Iowa. Then, after coming to Illinois, he was a teacher and principal of a high school in Palatine for six years, meanwhile studying law in various offices, most notably with Joshua C. Knickerbocker, first judge of the Probate Court after its establishment by the state legislature in 1877. Licensed in 1879, Cutting practiced for the next twenty years with assorted partners, concentrating on probate matters, served as a master in chancery, and, toward the end of 1899,

Probate Judge
Charles S. Cutting in 1900

when Probate Judge C. C. Kohlsaat was named to the federal bench, Cutting succeeded him in a special election.

Cutting's record of service in Probate Court was of the highest order. So versed was he in all aspects of that branch of law that lawyers often relied on him to correct mistakes in their petitions and orders in a genial and pedagogical manner. On the basis of his record, he was nominated in 1912 by President William Howard Taft for a federal judgeship but the Democratic majority in the Senate prevented confirmation of the appointment. This rebuff came shortly after the death of Wheeler and made Cutting amenable to an offer from Holt that he consider joining the firm. His reaction to the invitation was spurred by his irritation over the periodic need for engaging in political campaigning for re-election to the Probate Court; after completing the unexpired term of Judge Kohlsaat, he had been victorious in 1902, 1906, and 1910, in the latter year the only Republican to win on the county ticket in a Democratic landslide.

He held several meetings with Holt and Sidley, and on June 16, 1913, he announced his intention of leaving the bench. "I am resigning," he told reporters, "because of the annoyance caused by constantly recurring elections. A man is no longer judged on his merits while on the bench.

Judges are praised or blamed according to the parties they belong to. The constant worry and annoyance caused by this sort of thing has been too much for me. If it were not for that I would gladly remain on the bench." To Governor Edward F. Dunne he wrote, "A four-year term of office is absurd. As long as the permanency of judicial position depends on a political party there will be inefficiency."

Some weeks later, at a dinner in his honor under auspices of the Chicago Bar Association, Cutting amplified his comments before 500 friends and well-wishers gathered in the Mid-Day Club. After various judges and veteran attorneys praised his years of service in the Probate Court, Cutting urged greater participation by lawyers in the process of selecting candidates for judicial office. Reflecting the long-standing campaign by the association for reforms and improvements in that process, Cutting recalled an earlier speech in which he noted that on a particular political party committee that had named judicial candidates were five saloonkeepers, three aldermen, and a man convicted of a crime, but not a single lawyer. "Until the time shall come," he added, "when the lawyers who are the people who know not only about the legal attainments of judicial candidates but about their habits of industry, their ideals and their honesty shall have a direct but not exclusive influence upon the selection of judges we cannot hope for materially better things." Various speakers, while expressing regret that such an excellent judge had resigned, welcomed him back to the profession. "We believe," intoned John J. Herrick, an Association officer, "that Judge Cutting has the breadth of mind and the ability to adjust himself to new and changed conditions and that while we will lose the able, considerate and courteous judge we will find in him as the practicing lawyer the able, considerate and courteous opponent—or associate, as the case may be."

Innumerable opportunities would present themselves for Cutting to bear out that prediction. On the following September 1 his new affiliation began, an occasion marked by the renaming of the firm to Holt, Cutting & Sidley. His advent sparked the start of a period in which, because of Cutting's reputation on the bench, the firm experienced a steady increase in the array and variety of probate work of all kinds. Often, cases that seemed destined for extensive litigation would be referred to him for arbitration and a good deal of his practice emanated from lawyers outside the firm. And before long, Cutting's espousal of retaining clerks for longer periods than in previous years and offering them better prospects for advancement would produce rewarding results.

One of the first important—and complex—matters with which Cutting was concerned came in the wake of the death of Richard W. Sears, co-founder of the vast Sears, Roebuck & Company mail order business.

When Sears died in his summer home in Waukesha, Wisconsin, on September 28, 1914, he left an estate worth close to $16 million to his wife, Anna, named in his will as executrix. The inheritance tax of $313,616 assessed against Mrs. Sears the following March was the largest against a beneficiary of an estate in the history of Lake County, in whose suburb of Waukegan the Searses had been living for two years before the merchant's death.

Problems evolved after the Illinois legislature, on that July 1, amended the state revenue act of 1898 to permit retroactive personal property assessments despite whatever payments of such taxes had been made by a taxpayer in his lifetime. Consequently, on September 22, 1916, the Cook County Board of Review decreed that the Sears estate owed $1.8 million on property allegedly omitted from Sears' schedules from 1907 to 1912, when he and his wife maintained a home in the western suburb of Oak Park. Then, on the following May 9, a suit was filed in Cook County Circuit Court on behalf of the county assessor and other governmental bodies, including the Oak Park high school district and school board, to collect that amount from Mrs. Sears; it was transferred, on Cutting's motion, to the Lake County Circuit Court after he argued that Mrs. Sears had a right to trial in the jurisdiction in which she lived.

Final disposition of the case was some distance off, what with various legal actions and sessions before county boards and in the courts over the next fourteen years. In hearings before Judge Claire C. Edwards in Lake County Circuit Court at Waukegan, Cutting's prime contention was that at the time Sears died there was no liability for the payment of taxes of any decedent which had been omitted from assessment during his lifetime. He also pointed out to the county assessors that the amount of tax was grievously out of proportion to those levied against other Oak Park residents in the period in question. At one point, he obtained from Judge Edwards an injunction preventing the county from applying to secure judgment on its claim.

In February 1930, Judge Edwards ruled against Mrs. Sears, although he reduced the amount of taxes allegedly due to $776,877. Cutting appealed the ruling. In April 1931, the Illinois Supreme Court reversed Judge

Edwards' decree, sustaining Cutting's argument that the amended revenue act was not applicable to Sears' estate. The language of that statute, the court's ruling strongly noted, could not be extended "beyond its clear import to make the property subject to taxation," for when the legislature passed the controversial amendment Mrs. Sears was the sole and rightful owner by inheritance of the property—primarily stocks and bonds—of her late husband "and no change in the law thereafter made could disturb such vested rights." And the high court's decision emphasized: "It was not within the power of the State thereafter, by mere legislation, to impose upon her any additional obligations or to create any charge against her property. To do so would be a taking of her property without due process of law."

The opinion attracted attention and provoked considerable discussion among lawyers, especially those who specialized in problems affecting large estates. Cutting and those in the firm who worked with him on the case were given ample credit for carrying it to its successful conclusion, and the firm's reputation in the field of probate law was heightened.

6

In the early phases of the Sears case, Cutting had been assisted by a new clerk whom he assigned to appear before the county assessors to protest imposition of the huge tax. He was Edwin C. Austin at the start of a noteworthy career in which he would remain active in the firm for another sixty-eight years and would be highly influential in guiding its growth and shaping its policies.

He was born in Barrington, Illinois, on March 28, 1892, the son of a lawyer, Charles, a partner of Cutting's in the firm of Cutting, Austin & Castle. Only four months after the birth of his son, Charles Austin, then thirty-two, died of typhoid fever. Cutting assured his widow, Luella, that if Edwin should decide someday to study law he would find a place for him in any firm with which he was affiliated. That time came in 1914 when Austin was about to enter his final year at Northwestern University Law School. He had decided on a legal career after fleetingly considering whether to become a minister or a physician—for neither of which he adjudged himself especially suited—before graduating in 1912 from the University of Wisconsin. In his second year in law school he was a student editor of the *Illinois Law Review*, a task that required the digesting of

Edwin C. Austin in 1914

opinions of the Illinois Appellate Court; then and the next year he added
to funds from a partial scholarship by playing the piano for weekend
school dances and as head counselor at two summer camps—Keewatin for
boys, Pokegama for girls—near Mercer, Wisconsin.

After the camps shut down in the late summer of 1914, Cutting made
good his promise to Mrs. Austin. That September, in Austin's senior year,
during which he was elected class president, he was hired by Holt, Cutting
& Sidley on a part-time basis, attending classes half of each day and
working in the office the other half mainly at rudimentary clerical and
research duties. He was paid a monthly salary of twenty-five dollars and
just before Christmas he received a twenty-five-dollar bonus, Holt telling
him, "We would like you to share our Christmas well-being. Please accept
this check as a token, not a measure of our good will." When he
graduated at the top of his class the following July and before he handily
passed his bar examinations, Austin worked for a month at the camps and
then, at a salary of sixty dollars a month, he became a full-time clerk on
August 23, 1915.

As the newest of the clerks—the others, besides Harper and Dickerson,

79

were Ivor Jeffreys and Worth Allen—Austin was given the responsibility of docket clerk. He also did considerable research not only for Cutting but for the three other partners and the older and more experienced clerks who required memoranda in preparing motions and briefs. Although he had learned to smoke when he was still in high school, he was careful never to do so in the office, for Holt and Cutting not only were teetotalers but abhorred smoking.

Austin's very first client, that fall, was Dr. Claude Howard Searle, who was a fellow Sunday school teacher in Wilmette, where Austin lived with his mother while in law school, and whose sons, John and Howard, had spent summers at Camp Keewatin under Austin's guidance. Dr. Searle's father, Gideon, had established the manufacturing concern of G. D. Searle & Company in 1888 on Chicago's North Side, and he himself was now its general manager and prospective president, having joined the company in 1909 after graduating from Rush Medical College and practicing as a country doctor in Iowa. Austin drew Dr. Searle's will, the first of numerous services that would be performed by him and others in the firm for members of the Searle family, for individuals connected with the company, and for the company itself as it grew over the decades into a foremost international drug research organization and a maker of pharmaceuticals and diagnostic and hospital products.

Austin occasionally accompanied Cutting to court hearings and also was assigned small cases, from which he derived valuable basic experience and pragmatic lessons. In his first jury trial he defended Chicago Telephone Company against a Lake County farmer's claim resulting from an accident in which a company truck had killed one of his horses. Although such steeds were worth $75 or less, the jury, comprising mostly farmers, awarded the plaintiff $150. Austin was crestfallen, but the telephone company's official in charge of claims offered solace—and a realistic appraisal. "You made a fine argument," he said. "You really won a victory. I figure anything under $300 in such a case is a win for us. You will soon learn what to expect from a jury when a farmer sues the telephone company." In another trial, Austin's opponent, older in years and experience, showed his disdain by sneeringly alluding to him as "my young friend" and reading a newspaper while Austin made his opening statement or questioned witnesses. Noticing that the judge was irritated by such conduct, Austin referred frequently to his lack of experience in addition to citing court decisions supporting his arguments. The outcome was that the judge not only upbraided the older lawyer for his discourtesies to his young rival but also ruled in favor of Austin's client.

7

A month before Austin began his full-time employment, a terrible tragedy occurred in Chicago—one whose legal after-effects would keep him and others in the firm intermittently involved for nearly two decades.

On the warm, drizzly Saturday morning of July 24, 1915, four Great Lakes excursion steamers were lined up along the south bank of the Chicago River west of Clark Street, prepared to transport employees of Western Electric Company's Hawthorne Works, their families and friends —some 7,000 in all—across Lake Michigan to leafy groves near Michigan City, Indiana, for the fifth annual picnic of the Hawthorne Club.

First of the vessels scheduled to leave from the Clark Street dock was the *Eastland*, a sleek craft complete with a steam calliope on its main deck and below a restaurant, dance floor and jazz band, lounges, game rooms, and cabins. Proudly advertised by its owners as the "Speed Queen of the Lakes," it had plied the Great Lakes for a decade and developed a reputation as the fastest of these steamers.

For an hour after dawn, men, women, and children trooped happily and noisily aboard. By seven o'clock 2,400 persons crowded its decks, many of them in the lounges and game rooms, many strolling on the upper deck or standing along its rails. At 7:13 o'clock, Captain Harry Pedersen shouted orders for the *Eastland* to depart. At that moment, most of the passengers on the upper deck were bunched along the portside rail to look at a passing pigboat, a submarine-shaped freighter. As the stern line was cast off, the *Eastland* listed away from the dock, swayed back to an even keel as the passengers shifted away from the rail, but then lurched sharply, and, with a shudder rolled over on its port side in eighteen feet of water, with eight feet of her starboard side showing and her bow line still fastened to the dock.

Swiftly and horrifyingly, hundreds of screaming, panicky passengers were hurtled into the water and threshed and floundered there. Many drowned within seconds. Some managed to swim to the river banks or back to the ship to clamber aboard the exposed hull or cling to the starboard plates. Others hung onto boxes, barrels, and crates thrown to them by workers at an off-shore warehouse or to life preservers hurled by

The *Eastland*

sailors on the other excursion boats until they could be rescued by firemen, policemen, and bystanders who leaped ceaselessly from shore and from tugboats and other small craft that sped to the disaster. And hundreds more were trapped below decks, crushed to death or drowned in water that rushed down the grand staircase into the lounges, cabins, and other rooms.

Victims brought up from the water were laid in rows on the sidewalk, where physicians worked feverishly to revive those who showed signs of life. As word of the horror spread, the river banks became thronged with thousands of citizens, many of them friends and relatives of the picnickers. Emergency workers dispatched by Chicago Telephone Company installed telephones outside nearby store fronts for free use by survivors to call their homes or, sadly, to transmit news of the missing and the dead. Bodies dredged from the river or found inside by workmen cutting holes in the ship's hull with acetylene torches were taken in trucks to a West Side armory. By midnight, the dead numbered 810; later, when the hull had been refloated and towed to a shipyard, two more bodies were found. Twenty-two families were completely wiped out, and of the 812 victims, 465 were almost equally divided between men and women who worked for Western Electric, the rest were relatives or friends. In sheer numbers, the total dead would stand as the largest ever sustained in any calamity in the city's history.*

As general counsel and vice-president of Western Electric, Sidley was quickly involved with other company officials in establishing myriad relief measures. Promptly, the company appropriated $100,000 for use of the American Red Cross until establishment of a city-wide relief fund of $562,370, to which the company later contributed another $180,000. Special teams of relief workers were sent to surviving families that required financial aid. If surviving relatives of fatal victims requested it, the company paid all funeral expenses. Within a week after the tragedy, a permanent relief organization was established and a system of payments devised. Each employee with five or more years of service was eligible for death benefits totaling nearly $80,000 and survivors of those with fewer years also received monetary assistance. In addition, the company either cancelled or extended mortgage payments on survivors' homes. And widows of men who perished were given jobs with the company or, if they were unable to work, they received assurances that their children would be offered positions.

Amid clamor for punishment of whoever could be blamed for the tragedy, one of the first major developments among many to come was the indictment by a federal grand jury on manslaughter charges of Captain Pedersen, Chief Engineer Joseph Erickson, two officials of the St. Joseph-Chicago Steamship Company, the vessel's owners, and two federal steamboat inspectors. It was charged that the individual defendants had in various ways been negligent and that, in the light of testimony at a coroner's inquest, the *Eastland* had had a similar but non-fatal accident five years earlier, they were collectively negligent in permitting an "unseaworthy" craft to be used by the Hawthorne Club picnickers on that fateful Saturday. All the defendants were in Michigan when the indictment was returned and their counsel, including Clarence Darrow, argued before Judge Charles Sessions in Grand Rapids against the case's removal

---

*In succeeding months, others succumbed to injuries and exposure, bringing the ultimate toll to 835.

for trial in Chicago. The thrust of the defense argument was that the *Eastland* was seaworthy and that none of the defendants, singly or collectively, had been negligent. Darrow and the other defense attorneys cited a number of other possible causes, from the city's dumping of excessive rubbish into the Chicago River at the point of the fatal mishap to the Sanitary District's failure to keep the river's water level high enough so that the vessel would not possibly have listed so drastically. Judge Sessions ruled for the defendants, thereby negating possibility of a hearing in Chicago. "The majesty of the law," his decision read in part, "cannot be upheld and vindicated by forcing men from their homes to stand trial upon accusations which there is barely a scintilla of evidence to sustain. The evidence in this matter wholly fails to establish probable cause for believing any of these defendants guilty of any crime charged in the indictments."

But litigation stemming from the disaster was far from over and long in resolution. The various theories advanced by defense counsel before Judge Sessions as to other possible causes and persons, companies and civic agencies subject to legal action—and payment of substantial damages— spurred the filing of damage suits that numbered over 800. Many of these were instituted in the year after the tragedy, and because Western Electric Company and the Hawthorne Club were among the defendants, Austin in that year was kept busy as docket clerk keeping track of cases involving these clients. It would be another six years before the first of these cases would be heard and years more before ultimate disposition of all of them, and in each involving Western Electric and the Hawthorne Club the law firm would seek a favorable ruling.*

8

As the time approached for observance of the fiftieth anniversary of its founding, Holt, Cutting & Sidley was a firm small in size and numbers— four partners, four clerks, a lay staff of ten. Over the years it had not grown in proportion to the vibrant city's growth; its gross income was just under $100,000, and half of that amount came from work for two clients, Western Electric Company and Chicago Telephone Company. But its

*See Chapter VI.

standing in the legal community was without blemish and it enjoyed the goodwill and esteem of fellow-practitioners. And, as Holt emphasized at the anniversary dinner in the Blackstone Hotel on November 28, 1916, it had maintained an organic identity throughout the decades.

To the ninety-five men and women gathered to mark the happy occasion, Holt, in the evening's major address, spoke with pride about the firm as one whose partners had never left for an affiliation elsewhere and who, except for Cutting, had reached their high places through advancement within the firm. As for Cutting, now serving the second of two terms as president of the Chicago Bar Association and bringing in new clients seeking counsel in probate and estate matters, Holt expressed gratification at the compliment the distinguished ex-jurist had paid the firm by becoming a partner and "one of us in spirit as well as in bodily presence." Holt also traced the history of the firm from the earliest times of Williams and Thompson, characterizing the former as "considerate, wise and just, with a genius for friendship and loyal to the last heart beat" and the latter as "thorough, clear, a hater of shams and a hater of slovenliness, from whom no younger man could fail to learn lessons of clean and business-like methods of preparation and practice."

He talked, too, of other firms present and past, and of veterans in the profession, and of Arthur Wheeler, (". . . strong, sound lawyer, sagacious counsellor, loyal friend, high-minded Christian gentleman. . .") and of former clerks who had succeeded elsewhere as lawyers or, like Henry Bates, as dean of University of Michigan Law School. And he used the occasion to inveigh against what he saw as the prevailing trend to consider the amassing of legal fees more important than the rendering of excellent service. Recalling that in an earlier day whenever Norman Williams was asked, "How's the law?" he invariably replied, "The law is better than the profits," Holt declared, "It is a pity that this feeling should give place to the hard, rushing, devil-take-the-hindmost conceptions of commercialized practice, to personal antagonisms and business-grabbing, to advertising more or less disguised, to bad ethics and worse manners, in view of which one is sometimes tempted to treat the profession as a necessary evil and find his real enjoyment elsewhere."

He looked back on his forty years with the firm as a period in which a philosophy prevailed inside it that exemplified the ideals of both Williams and Thompson, principally the cultivation of "the human side of life . . . where success is appraised not merely with an eye to financial results but with a large door open to human fellowship and congenial intercourse with the sharers of our common profession, with sympathy and aid for the ambitions of subordinates instead of regarding them as mere hirelings or cogs in the wheels of a great machine, with loyalty to clients measured by the higher standard of loyalty to truth."

And he concluded on a lofty note of hope and optimism about the future: "Of an institution even as small as our firm, I love to think that however shifting its membership and with whatever adaptation to changing conditions, it may live, if not forever, at least for generations, and contribute its real though indistinguishable part toward the final establishment of justice and the oncoming Kingdom of Righteousness."

9

America's entry, on April 6, 1917, into the war that had been raging in Europe since 1914 had a sharp effect on the firm's personnel. Before the year was out, one of its four partners and three of its five clerks were in uniforms.

First to go was Austin. With the intention of joining the Navy if the country became involved, he and several friends had been attending night classes in navigation at Northwestern University in the preceding winter months. A few weeks after his marriage on June 9 to Marion Roberts, whom he had known and admired when she attended Camp Pokegama in 1915, he signed up for training as an officer in the Naval Pay Corps. That July 31 he and his bride were in Washington, where he attended officers' school and, upon graduation, was commissioned an ensign and assigned to the Puget Sound Navy Yard at Bremerton, Washington. There, his legal education and experience were put to use by his commanding officer by assignment to committees examining candidates for promotion, and before long he himself was promoted to lieutenant. Another clerk who left was James A. McLaughlin, who became a "90-day-wonder" Army officer. After the war, he gave up law practice and, with a change in his surname to the ancestral McLachlan, was for many years a recognized authority on the Harvard Law School faculty in fields ranging from real property to bankruptcy.

The partner who departed was McPherson. That November he was commissioned a captain in the Army and served subsequently in the War

Risk Insurance Division and the Bureau of Contracts and Adjustments in Paris and, under General Charles G. Dawes, as general purchasing agent for the American Expeditionary Force in Paris, Berne, and London. Holt, Cutting, and Sidley were well beyond the age limit for military service. But Sidley, who had been president of the board of managers of the Chicago Young Men's Christian Association from 1911 to 1915, was active as a foremost member of the organization's executive council in charge of constructing YMCA centers near Army camps in fifteen states from Kentucky to the Canadian border.

The need for personnel—as in every law office in the city—was pressing. As a consequence, two clerks were hired to do the work of the three who had departed; more importantly, William D. Bangs—whose partnership with Paul Harper and John Mechem was dissolved when they donned military uniforms—was brought in as a partner late in 1917. At thirty-two, he was the youngest partner ever to become a member of the firm directly from the outside. His academic credits were substantial, including a degree from Princeton University and a position on the editorial board of the *Harvard Law Review*, and his experience since graduation from that university's law school in 1910 had been with a solid local law firm before his affiliation with Harper and Mechem. Almost at once after joining Holt, Cutting & Sidley, Bangs performed much work for Chicago Telephone Company and would continue to do so through the difficult war months and thereafter.

10

At this time Nathan G. Moore, regarded as Chicago's foremost expert in real estate and condemnation law, was serving the firm as special counsel in behalf of a major client, James S. Kirk & Company, for nearly six decades the city's—indeed, the nation's—prime manufacturer of soap products.

The genesis of this affiliation lay in the city's efforts to carry out one of the many proposals in the imaginative Chicago Plan devised in 1908 by the master architect-planner, Daniel H. Burnham, under auspices of the Commercial Club. This involved the widening of heavily traveled Michigan Avenue and construction of a massive double-decked bridge at the Chicago River to eliminate perennial traffic congestion on the ancient, rickety Rush Street bridge a block to the west. After the stretch south of the river to Jackson Boulevard was broadened, it was time for work to proceed on similar improvement of the thoroughfare to the north and for construction of the bridge and its approaches. As in the first phase of the overall venture, condemnation proceedings had to be instituted against property that included scores of apartment buildings, a decrepit mansion or two, and factories of considerable vintage, including a portion of the Kirk plant, a squat, red-brick structure that stood on the river's north bank directly in the path of the proposed link.

The law firm's first step had been taken in 1911 with examination of authorities and opinions as to the city's power to condemn. By 1916, after the city had either won or successfully settled hundreds of suits brought by other involved property owners, Kirk executives—James, Milton, John, and Wallace Kirk, four of the seven sons of the founder—had need of a knowledgeable, prestigious condemnation lawyer. They did not oppose the link project and, in fact, had been among the signers of a petition favoring it. But they were determined that the amount offered by the city not wreak financial damage on their company.

In practice in Chicago since 1885, Moore was a senior partner in the highly-regarded firm of Wilson, Moore & McIlvaine. His reputation and victories in real estate cases were formidable, ranging from successful claims for damages caused by erection of the elevated lines to condemnation proceedings by which the Chicago and North Western Railway had secured land for a new passenger station. Although Moore and Holt had sometimes been on opposing sides in court hearings, they had been close friends for thirty years and worked together as lay leaders in Presbyterian church circles. So when Holt asked him to handle the Kirk defense, Moore agreed to take a leave from his firm.

The case came to trial in October 1917, before a jury in the County Court of Judge William L. Pond. Moore called many real estate experts and appraisers to support his basic argument that the portion of the plant slated to be removed for public benefit was a producer of income and differed, for purposes of remuneration, from a building that yielded no income; therefore the value of the section destined for removal needed to be based on its productiveness rather than on its worth as a physical property. During the trial, the *Tribune's* editorial cartoonist, John T. McCutcheon, portrayed the soap company as the only remaining obstacle to the project and wryly depicted a thoroughfare stretching around the old plant instead of running through it. In reply to the drawing and similar editorial attacks in other newspapers, a statement drafted by Moore emphasized anew the company's early support for the venture and added, "We realize that the public good is of paramount importance. . . . At the same time we believe that we are entitled to a fair and reasonable compensation. A manufacturing business employing more than a thousand people and running day and night cannot be moved instantly. A removal requires time. It costs money."

When the jury set compensation at $433,996, amounting to three-tenths of the total plant's value as property, Moore considered it inadequate. He appealed the ruling, but it was affirmed early in 1919 by the Illinois Supreme Court. The section of the soap factory was demolished—the company soon built a larger plant on North Avenue close by the north branch of the Chicago River—and work proceeded on the bridge and approaches. And on a warm May 14, 1920, Mayor William Hale "Big Bill" Thompson rode down a flag-bedecked Michigan Avenue with Charles H. Wacker, head of the Chicago Plan Commission, in an open limousine toward the south end of the span. While a band blared and a large crowd cheered him, Thompson snipped a silk ribbon, waved his big cowboy hat and directed the first automobile to cross the splendid new bridge.

11

While the Kirk appeal was pending, Holt underwent a mastoid operation. At first he appeared to have recovered well from the surgery and worked steadily in his office and made several court appearances. But within a few weeks, an infection developed and spread swiftly to his brain, causing his death on December 13, 1918, in his Cedar Street home. He was sixty-three years old, and he had been head of the firm since the death of Norman Williams in 1899. As well-known for his activity in civic and religious affairs as for his legal career, he had served as president of the Presbyterian Brotherhood of America, trustee of the Chicago Orphan Asylum, director of the McCormick Theological Seminary, alumni trustee of Williams College, and in varied capacities for the YMCA. His contributions to the firm were solid, although he had a tendency to be peppery in disposition and occasionally impatient with those who could not match his crispness and fluency in writing. And he had maintained the conservative policy regarding advancement, so that the rate of arrivals and departures of clerks had persisted in that period.

Nathan G. Moore

In the months after Holt died, Sidley proposed to Moore that he join the firm permanently as Holt's successor in status and compensation. The offer made much sense, for in addition to his expertise in the field of real estate law Moore was equally learned and experienced in corporate, trust, and tax law. He was now sixty-eight years old but still buoyant and vigorous, a dapper man who invariably appeared in court in a tweed cutaway coat. He affected a stern manner, especially with younger men in the firm, and was inclined to be—and would continue so—ultra-pedantic in correcting and rewriting incessantly, in a barely legible scrawl, documents he asked them to prepare. He was famed among colleagues and contemporaries for a keen memory and an ability to pinpoint with little hesitation or prolonged searching a precise quotation in the Illinois Supreme Court Reports or similar compilations that was pertinent to the matter under discussion. His stature in the legal community and his profound knowledge were undoubted, so that when he accepted Sidley's offer and became a partner on September 1, 1919, his affiliation was deemed a considerable boon. Appropriately and in accord with Sidley's proposal, the firm's name on that day was changed to Cutting, Moore & Sidley.

Cutting, Moore & Sidley
1919–1930

IN THE first postwar year, Sidley's immediate task as general counsel
for Western Electric was to spend several months in Europe, principally to gather evidence of extensive damage to the company's plant
and offices in Antwerp, an assignment that later resulted in his being
named chairman of the American War Claimants Association that
represented some 10,000 corporations and individuals whose claims
against Germany totaled over $10 million.

When Sidley returned to Chicago from Europe in 1920, he assumed
the role that he would fill for well over the next two decades, that of the
firm's active managing partner. He was now able to put into effect a policy
designed to stimulate retention of clerks with a definite aim of advancing
the ablest of them to partnerships instead of following the practice of the
past of allowing so many of them to train and derive valuable experience
there and then go elsewhere.

First to profit from the progressive concept were Austin and Dickerson.
After the war's end on November 11, 1918, Austin had been assigned for
a good part of the next year to service aboard the USS *Eurana*, a Navy
cargo ship converted to transport duty in bringing troops back from
Europe. When he returned to Chicago, he had a choice of two offers: to
come back to the law firm at a considerably increased salary of $250 a
month or to accept a higher-paying job in The First National Bank of
Chicago's trust department, headed by Roy C. Osgood, an old family
friend. Despite Austin's respect for Osgood and assured financial benefits,
the notion of a future that offered little variety and compulsory retirement
at sixty-five had no appeal, so late in November 1919, he returned to the

law firm to resume what would be a long, influential, and productive career. In addition to being in charge of the court docket, Austin was assigned by Sidley to handle various matters for Western Electric, mostly workmen's compensation cases, and he acquitted himself well.

In May 1920, Austin and Dickerson were officially designated as junior partners, in line with the salutary plan formulated by Sidley, with Cutting's strong backing, to promote from within more assiduously. Until adoption of this system, the only kind of partnership participation in the firm was that of underwriting partners whose earnings were based on percentages of total annual income. Now the two received specific financial guarantees and later a percentage of the firm's net income for the year. While each certainly welcomed compensation greater than when they were clerks, the basic benefit was the important shift in firm philosophy that would then—and in the future—stimulate elevation to the ranks of partners, especially as the firm's numbers of clients continued to expand.

Simultaneously, the firm moved to one of the city's newest skyscrapers, the Lumberman's Exchange Building—soon renamed the Roanoke Building—at 11 South LaSalle Street. Designed by William Holabird and Martin Roche, the sixteen-story structure had gone up in 1915 and was fully occupied until September 1919, when the north end of the tenth floor, comprising nineteen offices, was made available by the departure of Illinois Life Insurance Company. To Sidley, then in Europe on Western Electric business, McPherson wrote that he, Moore, and Cutting had looked elsewhere but had selected this space, despite a rent higher than that paid in the Tacoma Building, because it seemed especially well suited for the firm's purposes and "no space at a less figure is obtainable, nor will be obtainable for two or three years, as there is no building going on." Moreover, four rooms on the eleventh floor were available for use as a library, and in general, noted McPherson, "There is no better location for a law office in Chicago." That observation was fully justified. In addition to the Roanoke's proximity to banks and business establishments, LaSalle Street was aptly dubbed "the street of lawyers." A multitude of legal offices extended for almost a mile north of Jackson Boulevard, and plans were in the offing for the Chicago Bar Association to shift from cramped quarters in the Standard Trust and Savings Bank Building at Monroe and Clark Streets to the top floor of the twenty-story Burnham Building at Randolph and LaSalle Streets diagonally across from the huge edifice housing the City Hall and County Building, the Circuit and Superior Courts, and the civil branch of the Municipal Court.

Roanoke Building,
site of the firm's offices 1920-69

In the Roanoke Building the firm would remain for fifty years, with periodic expansion and improvement of facilities. In April 1924, after five stories and a tower had been added to the structure, a move was made to twenty rooms on the twentieth floor. Dickerson was in charge, and when the task was finished, he treated the clerks and other male personnel who had helped move files and other documents to a steak dinner at the Union League Club. Within five years, all that floor's thirty-nine rooms were taken over. Space on the floor below served as a library and what came to be called "the bull pen," with desks for incoming clerks, and later rooms were added for conferences, handling of mail, and other functions. By 1958, the firm also occupied the entire twenty-first floor and by the end of its stay in the building most of the rest of the nineteenth floor, too.

2

The decade following the move to the Roanoke Building was an eventful one for the firm—and for the city.

In the 1920s, Chicago experienced one of its biggest booms. Its population increased from 2.7 million to 3.4 million. Consumption of electricity rose 133 percent, the number of automobiles quadrupled. There was a vast rise in the amount of residential and commercial buildings; in a three-year period, 75 percent of building permits were for apartment houses, mostly in outlying areas for new residents arriving at an average rate of 60,000 a year. By 1923, the Loop had dozens of skyscrapers and more being built then and later. As in earlier times, there was violence and criminal turbulence, now occasioned by bloody warfare between gangs contesting for illicit riches to be gained by operation of illegal rackets and distribution of bootleg liquor. For most of these years, "Big Bill" Thompson reigned in the City Hall, and his admirers and cohorts, shrugging off corruption and chicanery in various sectors, shrilled "Throw away your hammer and get a horn!" in raucous emulation of the Booster-Boomer spirit of previous eras. There were many who deplored the civic iniquities but as many and more took a kind of perverse pride in them, and others were too busy building fortunes through heavy investments in real estate, stocks, and other securities to pay too much heed to the city's ills. The milieu and prevailing attitudes were deftly characterized by Mary Borden, a native Chicagoan and novelist: "No one is ashamed of anything in Chicago. Everything is moving much too quickly. Everyone is too specialized, and it is all too much fun. Each one, whether crook or politician or expert gunman, architect or banker or broker, is too good of his kind to be conscious of anything less positive and less exhilarating than his own power. Everything about the big, blustering place is positive and superlative." Other visitors praised and assessed, criticized and philosophized. To Sir Charles Wakefield, a British author and philanthropist, Chicago was "a city of tumultuous magnificence with all the qualities that entitle it to be admitted into that select circle of the world's titanic cities that are great in imaginative grasp of the possibilities of their situation and their corporate wealth as in numbers." Chicago was called "the dream of the industrial God" as writers traversed its vast tracts of factories and manufacturing plants and a "city of noise" as they listened to the clatter of street cars and roar of automobiles down constantly-improving Michigan Boulevard and elsewhere and "the city of hope, still fluent, still chaotic."

In much of this tumultuous decade, the firm was still relatively small, but it was strengthening its reputation as reliable, hard-working, efficient, and productive. As the range of clients broadened and increased, its income rose; by decade's end it would be four times as large as at the start. Throughout, Sidley constantly enunciated his philosophy that the firm's integrity and first-rate service to all clients at reasonable rates were paramount and unswerving. He counseled the younger men often and offered assistance whenever needed in complex matters, and he was steadfast in maintaining the pattern of promoting from within the ranks.

3

A consequence of gradually developing business was a growth in personnel. After a brief post-war stay in Paris as head of a J. P. Morgan & Company affiliate, Foreign Commerce Corporation, McPherson returned for good in 1921, and in 1925 Paul Harper, his business venture in St. Louis over, came back, within three years to be named a partner. And there were significant newcomers, all of whom would become partners in due time.

In April 1920, Merritt C. Bragdon arrived. A Phi Beta Kappa graduate of Northwestern University in 1913 and from Harvard Law School *summa cum laude* three years later, he practiced first with another Chicago firm, then served in the war as a lieutenant in an artillery regiment. A sound scholar who took extreme care in drafting documents, Bragdon started as an aide to Cutting in the field of estates, trusts, wills, and related tax matters. He rapidly won the esteem of his superiors, and of those who came under his tutelage. He became a partner in 1928. "A man who never makes mistakes," Sidley later said of him.

Edward D. McDougal, Jr., attending University of Chicago Law School (he had been urged to study law by ex-President William Howard Taft, a family friend), heard from an acquaintance of Bangs that the firm needed a law clerk. One June day in 1922, he showed up in Bangs' office and was then introduced to McPherson in an adjoining room, and would forever remember McPherson's appearance (". . . a crew haircut and his watch chain looped through his lapel with the watch in the breast pocket") and his quick and decisive manner of speech. There followed a session with Sidley and with Austin, who told him much about the firm's history and its high standards and requirements. At a lunch of braised ox joints with Bangs and McPherson at the nearby Brevoort Hotel, young McDougal was given some assurance that he might be hired later in the year. This did happen in October, at a salary of fifty dollars a month for part-time work while he finished the law school term the following January, when as a full-time clerk his salary was doubled.

Two years later came James F. Oates, Jr., son of a highly successful insurance agent who, as an officer of the central department of the YMCA in Chicago, knew Sidley well. After undergraduate work at Princeton University, Oates went to Northwestern University Law School and upon graduation in early 1924 started to make the rounds of Loop law offices. He was interviewed at length by Sidley, who was, as always, gracious and affable. On that February 17 Oates was hired as a clerk. "The firm had a reputation," he later recalled, "as a place where you had to work like hell. It took itself very seriously and its leaders—Cutting, Moore, and Sidley— and younger partners like Austin and Dickerson all had great qualities in various fields of the law. I was soon made aware that the heart of this firm was the acceptance by every one of the lawyers that our particular responsibility to the firm was to be part of a closely-knit, hard-working group and that we should never be offensive or arrogant and let the firm down in any way. I felt that I was lucky to be there."

At the end of 1926, Adlai E. Stevenson, then nearing twenty-seven, was the newest of the clerks. Like McPherson, Bangs, McDougal, and Oates, he had graduated from Princeton University, where he edited the *Daily Princetonian*. Then, although he would have preferred a career as editor or publisher of the *Daily Pantagraph*, the family newspaper in Bloomington, Illinois, he yielded to the strong urgings of his father, Lewis, and entered Harvard Law School. After two years, he returned to his home in Bloomington to work on the *Pantagraph* as a reporter, writing about, among other events, the John T. Scopes "monkey trial" in Dayton, Tennessee, and severe tornadoes in southern Illinois. Then he resumed his studies at Northwestern University Law School, received his degree, and was soon admitted to practice. After a European trip, he came to work for Cutting, Moore & Sidley at $100 a month and viewed the prospect of a legal career, as he wrote to a friend, "without the least eagerness."

Despite his qualms, Stevenson dutifully carried out chores invariably assigned to new clerks, whether doing research for older colleagues' briefs or making routine motions in court. He had little liking for trial work; in one of his few such cases—indeed, his very first—he secured, with considerable moral and practical support from Austin, an injunction preventing liquidation by a lessee of property in the trust established years back by Norman Williams for Sidney A. Kent. As the months progressed, Stevenson took on a range of other duties, from handling small estates to corporate financing. With the coming of the Great Depression, his

Adlai E. Stevenson
in 1927

assignments included foreclosure suits and others for repossession of articles whose buyers had defaulted on payments. Austin held Stevenson in high regard and saw in him prospects of becoming a first-class lawyer if he concentrated on his legal work instead of following through on his growing tendency to engage in outside activities and public life.

The latter trait then manifested itself in, most importantly, membership in the Chicago Council on Foreign Relations, an organization which met at weekly luncheons to hear speakers discuss events overseas and the nation's foreign policy; by 1932 he was its secretary and a year later its president. Earlier, he had shown interest in running as a Democratic candidate for the state senate but had not followed through. In Franklin D. Roosevelt's initial campaign for the Presidency, he served as its western division treasurer, and he also strongly supported the candidacy of Probate Court Judge Henry Horner for governor, endorsing him in *Pantagraph* editorials; Horner had succeeded Cutting in the Probate Court and knew Stevenson through the latter's occasional appearances before him in estate matters. After Roosevelt's inauguration, Stevenson made it known to several of his father's acquaintances in the administration—especially Harold L. Ickes, the new President's Secretary of the Interior—that he was interested in a government job, as were scores of young Democratic lawyers throughout the country. Early in 1933, Stevenson left Cutting, Moore &

97

Sidley for Washington to become a lawyer for the Agricultural Adjustment Administration; he wrote to his wife, Ellen, whom he had wed shortly after joining the law firm, that he was engaged primarily in preparing agreements for subsidies to crop-growers and hoped thereby to gain experience in administrative law, a rapidly-developing field in those early days of proliferating New Deal agencies. This departure—ending his longest period of sustained practice of law—was the first of several he would make from the firm in ensuing years.*

McPherson's brother-in-law, Mahlon Ogden West, who, like his sister, Frances McPherson, was a grandchild of Mahlon Ogden, one of the firm's earliest clients in the post-Great Fire days, was hired in 1928, a few years after graduating from Northwestern University Law School. Earlier, he had been a classmate of Stevenson's at Princeton. His career with the firm would be relatively brief; on January 17, 1936, a year after he was made a partner, he died suddenly of a heart attack in his Lake Forest home.

In 1929, came two men who were to figure significantly in the firm's history.

John Dern, the son of George H. Dern, Utah's governor and later Secretary of War in FDR's first cabinet, had been captain of the football team at the University of Pennsylvania. As graduation approached in 1924, he was offered a permanent job as freshman football coach. When he expressed no strong desire to have a lifetime career coaching football, his head coach suggested he enter the university's law school. Within days, Dern's future was determined, for he was readily fascinated by the idea of becoming a lawyer. He did coach freshman football, but also attended so industriously to his studies that he graduated in 1927 *cum laude* and, upon admittance to the New York bar, became a clerk that year for one of the city's august firms, Sullivan & Cromwell. When he wed Jean MacLeish, daughter of Bruce MacLeish, head of Carson Pirie Scott & Company, he decided to move to Chicago. He appeared at the offices of Cutting, Moore & Sidley with a strong recommendation from Arthur H. Dean, then a newly-named Sullivan & Cromwell partner, and was promptly hired, soon to become deeply involved in matters affecting public utilities.

Howard Neitzert wanted to be a sociologist after he graduated Phi Beta Kappa from the University of Michigan in 1927. After traveling for

*For Stevenson's later association with the firm, see Chapters VII and VIII.

several months around the world, he could find no satisfactory job in that field, so he took the advice of a favorite professor that he attend the university's law school for at least a year on the premise that it would be helpful to him as a sociologist to have some education in the law. The year stretched into two. Despite working in assorted jobs—cook, assistant manager of a country club, photographer for the university—to earn money for tuition and living expenses, Neitzert received nearly all top grades, and by the time he won his J.D. degree in 1929 he was ready for a career as a lawyer. The school's dean, Henry Bates, sought to dissuade him because he considered Neitzert's personality too abrasive, but he did write a "To Whom It May Concern" letter for him, citing his academic record. During that Easter vacation period, Neitzert visited forty-seven Chicago law firms and found no prospect of employment with any. On Good Friday, at Cutting, Moore & Sidley, he spent half an hour with Austin, afterwards recalling that, although he received no assurances of a job when he graduated, these words sprang to his mind: "I have a friend, an elder brother. I'll work for him, and for no other." That visit bore good results. Austin reported favorably to Sidley and when Sidley wrote to Bates for more specific information, he received a reply reading, in part, "I've rarely been able to recommend one of my students, but I can recommend this one." That September 16, two weeks after graduation, Neitzert was at work for the firm, beginning over four decades of service in which, in an assortment of assignments, he would achieve a deserved reputation as a brilliant trial lawyer.

In the opening year of the next decade, another Princetonian and Harvard Law School graduate arrived. Destined to have an estimable career with the firm and in civic and professional activities, William H. Avery, Jr., had given no thought either at the University of Chicago's secondary school or in his Princeton years to becoming a lawyer. But after signing up for an executive training program with the United States Steel Corporation, he was visited during commencement week in 1927 by two friends who had graduated a year earlier and who spoke enthusiastically about their initial year at law school. He enrolled at Harvard Law School, and in his third year he returned to Chicago during his 1929 Christmas vacation to explore post-graduation employment prospects. He paid a visit to his cousin, William S. Warfield III, a member of the firm of Cassels, Potter & Bentley, and asked him to make a list of firms other than his own for whom he would want to work if he were starting his career. Warfield jotted down thirteen, and Avery checked the list in the Martindale-Hubbell directory, noting well the number of Princeton alumni at Cutting, Moore & Sidley. On his job-seeking venture he soon found himself in Bangs' office. After a brief conversation, Bangs took him to meet Sidley, Oates, and McPherson. When Avery came back to Warfield, he told him that he hoped that when he paid another visit after graduation he would be hired. "I like the men I met," he said. "They seem to have a warm regard for each other and there's a certain positive feeling there." At this, Warfield pulled from his desk a copy of the list of firms he had prepared earlier; during Avery's absence he had checked Cutting, Moore & Sidley as the likeliest of them for Avery to join. "All these firms," said Warfield, "have integrity and ability. But this one has the greatest *esprit de corps* of any. These men really enjoy being together, practicing law together. Let's hope they pick you."

Warfield's wish was fulfilled the following summer. Avery had another meeting with Bangs, who was not certain that anyone would be hired because of the deepening economic depression. But that July, Bangs summoned him and asked when he would be ready to start. On that August 11, Avery joined nine partners and nine clerks of the firm and initiated more than half a century of valued service.

In keeping with custom, each of these newly hired men spent his early months doing legal research, assisting the docket clerk, checking real estate titles, and performing sundry rudimentary duties. As their predecessors did, they occasionally appeared in courtrooms either to answer court calls, ask for continuances, argue various motions, or even handle small cases.

4

Among myriad matters with which the firm was occupied in this decade were those relating to the Bell System and its affiliates.

Throughout 1920, Bangs worked with Eugene S. Wilson, Chicago Telephone Company's general counsel, on a plan for purchase of the still-ailing Central Union Telephone Company. On December 1, shortly after Wilson was transferred to New York to be American Telephone and Telegraph's vice-president for public relations, purchase was consummated of Central Union's sixty-one Illinois exchanges, which included Peoria,

William D. Bangs

Springfield, Rockford, Rock Island, Moline, Quincy, and thirty or more cities with 118,000 telephones and a system of toll lines; the price was $15.5 million in 5 percent notes of Chicago Telephone Company maturing in three years and assumption of underlying bonds of $520,000. Three weeks later, the CTC directors changed the name the company had borne since 1881 to Illinois Bell Telephone Company.

This was an important but uncomplicated event in the telephone company's history. More complex and long-lasting was litigation arising from rate changes. Shortly before the end of World War I, the federal government, by Presidential proclamation following passage of a congressional resolution, had taken control of all telephone and telegraph systems at first and later all railroad lines. In the ensuing months, Postmaster General Albert S. Burleson, delegated to assume possession and operation of the properties, was compelled, mainly by rising costs and ultra-rapid inflation, to raise rates on long-distance and local calls. These actions evoked nationwide protests from subscribers and state regulatory commissions to such extent that on August 1, 1919, a year after government control had begun, it was terminated. But sharp rises in costs and drastically reduced earnings continued; 1920 was adjudged the poorest

101

year Chicago Telephone Company had ever experienced with respect to earnings. Rate increases authorized that June and the following January helped to restore the company's earning power, but in September 1921, the Illinois Commerce Commission on its own motion issued a citation to determine the reasonableness of coin box rates in Chicago. This was the prelude to a long series of proceedings before the commission and in the courts.

On August 16, 1923, the commission, after nearly two years of hearings, issued an order effective that October 1 reducing rates for four classes of coin box services in Chicago. As general counsel for the company since 1922, Bangs countered by suing in the United States District Court to enjoin enforcement of the order. Before a special three-judge court, he argued that the order was confiscatory and violated the due process clause of the Fourteenth Amendment. That December 21, an interlocutory injunction was granted, and the ruling was affirmed by the United States Supreme Court on October 19, 1925, with the proviso that if the injunction, upon further hearings, were dissolved, the telephone company would refund to customers amounts paid by them in excess of the sums chargeable under the commission's order. The next hearing in the case did not occur until April 1929, when another three-judge court entered a decree making the injunction permanent. The commission and the city appealed that ruling. For two days toward the end of October 1930, Bangs argued before the high court. When he returned to his office, he appeared to be weary and tense. He discussed the proceeding with Oates, recalling what was said in the various arguments by him and the city's corporation counsel, Samuel Ettelson, and the state's attorney general, Oscar Carlstrom. The court's ruling on December 1 reversed the lower court's decree and remanded the case for further proceedings, the results of which would not be final for four years.* Bangs was never to know of this defeat, for three weeks earlier, on November 9, he was stricken with severe angina pectoris—superinduced, according to his physician, by nervous indigestion—and he died in his home in Geneva.

*See Chapter VII.

Early in the decade the first of a multitude of cases arising from the *Eastland* tragedy finally came to trial. For Western Electric and its Hawthorne Club—two of a number of defendants, including the city of Chicago—Cutting and Austin appeared before Circuit Court Judge Donald Morrill in January 1921, in a test case. Cutting served as adviser and consultant, and Austin bore the brunt of the task of preparing and presenting a defense based primarily on the argument that the company was not liable because all arrangements for the picnic on that tragic Saturday in 1915 had been made by the employees. At the close of the plaintiff's arguments presented by Charles Spencer, an attorney representing many of the victims' surviving relatives involved in the litigation, all the defendants except the city received a directed verdict. In November of the following year, the city, by stipulation, was the sole defendant in a jury trial before Superior Court Judge Thomas Windes in which Spencer, seeking $10,000 in damages for the family of a victim, charged that the city's failure to keep rocks and other obstructions out of the Chicago River had caused the excursion steamer to tip over. But Judge Windes, emphasizing that the river was not a highway and that the city could not be compelled to keep it clear of obstructions as it was required to clean streets, instructed the jury to disallow the claim. In 1924, a jury in the Superior Court of Judge John P. McGoorty reached a similar verdict in another damage suit.

Hundreds of other pending suits, by agreement between the defendants and plaintiffs, were placed on passed-cases court calendars for ultimate disposition either by settlement or trial. Periodically, new clerks at the firm were dispatched to make motions for dismissing the cases before whatever judge had them on his calendar, but invariably they returned to report that not only had their motions been denied but they had been upbraided by the judge. Early in 1931, Howard Neitzert was assigned the onerous task. The cases were then on the calendar of Circuit Court Judge John R. Caverly, a crusty veteran who six years earlier had achieved renown—and, in some quarters, strident criticism—for meting out life sentences instead of the death penalty to Nathan Leopold and Richard Loeb for the murder of young Bobby Franks. Confidently, Neitzert offered his motion to dismiss Western Electric and the Hawthorne Club as defendants in some 800 cases. Surprisingly, Judge Caverly ordered both sides to attend hearings exploring the nature and scope of the agreement for placing the suits on passed-cases calendars. After the hearings, Judge Caverly announced he would hear arguments on Neitzert's motion. Neitzert's main point was that the purpose of the agreement had failed because the passage of time since the filing of the suits precluded settlement. He urged that dismissal of his clients be granted for want of prosecution. The arguments for each side lasted only an hour. Then Judge Caverly ruled in Neitzert's favor, stating that too much time had gone by without settlements or trials. When Neitzert informed Sidley and others at the firm of Judge Caverly's decision, they expressed astonishment at this feat of a newcomer, along with pleasure that the vexing matter was finally disposed of.

Judge Caverly's action ended the involvement of Western Electric in the legal aftermath of the *Eastland* calamity. But other aspects had yet to be resolved. In 1927, some 600 suits for claims totaling $8 million had been filed in the United States District Court against the vessel's owner, the St. Joseph-Chicago Steamship Company. After considerable delays and scores of hearings, Special Master in Admiralty Lewis F. Mason in 1933 issued a lengthy report which found that the claims were justifiable but that the company had no funds to satisfy them and was liable only for the value of its interest in the ship. That value no longer existed, for even the $42,000 the company had received in selling the ship to a group of Chicago business men headed by Samuel Insull had been depleted by the costs of salvaging it from the river bed and by legal expenses. Moreover, Mason's report offered the opinion that the *Eastland* had capsized because its chief engineer had improperly distributed the water ballast; testimony was that the port side tanks were full and those to starboard were empty, keeping the ship from achieving stability. This negligence was not, in Mason's view, the company's responsibility, for the ship was otherwise seaworthy in all respects and properly manned and equipped for carrying passengers. Judge John P. Barnes affirmed Mason's conclusions, as did the United States Court of Appeals, and three years later the United States Supreme Court refused to review that ruling, thereby putting a decisive end to litigation. As for the ship itself, it was by then the USS *Wilmette*, converted since the Navy had taken it over in 1917 into a training ship for naval gun crews. It served as such through World War II, and, after it was decommissioned in 1945, was sold a year later for $2,500 to Hyman-Michaels Company and cut up for scrap metal.

6

Another case that evoked considerable interest in this period emerged from a complaint by the Federal Trade Commission that James S. Kirk & Company, among many soap manufacturers, was engaging in unfair trade practices by labeling one of its many products "Cocoa Hardwater Castile." The action came in response to charges from importers of castile soap from Italy, France, and Spain that the Chicago company and other major soapmakers were using the word "castile" deceptively. Authentic castile soap, they maintained, had olive oil as its sole fat ingredient. The Kirk product was made of substances other than olive oil—almost entirely coconut oil—and consequently, in the words of the FTC complaint, its "labeling or marketing have the capacity and tendency to deceive the trade and public into the erroneous belief" that "Cocoa Hardwater Castile" contained olive oil.

The other companies halted use of the allegedly offensive word, but Edwin G. Holloway, Kirk's doughty president, insisted on fighting the action. Donald McPherson headed the law firm's team representing Holloway's company, with Oates and McDougal to gather evidence to refute the commission's claim and Stevenson to research points of law. After the commission issued an order on May 12, 1926, to cease the use of the word, Oates and McDougal set out on a cross-country trek to get statements from scores of people—grocers, scientists, pharmacists, physicians, nurses, soap-makers, housewives, and other consumers—that they had never considered "Cocoa Hardwater Castile" a soap made of olive oil but primarily a free-lathering toilet soap, especially effective in hardwater areas. They did their work well, for in hearings before the commission's trial examiner, Edward M. Averill, from that October 4 until the following July 19 in a number of cities, among 800 witnesses called in the Kirk company's behalf were twenty-nine soap manufacturers, 400 representatives of every branch of the American soap distributing trades, doctors and representatives of such institutions as Harvard University School of Medicine, the College of Pharmacy of Columbia University, and the Mayo Clinic. And this impressive array presented a nation-wide cross-section of opinion that the use of "castile" had been in accord with the practice of American soap manufacturers for over seventy-five years and conformed to the understanding of the soap trades and of ultimate consumers that no deception had been involved as to the kind of oil contained in products bearing that name. One of the telling pieces of evidence pertaining to the

105

long-standing use of "castile" in soaps with no intention to misrepresent its composition was offered by three sons of James S. Beach, owner of a soap factory in Dubuque, Iowa. Asked by Oates if their father had ever made castile soap, the sons replied that he had, back in the 1880s, and that it contained coconut oil. Moreover, one of them found an 1884 company advertising card with a photograph of a beach house on one side and on the other a poem titled "Castile," whose last verse read:

> For Beach's castile
> Be pleased now to hark
> Is not made from the grease of the
>   scavenger's cart
> But from coconut oil from the land of
>   the palm
> Where the Indian Ocean encircles Ceylon.

In May 1928, the trial examiner ruled in the Kirk company's favor, citing particularly "overwhelming evidence" that for three-quarters of a century castile soap produced in the United States had not been misrepresented as containing olive oil. But that December the full commission rejected Averill's decision and issued a formal cease-and-desist order. Charging that this order was unlawful, the firm petitioned the United States Court of Appeals to set it aside. That plea was granted in a unanimous opinion April 15, 1932, and at the end of that year the company emerged the final victor when the commission's petition for a writ of *certiorari* was denied by the United States Supreme Court. By this time, the Kirk company had been absorbed by Procter & Gamble Company, which had purchased its $2 million manufacturing plant on North Avenue close by the Chicago River's north branch. Cutting, Moore & Sidley had represented the Kirk company in that transaction and it and its successors in years to come continued representation of members of the Kirk family in estate, trust, and income tax matters and Procter & Gamble in problems in the Chicagoland area.

The time and expense involved in contesting the commission's action proved to be well-spent. Under the Federal Trade Commission Act, until final resolution of the case the company was not prohibited from engaging in the practice in question. As the sole manufacturer still using the disputed word—along with "Made of 100% Pure Coconut Oil" on its wrappers—its market for "Cocoa Hardwater Castile" expanded greatly in the years of legal conflict, and the resulting profits made up many times over for the considerable costs of the litigation.

7

Toward the end of the decade, as it had numerous times in the years since its beginnings, the firm acted in support of an important cultural institution in a dispute: the world-famous Art Institute, the impressive Renaissance-style two-story structure standing, since the World's Columbian Exposition of 1893, in Grant Park on Michigan Avenue at the foot of Adams Street. In 1928, its trustees proposed to erect a $5 million addition, 800 feet long and facing Lake Michigan, not only to house part of its ever-growing collection of art works but also a school for aspiring painters and sculptors. A contract with the South Park Board was duly signed and public announcements were made to the effect that the expansion was necessary for the Art Institute to keep step with the growth and development in coming decades of Chicago and the Middle West and that a competition would soon be conducted among foremost architects in the United States and Europe to determine the most feasible and attractive design.

The project was generally adjudged to be especially valuable in view of the surge of contributions of art works from Chicago collectors and the resulting need for gallery space. But on February 16, 1929, the owners of the Stevens Hotel, half a mile south of the institute on the west side of Michigan Avenue and advertised as "the world's largest," filed suit in Circuit Court to enjoin construction of the addition. They claimed that a new structure might be so tall that it would obscure the view of Lake Michigan from the hotel windows and contended that all land east of Michigan Avenue was meant to be preserved for park purposes. They based their action on earlier court rulings in years of legal conflict touched off by the zealous merchant, A. Montgomery Ward, to keep the Lake Michigan front forever open, clear, and free of buildings and other obstructions. Actually, Ward had relented in his campaign when plans to build the Art Institute had been made known in 1891 because adjacent property owners had given their consent to construction, but his assault on all other such ventures had continued with persistence and frequent suits until his death in 1913.

To fight the hotel's action, Percy B. Eckhart, the Art Institute's vice-president and general counsel, sought the firm's aid. Moore took charge, with Oates to do research and help prepare motions and other pertinent documents. After Judge William V. Brothers, holding that previous rulings barred construction within the limits of Grant Park, granted the injunction, an appeal was filed with the Appellate Court. There, Moore and Eckhart made a number of forceful arguments beyond one for the obvious need for the addition. They emphasized that when approval was given by the city council in 1891 for constructing the Art Institute the ordinance specified the "permanent accommodation" of the structure and that five years later a decision in one of Ward's suits that ordered the removal of lumber, timber, dirt, rubbish, garbage, and other offensive matters from portions of Grant Park not only excepted the Art Institute as the sole building in the area but, even more to the point in question, placed no restraints on "necessary enlargement and expansion" in the future. Consequently, in the time since, periodic essential additions had been made, including Fullerton Hall in 1897, Gunsaulus Hall in 1913, and the Kenneth Sawyer Goodman Memorial Theater in 1923. On March 27, 1931, the lower court's verdict was reversed in a ruling that did, however, block extensions beyond Monroe Street on the north, Jackson Boulevard on the south and the Michigan Avenue frontage and limited the height of the proposed new structure to that of the existing building "unless merely by way of ornament, pinnacles or flagpoles."

When the Illinois Supreme Court denied the hotel's petition for leave to appeal the following June 19, the way was clear for proceeding with the addition and for all similar undertakings thereafter. But the institute's building fund, said Eckhart, was depleted and with the Great Depression well under way prospects for raising the necessary money were dim. Two years later, Eckhart announced that accumulated income from a bequest of $1 million in a trust fund established in the will of B. F. Ferguson, a wealthy Chicago lumberman who had died in 1905, would be used to construct the first portion of the proposed adjunct. This spurred years of controversy in and out of the courts because Ferguson's will had provided that his bequest be used for "the erection of monuments in bronze, stone and granite in parks and on boulevards." Local sculptors agitated against use of money from the fund, whose trustee was The Northern Trust Company, for any purpose other than that designated in Ferguson's will. Not until 1958 was the plan of thirty years earlier consummated, after Eckhart's partner, William McSwain, and Avery, as attorney for The Northern Trust Company, obtained an Appellate Court decision that the addition could legally be declared a "monument." In that year, the B. F. Ferguson Memorial Building was constructed, but with changes wrought by the passage of three decades; it was placed north of the institute instead of to the east and it housed, instead of galleries and the institute school, offices of the administrative and curatorial staffs and technical services. In subsequent years, more structural additions were made, climaxed by a multi-million dollar Columbus Drive extension to celebrate the founding of the first Art Institute of Chicago back in 1879. In addition, a B. F. Ferguson Monument Fund was set up for the erection and maintenance of statuary in parks and public places; one of the notable works thus sponsored was the striking fountain sculpture by Isamu Noguchi in a reflecting pool adjacent to the Columbus Drive entrance.

8

Besides its representation of clients in assorted litigated matters in the 1920s, the firm played a crucial role in other sectors of its practice.

By the early 1880s, William H. Miner had invented a number of devices for railroads, notably a friction draft gear designed for the coupling of the heavier passenger and freight cars and locomotives then in general use. Over the years he amassed a considerable fortune from the sale of draft gear and other railroad supplies. Near Chazy, the upstate New York farming community of his boyhood, he maintained a 14,000-acre farm named "Heart's Delight." In addition to encompassing the gamut of farm crops and domestic, pure-bred animals, the farm served as a sanctuary for buffalo from Western states and deer from Japan. He also contributed substantial funds for the establishment in 1916 of the Chazy Central Rural

School, one of the country's first consolidated schools, and gave financial aid to needy farm workers and other young men and women who could not afford college tuition.

Miner hoped to attain other philanthropic aims, but in the years following World War I he had been increasingly hampered by ever-higher federal income taxes. Early in 1923, after a board meeting of Western Electric Company—in which Miner was a stockholder second only to American Telephone and Telegraph—Miner met with Sidley to discuss how he could best continue his benefactions without undue monetary loss in his lifetime and after his death. Sidley's initial proposal was for Miner to incorporate his thriving railway supplies business so that he could contribute funds directly to philanthropic ventures before imposition of income taxes. By 1925, Sidley, assisted by Bangs and Austin, established several trusts and the William H. Miner Foundation, in which were placed Miner's many patents and total equity of his company. One of the early results of these actions was to help finance construction in 1926 of the Physicians Hospital in Plattsburgh, some twenty miles south of Chazy.

When Miner died in April 1930, his trusts withstood federal tax challenge. He left all shares of stock in his company to the foundation, except for those held in trust for certain company officers and other employees to be transferred to the foundation upon termination of employment. As the years progressed, in good times and bad, income accumulated in the foundation. Consequently, with interest, dividends and patent royalties, and gains from sales of securities, the foundation became able to furnish money with which to put up a new Chazy School building and assist in its support, as well as to pay for modernizing the Physicians Hospital, the purchase of medical equipment, and the erection of a nurses' residence. Sidley had been named a trustee in the original foundation instrument, which was notarized by Stevenson in his first months with the firm, and Austin had become a trustee after Miner's death. He and Sidley were so serving in 1957 when another of Miner's long-hoped-for projects was realized with the dedication of the $4 million William H. Miner Agricultural Research Institute, close by the site of Chazy's one-room school house Miner had attended as a boy. "A fabulous array of buildings with equally fabulous equipment and furnishings," the *Plattsburgh Press-Republican* exulted. The firm's relationship with the foundation remained close. Upon Sidley's death in 1958, Middleton Miller, a 1932 Harvard Law School graduate and a partner since 1948, replaced him as a trustee. During Austin's chairmanship starting in 1968, the foundation's contributions for the support of its several charitable beneficiaries grew to more than $1 million a year.

While carrying out plans in Miner's behalf, Sidley continued to make periodic trips to Europe for Western Electric and for other members of the War Claimants Association. And he was also instrumental in facilitating an innovative venture affecting Western Electric's supplies distribution division. This department had kept pace over the decades with the company's unit that manufactured telephones and related equipment. It also carried in stock and sold, through a network of fifty-five warehouses in various parts of the nation, products not made by Western Electric that ranged from motors and generators to lamps and radio broadcasting apparatus and went to customers in the industrial, railroad, and other fields. By 1924, its sales amounted to $66 million, making it the biggest enterprise of its kind in the world. Because telephone manufacture and the distribution of electric supplies constituted two distinct lines of business, each requiring specialized organizations and management, separation of the two seemed advisable. So, at the start of 1926, with Sidley overseeing the legal details, the distribution unit was split from the parent company and incorporated as the Graybar Electric Company, with an office in New York and Chicago headquarters on South Clinton Street and capitalized at $9 million. Its name was derived from the two men—Elisha Gray and Enos M. Barton—whose small firm of Gray and Barton, set up back in 1869 to manufacture electrical equipment, had grown to be the giant Western Electric Company.

By the end of 1928, Graybar's annual sales had risen to $75 million. Then came an event even more novel than the 1926 split and adoption of the name based on that of the original firm. This was the transfer of Graybar to its officers and employees, the first time in American business annals that a company of such a size had been reorganized in this way. A check for $3 million, representing a down payment on the purchase price of $9 million for 30,000 shares of common stock, was handed to Western Electric's president, Edgar S. Bloom, by Graybar's chief executive, Albert L. Salt, who had started his career as a Western Electric office boy forty-four years before, with the rest to be retired over a period of time. "One of the most unusual records in American industrial life," the *Tribune* characterized the transaction, and it and other observers of future progress of the employee-owned company would have occasion to comment anew as Graybar weathered the Great Depression and in 1941 reached a sales volume of over $100 million, an increase in the number of its distribution centers from fifty-nine to eighty-six and the purchase of the remaining outstanding shares of stock for $1 million. Nor did Graybar's growth and attendant success languish in succeeding years. By the 1970s, it attained and maintained sales revenues in the billions and held topmost rank among similar companies. Various legal matters for Graybar in Chicago continue to be handled by the firm.

9

During this decade, Chicago became the Midwest center of the emergence of a number of new public utility systems. One of the biggest became a client, thereby giving the firm experience with large-scale acquisitions and public utility financing.

Starting in 1927, an energetic ex-Army colonel named Albert E. Peirce began to gather into his Central Public Service Corporation many small public and privately owned electric, gas, water, steam heat, street railway, and bus firms, all held together by a complex of holding and sub-holding companies. Before long, the corporation's operating properties were scattered in twenty-four states from Maine to Oregon and in seven foreign countries, with total assets of $360 million. Donald McPherson served as its general counsel and a vice-president, overseeing all the legal work entailed in the corporation's sale of its securities. He spent as much or more time in Central Public Service's offices atop the Railway Exchange Building at Michigan Avenue and Jackson Boulevard as in his quarters in the Roanoke Building.

As was the case with other public utility combines new and old in this bullish time, thousands of customers eagerly responded to the stock offerings of Peirce's corporation. Business stayed brisk until the 1929 stock market crash and the onset of the Great Depression. Then, one after another, Central Public Service's various operating properties suffered sharp declines in earning power. By mid-1931, the value of the corporation's debentures had fallen to 63 from a high of 96½. To ease its financial problems, Peirce's corporation underwent a complicated reorganization in the summer of 1932 that involved, among other things, the shifting of

Donald F. McPherson

control from Central Public Service to two newly-formed units, Central Public Utility Company and Consolidated Electric and Gas Company. McPherson helped to formulate these adjustments in the corporate and financial structure, after which the firm ceased its representation. The reorganization proved to be of little avail. Various holders of the corporation's debentures filed petitions in the United States District Court for involuntary bankruptcy, and at year's end a receiver was named for the once-thriving empire.

10

Beyond the practice of law in diverse areas and the accompanying development of a wider range of clients, the decade was marked by efforts of Sidley and other senior partners to maintain and heighten morale and camaraderie. Despite heavy responsibilities to clients, Sidley took special pains to give time to younger men for discussion not only of legal matters with which they were concerned, but any personal problems. Years later,

Austin—who came to resemble him in many ways personally and professionally—recalled Sidley's solicitude and many kindnesses: "I felt we had as perfect an understanding as an older and a younger man could have. He was a gentle, tolerant man, moderate in personal habits, and a thoroughly lovable person." Once each summer, all the lawyers, secretaries, office boys, and other lay employees were invited to an outing on Sidley's farm near Barrington. And on many summer weekends, Bangs invited young lawyers and their wives to his handsome Geneva residence for a day of tennis, golf, or swimming in the pool. McPherson invariably commended clerks for work well done, scrawling his compliments with a red pencil atop the draft of a memorandum; he also rode herd on fledgling clerks to answer, whenever possible, letters or other communications without fail within twenty-four hours after their receipt—and to assure that his instructions were strictly followed he directed that all outgoing and incoming correspondence be delivered to him each day.

Additionally, internal events and customs were instituted that made for closer personal relationships and would, for the most part, endure for the lifetime of the firm.

One such, begun in 1920 and repeated annually, was a Christmas luncheon, held on the last day of business before the holiday, at first at the Blackstone Hotel and then and subsequently at the Chicago Club, except in the few years after women became lawyers with the firm but were not then permitted in that all-male club. It was preceded in the morning by the awarding of bonuses and year-end salary raises to associates and lay employees. Each man would wait in line in order of seniority in the corridor outside Sidley's office. Upon entering, he would find Sidley at his desk; in the early 1930s Austin sat beside him. After a brief but genial appraisal of his work in the year, he received a bonus check with a comment similar to the one Charles Holt had made to Austin at his first Christmas with the firm in 1914, "Please accept this check as a token, not a measure, of our esteem." After this ritual was completed, the lawyers walked leisurely to the Chicago Club for lunch while the secretaries and other women staff workers lunched in a private dining room in the Union League Club. Boys and men on the staff stayed in the office to take calls and handle any emergency matters, to be luncheon guests of the firm's office manager later.

Preceding a report by Sidley on activities of the past year, McPherson's elegantly expressed tribute to the zeal of the clerks and a speech by a local

William P. Sidley
on his Wyoming ranch

judge or law school dean or the general counsel of a long-time client, a
skit, complete with jibes and satirical verses, was presented by clerks and
younger partners. Typical was the set of rhymes by John Paulding Brown,
a bright young clerk and inveterate prankster and wit, at the 1929
luncheon. To the great glee of the assemblage, he directed sharp,
humorous barbs in all directions.

At Paul Harper, who had been elevated to a partnership a year earlier:

> *Great pundit neath whose shiny dome*
> *All knowledge finds at last its home.*
> *His humor's agile though his jowls are*
>   *thick,*
> *He'll quote you Hebrew, Greek or Arabic.*
> *This scholar's learning's now for sale,*
> *A legal walrus piercing through the*
>   *corporate veil.*
> *Script on his tusks and charters on*
>   *his tail—*
> *When Harper speaks, no other's arguments*
>   *avail.*

115

At Adlai Stevenson:

> *A fragile bloom from Bloomington,*
> *Where Pantagraphic lawyers run.*
> *He squanders pounds but guards his*
>   *pence—*
> *Sly rabbit of the legal fence.*

At James Oates:

> *With mighty voice and puissant eye,*
> *He booms and glares where others sigh,*
> *And o'er his dazzled victims gloats—*
> *No horse's fodder this, although its*
>   *name be Oates.*

At John Dern:

> *Who is this timid clerk now we see*
> *Fresh from the Salt Lake's salty sea?*
> *Much to forget, and yet still more to*
>   *learn.*
> *Gol' derned if it's not John Dern!*

After recital of these and other stanzas came this impish chorus:

> *I'm only a hard-pressed law clerk,*
> *Or an almost-law-clerk am I.*
> *I can't get the hang of the legal slang*
> *No matter how hard I try.*
> *So be damned to the corporate fiction,*
> *And to hell with the corporate veil,*
> *And let every man now empty his stein*
> *As he joins us in drinking his ale.*

Besides concocting such rhymes, Brown delighted in joining his closest friends at the office, Stevenson and West, in playing practical jokes on one another. An especially hirsute young man, West returned from a vacation to find that Brown and Stevenson had placed a tailor's dummy covered with a huge fur coat in his desk chair. On another occasion, when Brown embarked on a voyage to Europe, West, encouraged by Stevenson, wrote

116

to the ship's surgeon to warn him that Brown was mentally deranged despite periods of apparent rationality and needed constant watching. The prank caused Brown some discomfort until he could unravel the source of the problem and explain to the surgeon about his prankish friends back in Chicago. And when Stevenson returned from his honeymoon, West and Brown piled his desk high with mounds of files and spurious memoes from each of the partners assigning him work that needed doing urgently; when Stevenson telephoned to his bride to lament that he would not be home for dinner that night or even on subsequent nights, half a dozen associates listened in on his plaintive conversation through the cooperation of the switchboard operator in plugging them into his line.

Brown continued his irreverent versifying at the yearly convivial gatherings until he left in 1935 for a government post in Washington. But the tradition endured, occasionally extending to a speech by a former clerk or partner who had joined a company that had become one of the firm's clients. The partners generally approved of this frivolity as an excellent morale-booster and a way of relieving the pressures of heavy work loads. Moreover, Austin had become involved in the production and performances of the Chicago Bar Association's "Christmas Spirits" shows that, starting in 1924, poked fun—often good-naturedly but sometimes with savage wit—at lofty personages in national and local government and politics and, of course, at the profession that afforded its members their livelihoods. He had first been enlisted by John D. Black, one of the city's best trial lawyers and a noted wit, as pianist to accompany singers of mocking ditties in similar programs staged by The Law Club of Chicago; when these early Law Club shows became part of the CBA's annual holiday dinners as "Christmas Spirits," he joined Black and others in writing and acting in the satirical skits.

Another long-standing tradition was instituted in 1924, shortly after the Chicago Bar Association, upon its fiftieth anniversary, moved into expanded quarters atop the twenty-story Burnham Building at LaSalle and Randolph Streets. To help increase patronage in the association's dining room, Sidley—who would be the association's president in six years—initiated the practice of having a round table set aside there primarily for associates every Monday and offering them lunch without charge. This came to be called "The Crib" and it was highly popular. The weekly lunch sessions, continuing for many years after the association moved in 1937 to permanent headquarters at 29 South LaSalle Street, proved

117

effective as another means for the firm's lawyers to meet informally and become better acquainted, thereby strengthening the firm's *esprit de corps*, that quality which influenced so many law school graduates then and later when they were deciding with which law firm to start a career.

Cutting, Moore & Sidley
1931–1936
Sidley, McPherson, Austin & Burgess
1937–1944

A MOST SIGNIFICANT and far-reaching event in the firm's long history was the admission to partnership early in 1931 of Kenneth F. Burgess, a leader in the top-most ranks of railroad attorneys.

Born in Oshkosh, Wisconsin, in 1887, Burgess graduated in 1910 from the University of Wisconsin and two years later from its law school, where he was an instructor while completing his studies. In the next three years he engaged in general practice in Lancaster, Wisconsin, represented the Chicago, Burlington & Quincy Railroad as local counsel and also wrote a textbook, *Burgess' Commercial Law*, for use in high schools and commercial colleges. He so impressed the Burlington's top executives—in one case securing the acquittal of a conductor charged with murder—that in 1915 they hired him for the legal staff in Chicago to handle rate cases before the Interstate Commerce Commission and other regulatory tribunals. He advanced to general attorney in 1917 and, after two years as western regional counsel for the wartime's United States Railroad Administration, to general solicitor in 1924. Steadily, he built an impressive reputation as an expert in railroad matters, serving the Burlington in a wide range of issues from rate and service cases to labor wage disputes, and he supervised the Burlington attorneys who handled valuations, taxation, rate and service regulations, undercharges and overcharges, and property damage suits. He continued to turn out books—*Railroad Rates, Service and Management*, with Homer B. Vanderblue, a Northwestern University professor, became a standard college textbook—and scores of technical,

Kenneth F. Burgess
in 1931

authoritative articles on varied elements of railroading. And he was gaining renown as an expert in the field of public utilities. One of the early members of the American Bar Association's Public Utility Law Section in 1917, he became its chairman in 1928–29 and in 1930 also headed the ABA's Committee on the Boundaries Between Regulation in the Law of Public Utilities; in these capacities, he spoke often at professional and public meetings.

In the months after William Bangs' death in October 1930, it became evident that a lawyer deeply-versed in public utility law was needed to be the new general counsel of Illinois Bell Telephone Company and a partner in the firm. Although Sidley was relying increasingly in various ways on Austin, who had been named a senior partner in 1929, an additional lawyer of ability and repute was needed.

The choice lay between Burgess and Ernest S. Ballard, an excellent lawyer who had earlier served for a decade as general solicitor of the New York Central Railroad. McPherson favored Ballard's selection. Austin had become acquainted with Burgess when they—Austin as a freshman, Burgess as a senior—attended the University of Wisconsin. In discussions with Sidley, he enthusiastically spoke for Burgess, and strong support came from Charles M. Bracelen, AT&T's general counsel, because of Burgess' broad experience with the Burlington in rate proceedings, and from Henry A. Scandrett, president of the Milwaukee Road, whose

120

opinion of Burgess was high as a result of having worked with him successfully in a large amount of litigation ("an outstanding figure at the Bar" is how he characterized him to Austin). A decision was soon reached. On March 1, 1931, Burgess became general counsel of Illinois Bell Telephone Company and was named a partner—as were McDougal and Oates—in Cutting, Moore & Sidley.

2

Burgess' advent and subsequent career with the firm made him a formidable asset, a partner who proved most influential in its growth and development. Just as Cutting had attracted probate and estate business after joining, Burgess' arrival and elevation to a senior partnership at the start of 1933 signaled an influx of railroad clients who would continue to rank high among sources of the firm's practice.

Of immediate importance, however, was the resumption of steps to nullify the results of the United States Supreme Court decision shortly after Bangs' death that had reversed a District Court ruling enjoining the 1923 order of the Illinois Commerce Commission which had originally prescribed reduced rates for four classes of telephone coin box users in Chicago. After the high court had remanded the case for further hearings, Burgess joined Bracelen and other lawyers in behalf of Illinois Bell Telephone Company's effort to secure a permanent injunction against enforcement of that order. Once again, responding to the argument that the commission's action was confiscatory, a three-man court granted the injunction. Again, the commission, now headed by Benjamin F. Lindheimer, carried the case to the Supreme Court, and, on April 31, 1934, the verdict went against the telephone company.

It now became necessary to refund money to subscribers for the years from 1923 to 1934. The refunds began in June with an announcement from Burgess: "We do not anticipate difficulties in making them, aside from the time required for checking the vast number of telephone bills covering the eleven-year period. This will be done in an orderly manner under the direction of the court." Month after month, the refunds continued under supervision of Judge Evan A. Evans, senior judge of the federal Court of Appeals, who had presided over the three-man court that had heard the case from the start. Ultimately, the total amount subject to refund was calculated to be $17 million. Despite the best efforts to locate all subscribers entitled to refunds, toward the end of the decade there remained a substantial sum of unclaimed money—$1.7 million, including interest. Asserting alleged rights under the law of escheat, Illinois then claimed that amount, and various other parties also claimed the fund. Burgess fought their efforts successfully in 1940 in the United States District Court, arguing that the unclaimed money should be kept by the company to offset $2.8 million in costs incurred by it in making the refund. The final amount retained by the telephone company was $1.6 million, which remained after court-ordered payments of $60,000 to Illinois and $30,000 to Chicago as reimbursements for expenses incurred during the rate litigation.

Aiding Burgess was D. Robert Thomas, a 1935 graduate of Harvard Law School who had come to the firm in 1937. Thomas had clerked for Judge Augustus N. Hand in the federal Court of Appeals in New York and had been with a New York law firm until he and his wife, both from the Midwest, concluded that life in Manhattan did not appeal to them. Thomas traced the law of escheat through American and British history and prepared the brief that helped attain the victory. (Years later, he recalled an interesting tidbit uncovered in his intensive research, namely that an exception to the general rule about a king's rights held that when a whale foundered on the shore the queen was entitled to the whalebone for use in corsets for herself and her ladies.)

3

The deepening depression that came after the 1929 stock market crash brought woes to the nation's railroads. In the next three years, net operating income dropped from $1.3 billion to $325 million. Car loadings and freight shipments ebbed by 50 percent. Employees by the many thousands were discharged, and many who remained had their work weeks reduced. Purchase of new equipment was minimal. The decline in economic activity was intensified by increased competition from other kinds of transport—trucks to carry freight on extensive highway systems, buses and airplanes for passenger travel.

A measure of relief was provided by emergency loans from the Reconstruction Finance Corporation, established by Congress early in 1932 at the behest of President Herbert Hoover. But more needed to be done as conditions worsened. In 1935, amid continuing actions in Franklin D.

Roosevelt's New Deal era, Congress initiated crucial hearings to consider amendments to the year-old Section 77 of the Federal Bankruptcy Act that would enable faltering railroads to file voluntary petitions for reorganization. Before House and Senate committees, Burgess testified in behalf of large insurance companies that held railroad bonds. After enactment of the amendments, the first of scores of railroads seeking to adjust their financial structures was Chicago and North Western Railway Company, which filed its plea for reorganization in United States District Court that June 29. In subsequent proceedings before Judge John P. Barnes and, later, the Interstate Commerce Commission, Burgess headed the firm's team representing creditor interests and, after approval, assisted the railroad's reorganization managers who were charged with drawing up new charters, by-laws, mortgages, and other security documents, preparing new stock certificates, bonds, and debentures and exchanging old securities for new ones.

The complex work by the firm for the Chicago and North Western went on for another nine years. And, continuing into the 1950s, the firm performed similar duties in connection with the reorganization of other lines: Minneapolis, St. Paul and Sault Ste. Marie; Chicago, Milwaukee, St. Paul and Pacific; Chicago, Rock Island & Pacific; Denver & Rio Grande Western; Chicago, North Shore & Milwaukee; Duluth, South Shore & Atlantic; and the Wisconsin Central.

Foremost among those in the firm who worked closely in this decade with Burgess on railroad matters involving complex legal problems was Douglas F. Smith, whom Burgess had persuaded to join as a partner on March 1, 1935, after fifteen years as commerce counsel for Union Pacific. Paul Harper was another member of Burgess' team and drew the mortgages for the Chicago and North Western when it emerged from bankruptcy in 1944. Another was George Ragland, Jr., with the firm since 1931 after graduate work at the University of Michigan Law School and author of *Discovery Before Trial*, a highly regarded treatise that was credited with influencing the nationwide development of extensive discovery procedures. In the following years, more men—partners and associates —would become involved under Burgess' direction not only in railroad reorganizations but in other sectors of the industry, especially in important mergers.*

*See Chapters X and XIV.

4

Early in 1933, Burgess was elected to Northwestern University's board of trustees, thereby initiating twenty-six years of valued service, twenty-two of them as board president—a term longer than that of any other in the university's history. And within a few months the firm began its long-enduring representation of the university.

This came about as the result of a proposal that May by Robert Maynard Hutchins, president of the University of Chicago, that the two institutions merge. In a letter to Northwestern's president, Walter Dill Scott, Hutchins cited the economies that could be realized without impairing educational and scientific effectiveness. Such a move, Hutchins predicted, would create "the greatest educational enterprise in the world." Scott was receptive and joined Hutchins in preparing a memorandum for a trustees' merger committee that delineated all aspects of the plan of unification. The merged institution was to be called The Universities of Chicago. In addition to streamlining the administration, duplication would be eliminated in the fields of law, education, commerce, medicine, and the liberal arts. Graduate work would be concentrated on the University of Chicago campus, undergraduate training in Evanston, and professional schools on Northwestern's Chicago campus. The result, according to the Scott-Hutchins document, would be an annual saving of $1.7 million.

All that summer and beyond, the proposal aroused strong reactions. As rumors of the plan spread through Evanston, its city council and chamber of commerce expressed opposition, one business leader stressing that the university was "the city's largest industry" and that the proposed merger would cause a drop in trade volume and real estate values. The *Evanston Review* charged that the Rockefeller Foundation was prepared to make available an added $25 million endowment if only one major university were in the Chicago area; it headlined its story "Call Merger Rockefeller Plan to Wipe Out NU." Northwestern alumni were generally against the plan, voicing fears that traditions and loyalties to their school would vanish with assumption of the new name. Most vigorous in their antagonism were teachers and students of Northwestern's Medical School, whose pragmatic educational method and philosophy differed from Chicago's greater emphasis on research and instruction in the more theoretical aspects of medicine. In a huge anti-merger rally on Northwestern's

Chicago campus, medical students burned effigies of Scott and Hutchins.

At a July meeting, one of several crucial questions that concerned Northwestern's committee and a similar group of Chicago trustees was whether the merger could be undertaken without resulting in the loss of the tax-free status granted Northwestern in its 1851 charter obtained from the Illinois legislature by its founder, John Evans. Opinions were asked of Leon Green, Northwestern's Law School dean, and of Cutting, Moore & Sidley and two other law firms, Winston, Strawn, Shaw & Black and Mayer, Meyer, Austrian & Platt. By late September, the opinions were ready, and they varied. The one prepared by Nathan Moore, with use of George Ragland's considerable research, warned of legal perils to Northwestern in the proposed merger. The original tax exemption accorded the school was protected under the landmark Dartmouth College case, which, by a United States Supreme Court ruling in 1819, placed a charter of private corporations—in that instance, a college—outside the scope of control by the state that had granted the charter. The power to give such tax exemptions was narrowed in the revised Illinois constitution of 1870, and, in Moore's judgment, it was important for Northwestern not to take any action that would impair its contractual right to the full exemption in its pre-1870 charter. To carry out a merger now would run the risk of waiving the right to escape the burden of being limited to narrower exemptions—or none at all—specified in post-1870 statutes. The other two firms were divided in their opinions. Dean Green disagreed strongly with Moore, maintaining that the university's tax-free position was protected by a statute adopted in the late 1890s that purported to say that no tax exemptions provided before 1870 would be lost in any subsequent actions after that year.

Whatever effect these legal interpretations could have had on an ultimate decision, the issue was resolved because of other factors. One was the death the next February 15 of Melvin A. Traylor, The First National Bank's chief executive who, as chairman of the merger committee, had been an especially ardent proponent of unification. Faced with this loss, sustained agitation from civic groups, disagreements among trustees and a report from a faculty committee that educational disadvantages of unification would outweigh advantages, Scott and Hutchins agreed to end negotiations. But each continued to retain faith in the fundamental idea. Said Scott: "The more I studied the merger the more desirable I found it to be. It is a great regret to me that conditions were such that it could not

125

become a reality." And Hutchins: "I shall never cease to regret the failure of this plan, for I regard it as one of the lost opportunities of American education."

5

The months that followed the start of Franklin D. Roosevelt's first Presidential term in March 1933, were marked by a plethora of legislation affecting industry, agriculture, banking, labor, and millions of jobless. Some of the many acts passed by Congress in the sustained period from that month through mid-June that came to be called the "Hundred Days" were later declared to be unconstitutional by the United States Supreme Court. Many others endured and, through establishment of new regulatory agencies, considerably expanded then and for decades to come the practice of administrative law, with attendant complexities and conflict over rules and regulations that some considered constricting.

Among the early measures that year were the Emergency Banking Relief Act to confirm the steps taken since the inauguration to check the money panic, the Beer-Wine Revenue Act that legalized sale of wine, beer and ale and presaged repeal of the Eighteenth Amendment that December, the Civilian Conservation Corps Reforestation Relief for a quarter of a million unemployed young men in reforestation, road building, soil erosion prevention, and national park and flood control projects, the Federal Emergency Relief Act that appropriated $500 million for aid to the nation's indigent, the Agricultural Adjustment Act aimed at restoring the purchasing power of farmers and, by far then the most controversial, the National Industrial Recovery Act that established the National Recovery Administration—the NRA—to devise and enforce "fair competition" codes in various industries and, through a National Labor Board, guarantee workers the right to bargain collectively with their employers. (After the latter act was declared unconstitutional in 1935, the National Labor Relations Act was passed, re-asserting the rights of employees to organize and join labor unions and to engage in collective bargaining.)

One that immediately affected some of the firm's clients was the Federal Securities Act of May 27, 1933, designed to compel full disclosure to investors of information about new securities that were offered publicly or sold through the mails or in interstate commerce. Initially, such issues had to be registered with the Federal Trade Commission by filing of sworn statements placed on public file but this was shifted to the Securities and Exchange Commission after that agency was established a year later.

The securities work done by the firm in the latter years of the 1920s had diminished considerably after the stock market crash of 1929. But the experience gained now proved valuable. The firm prepared, in 1935, one of the first issues in the nation of securities under the newly-enacted legislation, that of $45 million in first mortgage bonds of the Illinois Bell Telephone Company. Burgess negotiated clearance of this issue with Joseph Kennedy, the first chairman of the Securities and Exchange Commission, who was anxious to show the financial community that the new legislation did not stifle corporate financing. The first underwriter the firm represented under the new act was Halsey, Stuart & Company for an issue of Peoples Gas Light and Coke Company in 1936, and a year later the firm handled Commonwealth Edison Company's initial bond issue. These and other matters of this sort required long hours of work in drafting mortgages and preparing registration statements. For two summers Burgess and Austin gave up their vacations to engage in such labors and to supervise others. (James E. S. Baker, who had worked for the firm in the summers of 1934 and 1935 while attending Northwestern University Law School and in 1936 had become a full-time clerk after graduating at the top of his class, later recalled that his task was to read, digest, and summarize all of the franchise ordinances of Commonwealth Edison, Public Service Company of Northern Illinois, Western United Gas & Electric, and Northern Illinois Utilities—"well over 600 of them.")

These early representations started activity for corporations, underwriters, and stockholders making secondary offerings that grew to become a major part of the firm's business, involving billions of dollars and with primary emphasis on public utility issues. In addition, the firm handled a large volume of work with securities, such as the sale of long-term bonds and notes by manufacturers, retailers, and mining corporations and insurance firms, pension funds, and financial institutions buying such securities for investment individually or in small groups.

A major client in the early New Deal years and later was United Light and Power Company, a $570 million holding company with sixty-four utility subsidiaries in Ohio, Michigan, Wisconsin, Illinois, Iowa, Missouri, Nebraska, Kansas, and Texas. In 1934, the vast combine's new president at Chicago headquarters was Charles H. McCain, the recently-resigned chairman of the board of New York's Chase National Bank. Cutting, Moore & Sidley became the principal law firm for United Light and Power after Burgess helped to secure a satisfactory settlement in an action brought by holders of bonds of a small electric interurban railway it owned. Soon, there was need for services in a much more crucial matter.

For some time, Roosevelt had advocated action against what he called "the evil of public utility holding companies." Early in 1935, in a message to Congress, he called for rigorous control of such combines, with virtual dissolution of those that he maintained were not serving the public interest. "Except where it is absolutely necessary to the continuing functioning of a geographically integrated operating utility system," he asserted, "the utility holding company with its present powers must go. It is a device which does not belong in our American traditions of law and business. In its destruction of local control and its substitution of absentee management, it has built up in the public utility field what has been justly called a system of private socialism which is inimical to the welfare of a free people." Vexing as these words may have been to heads of such companies, far more obnoxious—dangerous, some charged—was the President's call for imposition of a "death sentence" on holding companies within five years after passage of pending legislation if they could not demonstrate localized, useful, and efficient purposes.

The Public Utility Holding Company Act embodying the "death sentence" clause and other provisos was introduced by Senator Burton K. Wheeler and Representative Sam Rayburn. Supporters hailed it as a way to eradicate practices indulged in by some holding companies in the previous decades—especially in the 1920s—of pyramiding subsidiaries into intricate financial structures by which prices for gas and electricity above all could be kept high and investors milked of funds. Since the 1929 crash, companies had failed not only because of the dire events that followed but also either through inefficient management or dubious financial manipulations. Reform of the system, the bill's backers said, would benefit private enterprise; the spirit of the proposed legislation, principally its "death sentence" clause, was, in the words of Walter Lippmann, "the spirit of American individualism in its original form." Opponents raised strong doubts about the constitutionality of the act and charged its backers with attempting to nationalize the country's power business. Spokesman for the companies was Wendell Willkie of Commonwealth and Southern Corporation. While he admitted that some holding company executives had engaged in dubious practices, he praised the system itself as an indispensable element of the utility industry and warned that passage of the bill would throw that industry into "a chaos of liquidation and receiverships" and do great damage to holders of utility stocks.

All spring and summer of 1935 the conflict continued. Thomas Corcoran, one of the President's top aides, led a strenuous campaign to persuade members of Congress to vote for the bill. Lobbyists for public utilities applied their pressure on legislators, and publicists for the industry organized an extensive program among holders of utility stocks to send wires and letters asking for "No" votes; a freshman senator from Missouri, Harry Truman, later recalled that he received 30,000 such messages. To reports that Roosevelt was prepared to back off from the death sentence, the President scribbled a pencilled statement to Wheeler to the effect that any changes in that clause would strike at the bill itself and would be contrary to the recommendations expressed in his congressional message.

In June, a vote in the Senate on the death sentence clause narrowly won, 45-44, and later the House, which had at first rejected it, followed suit after certain compromises were injected into the act's language. That August 26, the President signed the bill. By its terms, the Federal Power Commission was authorized to regulate interstate transmission of electric power and the Federal Trade Commission to do likewise with gas. Full supervisory control of the holding companies' financial practices was placed with the Securities and Exchange Commission. Electric and gas holding companies were to be restricted to operations as concentrated systems confined to a single area, and, to eliminate pyramiding, their corporate structures were to be simplified.

The deadline for all utility holding companies to register with the Securities and Exchange Commission in fulfillment of the requirements of the new act was set for the following December 1. Before that time, the firm had prepared a detailed opinion, based on an elaborate review and analysis of authorities, that condemned the Public Utility Holding Company Act as illegal and abhorrent to constitutional principles. Copies were printed and distributed not only to McCain and other officers at United Light and Power and to smaller utility holding companies among its clients but also to law firms that asked for them. Legal action soon followed. In behalf of United Light and Power a suit was filed in the United States District Court in Washington—one of the first such in that jurisdiction—asking that the act be held unconstitutional because, among other reasons, its scope was excessively broad and seeking an injunction against its enforcement. Some fifty similar suits soon were on file in various other cities. To counter these efforts, Corcoran and his New Deal associate, Benjamin Cohen, instituted in the Federal Court in New York action to enforce the act. In the Washington case, Attorney General Homer J. Cummings made a rare appearance to ask that the court stay any hearings until the New York proceeding could be completed.

The Washington firm of Covington & Burling had been employed to assist the plaintiff utility in pressing for the injunction against enforcement of the act. One of its foremost members was Dean Acheson, who asserted it was unfair for the plaintiff "to stand in a breadline for justice," and joined Oates and others in the firm to argue in support of a motion to reject Cummings' request. That motion was denied, but the Court of Appeals reversed the lower court's decision, upheld the contention that there was no merit in the government's position, and directed that the Washington case be heard. Appeal was then taken by government attorneys to the Supreme Court and considerable time elapsed before the justices ruled that there had been unjust deprivation of the plaintiff's rights through undue postponement of the hearing. But meanwhile the New York case had made its faster way to the Supreme Court. On March 28, 1938, the Public Utility Holding Company Act was decreed to be constitutional; a vital section of that decision virtually granted unlimited authority to Congress under the interstate commerce clause. While awaiting that decision, McCain, a month earlier, had registered his company in accordance with terms of the act. He had done so on the advice of Austin, who believed that the Supreme Court was growing increasingly liberal and, augmented by Roosevelt appointees in the aftermath of his smashing victory in the 1936 election, would be inclined to deem the act constitutional.

In 1939, McCain left United Light and Power for a high executive position with the Dillon, Read investment house in New York and was replaced by William G. Woolfolk. John Dern was assigned the task of preparing the myriad details of integrating the vast holding company. Working with Harry Munsell of United Light and Power's legal department, he headed a team that, by May 1940, was ready with a preliminary plan to submit to the Securities and Exchange Commission that provided for disposal of $135 million in utility assets and replacement by an equal

John Dern

amount of assets located in three contemplated areas of operation mainly in the Middle West. The plan stressed the company's willingness to avoid litigation and sought the SEC's cooperation in solving problems created by the legislation "in a constructive manner and with due regard for the interests of all security holders in the system." After considerable study and conferences in the next year or more, the SEC issued a geographical integration order on August 5, 1941, which, in effect, would eliminate United Light and Power as the parent unit and elevate one of its subholding units, United Light and Railways Company—of which Dern was now general counsel—to head a system centered in the Kansas City, Missouri, area. In a letter drafted by Dern and Munsell, Woolfolk informed stockholders that the company had decided that "frank cooperation" with the SEC would be expeditious but he emphasized that individual stockholders could still contest the SEC order in the courts. Final resolution of the matter was nearly a decade away. Much work remained to be done, with varied problems yet to be solved in carrying out the requirements of the legislation. The years ahead would be arduous for Dern and his colleagues as they sought to carry out complicated procedures that resulted in the sale of some United Light and Power properties to

131

public power districts or municipalities and the creation of publicly-owned independent operating utility firms and, as in the case of American Natural Gas Company, a publicly-owned holding company.* And, gratifyingly, in the ultimate breakup of the system no investor lost a single dollar of principal or interest.

6

Services in an entirely different area of the firm's practice were rendered to Edith Rockefeller McCormick, a relationship that had started early in the 1920s and was now entering its final—and complex—phase.

For most of the middle years after her marriage in 1895 to Harold F. McCormick, youngest son of Cyrus Hall McCormick, the reaper's inventor and founder of International Harvester Company, she was the acknowledged successor to Bertha Honore Palmer as the queen of Chicago society, a *grande dame* who lavished money on assorted charities and on the arts—she and her husband created the Chicago Opera Company in 1910—and bore a reputation for extremely grandiose ways and assorted eccentricities. The McCormick greystone mansion on Lake Shore Drive between Oak Street and Bellevue Place was a veritable palace, built in 1888 by Solon Beman for a wealthy stock trader and given to her as a wedding present by her father, John D. Rockefeller. Its forty-one rooms were filled with treasures and costly furnishings from many parts of the world. Mrs. McCormick's array of jewels—emeralds, pearls, diamonds, rubies—was awesome.

In addition to the Lake Shore Drive mansion, there was a baronial country house in the northern suburb of Lake Forest. This was the forty-four room Villa Turicum, erected in 1912 at a cost of $5 million on a knoll overlooking Lake Michigan amid 300 heavily-wooded acres and on its meticulously landscaped grounds were Italianate sculptures and a large outdoor swimming pool, a lily pond, a bowling green, and a formal garden.

For all the splendor, neither McCormick was to spend much time at Villa Turicum. A housewarming planned for shortly after its completion had been cancelled without explanation, and barrels of china and several Italian Renaissance pieces remained uncrated for years thereafter. Such

*See Chapters IX and X.

Edith Rockefeller McCormick

untoward events were manifestations of stress in the marriage. McCormick complained to his sister, Anita Blaine, that his wife lacked understanding. Mrs. McCormick was subject to spells of depression, occasioned, friends believed, by the death of her first-born, John, when he was four years old.

In 1913, Mrs. McCormick went to Switzerland with her three other children, and there she stayed for the next eight years. McCormick visited her occasionally, but late in 1920 he told her he wanted a divorce. When Mrs. McCormick returned to Chicago in September 1921, she sought the services of Cutting, Moore & Sidley, to whom she had been referred by E. Parmalee Prentice, wed since 1901 to her older sister, Alta, and now in private law practice in New York. On that December 28, less than fifty minutes from the time Cutting filed a bill in Superior Court charging McCormick with desertion and an answer by his three lawyers headed by Clarence Darrow admitting that he and his wife had lived separate and apart since May 27, 1918, Judge Charles A. McDonald granted the decree after brief testimony by Mrs. McCormick and two servants.

In 1923, the firm set up, at her request, the Edith Rockefeller McCormick Trust to consolidate certain of her holdings and "to engage in the business of acquiring, subdividing and selling real property and . . . building, erecting and constructing buildings of any and all kinds." As capital, she pledged $5.2 million, principally in stocks of Standard Oil companies. When her father received the trust's prospectus, he wrote to advise her that although he considered her "a brilliant and mature woman of great mental capacity," perils lay ahead: "It seems to be my duty to warn you of the pitfalls and vagaries of life. I would urge you to select an

133

honest, courageous and capable man to advise you in these affairs.''

The man Mrs. McCormick chose was Edwin D. Krenn, an architect she had come to know in Switzerland. Krenn had established a real estate firm in Chicago with a onetime schoolmate, Edward A. Dato, an experimental engineer for the International Harvester Company. From their Michigan Boulevard office and with funds furnished by the trust, the two rapidly became leading entrepreneurs in the prevailing real estate boom. They bought and sold hundreds of commercial and residential properties in various parts of the city and thousands of lots and bungalows in and around the northern suburb then known as Niles Center and later as Skokie. At its height, their firm's assets were estimated to be worth $16.4 million. Mrs. McCormick took little part in their manifold operations beyond discussions of a grandiose—and never completed—project to be called Edithton and built on 1,500 lakeside acres near Kenosha, Wisconsin, in the manner of Florida's Palm Beach. In June 1929, a new prospectus for the trust announced the sale of $11 million in gold notes, the proceeds to be used toward payment of bank loans and obligations on real estate owned by the trust. For this issue Mrs. McCormick pledged securities with a total market value of more than $18 million. More than half was in 175,400 shares of Standard Oil Company of New Jersey and the rest in stocks and bonds of other Standard Oil companies and various utilities and railroads.

The stock market crash that October and the gradual waning of the real estate boom precipitated considerable financial distress for Mrs. Rockefeller. As her pledged securities dropped sharply in value, she pledged additional stocks. To help pay off notes of the trust, she mortgaged her Lake Shore Drive mansion and Villa Turicum and adjacent property for $777,500. A slight measure of relief might have been gained had she been willing to let Krenn & Dato foreclose mortgages on hundreds of properties on which payments were long overdue or to institute eviction proceedings against delinquent apartment tenants. But she refused to do so. By the end of 1931, with the continuing drop in the worth of her stock—at one point the annual Standard Oil dividend was only twenty-five cents—and further slippage in real estate values while her living expenses and the cost of maintaining her palatial home and retinue of servants remained constant, a large portion of her financial resources was depleted. Moreover, her health had not improved after a cancer operation the previous year, and her social activities were now greatly curtailed.

Early the next July, after her brother, John D. Rockefeller, Jr., made arrangements for $1,000-a-day support for her, Mrs. McCormick moved into a three-room suite in the Drake Hotel. Nearly all of her priceless belongings were placed in storage and most of her servants were dismissed. Ordered by her physicians to maintain what they called "a regime of repose," she delegated Krenn to speak for her. He held press conferences in his hotel rooms at which he expressed optimism: "It is true that Mrs. McCormick is economizing, like the rest of us. It is true that her income has been sharply reduced. It is also true that, out of consideration for others, she declined to take such action as would have protected her against these reverses. But she is not broke. She is able to meet her obligations and she is holding property and securities whose value will be restored in the general recovery from this economic depression."

Krenn's roseate predictions were never realized. On August 4, Cutting came to Mrs. McCormick's suite for the execution of a new will, with Oates and W. Clyde Jones as witnesses, to replace one Cutting had prepared in mid-1931. She received them graciously, but day by day thereafter she grew weaker, at times losing her power of speech. On the afternoon of August 25, six days short of her sixtieth birthday, Mrs. McCormick died. At her bedside were Krenn, her three children, and her former husband who, Kathleen McLaughlin revealed in her headline story in the *Tribune*, had sent her a red rose on each birthday since their 1921 divorce and had visited her daily in the last weeks of her life.

Settlement of Mrs. McCormick's estate—and attendant legal matters—was destined to be complicated and lengthy. The will, designating Chicago Title and Trust Company as executor, named Krenn as the recipient of five-twelfths of the estate, with the remainder in smaller shares to her three children. To assembled reporters, Cutting said that Krenn had given the trust set up for Mrs. McCormick $1.2 million in cash and securities late in 1931 and was prepared to give more. Cutting also sought to clarify an association that had kept Chicagoans intrigued and perplexed for over a decade: "Their relationship was like that of a son and mother, one of the most beautiful friendships I have ever witnessed." He disclosed that several days before Mrs. McCormick's death Krenn had surrendered to Dato whatever portion of the estate he might receive in exchange for an annual lifetime annuity of $24,000 on which he could retire and return to Switzerland. But that arrangement was cancelled when the inventory of Mrs. McCormick's estate showed personal property worth $1.03 million—

less than a third of the amount owed in taxes and assorted bills and to various claimants charging defaults of interest payments on bonds of the real estate trust. By the following March, Cutting took dour note of the estate's condition. "No one can tell what the assets will bring when the estate comes out of probate next September," he said. "But it may be that they will not bring enough to pay the bills. In that event, Mr. Krenn's five-twelfths share will amount to nothing."

Before Cutting could be proved correct, Krenn severed all legal and financial ties with Dato in their firm and put his claims to real estate and property of the estate, his rights under the will's provisions, and claims against the trust into the hands of a real estate dealer who held a Circuit Court judgment for $109,000 against Krenn & Dato. Austin and Douglas Smith successfully fought that claim and Probate Judge John F. O'Connell upheld their contention that the $1.2 million in cash and securities had been passed on by Krenn in 1931 to the real estate trust and not to Mrs. McCormick personally and therefore her estate was not liable. The ruling was appealed. In hearings before Circuit Court Judge Daniel P. Trude, Smith scored vital points when Krenn was placed on the witness stand by his attorney, Samuel E. Hirsch. In addition, Smith read into the record a list showing that in the eight years from the creation of the real estate trust until Krenn made his loan, Mrs. McCormick had bestowed innumerable gifts upon Krenn—$1 million in securities, $564,000 in cash, and $15,000 in jewelry. Judge Trude ruled for the defense, and in 1938 the Illinois Appellate Court affirmed his decision, thereby ending that litigation.

By now, the sale was under way of many of Mrs. McCormick's possessions. Two of her necklaces, with gems reportedly part of the Russian crown jewels, were sold in 1935 for $600,000 to a buyer whose identity was kept secret. Another necklace, said to have been owned by Russia's Catherine the Great, had ten large emeralds spaced on a strand made up of 1,600 diamonds, and its value, at the time of Mrs. McCormick's death, was estimated at $2 million. The firm notified all the estate's creditors of the necklace's availability, and Henri Cartier of the famed jewelry house came to Chicago to testify as to its authenticity and value, but no purchasers stepped forward. Tentative authority was given by Judge O'Connell to break up the necklace and, if necessary, to cut up the emeralds, the largest of which weighed 100 carats, to smaller sizes. This intended boon to potential purchasers proved to be unnecessary.

Acting as agent, the Cartier firm located a buyer in Paris. Early in 1936, Judge O'Connell approved the terms of a sale. Again, the purchaser's identity was not disclosed but the price was entered into Probate Court records: $800,000.

Month by month, year after year, the estate wound its tangled way through Probate Court. The Emperor carpet of Peter the Great, once appraised at $125,000, was acquired by an unidentified buyer for $75,000. A rare manuscript once valued at $10,000 was sold for $2,250. Other holdings in the mansion on Lake Shore Drive and at Villa Turicum in Lake Forest ultimately went, too, invariably at small percentages of their initial worth. Within a few years, both McCormick mansions were disposed of. On November 14, 1951, nineteen years after Mrs. McCormick's death, William Avery filed a final accounting with Probate Clerk John W. Tauchen with a request for Probate Judge William F. Waugh to approve distribution to creditors of the small amount of assets remaining in the estate. The request was granted the next month and the complex estate was finally closed, with creditors receiving fifty-six cents on the dollar for their claims.*

7

Considerably less complicated and demanding was the work involved in the firm's handling of the estate of William Wrigley, Jr., after the chewing gum mogul died at seventy on January 26, 1932, in Phoenix, Arizona, where he maintained a winter residence—in addition to another in Pasadena, California—and was owner of the resplendent Arizona Biltmore Hotel designed by Frank Lloyd Wright.

Wrigley had entered the gum-making business in Chicago in 1892 after working as a salesman of products of his father's soap factory in his native Germantown, Pennsylvania. He made the switch because he became aware that many of his customers were more delighted with the packages of gum that were given as premiums than with the soap. From the start, Wrigley prospered in his new venture. A genial, enthusiastic promoter, he initiated widespread advertising campaigns and projects to educate the general populace to the gum-chewing habit. Twice, he sent

*Although Mrs. McCormick's children received nothing from her estate, they shared in a $14 million trust fund that had been established in 1917 by their grandfather, John D. Rockefeller.

packages of gum to everyone listed in all the phone books in the United States. During recurring financial panics, he doubled his advertising budgets; in 1907, when Spearmint with the Wrigley-designed gnome on the pack was first produced, he spent lavishly on billboard and newspaper advertisements, countering the counsel of associates to be more conservative in that economically dire year with "People chew harder when they are sad." This kind of philosophy and attendant hard-driving sales methods produced ever-increasing revenues; two decades after he embarked on his venture, the public was paying $30 million for his products every year and by 1930 annual sales were well over $70 million.

Wrigley spent a good deal of money on other enterprises. In 1919, he and several others bought for $3 million Santa Catalina Island, a 48,000-acre tract twenty-six miles off California's southern coast. In the years that followed he bought out his partners in the Santa Catalina Island Company and expended nearly $30 million more in the construction of roads and parks in and around the isle's sole city of Avalon and the building of hotels, private homes, a movie theater, restaurants, a yacht harbor, and the world's largest ballroom, the Avalon, with room for 3,000 dancers and to which would eventually come bands led by Benny Goodman, Glenn Miller, Freddy Martin, and Harry James. Four years earlier, he had become a partner with J. Ogden Armour, the Chicago meat packer, and others in acquiring the Chicago Cubs baseball club and later bought the Los Angeles minor league team. The Cubs established a spring training camp on the island and Wrigley attended their sessions as often as possible while gradually gaining majority ownership. He regarded baseball as "the red-blooded American game. Like American business, the game is played to win and a game is nothing until it is won." Prominent in Chicago civic affairs and involved in extensive real estate ventures there—his Wrigley Building in 1924 was the first in a cluster of skyscrapers at Michigan Avenue and the Chicago River—and elsewhere, Wrigley was also a generous but unostentatious philanthropist. Among many benefactions was a large gift to Chicago Memorial Hospital and substantial donations to Illinois Home for Crippled Children, and after the onset of the Great Depression he turned over to the Salvation Army one of his Chicago properties, a six-story building, to be used as a shelter for jobless men, and provided a $5,000 monthly stipend for its maintenance.

A few months before his death, a new will had been drawn for Wrigley by Paul Harper, whose association, both as lawyer and friend, with

Paul V. Harper

Wrigley's son, Philip, had been maintained ever since the 1912 world tour on which Harper had served as Philip's tutor. The elder Wrigley had been impressed with the brief summary of the will that Harper had prepared for Philip and asked Harper to draft his will.

When the will was filed in Cook County Probate Court two days after a brief funeral service in Wrigley's Pasadena home, his fortune was listed in Harper's petition as $20.2 million. This referred to property in Illinois and did not include his out-of-state holdings—including his estate on Santa Catalina Island, his Phoenix and Pasadena residences, and hotels and other properties in Arizona and California, a summer home in Lake Geneva, Wisconsin, and mining lands in the west and southwest—whose worth was estimated at between $10 million and $15 million. Philip was bequeathed the Chicago Cubs, and after cash bequests to him, Wrigley's widow, Ada, and his daughter, Mrs. James Offield, of $100,000 each, and smaller amounts to other relatives, friends, business associates, and servants, the will directed that the balance of the estate, consisting mainly of nearly half a million shares of stock in the William Wrigley Company, be kept intact in a trust whose income was to go to Ada Wrigley until her death, at which time the trust was to be dissolved, with Philip receiving the major portion of assets remaining after payment of inheritance taxes and other costs. By 1937, when Harper's final accounting in Wrigley's estate was approved by Probate Judge John F. O'Connell, rising market prices had boosted its value by another $10 million. Harper also reported that more than $10 million had been deducted from the total amount for taxes and administrative costs, the largest item being federal, state, and other taxes totaling $8 million.

Another estate case that evoked far less—or minimal—public interest posed an interesting legal question.

Shortly after the death in Miami Beach early in 1934 of E. Mead Johnson, the eighty-one-year-old president of Mead Johnson Company, a major manufacturer of baby food in Evansville, Indiana, Paul Butcher, a senior trust officer at Continental Illinois National Bank and Trust Company, came to Austin with a potentially serious problem. This stemmed from the claim by Johnson, for whom the bank had set up a substantial trust, that he was technically a citizen of Florida, where he had long kept a winter home, although he also had a summer home in Michigan and his long-time Evansville residence. Now that he was dead, there loomed the prospect of efforts by all three states to collect inheritance taxes on his estate.

Austin faced the multiple domicile dilemma that had similarly plagued the $115 million estate of Dr. John Thompson Dorrance, founder, president, and sole owner of Campbell Soup Company. When Dorrance died in September 1930, at his farm near Mount Holly, New Jersey, he also had a residence in Radnor, Pennsylvania, and each state entered claims for inheritance taxes. The executors of the Dorrance estate contested the claims in the courts of both states, and in each state the ruling was that Dr. Dorrance was legally domiciled in that state. As a consequence, after lower court decisions were upheld by both states' supreme courts and the United States Supreme Court denied relief, New Jersey received $15.6 million and Pennsylvania $14.5 million.

To avert a similar outcome in the Johnson matter, Austin began negotiations with the tax authorities of each state, but progress was disappointingly slow. The attorneys general of Indiana and Florida were especially unyielding in their quest for a full domiciliary tax; Michigan had slight basis for its claim. Austin did considerable traveling to the capitals of the tax-seeking states. On a trip to Tallahassee, when he was compelled to wait while the attorney general was confronted with an emergency court battle, he spent many hours studying the Federal Code in the Florida Supreme Court library. The time there proved valuable. In his reading, Austin found language that prompted his decision to institute action in the United States District Court in Chicago because the assets on which each state sought liens were held by a bank in that jurisdiction and therefore that court had the power to decide the validity of the respective liens involving the controlling domiciliary question. The result was that a settlement was worked out in which a single tax was divided mainly between Indiana and Florida, with Michigan receiving a minute portion. (Long after the conclusion of this matter, it was discovered that Johnson had a one-third interest in a large tract of Mississippi River delta land which he evidently had forgotten about and was not known by any member of his family at the time of his death. The firm resolved the problem of omission of the extremely valuable land on a favorable basis and established the respective Johnson family interests in the property, all of which led to huge royalties for the Johnson family members after oil was struck there.)

8

A salient case in the decade outside the area of estate law involved the Young Men's Christian Association, with which the firm and some of its partners had maintained a close legal and personal relationship for many years.

In 1874, as a result of his friendship with Dwight L. Moody, the energetic evangelist then president of the YMCA's Chicago branch, Norman Williams had begun to serve as its counsel and continued to do so until his death. Charles Holt and Arthur Wheeler filled the same capacity, in addition, like Williams, taking strong interest in the organization's manifold activities. William Sidley was an even more assiduous supporter, first as a member of the YMCA's board of managers in 1899 and from 1911 to 1915 as the board's president. In the latter role, he was instrumental in enlisting the financial support of such eminent Chicagoans as Julius Rosenwald, John G. Shedd, Cyrus McCormick, J. Ogden Armour, and William Wrigley for construction of the YMCA Hotel, a $1.4 million, nineteen-story structure at 826 South Wabash Avenue whose avowed purpose was to serve, at minimal rates, "the self–respecting young man at the threshold of his city life—men of moderate means passing through the city and those temporarily out of work." At its dedication on May 21, 1916, Sidley, chairman of its committee on management, emphasized the hotel's role in providing young newcomers and transients with a wholesome environment to counteract "dangers to physical and moral and spiritual health that lurk in the cheap hotels and lodging houses to which they are compelled to resort, and in the adjuncts of such lodging houses—the saloon, the gambling house, and the brothel." The "dangers" cited by Sidley had been uncovered by a group of University of Chicago students recruited by the YMCA's general secretary, Wilbur Messer, to dress as tramps and live for a brief time in hotels in the general vicinity; typical among the students' findings was that there were scarcely half a dozen "where a man may go and be reasonably sure of coming out uninfected and uninfested."

Initial rates at the new 1,800-room hotel were thirty to fifty cents a night. Revenues from that source and various facilities, even after prices were later raised and an addition erected in 1927 increased the number of rooms to 2,700, were not enough to cover operating costs and other expenses, which had to be made up mainly by contributions large and small. Yet, through operation of the hotel, the YMCA was faced for nearly five years in the 1930s with a challenge to the validity of benefits granted when it was chartered by the Illinois legislature in 1861. In 1932, Cook County Assessor J. L. Jacobs levied a personal property tax for the preceding year of $6,364 upon the hotel and its cafeteria, newsstand, haberdashery, laundry, and other internal properties. YMCA officials protested the action in vain. When the county brought suit in Circuit Court to collect the tax, Burgess, assisted by Avery and Ragland, represented the association in a crucial legal contest of the assessment, the first of its kind ever made against the organization. Burgess based his defense on the original charter and an amendment of 1867 which stated unequivocally that all such YMCA holdings were exempt from taxation because the organization had been created for "benevolent and religious purposes." Neither the hotel nor the designated enterprises, he effectively showed with ample evidence, were a means of making profits or gain but fit the charter's characterization of a charitable institution. "The work in the YMCA hotel," he asserted, "is largely different from the ordinary hotel. Religious services are held, advice is rendered the young men guests and scores of services are rendered which would be unknown in the ordinary hotel." The YMCA, he said, was still working to improve the moral character of its young residents and the hotel had been built to assist in achieving that objective.

Judge John Prystalski ruled in the YMCA's favor. As anticipated, the county appealed. Burgess argued the case before the Illinois Supreme Court. In a sweeping decision on December 10, 1936, the high court affirmed Judge Prystalski's judgment with emphasis on the fact that the YMCA's charter constituted a nonrevocable contract in accord with the 1819 ruling by the United States Supreme Court in the Dartmouth College case. A key conclusion of its opinion accentuated the hotel's charitable nature: "Upon the statement of facts shown by the record it is clear the appellee is a charitable organization engaged in charitable work. Its primary object is charity—not the making of a profit. The rates charged for its rooms are not based, alone, on the cost of services rendered but the object . . . is to furnish wholesome living conditions to young men at a price they can afford to pay and thereby correct the social evils that surround men who would otherwise be compelled to live in cheap rooming houses, amid sordid environments." The services furnished by the cafeteria and the other enterprises were "purely incidental to the furnishing of the rooms in which the men should live and . . . likewise exempt from taxation. The word 'benevolent' found in the first section of the charter means 'charitable.' " The ruling stressed, too, that, in law, charity was not confined to the relief of poverty or distress or to mere alms-giving "but embraces the improvement and promotion of the happiness of man."

In later years, the important opinion was successfully invoked when further efforts were instituted by taxing authorities to make assessments against the hotel and other properties, including the twenty-four-story Lawson YMCA, which had opened late in 1931 at 30 West Chicago Avenue with the aid of a substantial bequest from Victor F. Lawson, founder and publisher of the *Chicago Daily News*. Sidley remained active in the affairs of the YMCA, serving as president of its board of trustees from 1944 to 1948 and enlisting other members of the firm to take on varied duties for the organization in and out of courts.*

9

The depression-ridden 1930s were reflected in diverse forms—the ever-rising ranks of the unemployed, the failures of hundreds of banks large

---

*The hotel on Wabash Avenue continued to carry out its original purposes for over four decades more. Thousands of indigent persons were given reduced rates on rooms and free meals. During World War II, it housed and fed soldiers in the Army Air Corps' mechanic training courses. Rising energy costs, inflation, and ever-increasing annual deficits compelled the YMCA board of managers to shut it down late in 1979.

and small, scores of railroad and industrial bankruptcies, foreclosures of mortgages owned by bank and trust company clients, decreases in national purchasing power and wages, hard times for some of the city's oldest clubs. In 1935 Austin, as president of the Union League Club, performed a valuable service for that venerable institution. Beset by depression-era woes caused by a decline in membership and income, the club was unable to meet principal and interest requirements on two mortgage loans totaling $3.8 million secured for construction of its new building on Jackson Boulevard. Austin worked out a reorganization plan, approved that July 15 by United States District Judge William H. Holly, by which past-due interest was waived and interest rates reduced, with payments to second mortgage bondholders deferred until the principal of the first mortgage had been reduced to $1 million.

Nor was the firm itself spared the effects of the depression. By 1931 its income had reached the highest point in its history, but from that peak until 1935 it dropped nearly 40 percent. In that period, a committee made up of Austin, McPherson, and Oates met frequently to handle operating problems, and at these sessions there was occasional discussion about instituting cuts in the salaries of clerks and lay personnel. Approval of such reductions was up to Sidley as head of the firm—and that approval did not then materialize because he and other senior partners decided to bear the burden of the decline in income. "It was recognized," read a typical statement in the minutes of one of the committee's meetings in September 1931, "that this was one of the few large firms in this and other leading cities where lawyers and stenographers have not been let out or their wages considerably reduced."* By July 1932, however, after the firm recorded the first of several decreases in annual income over the next three years, wages of lay help but not of law clerks were cut by 10 percent, reflecting that the depression's deflation in prices had reduced the cost of living; the amount saved thereby was set aside and used for distribution of that year's Christmas bonuses. Three years later, what with a slight easing in economic conditions and the acquisition of clients beset with problems arising in large part from requirements to comply with regulations of new federal agencies, periodic salary increases were resumed, and starting salaries for clerks were set, the next year, at $100 a month.

Throughout the difficult times, steps were taken, too, that were

144   *In the worst of the depression, 10 percent of Chicago's lawyers were on relief.

designed to improve efficiency and working methods. McPherson strongly stressed the need for close supervision of all work done by clerks so that, as the committee's minutes stated, "this work is constructive and that no time is wasted." It was also agreed that no additional stenographers would be hired for a time, necessitating the assumption of additional tasks by those so employed and by partners' secretaries. To offset any need for salary reductions if economic conditions worsened, Sidley directed that all the lawyers, principally newer men—who, he noted, seemed to waste time in their early hours—should start dictation at 9 o'clock each morning. Wherever and whenever possible, economies were effected. At one point, Burgess and McPherson checked respectively at Illinois Bell Telephone Company and Central Public Service Corporation how much it was necessary to spend on an adding machine that Natalie Olander, the firm's longtime bookkeeper, had suggested purchasing; the result was that instead of a large Burroughs machine for $340, a smaller Burroughs model was acquired for $205. And, as indicated by this statement in the minutes of a meeting in October 1933, strict economizing continued to prevail in relatively mundane matters: "It was determined not to invest approximately $100 in the washing of rugs, in view of the fact that they are cleaned daily by vacuum cleaner."

Along with essential frugalities, a number of internal processes and systems were established that would endure, with major or minor adjustments and refinements adjudged necessary in subsequent years.

In 1931, as Burgess was preparing to join the firm, it was determined by the partners that lawyers would be assigned to work in four principal departments. One encompassed corporate finance and public utilities under supervision of Paul Harper, another probate and federal taxes under Merritt Bragdon, another real estate under Edward McDougal, and the fourth, under James Oates, litigation. Assignment to a specific department, it was stressed, simply fixed a lawyer's primary responsibility and did not mean that he was to be excluded from work in another area, if needed. Work could be assigned according to clients as well as by departments and the several lawyers having contacts with clients would maintain them although the work involved would be done through the appropriate department. Each department head was directed to supervise work carefully, approve all legal opinions, and read all letters written by his department's members in connection with the department's tasks.

Shortly after these departments were set up, Austin proposed the

Merritt C. Bragdon

adoption of a policy of employing one outstanding law clerk each autumn from among members of the graduating classes of several leading law schools in the country. This was the initial move toward creating an organized recruiting system that, in mid-decade, was further formalized by proposing that specified members of the firm, each spring, communicate with likely candidates whose names and scholastic data would be acquired from deans of designated law schools—University of Chicago, Harvard, Columbia, Northwestern, Pennsylvania, and Yale—and request such candidates to come to the office to be interviewed.* During this time, too, the designation of each newly-hired man was altered from "clerk" to "associate lawyer" and then to "associate."

As in the past, newcomers, with rare exceptions, were assigned to duty as docket clerks. For years, the records of cases—dates of filing of papers, continuances granted, orders entered, and other steps in the legal process— had been entered on looseleaf sheets in large volumes, much as they were in court clerks' offices. Then, a streamlined method was devised by J. Rockefeller Prentice when he was hired as a clerk after graduating from

*This was not put into actual practice then, and the less formal hiring system continued to prevail. For subsequent recruiting, see Chapters VIII and XVI.

Yale Law School in 1931. He came to the firm at the behest of his father, E. Parmalee Prentice, whose friendship with Sidley went back to the "Croatian Episode" of the 1890s. During a hiatus in his undergraduate years at Yale, young Prentice had worked at a wholesale hardware firm in Boston whose inventory records were virtually non-existent or, at best, thoroughly muddled. Before returning to school, he organized a system of index cards that enabled his employer to know, at a glance and in essential detail, the amounts, costs, whereabouts, and other pertinent data relating to many hundreds of items in stock or that needed to be ordered from manufacturers. After mundane duties in the firm, Prentice was delegated to take charge of the docket ("The lowest job is docket clerk," he had written earlier to this father, "and I am working up to that!"). Drawing upon his successful experience at the Boston company, Prentice, with the approval of Sidley and other senior partners and at his own expense, replaced the loose-leaf method with a system of cards to keep the docket current. Records of active cases were kept on visible index cards, while cards for cases that were disposed of were filed in a drawer. Later, as the firm and the number of lawyers and cases expanded considerably, various improvements were instituted to keep lawyers aware of assorted matters relating to cases in their charge, and the corps of docket clerks and assistants grew ever larger. But Prentice had laid the basis for all that came later.

10

In the autumn of 1934, Adlai Stevenson returned to the firm after his year and a half in Washington, where he had worked in his final months as chief attorney for the Federal Alcohol Control Administration, created by Presidential order to police the liquor industry in anticipation of the repeal of the Eighteenth Amendment. He was encouraged in his intention to rejoin the firm in letters from McPherson, who assured him that his work would not be confined to routine matters but would be based on his recent experiences in administrative law, and from Burgess, who said Stevenson's decision was a wise one yet expressed his occasional qualms about practicing law: "It frequently seems to me as though I am doing little of a really worthwhile nature, and there are times when all of us get discouraged. I suppose that is a human tendency . . . . As you know, I have greatly feared that if you stayed too long in Washington you might unfit yourself for a more routine existence such as is called for in the practice of law."

The first partner Stevenson conferred with upon his return that October was Sidley, who expressed hope that Stevenson would renew his activities with the firm with increased enthusiasm, and assigned him to handle top-level tax work and chancery litigation, notably court contests under the new federal bankruptcy statute, and matters in which he could make use of his Washington experience. He worked closely with C. Bouton McDougal, a University of Chicago Law School graduate who had been hired in 1933 as a $50-a-month clerk, in financing bond issues under McPherson's supervision, and he was also given duties for Illinois Bell Telephone Company. Later, he and George W. Ball, another ex-New Deal lawyer (and a future Undersecretary of State and diplomat) who came in 1939, worked on varied matters, including the refinancing of an Omaha gas company. In the spring of 1936, he was named a partner. But outside affiliations made demands on his time and often intruded on his law practice. As president of the Chicago Council on Foreign Relations, he made frequent speeches about the growing crises in Europe and the role of the United States in confronting them, and after war broke out in Europe he was a leader in forming the Committee to Defend America By Aiding the Allies, the group whose views ran counter to those of the isolationist America First Committee. Foremost among the partners who shared Stevenson's views on foreign affairs and held active membership in both the Council and the interventionist organization was Sidley, for all his opposition to many of the Roosevelt administration's domestic policies. As the national debate between advocates of intervention and non-intervention heightened, Stevenson traveled about the country making speeches and arranging rallies—and giving less time to duties at the law office. Soon, he was once more seeking a job in Washington. It came at the end of June 1941. He was appointed principal attorney in the office of Secretary of the Navy Frank Knox at $5,000 a year. Fearing that in this position conflicts of interest might arise because some of the firm's clients held government contracts, Stevenson wrote to Sidley proposing a formal, but possibly temporary end to his partnership rather than a leave of absence earlier agreed upon. His superiors accepted this decision with regrets but with good wishes. "I hope, very sincerely," Austin wrote, "that your absence will not be for long." Prophetically, he added, "At the same time, I rather have a feeling that the lure of public service will be quite strong and you will stay beyond the time now anticipated. I am confident that you will do a good job."*

11

Except in some matters pertaining to Edith Rockefeller McCormick, Charles Cutting was relatively inactive as a "retired" senior partner in the early 1930s. He still came to his office periodically and, despite an occasional loss of memory, he always made himself available, as in the past, to younger men seeking guidance in probate matters. His portrait now hung in the Probate Courtroom, over which he had presided for thirteen years before joining the firm in 1913.

Early in 1934, he spent several weeks in the Presbyterian Hospital in treatment for exhaustion, but on that March 3 he was well enough to celebrate his eightieth birthday by lunching at the "judges' table" in the Union League Club with such friends as Federal Judges James H. Wilkerson, William M. Sparks, and Evan A. Evans and responding to a demand for a speech only with "My appetite improves with age." His appearances in his office were more sporadic in the months that followed. On April 7, 1936, he was back in the hospital after suffering a severe stroke, and ten days later he was dead. At a memorial service in Palatine Township high school's Cutting Hall, Austin recalled Cutting's years of service on the Probate bench and those with the firm: "He represented alike the rich, the poor, the great and the lowly—but one inflexible line he would not cross in accepting retainers. He refused any cause which he did not consider just." And he also enumerated Cutting's innumerable outside activities that included being president of the Chicago Bar Association twice and of the Law Club of Chicago, a member of the state board of law examiners, head of the Cook County Board of Education, one of the originators of The Chicago Community Trust, a pioneer philanthropic foundation, a trustee of Lewis Institute, and a director of Chicago Title and Trust Company. Underscoring his "great intellectual power" and "great professional talent and fine ethical sense" and vital contributions to the firm—not least among them his constant espousal of promotions from within the ranks and as a knowing guide to younger men—Austin fittingly declared, "Judge Cutting has enshrined himself in the hearts of

*For Stevenson's later affiliations with the firm, see Chapter VIII.

Judge Cutting in mid-1930s

his partners, and he will live with us always, so long as any of us remain. His place there is secure."

Two days before Cutting's death, announcement was made of Nathan Moore's retirement; actually, he had not practiced with the firm since the preceding September. Moore was eighty-three years old and had been a lawyer for fifty-seven consecutive years, most of them filled with distinction and accomplishment. To reporters, he proclaimed his intention to practice some law but mainly to devote his time to writing his memoirs and to painting in a studio that he had added to his Oak Park home. He also used the occasion to reflect on the past and present of the profession in which he had so long been engaged: "Young lawyers nowadays are more competent and better trained. They attend better schools and come out in much better shape. Fifty years ago, the judges and the Bar operated on a basis of mutual trust and respect. Now the courts are so numerous and the lawyers so plentiful that the Bar and court haven't much chance to get acquainted. I don't know more than 250 of the 10,000 lawyers listed on the Illinois Bar Association rolls. But the Bar is still honorable in the main. Some may sully the profession, but I've never come into contact with them." Moore lived on, turning out oil paintings mainly of landscapes, until August 1946, when he died at ninety-three.

Cutting's death and Moore's departure prompted consideration of a new name for the firm, as had been the custom in the past under similar circumstances. Some friends urged that there be no change; at a dinner meeting in New York, Irving Olds of White & Case and Arthur Dean of Sullivan & Cromwell advised Austin and John Dern to retain the name because as Cutting, Moore & Sidley the firm had become well-known outside Chicago, especially in New York and Washington. But Austin, cognizant of Moore's stated intention of practicing law occasionally, deemed this impossible. For months, there was much discussion of the matter by the partners. Finally, on the last day of the year, the firm assumed a name longer than any since its founding seventy years earlier: Sidley, McPherson, Austin & Burgess. McPherson remarked that it sounded like a trunk falling downstairs.

12

In the last half of the decade, with the easing of financial stringencies and the acquisition of clients facing predicaments arising from regulations imposed by new governmental agencies, additions—besides those already cited—were made to the firm's legal and lay personnel.

New associates who would be with the firm for some time ahead as partners included Middleton Miller, who came in 1935 after three years with a firm in Louisville, Kentucky, and was assigned to work primarily in the area of trusts and estates; J. Edward Day, who formed a close friend-ship with Stevenson after arriving in 1938 upon graduation from Harvard Law School; and George A. Ranney, a 1939 newcomer from Yale Law School who had been recommended by Stevenson.

In 1939, an affable man with a penchant for organization was hired as office manager, a post filled earlier in the decade by two others, with the book-keeping assistance of Natalie Olander and Edith Miller. William Jensen had formerly served in that capacity at a local business firm and, in the early dark days of the depression, had lost his haberdashery in a Loop building. Among his immediate predecessors was Lawrence E. Emmons, an associate who worked as manager on a part-time basis from 1930 until departing in 1936 to open a law office in his home town of Quincy, Illinois. Jensen would fill the position for the next thirty-three years in which the firm's growth required departmentalization of duties that he now and for the following several years handled by himself—

hiring and supervising and, when necessary, firing lay employees, purchasing supplies, distributing copies of office memos, making train and airline reservations, and even filling in at the office switchboard and at the reception desk.

Jensen also saw to the placement, when needed, of additional desks for associates in the crowded nineteenth floor "bull pen" adjoining the library. "There was a wonderful spirit there, a wonderful feeling of friendship," Ranney recalled later. "We used to have tea every afternoon, somewhat remote from the eyes of the seniors. We did the work assigned us, but there was not the sense of competition among us that became true of large firms of the future. We did struggle hopefully with the thought of becoming partners, but there was also a sense of fun in being an associate, a sociability in the office and even more when, as a group, we went to theaters or held our loud and pretty raucous parties."

And, as in the preceding decade, conviviality manifested itself at the Christmas luncheons in the Chicago Club. At the one in 1939, whose guest of honor was Chief Justice Francis S. Wilson of the Illinois Supreme Court, Ball and Ranney offered a reading of their "An Afternoon in the Zoo" that included such jocular verses as these:

About William Avery:

> *A moral beastie is the Avery.*
> *It thinks all vices quite unsavory;*
> *That taking drugs*
> *Is just for thugs*
> *And that white slavery is knavery.*

About Middleton Miller:

> *The Miller bird cavorts along*
> *The Iowa-Kentucky axis,*
> *And as it soars, it sings a song,*
> *A morbid song of death and taxes.*

About Howard Neitzert:

> *The Colonel's a Missouri Mule,*
> *Half horse, half ass, and half damn fool.*
> *Its specious southern eloquence*
> *Conceals its lack of common sense.*

152

About James Baker:

> *The noisy Baker*
> *Is an otter*
> *That chases mermaids*
> *Through the water.*

About William Jensen:

> *What bane that bird atop the fence on?*
> *Ay tank the sign says "Willie Yensen."*
> *You're wrong. That ain't no Swedish tanager.*
> *It's just the Sidley's office manager.*

About Ralph Himmelhoch, who excelled in pugnacious and invariably successful defense of Illinois Bell Telephone Company in "bang-in-the-ear" cases brought by those who charged that their hearing had been damaged by faulty receivers:

> *Behold the frumtious Himmelhoch!*
> *Mother Nature's funniest joke.*
> *It perches on the Illinois Bell*
> *And shouts like hell.*
> *It climbs upon the telephones—*
> *And moans.*

Nor did the poetizers spare themselves. About Ranney, then the docket clerk, they recited:

> *On its fanny sits the Ranney*
> *In the docket.*
> *It has you where the hair is short*
> *For it could throw you out of court*
> *By simply failing to report*
> *If you should mock it.*

And about Ball:

> *The Ball is neither fish nor bird.*
> *It's just absurd!*
> *Though neither man, nor mouse, nor moo,*
> *The Ball lives up above the Soo.*

It frightens widows, babes and orphans
By peeking 'neath the lids of corfins
Of corpses who one time invested
In bonds in which it's interested.

This seasonal jollity signaled the end of a decade that had been a difficult one. Diverse problems arising from the Great Depression and the fresh array of numerous governmental agencies had beset the firm and many of its clients, old and new, and they had been weathered. Of paramount importance had been the strengthening of the firm as one steadfast in its unstinting service to clients of whatever nature or status, the addition of strong, skilled lawyers, and the maintenance of solid morale and a helpful spirit of camaraderie and cohesiveness. These qualities would be sorely needed as, soon enough, new problems and new challenges presented themselves.

13

Shortly after the outset of the 1940s, soon to be so eventful, the firm acquired one of its most innovative, interesting—and enduring—clients. He was Arthur C. Nielsen, who had started a market research company in 1923 with capital of only $45,000, partly his own funds saved while working for an advertising agency and some from fellow-members of Sigma Phi fraternity in his years at the University of Wisconsin. As in the case of the G. D. Searle pharmaceutical-making house and Searle family, the Hoover Company and its vice-president, Earl Hoover, and other Hoover family members, and the Brooks-Scanlon lumber firms and their dominant executive, Edward Brooks—all clients over many years— Nielsen came to the firm through his friendship with Austin, a Sigma Phi at Wisconsin a few years before Nielsen enrolled in its engineering school to emerge, by 1920, as the graduate with the best scholastic record up to that time.

Nielsen had founded A. C. Nielsen Company with only five employees to conduct what he called "Performance Surveys," a special kind of marketing research that provided economic and engineering analyses of how well—or how poorly—the products of manufacturers of industrial machinery and goods were performing in the plants and stores of their customers. Later, after teetering on the brink of bankruptcy in the depression years, Nielsen devised a more complex research service known as the Nielsen Drug Index that, through interviews and on-the-spot checks of inventories, kept manufacturers apprised of results of the retail sale of their products and then a parallel service for the food industry called the Nielsen Food Index and still later the Nielsen Retail Index Services for not only food and drug store merchandise but also tobacco products, confectionery, alcoholic beverages, photographic equipment and supplies, and electrical appliances. Services and clients proliferated throughout the United States. By 1939, after eighteen months of difficult preparatory work, a British subsidiary was incorporated in Oxford, thereby inaugurating the company's first business abroad.

During the earlier part of the company's growth and increasing profitability, Nielsen's attorney was Robert McCurdy, a former judge whose devotion to the Wisconsin chapter of Sigma Phi fraternity was intense. But by 1940, what with the company's expansion and prospects for an affluent future, Nielsen and McCurdy felt that a younger man with an office organization was needed. So Nielsen sought out Austin and thenceforth the firm became his counsel for both business and personal matters. The Nielsen firm was then engaged in conducting research and pilot operations of an inventive device called an "Audimeter" that had been developed by two Massachusetts Institute of Technology professors, Robert F. Elder and Louis Woodruff. Use of the ingenious appliance installed in representative homes in scientifically selected parts of the country was initially designed to provide detailed and reliable estimates of the size and other characteristics of audiences for radio programs. By 1942, the tests were deemed satisfactory and a commercial service for network radio was inaugurated. Eight years later, network television was added, and in subsequent years the Nielsen Television Index Service became—and has remained—the best-known of the many services offered by the company, although comprising about 16 percent of total sales and a somewhat smaller share of total profit.* At the heart of the research system, Audimeters record every minute whether the television sets are on or off and if on, which channel is tuned in. The resulting records, in code on photographic strip film, are converted to International Business Ma-

*In 1964, the radio portion of the service was discontinued for technical and economic reasons.

chine cards in automatic coding machines at central offices and then put through a battery of electronic data processing machines that turn out printed results and dozens of types of information—ranging from the number of families watching telecasts to minute-by-minute fluctuations in audiences—for networks, local stations, advertisers and agencies, and program producers. Beyond recipients of television ratings, the ranks of clients supplied with over ninety other services through different market research techniques increased steadily in other areas as the company grew to be the world's largest of its kind. These clients included foremost manufacturers of a wide variety of consumer products, major advertising agencies, large oil companies, magazine and newspaper publishers, and scores of other companies and industries in two dozen countries around the world.

In the years since the initial affiliation—a period in which the Nielsen company's physical facilities expanded from a small office building on Chicago's northwest side to a complex of handsome structures in suburban Northbrook—Austin took the lead in handling diverse legal aspects of the Nielsen company's manifold activities, along with personal matters for the company's founder and members of his family. He helped steer Nielsen through financial shoals in the late 1940s when the radio audience measurement work was eating up much of the profits derived from the food and drug indices. He also rearranged the company's capital structure through creation of conventional voting and non-voting stock, as well as a special class of voting stock without substantial value, all of it retained by Nielsen. By this, Nielsen was able to sell some stock without losing voting control of the company. The firm also handled a number of acquisitions for the company. In these actions, Austin was aided primarily by Robert L. Foote, who had come to the firm upon graduation from Harvard Law School in the summer of 1941 and became a specialist in stock and bond issues, contract negotiations, general business advice, and phases of corporate law. Foote's relationship with the Nielsen company, both before and after Nielsen was succeeded by his son, Arthur, Jr., as head of the company, continued to be close, involving, beyond services cited, extended trips to England and France for negotiations for the sale there of several Nielsen interests. Not only did he become its general counsel when Austin relinquished some of his duties but in the mid-1970s, when Austin's numerous years on the company's board of directors ended at his request, Foote took his seat. In personal matters, Austin set up Nielsen family trusts and effected provisions in Nielsen's will that, upon the engineering-marketing genius' death in 1980 at eighty-two, characteristically provided not only substantial bequests to his wife, Gertrude, and children and other relatives and his college alma mater and Northwestern University but $2.4 million to forty-five charitable organizations in amounts from $5,000 to $150,000.*

14

As the firm headed for its seventy-fifth anniversary in 1941, its ranks comprised ten partners and twenty-one associates.

Harbingers of a major problem came when, in mid-year, two associates left for military service. Rockefeller Prentice went on active Army duty and became first a captain and later a major of a field artillery outfit. James Baker, a Navy reservist, was called into active service as a lieutenant junior grade, rising to commander before the end of the war. Before long, there would be other departures, but, meanwhile, plans and preparations were afoot for a reception to mark the anniversary. Meticulous attention was paid to all details, from selection of the Mid-Day Club on the seventeenth floor of the First National Bank building for the affair and the drawing up of a list of invited guests to the hiring of the well-known Arthur Herbert Heineckel Quartet (two violinists, a cellist and a pianist) and correspondence with Heineckel about appropriate musical numbers. The latter task fell to Edward McDougal, who was duly informed by Heineckel that the selections would include the overture to Mozart's *The Magic Flute,* the second movement from Tschaikovsky's *Fifth Symphony* and arias from Puccini's *Madame Butterfly.* The three-hour reception, with wives of the partners as hostesses, was scheduled for that December 12—five days after the Japanese attack on Pearl Harbor. Despite the sudden turn of events with the country's entry into World War II, no changes in anniversary plans were considered, except that McDougal asked Heineckel to be sure to include familiar songs from the World War I period—"Tipperary," "The Long, Long Trail," "Smile, Smile, Smile," and "Over There"—and, of course, "The Star-Spangled Banner" and "Battle Hymn of the Republic."

*During his lifetime, especially as his company prospered, Nielsen's benefactions extended from contributions of funds enabling Scandinavian students to study business administration in the United States to paying for most of the cost of restoring the Sigma Phi house in Madison after it was destroyed by fire early in 1973.

157

Six hundred persons attended the event, characterized by Sidley as "a somewhat unique gathering in Chicago history" not merely because of the firm's longevity but because among the diversified guests were many of the city's foremost lawyers and jurists, civic leaders, political chieftains, deans of law schools, newspaper publishers and reporters, and industrialists. Also in attendance were such representatives of an earlier generation of the firm's and the city's legal history as Charles Holt's sister, Ellen; Lessing Rosenthal, a classmate of Sidley's at South Division high school back in the 1880s and at the Union College of Law in 1891;* Frank J. Loesch, a veteran legal luminary who had known all members of the firm since the days of Norman Williams and John Thompson; Kenesaw Mountain Landis, the former federal judge who was the nation's baseball commissioner; ex-Vice President Charles G. Dawes; and John Henry Wigmore, dean of Northwestern University Law School who noted, in a follow-up letter to Sidley, that many in the firm had been his students in his professional days and described the anniversary reception as "the most distinguished social-professional occasion ever known to me in Chicago." Present, too, was Marshall Field III, whose new newspaper, the *Chicago Sun*, had emerged on that December 4; in a letter accompanying the invitation to Field, Sidley reminded him of services rendered by the firm many years earlier to his grandfather and congratulated him on the *Sun*: "It is indeed a good newspaper with an ideal program and an alternative setup of the news divorced from propaganda, which is what we are all seeking in these troubled times and which is so difficult to secure."**

The celebration also enabled Sidley and Austin to underscore anew the distinctive nature of the firm and its traditions and philosophy. Acknowledging a letter from Martin H. Foss of the city's legal department containing special praise for the abilities of the associates and younger partners, Sidley wrote, "I attribute our continuity as a firm and such success as we have achieved largely to the fact that it has been our policy to recruit our partners almost exclusively from our clerks whom we have most carefully educated with that possibility in view. Throughout the more

*Rosenthal sent boutonnieres for everyone in the firm to wear, plus a large candle to be lighted. The latter was overlooked, but was put to use at the annual Christmas luncheon two weeks later.

**Nearly four decades later, the firm acquired as a client Field Enterprises, Incorporated, parent organization of the newspaper (known then as the *Sun-Times*) and other properties.

William P. Sidley and Edwin C. Austin
greet guests at 75th anniversary party

than fifty years of my connection with this office it has been our uniform policy to choose these associates of ours with a view to their character as potential partners." To a congratulatory letter from John Searle, with whom he had maintained so long a professional and personal relationship, Austin replied, "A law firm has no plant. The rules of ethics forbid advertising. And its research results in no product except service to clients —all that a firm can sell. Because of these factors, your good will is the more important to us."

15

At the end of its seventy-fifth year, the firm faced an accelerated exodus of personnel. "The boys are all getting the fever now," Austin wrote to Baker, serving as navigator aboard the USS *Pelias*, a submarine tender that had escaped damage when Japanese bombs rained down upon Pearl Harbor. Steadily, men enlisted in the Army or Navy, most of them headed for officers' commissions, and a few reported for governmental duties in Washington. Some newly recruited associates like Edward W. Saunders, a 1939 Princeton alumnus and recent graduate of the University of Chicago Law School, and James W. Kissel, a 1938 University of Wisconsin alumnus and a graduate of John Marshall Law School, served only a few months before donning uniforms. Austin himself inquired of naval authorities whether he might become an officer once more but was told that, at fifty, he was too old for service.

By the following August, the number of lawyers at the firm had shrunk from the thirty-one of pre-war days to only nine. Hard-pressed to fill the needs of clients—"On numerous occasions," Austin later recalled, "I and others in our reduced ranks had to work all night and sometimes for two successive nights without sleep"—the firm sought to employ lawyers from other cities who wanted to work in Chicago, law professors whose classes had been depleted because of student enlistments and demands of the selective service system, and men who had been adjudged physically unfit for military service.

Although replacements were hired with no guarantee that they would be retained at war's end, several with considerable experience who came in 1942 would remain, as partners, long after the war was over: Harlowe E. Bowes, from a seventy-lawyer firm in New York where he excelled in securities and corporate areas; Ray Garrett, a specialist in corporate law who had written the Indiana Business Corporation Act and helped devise a similar act for Illinois; Howard P. Robinson, who had been the Phillips Petroleum Company resident lawyer in Chicago; J. Dean Vail, Jr., a tax expert who had been a law school classmate of Baker's; and Robert Diller, a former Department of Justice lawyer who, in addition to practicing corporate law, would become the firm's diligent historian.

And for the first time in its long life, the firm engaged a woman lawyer. She was Alice M. Bright, who had graduated second in her class at the University of Chicago Law School in the summer of 1941. She had already accepted a position in military intelligence in Washington when she received a call from Paul Harper who, like other senior partners, was on the lookout for bright draft-exempt prospects. Informed about Miss Bright and her scholastic stature by Philip Schofield, an associate about to leave for a position in the Washington office of the Alien Property Custodian, Harper persuaded her to come to the Roanoke Building offices to be interviewed by him, Burgess, and other partners. When she accepted employment on the next June 1 at $150 a month, Miss Bright was quite a rarity as one of only three women then at major Chicago law firms, although there were several who practiced alone or with one or two male partners. Assigned at first to probate work, assisting Bragdon and Austin and also Harper with Harper's mother's estate, she soon, in the prevailing

Alice M. Bright,
firm's first woman member

manpower shortage, also assumed tasks in real estate, contract negotiations and other areas. In the years that followed, during which she was made a partner, her practice became more diversified and ranged from child custody matters and complex divorce cases to drawing up wills and trusts; in the latter, as she said later, she enjoyed the role of a family counselor in working with second and third generations of clients she had served in her early days as the firm's first "lady lawyer."

Among those who served during the war period and some for a time thereafter were Walter V. Schaefer, a bright young professor at Northwestern University Law School who stayed until he returned to his classes at the end of 1945 and later became an Illinois Supreme Court Justice; Robert A. Sprecher, subsequently on the bench of the United States Court of Appeals; and Lloyd McClelland, a future vice-president and general counsel of Sears, Roebuck & Company. Hired as full-time librarian was Sidley's brother-in-law, Eugene Dupee, at eighty a man with years of experience behind him as a condemnation expert for the city and filled with political lore he would delight in passing on to freshly-arrived associates until his retirement in 1960.

On the first anniversary of the Pearl Harbor assault, Sidley wrote to Baker, "We have half a dozen or more new faces in the office who are valiantly aiding us to keep on top of our work." His letter was one of scores he and other partners who remained in Chicago regularly dispatched throughout the war years to sustain the morale of men overseas or in stateside posts. In the immediate post-Pearl Harbor weeks, Austin's letter to Baker told of the anniversary festivities, then went on, "We are in the fight now and the only course is to keep our chins up and see it through. I have faith that we can do this. And I am strongly tempted to go back and see that personnel man who told me I was too old to get back in the navy and find out whether he has changed his mind." Douglas Smith wrote regularly, in one early missive to Baker telling of recent departures and adding, humorously, "You can see from all this that if we keep the shop open the partners are going to have to go to work, provided, of course, that there should be any work to do. I should think it not all unlikely that in another year or two they might have a lot of us oldsters in the factories making munitions for you fellows, which would be all right with me."

For the war's duration, in addition to such letters, a mimeographed sheaf of news items about men in service, communiques from them, and jottings about activities at the office was sent periodically to all who had left. Each report, headlined "Unofficial Bulletin" and ending with "Your Fellow Cribbers," offered information about Prentice's marriage, while on leave, to Abbie Cantrell, one of the firm's receptionists, and Baker's promotion to a full lieutenancy, with occasional duty as a legal officer in courts-martial at Pearl Harbor ("Not exactly LaSalle Street law but it does help to remind me that basically I'm a lawyer, not a naval officer"). Other items dealt with the hiring of such newcomers as Miss Bright ("appropriately named") and accounts of jovial gatherings of colleagues stationed in and near Washington at Adlai Stevenson's home. The newsletter also told of Howard Neitzert's elevation to a partnership in 1942. He was by then possessor of a formidable reputation as an excellent trial lawyer. "It was hard work," he recalled in later years, "but I liked it, always enjoyed being in court, looked at it as a kind of a game I invented in the office and played in the courtroom." Some opponents—and even cohorts—considered him intractable on occasion, but few questioned his brilliance. He would continue to exhibit his skills as counsel for railroads in a series of confrontations with labor unions and in other often complex matters.*

16

On the home front, the bulk of the firm's work continued to be performed for such important clients as utilities, banks, and railroads. Paul

*See Chapter X.

Harper led the team that drafted the mortgages for the Chicago and North Western when the railroad finally emerged from bankruptcy in 1944. He was also involved, in overseeing matters related to the Wrigley interests, in a project of lesser import but of interest to sports fans. In 1942, Philip Wrigley, apprehensive over the possibility that organized baseball might become a wartime casualty because of the drafting and enlistment of scores of players, proposed the formation of a girls' professional softball league. As attorney for the Chicago Cubs and a member of its board of directors, Harper organized a non-profit corporation headed by Wrigley, Branch Rickey, president of the Brooklyn Dodgers, and himself. Territorial tryouts got under way early in the following spring, and by mid-May sixty players were selected, fifteen to go to each of four clubs in Kenosha and Racine in Wisconsin, Rockford, Illinois, and South Bend, Indiana, none of which had ever had major league baseball teams. The first season was reasonably successful, with total attendance of over 176,000. But when the league went into Milwaukee and Minneapolis, which had regular baseball teams and ball parks, attendance was skimpy. Wrigley sought to attract crowds by hiring the Milwaukee Symphony Orchestra to present a one-hour concert before games, but customers continued to stay away there and attendance languished elsewhere, too. By the end of 1944, foreseeing the end of the war and the return of players from service—and having borne most of the costs of his well-meant venture with very little income—Wrigley withdrew and the league soon disbanded.

17

On March 17, 1944 Donald McPherson, who had been relatively inactive at the firm for three years because of poor health, died in his Lake Shore Drive home. He was fifty-nine, and obituaries took note of his long years of practice with the firm in corporate areas and his leadership in innumerable civic activities and organizations ranging from the Chicago Council on Foreign Relations, whose president he was in 1939 and 1940, to the Illinois Legislative Voters League.

A memorandum Sidley drew up for the *Chicago Bar Record* and personnel at the firm included excerpts from letters of condolence to Mrs. McPherson and to him that stressed McPherson's qualities as "a rare individual who combined an absolute white-hot intensity of purpose with a great decency of thought and action and a method of expressing himself which at times approached the speech of an articulate rapier" and as a lawyer whose clients could see in him "almost a knight in armor charging furiously into the lists for them."

McPherson's death resulted in a change in the firm's name that September to Sidley, Austin, Burgess & Harper. In that year, too, four of the associates became partners: Avery, Bowes, Garrett, and Ragland.

Sidley, Austin, Burgess & Harper
1944–1949
Sidley, Austin, Burgess & Smith
1950–1956

AFTER THE war was over, most of those who had left returned to the firm, so that by the summer of 1946 there were fifteen partners and twenty-six associates. It was soon evident that there would be plenty of work for all. Resumption of the manufacture of consumer goods, severely curtailed in the war years, and company expansions brought a need for infusions of capital and issues of client companies' securities. Regulatory agencies of the Roosevelt era still prevailed. New ones and statutes enacted by the Congress and state legislatures resulted in more regulations and a consequent heightening of administrative law practice. More taxes were imposed by state and local governments. The war's cost had already raised federal income tax rates to higher levels, with probabilities of further boosts, and there was need for counsel to clients encountering new tax problems.

Especially illustrative of the range of expanding activities in the immediate and later postwar years was what was being done by lawyers specializing in corporate practice.

During the war, many corporations of modest size had been called on by the government to manufacture materiel and equipment for use in the war effort. Because they had insufficient capital, they found it necessary to secure financing from banks, much of it in the form of what were called "V loans." The Northern Trust Company consulted the firm regarding such loans, thereafter handled by Bowes, whose experience with banks in New York in his eleven years of practice there proved of inestimable value. So impressed were many of these borrowers that they retained the firm after the war so that they might have the benefit of Bowes' service in all corporate matters. Bowes was also a central figure in corporate matters of larger magnitude. He was joined by Foote, upon the latter's return from naval service, in assisting Dern with the United Light and Power system, in addition to serving Illinois Bell Telephone Company and Iowa-Illinois Gas and Electric Company and underwriters for securities issues for Commonwealth Edison Company and Public Service Company of Indiana, and others. Garrett and Harper were engaged mainly in facilitating reorganization of railroads emerging from depression-era bankruptcies. Edward McDougal worked on utility financing, and Bouton McDougal continued the kind of financing work he had started with Austin in the latter 1930s, now representing insurance companies and other buyers of issues of bonds for Central Telephone Company and its subsidiaries and similar firms. George Ranney aided Garrett on various corporate matters, along with duties in labor cases with Neitzert after he became a partner in 1951 following trial work in 1946–47. Adding to the representation of Halsey, Stuart and Company that had begun earlier, the firm now became Middle West counsel for two of the nation's highly respected investment banking firms—Smith Barney & Company and White, Weld & Company—on securities issues which they took the leadership in underwriting.

Into the 1950s, the corporate practice continued to expand. Vail and Foote helped guide Brooks-Scanlon Lumber Company through a major change in its operations, including the merger of its affiliates and the sale of its southern timberland to Procter & Gamble as a source of lumber for that firm's Buckeye box board mill. The proceeds were invested in oil operations which became Ambassador Oil Company and Kingdom Oil Company.

In this decade, a number of clients went public for the first time. Foote and Bowes aided Austin in an initial offering by G. D. Searle & Company, and Foote continued to do corporate work for the pharmaceutical company along with others in the group. In short order came stock offerings by A. C. Nielsen, as related earlier, Ambassador Oil Company, Brooks-Scanlon, and R. R. Donnelley & Sons Company. For the latter, Foote wrote the registration statement. He later recalled this as "a particularly interesting experience" because the company had always been especially secretive about its financial affairs and wished to remain so in case the proposed public offering was abandoned—a problem solved by Foote by working in an isolated room in the huge Donnelley plant to avoid causing any speculation about why he was there until the registration statement was actually filed. Subsequently, the firm handled a number of other stock and debenture offerings for the printing company.

Throughout the decade, the corporate group gradually evolved into three sub-groups. One, headed by Bowes, spent most of its time on utility financing and as underwriter's counsel in connection with a substantial amount of competitive bidding underwritings where a company had to select counsel to represent the underwriter making the successful bid. The second was headed by Garrett and worked primarily in railroad reorganizations, financing, and acquisitions. Foote headed the third group that devoted itself to more disparate matters such as public offerings, general corporate acquisitions, and contracts for such clients as A. C. Nielsen, which he served as general counsel, Brooks-Scanlon, and others that needed corporate work outside the utility and railroad fields.

An example of such a client was the Chicago Musical Instrument Company. It had been founded in 1920 by Maurice H. Berlin, who at thirteen had been a $3.50-a-week messenger for the Wurlitzer Company and later an army bugler in the First World War. In the late 1950s, after the death of his lawyer, Berlin and his son, Arnold, came to Avery, who became their and the company's lawyer. While Avery handled most personal and corporate matters, he had Foote handle a number of corporate acquisitions. By this time, CMI had achieved a national reputation as a foremost distributor of musical instruments through the acquisitions of the Gibson Company, the nation's largest producer of guitars, and F. E. Olds and Son, a leader in the band instrument field, and the sale of thousands of plastic bugles to the armed services. A major move came in 1956 with the acquisition by CMI of patent rights to the Lowery electric organ from its developers and contracting with the Hallicrafter Company, a Chicago electronics firm, to produce it. From 1957 to 1961, total CMI annual sales rose from $11 million to $25 million. In the latter years, fourteen months after CMI's first public stock offering, the value of a share of its stock rose from twenty-four dollars to fifty-four dollars. The firm continued to have a key role in further developments—additional offerings of stock and debentures with Smith Barney as underwriter and the procurement of more instrument companies, notably the 104-year-old family-owned Story & Clark Piano Company of Grand Haven, Michigan, and the Hallicrafters organ manufacturing facilities.

In the following years, corporate practice of the firm continued to expand, partly by virtue of the growth and increasing problems of existing local, regional, and national clients, and partly as a result of the acquisition of a host of new clients, so that the corporate group became the second largest of the firm's functional groups.* In addition to normal corporate work, the firm's services included advice and representation in various types of financing, acquisitions, mergers and sales, real estate transactions, litigation and federal, state and local taxes, and administrative law matters. As usual, the firm was called upon by growing numbers of individuals in connection with their varied personal and financial problems.

2

Those who did not return from the war included Prentice, Daggett Harvey, and George Ball. Prentice had long been interested in artificial insemination of dairy cattle, about which his father had written several books after retiring from his New York law practice. He now decided to set up a firm that would furnish such a service to dairy farmers on a nationwide scale; in a few years his American Breeders Service was one of the foremost companies in that field, and he gained considerable renown as a pioneer in the technology of artificial breeding of cattle. Harvey, a bright and witty associate since 1933, became an executive with his family's famous Fred Harvey restaurant chain, retained in the future as a client. As counsel for the French Purchasing Commission, Ball had many European clients, so New York seemed a logical place to join in establishing a law firm known there as Cleary, Gottlieb, Friendly & Cox and in Washington as Cleary, Gottlieb, Friendly & Ball; he wrote later that he sought to have the firm reflect qualities he had found "most exemplary in the Sidley office, such as exceptionally high professional standards, humane principles of administration, congeniality fostered by senior partners and work that was hard but stimulating and intellectually gratifying."

After a period as an assistant to Secretary of State Edward Stettinius and chief of the American delegation to the United Nations Preparatory Commission in London, Adlai Stevenson came back to the firm early in 1947. Although he attended to duties, he concerned himself with other matters. He pondered the idea of starting his own law firm, as he also had

*See Chapter XIV.

done in the final stages of his wartime service; he organized a series of monthly lectures on foreign relations to be given at Northwestern University Law School by him and others; he made many speeches before groups ranging from the Chicago Council on Foreign Relations and the Commercial Club to the Chicago Bar Association and Springfield's Lincoln Library Forum. And he talked politics, one result of which was that toward the end of the year the chieftains of the Democratic party in Illinois asked him to run for governor in 1948. Stevenson had hoped for a bid to be a candidate for the Senate—friends had formed a Stevenson-For-Senator committee—and he found it difficult to reach a prompt decision. He sought the counsel of friends and colleagues, prime among them Austin. With prescience, Austin told him in a long afternoon of discussion: "You're now twenty years out of law school and you've never quite decided if you want to be a lawyer or be in public life. I think it's public life, although I think you could be a great lawyer. If you want public life, this is the opportunity of a lifetime. You'll be elected. And if you retain your health, you'll be an outstanding candidate for President in 1952." (Stevenson handily defeated the incumbent governor, Dwight Green, and Edward Day went to Springfield with him as a legal and legislative assistant. Although he never again was a member of the firm, he kept the close friendships he had made there. After his defeat by Dwight Eisenhower in the 1952 Presidential election, he was given space in the firm's offices for himself and his close aide, William McCormick Blair, Jr., and two secretaries, and he used the rooms as his Chicago headquarters until he organized his own law firm in 1955. And in 1962, when Stevenson applied for admission to the New York bar while he was United States Ambassador to the United Nations, Austin wrote a highly laudatory letter vouching for his character and fitness and calling him "a high-minded gentleman of unquestioned character and of the highest integrity—an affable, friendly human being and one whose presence we miss in the office.")*

Before the decade was out there were departures of three more partners, none to other law firms. In 1947, Edward McDougal left to become counsel and secretary—later vice-president—of International Minerals and Chemical Corporation. The following year, James Oates was named board chairman and chief executive officer of Peoples Gas Light and Coke

*For later references to Stevenson, see Chapters IX and XII.

Company. In 1957 he moved to New York to become chairman of the Equitable Life Assurance Society of the United States. C. Bouton McDougal took the position of secretary and, later, vice-president of R. R. Donnelley & Sons Company. All were clients except for the gas company, although it and one of its subsidiaries, Natural Gas Pipeline Company of America, retained the firm from time to time.

3

Late in 1949, the ebullient Paul Harper died of a coronary thrombosis. As the new year began, the firm's eighth name since its founding in 1866 became Sidley, Austin, Burgess & Smith. Austin took over representation of Harper's longtime friend and client, Philip Wrigley, and maintained a close professional and personal relationship with Wrigley and his wife, Helen. In the years since, others in the firm—notably W. Sterling Maxwell, a 1949 graduate of the University of Michigan Law School and a partner since 1962—also served members of the family. Included was the probating of the will and distribution of the assets of William Wrigley, Jr.'s widow, Ada, after she died at the end of 1958 in her Pasadena home, where she had lain for eleven years in a coma induced by a severe stroke. After the deaths of Philip and Helen Wrigley within two months of each other in 1977, their estates were handled by a team headed by Maxwell and Alice Bright, with Bright obtaining a particularly favorable valuation of the large holdings of Wrigley Company stock. Beginning in the early 1970s, Miss Bright successfully represented the younger William Wrigley in tangled, embittered, and extended marital proceedings brought by his wife, Joan, which, however, ended in an annulment sought by Wrigley.

In baseball matters, Avery, in addition to seeing to financial and corporate aspects of the Chicago Cubs' operations, worked out details of the sale in 1956 of the Los Angeles Angels, the minor league team that the senior Wrigley had acquired years before and which, since 1941, had been a Cubs farm club. The purchaser was Walter O'Malley, who had long been unhappy with aged Ebbets Field as the home park for his Brooklyn Dodgers and sought a replacement. The agreement between Wrigley and O'Malley provided for payment to the Cubs of $2 million and transfer of the franchise and field of the Fort Worth, Texas, league team in exchange for the Angels' field and the players' contracts. By the opening of the 1958 season the Brooklyn team was ensconced on the West Coast as the Los

Douglas F. Smith

Angeles Dodgers, much to the displeasure of its rabid New York followers but to the delight of the ever-expanding hordes of fans in Los Angeles and environs.

Meanwhile, Baker handled radio and television contracts, National League relations, and litigation for the Cubs. He also became involved in kindred matters. One that drew considerable press attention was a suit by Gordon McLendon against thirteen major league baseball clubs for $12 million because, he claimed, his Liberty Broadcasting System was denied access to the teams' parks to broadcast the "Game of the Day" to his 400 stations in cities which had minor league teams. Trial dates were continued many times after institution of the action early in 1952. In their midst, McLendon's network went out of business. By 1955, the litigation ended with Baker working out a compromise settlement with McLendon for a minute fraction of what he sought. During the course of the McLendon suit, Bowie Kuhn, then a New York lawyer, worked in the office in Chicago with Baker and others on the case, and after becoming baseball commissioner, he hired the firm to represent him in several matters, including the successful defense of a suit arising out of Kuhn's voiding of the sale of three major league players as not being in the best interests of the sport.

In 1981, the firm's connection with the Cubs came to an end when   *171*

Maxwell represented the younger William Wrigley and the team in its sale that summer to the Tribune Company for a reported $20.5 million.

4

The postwar increase in legal personnel continued as the heightened business economy fostered the need for considerable expertise in dealing with clients' problems. In addition to litigation and corporate transactions there was an intensification of lawyers' roles as advisers and counselors, especially in matters stemming from complex rules and regulations so that cases would not have to be taken to court with attendant consumption of time and manpower in prolonged and expensive lawsuits.

To insure that the office would be more efficiently organized to handle business, the prevailing system of assigning lawyers was revised. A "general assignment" group in 1946 was made up of senior associates of ability and experience who had become specialists in one or more types of work and could be generally available to take a high degree of responsibility for matters referred to them from time to time by firm members. In an internal memorandum to all partners and associates, these lawyers were designated as a "floating reserve" to whom partners could delegate matters and upon whom they could call for assistance. Lawyers particularly fitted for work they had been performing, such as probate and real estate matters, were expected to continue to do so for some time to come and were designated as being given a "departmental assignment." As before, younger lawyers were to be assigned to the docket department only after spending a year or more after arrival from law school on legal research and other services for partners and senior associates.

Lawyers not given general or departmental assignments were assigned to individual partners but could be called on for other work in emergencies or when not needed in their designated activity. Stress was laid anew on a long-standing firm tenet: "A partner to whom a staff lawyer is assigned is under a duty to develop, guide and instruct the staff lawyer so assigned." Those in specific types of work were designated as being available also for rotation or other assignments when not engaged in their specialties. No staff lawyer was to be assigned to a particular partner for more than a year except in special circumstances, "the object being," advised the memorandum, "to give the assigned staff member a broad experience in office work as well as the experience of working under several men and to enable more than one partner to become familiar with the talents and qualifications of each associate." In 1949, the organizational and assignment setup was further altered, with division into six departments—corporation, litigation, real estate, tax, trust, and general. Among new rules was one that specified that whenever a lawyer completed assigned work, the department chairman was to be notified, and if no further work was required of him or her the chairman was to advise other department heads of the lawyer's availability for work in other areas. In ensuing years, as the firm grew larger and the ranks of lawyers increased greatly, new procedural rules were instituted whose overriding aim was to insure topflight service to clients.

5

By this time, the two men most deeply involved in managerial duties were Austin and Burgess. Sidley had begun to turn over many responsibilities to them in the late 1930s as he reached his seventies, and increasingly

Name partners in 1951: (*Left to right*)
Douglas F. Smith, William P. Sidley,
Kenneth F. Burgess, Edwin C. Austin

in the years that followed he relied on them for decisions on the firm's policies and procedures.

Their respect for each other's abilities and long years of friendship created what Austin later recalled as "a splendid understanding," with minimal differences of opinion. Austin oversaw corporate financial and probate work and office finances. Burgess supervised all litigation and took an intensely active part in recruitment of associates and assigning lawyers to their offices. In case of unusual problems affecting the office, they consulted other senior partners.

Although they were looked upon as "father figures," especially by younger associates, their personalities contrasted markedly. Austin was benign, gentle, and calm, with the ways and manner of an earnest teacher. Burgess, strong-minded and forceful, was at times quick to lose his temper, although he would almost always apologize to those he occasionally upbraided for arguing or disagreeing with him. Burgess appeared to some, as one associate put it, "to resemble what we imagined God should look like in the original fire and brimstone stories, but he inspired our integrity and determination to work very hard," while Austin was "a perhaps more dignified version of what small children imagine Santa Claus to be like, with friendly twinkling eyes that always seemed to say, 'Don't worry, all is well' and he inspired our conviviality and determination to pay attention to being business-getters and business-keepers for the firm." Both men paid scrupulous attention to tasks that needed to be done, and they made themselves available to any of the lawyers for discussions of professional or personal problems. Unless a case required that he be out of the city, Burgess invariably showed up on Saturday mornings to make the rounds of the premises with the office manager and sometimes stride into the office of an associate who was putting in extra hours preparing a brief or some other document with the commendation, "Good to see you busy. If you weren't worth more than I'm paying you, I'd fire you." This emphasis on diligence was also underscored on each day before all holidays except Christmas, New Year's, Thanksgiving, and Independence Day by Burgess' notice on the office bulletin board: "The firm will be closed for all those who have no work to do." Walter J. Cummings, who came to the firm in 1946 after six years in Washington on the staff of the United States Solicitor General and as a Department of Justice lawyer, remembered that message long after his years there and during his service, starting in 1966, as a judge of the Seventh Circuit United States Court of

Appeals: "You can imagine that such a notice required all the younger lawyers to report, if only to save face."

Austin enjoyed engaging associates in congenial conversation not only about their cases and the firm's history and leaders of the past but about its philosophy and pragmatic purposes. "It's easy to fry the fish," he often said, "but the trick is to catch it." He emphasized that new clients could best be obtained by doing work of high quality so that it would be noticed by others in need of representation. He also advised the young lawyers, "Think of this firm not as a pie of fixed size to be divided up but as a pudding of indefinite size to which we all contribute and in which we all share." And he laid stress, in such conversations and in talks to students at Northwestern University Law School and elsewhere, on qualities needed in having a successful law practice—"integrity, intelligence, industry, imagination, and initiative."

6

Of the partners who were becoming engaged in recruiting, Burgess was most assiduous. He made regular visits to the top-rated law schools in the East, but he kept an eye out for law students of proven ability in other parts of the country. He especially favored those with excellent records and accomplishments at midwestern schools, sometimes saying, "I prefer small town boys from the Midwest because they have the ambition and expect to work." While not all those who were hired in the postwar years and in the 1950s precisely fit that description, many of them came—as had some others earlier—from such places as the Universities of Wisconsin, Michigan, Minnesota, and Iowa and, in the Chicago area, the University of Chicago, Northwestern University, and Loyola University. Whatever their origins or social standing or schools, it was paramount to Burgess that they be truly the best and the brightest of likely associates.

Three men recruited by Burgess in this period amply filled those requirements, and each was to become an important member of the firm.

In the fall of 1948, when Howard J. Trienens was in his final months at the Northwestern University School of Law and editor of its law review, Burgess invited him to his office for an interview. Because Trienens intended to move to California and practice there, he turned down Burgess' bid to join the firm as an associate. After Trienens graduated early in 1949 and was engaged by the law school to teach a course in criminal law while making his California plans, Burgess asked the school's dean, H. C. Havighurst, to arrange Trienens' teaching schedule so that he could work part-time for the firm on an anti-trust case involving the Chicago Medical Society. For a semester, Trienens spent his mornings teaching and the rest of the day at the firm. He did take a trip to San Francisco, where he had interviews with railroad and telephone attorneys from which he concluded that he would find practice there less satisfying than with the firm. Trienens stayed with the firm until June 1950, when he left for Washington to serve for two years as a clerk to Supreme Court Chief Justice Fred M. Vinson. When he returned to Chicago in 1952, he went to work with Burgess and Douglas Smith, mainly on rate cases for Illinois Bell Telephone Company and for a group of western railroads. Very early, Trienens began to acquire a deserved reputation as an extremely bright lawyer, always prepared to present complex data and figures with clarity and persuasive argument directly and without rhetorical embellishments. Such qualities and others would be even more evident as he advanced within the firm and as he grew in professional stature and degree of accomplishment. In 1956, he was named a partner.

Trienens' predecessor in clerking for Chief Justice Vinson was Arthur R. Seder, Jr., also a Northwestern University Law School graduate. He was twenty-five years old, with a wife and child, when he entered law school late in 1945 after war-time service as a B-17 pilot who had flown twenty-five missions over Germany and France. At Northwestern he co-edited the law review with a close friend, John Paul Stevens, the future justice of the United States Supreme Court, and for a time after graduating taught a course in contract law. Before going to Washington in 1948, he met with Burgess and after a friendly conversation filled out a job application form; he was strongly influenced to seek employment there, he said later, by the esteem in which the firm was held by his father, a financial vice-president for the Chicago and North Western who had worked closely with Harper and his team during the time of that railroad's reorganization. Toward the end of Seder's second year at the Supreme Court, Burgess invited him to dinner in Washington. Seder had offers to teach at the University of Pennsylvania Law School or stay in Washington with Covington & Burling. But when Burgess asked him to join the firm, he readily assented and did so in the summer of 1950. His varied duties included preparing briefs for cases on appeal in higher courts, successfully trying assorted cases for Illinois Bell Telephone Company and starting to aid John Dern in work for American Natural Gas Company, where, as its general counsel, Dern was known as "the conscience of the organization" and where Seder absorbed Dern's skills and considerate ways that would be of great value to him after he was made a partner in 1956.

A 1951 graduate of the University of Iowa Law School, where he was a co-editor of the law review, H. Blair White had intentions of getting a government job in Washington. At the suggestion of one of his professors who had recommended him to Burgess, he stopped in Chicago on his way to the capital and spent several hours with Burgess and other partners. "As I got back on the train," he recalled later, "I knew I was very interested. I liked the openness and warmth of the firm. I got to Washington but was turned off pretty fast and came here." Two days after his arrival that June 29, he became part of the team—"I was the low man on the totem pole" —that defended Borden Dairy Company in an anti-trust suit brought by the government against it and four other dairies. In his years afterward, he figured prominently in many major matters in addition to heading up and sharpening recruiting programs whose basic tenets stemmed largely from Burgess' philosophy of placing greatest emphasis on scholastic merit and attainments.

Not all of Burgess' outstanding recruits stayed long enough to become partners. Darwin E. Smith, who joined the firm in 1955 upon graduating from Harvard Law School, was one such associate who proved his legal ability but displayed an interest in business management. In 1958, he joined Kimberly-Clark's law department and in 1962 he became vice-president and general counsel. His potential for management led to his becoming Kimberly-Clark's president in 1970 and board chairman and chief executive officer the next year.

As a further aid in recruitment, an important project was instituted, under the direction of James Baker, for summer associates who were still in law school or were recent graduates and had been singled out as good prospects either by the firm's recruiters or recommended by professors. This program had two aspects: working assignments and a series of survey meetings. Initially, each man or woman worked full time with a single partner, usually on one or two matters, and rarely for longer than two weeks; later they were given assignments that furnished experience in such fields of law as general and specialty litigation, real estate, probate and corporate, tax and anti-trust matters. The survey meetings consisted of weekly luncheons in the president's room of the Chicago Bar Association at

177

which a single partner or a group of partners would tell of their special fields of expertise and some typical experiences in handling difficult or unusual cases and offer advice on the skills needed to practice in a particular field. Each partner's statement was followed by a question-and-answer session marked by candor and pragmatic approaches to the legal profession generally and the firm specifically. The programs constituted so excellent a method of orientation that it was decided to invite new full-time associates, a beneficial move that allowed for interaction with the students and created an atmosphere in which proposals from the recruiters might receive favorable responses. In each of the more than ten years that Baker was in charge of the project before turning over his task to others who have carried on into the present, he enlisted the aid of at least two younger partners, with a gradual turnover so that many such partners came to be involved. Moreover, the firm received innumerable favorable reactions to the summer sessions from law school deans and professors, and the program served as a model for others instituted elsewhere.

7

The firm's policy of anti-nepotism came up for reconsideration in the postwar period.

No child of a partner had ever been employed as an associate or made a partner, except for Leverett Thompson, the co-founder's son who worked in the mid-1890s, several years after his father's death. Two partners' daughters were married to associates—Barbara Austin to Robert Foote and Mary Louise Burgess to Edward Day. In each instance, the marriages took place after Foote and Day had been recruited, had become associates, and had demonstrated abilities that led to subsequent admission to partnership along with their contemporaries.

In 1949, the sons of Merritt Bragdon and Ray Garrett were both excellent students at Harvard Law School, but neither, in accord with tradition, was proposed by his father for association with the firm. Rather than decide for themselves whether to depart from past practice and offer them employment, Austin and Burgess delegated the task to four younger partners—Dern, Avery, Ragland, and Bowes—and asked them to express their views to other partners. The four met on a Sunday afternoon in Dern's Glencoe home and agreed unanimously that the established anti-nepotism practice be continued. They felt that this would be in the firm's

Partners in 1951: *Front row* (*left to right*): Douglas F. Smith, Ray Garrett, Howard Neitzert, William P. Sidley, John Dern, Kenneth F. Burgess, Edwin C. Austin. *Middle row*: James E. S. Baker, Walter J. Cummings, Jr., Robert L. Foote, Harlowe E. Bowes, Howard P. Robinson, George A. Ranney, William H. Avery. *Back row*: Merritt C. Bragdon, Robert Diller, Middleton Miller, Edward W. Saunders, D. Robert Thomas, George Ragland, Jr.

best interests and in those of partners' sons or daughters. The firm would thereby avoid serious personnel problems and individual feelings about over-preferment or unequal treatment because of blood relationships. In the case of an outstanding success of an offspring in practice elsewhere, it would be recognized by all concerned that it was achieved by individual merit and not because of that relationship.

The recommendation of the four—each, incidentally, with a son or daughter under twenty-one who might attend law school—was accepted and the policy has been maintained ever since.*

---

*One of these sons and Ray Garrett, Jr., did join leading Chicago law firms after they graduated and gained success there as partners. The younger Garrett also later served for several years as chairman of the Securities and Exchange Commission.

8

Among major cases in the post-war decade was one in which the amount of money involved was the largest in the firm's history up to that time.

Between June 20, 1946, and October 4, 1948, the Department of Justice filed seventeen complaints with the Interstate Commerce Commission alleging that the nation's railroads had overcharged in the war years for transporting to coastal ports for shipment overseas masses of materials ranging from bombs and soldiers' packs to airplane landing mats and jungle hammocks. Total reparations sought were over $2 billion, the highest proportion of which involved the western railroads because of their long hauls and concentrations of shipments to the Pacific Coast. Burgess was chief counsel for the western railroad group in the reparations cases while Windsor Cousins, the Pennsylvania Railroad's general counsel, headed the defense for the eastern roads and Joseph Johnston, a Birmingham, Alabama, lawyer, represented the southern roads. Initially, Burgess' team was made up of Douglas Smith, Robert Thomas, and George Ragland; they were joined by Emerson T. Chandler, who came to the firm in 1949 after graduating from the University of Michigan Law School.

To counter the government's allegations, many months were spent in amassing evidence to show that the freight rates for sending the war materials were considerably lower than those that would have been charged along the same trackage to commercial shippers. Expert witnesses were sought to testify on the many elements in the complaints. One such, whom Thomas vividly recalled years later, was Louis Feiser, a Harvard University chemistry professor. At the war's start, thousands of incendiary bombs had been made, shipped to England and stockpiled. When bomber aircraft began to use them, it was found that far too many were inefficient because the solidified gasoline in the bombs had turned back to liquid. By adding coconut oil as a primary ingredient, Feiser had determined, the gasoline would remain solidified so that neither heat nor vibrations in transporting the bombs would affect the solid, which was named "napalm." Because the napalm bombs were shipped without the detonators and explosive charges that would break open the casings, igniting and scattering the napalm, the government claimed that the articles shipped were not "bombs" within the meaning of the tariffs and were no more hazardous than gasoline, for whose shipments the rates were lower. During a visit to Feiser, Thomas and Ragland watched him pour gasoline into a pan on the floor and calmly toss a match into it. Thomas later recalled: "At the puff of flame George and I jumped back but no harm resulted. We employed Dr. Feiser and his testimony as to what would happen if a carload of napalm bombs caught fire in a town or city was very convincing. He also made movies of small amounts of napalm and liquid gasoline as they were ignited near wooden boxes to show how much more destructive napalm was."

In hearings before the Interstate Commerce Commission that began in 1949, Feiser was one of many witnesses, and Thomas also succeeded in having his movies shown and received in evidence. Government attorneys sought to have each of the seventeen complaints considered separately. Burgess fought this successfully with arguments that while the individual complaints raised issues which technically were separate, all had common background and most involved questions which generally were similar, and their consolidation would facilitate the hearings and decisions. Other telling points were made as the hearings proceeded. One was that railroad earnings during the war represented only a moderate rate of return on invested capital. Another was that in the war period the rail carriers paid between $3 billion and $4 billion in federal income taxes while in World War I the government incurred an out-of-pocket loss of $1.5 billion through its operation of the railroads. Concern was expressed, too, over the defendants' inability to pay the amount sought out of existing resources as the total net working capital of all the American railroads was less than $500 million. The award sought would therefore have to come from freight payments by other shippers, an eventuality certain to result in either inferior service or higher rates or both, with a high risk of bankruptcy of many railroads. Trade associations, agricultural organizations, railroad employee unions, and chambers of commerce joined in the defense. The final ICC hearing was on December 2, 1954—five years after the case began. After briefs were submitted, the commission dismissed all seventeen complaints, stressing that the charges made by the railroads for the wartime shipments were not unreasonable. That decision was affirmed when the government appealed the napalm bomb case to the United States District Court in Washington, with Thomas arguing in the railroads' behalf.

Important services for Pullman, Incorporated, were furnished by the firm in the aftermath of action by the Justice Department. In 1940, a suit was filed in United States District Court in Philadelphia charging the company with monopolistic practices by preventing railroads and other car builders from introducing modernized sleeping cars. The government's eighty-page bill not only cited Pullman's alleged restrictive policies but demanded disposal of either its sleeping car division or its manufacturing business. In response, Pullman maintained that if it was a monopoly it was a "benevolent" one and acted in the public interest. To charges that its rolling stock was outmoded, it replied that it had spent $30 million in air-conditioning its cars in the previous decade and was contemplating other improvements.

When a hearing was scheduled before a three-judge Federal Court, Austin was asked by Pullman's president, David A. Crawford, and Champ Carry, the other senior officer, to sit in as an observer. In May 1944, the court ruled that Pullman Company had to sell either its railroad car manufacturing business or its sleeping car unit within a year, and gave it ninety days in which to make a decision. Pullman's choice to divest the monopoly sleeping car business came as a surprise because the post-war drop in passenger travel was yet to come. Among leading bidders for Pullman's 600 streamlined cars for a time was Robert R. Young, the kinetic financier and frequent critic of what he considered the hidebound ways of the railroad industry. He proposed to carry out a $500 million modernization program. But subsequent court hearings resulted in a ruling in 1946 that a consortium of railroads could purchase the Pullman cars. The Justice Department appealed to the United States Supreme Court to bar that sale because ownership by the railroads would maintain the traits of a monopoly. But in March 1947, that appeal was rejected by a 4-4 vote and the sale was approved. The sales contract, involving the transfer of shares of stock worth over $40 million to fifty-seven railroads in the consortium, was complex and minutely detailed. Austin and Harlowe Bowes worked for weeks with Pullman officers in preparing it and setting up a new Pullman Company with Carroll R. Harding, a former executive with the Southern Pacific, as its president. Despite a promising start, the company began a decline in 1948 that persisted through the next years, hastened by large shifts of passengers to air and bus traffic and increased use of ever-expanding hard roads and interstate highways by motorists. By 1968, the company was operating, with a drastically reduced work force of conductors and porters, on only twenty-seven railroads, with losses amounting to $27 million. At the start of the next year, all its activity ceased, the *Chicago Sun-Times* describing the event with an apt heading on its story: "Pullman Ends a Gilded Era of Sleeping-Car Operation."

As it looked ahead to new ventures, Pullman retained the firm to settle federal income taxes that had been open and unresolved since 1938. Middleton Miller worked on this problem for the next seven years, with counsel from Austin. After carrying successful appeals of a $67 million tax deficiency assessment to the Tax Court in seventeen separate suits, recovery was obtained of some $5 million of taxes previously paid. Subsequently, the firm was called upon when it appeared that a controversy with the Internal Revenue Service could end up in court. Robert R. Frei, who had become the acknowledged specialist in federal income tax practice after coming to the firm in 1949 *magna cum laude* from the Harvard Law School, handled two cases in which refunds were sought. One involved the question of whether the company could write off the remaining cost of its old Michigan Avenue building in the year when the decision was made to demolish the structure or if the loss had to be deferred until the actual razing. The other concerned taking a worthless stock loss in connection with a railroad-car manufacturing subsidiary in France that had been inactive since the end of World War I. After hearings on the first in the Court of Claims and the second, with Howard Robinson in charge, in the federal court of Judge Julius Hoffman, both cases were settled favorably with refunds of over $1 million each.*

---

*Pullman continued to produce railroad freight cars and subway cars and even occasional passenger cars and truck trailers and concentrated on developing into an international firm that by the 1970s had diversified projects like construction of ammonia plants in China and a $360 million facility in Kuwait for converting flared gas from oil refineries into liquefied petroleum gas. Losses in mass transit projects and large cost overruns produced vexing problems. On August 22, 1980, it was acquired by Wheelabrator-Frye, an environmental and energy systems manufacturer, for $497 million and became a subsidiary of the Hampton, New Hampshire, firm.

10

Another Chicago manufacturer of railroad cars, Pressed Steel Car Company, was involved in an interesting test case engaged in by the firm in this period.

Early in 1940, William Avery had taken to the United States Court of Appeals a lower court decision—in a case tried in the District Court by another law firm—that sustained imposition of the Illinois retailers' occupation tax against Globe Varnish Company, a Chicago railroad supplier then in reorganization proceedings under the federal bankruptcy act, on many dozen gallons of black paint shipped from within the state to an out-of-state destination, specifically the Milwaukee shops of Chicago, Milwaukee, St. Paul and Pacific Railroad over that road's lines. That decision prompted Burgess, on behalf of railroad clients who were apprehensive about the possibility that taxes so inflicted on other Illinois suppliers with whom they dealt would be passed on to them, to assign Avery to seek a reversal of the ruling. With the aid of Edward Day, Avery prepared the appeals brief and then argued the case in the court's stately building on Lake Shore Drive. By a 2-1 decision the earlier judgment was reversed on the ground that the shipment constituted an interstate transaction and later the United States Supreme Court denied *certiorari* on procedural grounds.

Accordingly, the Illinois Department of Revenue changed its rules to exempt such interstate sales from the tax. But early in the 1950s the United States Supreme Court, in a similar case that developed in Mississippi, handed down a decision directly opposite to the previous rulings. On November 5, 1953, Illinois' Department of Revenue revised its rules again to make the tax applicable. Especially irksome—and potentially costly—was the provision for taxes to be imposed retroactively to periods before the rules were changed on the theory that the tax statute had not been changed but had always applied to such sales, regardless of prior court decisions. Deficiency notices were sent to all railroad suppliers; for example, the Electromotive Division of General Motors Corporation, a supplier of diesel locomotives and other equipment, received such a notice for $95 million, for which it was indemnified by the railroads.

Burgess and Avery held numerous parleys with railroad attorneys, and it was decided to take a test case to court with Pressed Steel Car Company as plaintiff. After a four-week trial in which Pressed Steel was represented by Avery and the state by its attorney general, Latham Castle, and special counsel retained for the important case, Judge William V. Brothers in the Cook County Circuit Court held for the company on the ground that levying the tax was forbidden by the commerce clause of the federal Constitution. Richard J. Lyons, the state's revenue director, filed an appeal to the Illinois Supreme Court, and the argument there was held in September 1955, with Avery arguing the case and being assisted on briefs by Emerson Chandler and Arthur Seder. In its decision rendered that November, the court held that it had to follow the latest of the United States Supreme Court rulings in the Mississippi case. But more significant from a pecuniary standpoint was this part of the decision: "In our opinion it is unreasonable and inequitable to apply the revised regulation retroactively in this case after the taxpayers had entered into contractual relationships upon the basis of the existing regulation." Thereby, after hearings at the Revenue Department, assessments against Pressed Steel Car Company and other railroad suppliers were reduced in line with the high court's finding; the largest cut applied to General Motors, whose levy was set at $2 million instead of $95 million.

11

An important case in zoning of public utilities evolved in 1947 when Illinois Bell Telephone Company applied to Chicago's building commissioner for a permit to build a telephone exchange building in a West Side neighborhood. When the application was turned down because, in the city's opinion, the proposed improvement did not conform with requirements of the zoning ordinance, an appeal was filed by Avery with the city zoning board of appeals. At public hearings, some twenty property owners in the area, including several city officials, protested primarily on the grounds that the site for the exchange was in the center of a long-established residential district and the projected construction there would make the neighborhood less attractive as a home community and depreciate property values. Engineers for the company denied that charge and, more importantly, testified that the exchange would furnish better service for customers through an expanded automatic dial system, that selection of a different site would increase costs, and that with the employment of only ninety persons instead of the usual 300 at a manually operated exchange of the same size there would be none of the traffic congestion or noise feared by nearby residents.

A major point brought forward for the company was that the physical dimensions of the proposed exchange qualified the telephone company for "special use" as defined in the city zoning ordinance. But despite this telling argument, the board denied the application, whereupon *certiorari* proceedings were started in Circuit Court. In hearings before Judge Harry T. Fisher, Avery introduced vital exhibits and testimony to show that the zoning board had earlier approved seven different applications for new exchanges or additions elsewhere that exceeded either area restrictions or maximum height limitations. Besides, a 1941 letter from the chairman of the City Council's subcommittee on rezoning to a telephone company official was presented with telling effect: "Telephone exchanges . . . are a special use," it read, "and the coverage height and volume provisions of the district in which the exchange is located do not apply to the public utility." Judge Fisher reversed the board's decision. A special use of the property as a telephone exchange was necessary for the public convenience, he ruled, and he directed the zoning board to issue a written approval of the phone company's application and the building commissioner to grant a permit.

Judge Fisher's ruling was challenged by an appeal to the Illinois Supreme Court. On the day of the argument, while Avery and Burgess, who was in Springfield on another case, waited in an antechamber for their cases to be called, Burgess asked Avery how he felt. "I feel just the way I did before a track meet in high school years ago," Avery replied. "My hands are sweaty, my stomach disturbs me, I feel terrible." When Burgess responded that he felt the same way and Avery expressed surprise that he did after all the appearances he had made before courts high and low, Burgess said, "I certainly do, and let me tell you something. If you ever get so you don't feel that way you haven't got the adrenalin running and you're not going to do a good job. You've got to feel that way in order to do your very best."

On March 24, 1949, Judge Fisher's decision was upheld by the Supreme Court, which unequivocally rejected the city officials' arguments. Uncontroverted evidence had been presented, the opinion stated, to disclose "that a new telephone exchange is needed to meet the increasing demand for service, that the proposed site is at the exact wire center of the telephone district and that the wire center is the most practical, convenient and economical location for the new exchange." As for the section of the city zoning statute providing for approval by the zoning board of "any special use where the use is necessary for public convenience," the telephone company, stated the justices, had made an affirmative showing that made mandatory the approval of the application for construction of the West Side telephone exchange building. The case—and its outcome—had significance for other lawyers representing public utilities and requests for his brief came to Avery from many states.

Firm Matters
Sidley, Austin, Burgess & Smith
1957–1967
Sidley & Austin
1967–1972

IN 1957, when the firm had twenty-nine partners and twenty associates, Austin was afforded an opportunity to set down for public perusal his thoughts and facts about large law firms.

This came about as a result of an article in the November 1956 issue of *The Practical Lawyer*, a publication of the American Law Institute. In it, Roger B. Siddall, a former New York attorney then practicing in St. Thomas in the Virgin Islands, cited what he considered weaknesses of large law firms and offered proposals for remedying them. Too many such firms, he wrote, were "fraught with personal tensions which may lead to crackups of one sort or another if, however unwittingly, members depart from proper partnership etiquette and procedure." Basing his statements on his own experience in New York, he told of how partners had differing percentages of participation which, every two or three years, were shifted around by the firm's chief partner on his own private appraisal and not on formal records of partners' productivity. This, he asserted, prompted partners to play up to the firm's head to a point where no partner dared to congratulate another on a job well done, and some even spread defamatory stories about other partners. It was possible, Siddall acknowledged, to have big law firms that might operate smoothly. "But every large law firm is in constant danger of developing tensions." He propounded the questions of whether clients were the office's or of one or more of the lawyers and how matters of firm policy were decided—"by the vote of those who can shout the loudest, or show the most hands, or add up the highest percentage of interest in the firm, or how?" To prevent inequities and problems, Siddall suggested development of a new legal specialty: independent consultants to large law firms regarding partnership organization and arrangements. Such consultants would associate themselves in an organization called "American College of Large Law Firm Consultants" and make themselves available for individual conferences, interviews, and examination of pertinent documents and familiarize themselves with whatever partnership problems of their clients developed and periodically make reports and recommendations which could be relied on as outside, impartial, and unbiased judgments on the smoothness of the firm's operations.

As a senior partner of a moderately large firm, Austin was asked by the magazine's editor, Judge Herbert Goodrich of the United States Circuit Court of Appeals in Philadelphia, to reply. He had no wish, Austin responded, to engage in a controversy with Siddall, but he wrote an article for the April issue—"purely objective," he stressed—on the large law office. Delineating a firm as large whenever it reached a size that made it difficult for every senior to know intimately the work of each junior member or associate and for each associate to know each senior, he put forward this question: "Is any particular type of 'large firm' best for its members, associates, lay personnel or the community?" Answering this question, he traced the expansion in the number of big law firms to the end of World War II and attributed it to the growth of business enterprises and consequent complex needs: "When this is accompanied by an enormous mass of state and federal regulations, laws in the field of labor relations, security distributions, trade practices, and by incredibly complex and sometimes incomprehensible tax legislation, the problem of adequate legal service goes beyond the capacity of the lone practitioner or of a small group." Moreover, the creation of administrative bodies with quasi-legislative power and their issuance of regulations—"government by loose-leaf service"—compounded the problem: "No one lawyer, however brilliant, can keep at his fingertips the latest regulations as well as the decisions of a multitude of federal and state courts."

To criticism that large firms were "law factories," Austin replied that their real products were legal services and advice—"these are more hand-tailored than factory-produced." No firm could become or remain large unless its services were highly-skilled and effective and reflected conscientious and industrious efforts for its clients. The large firm could render types of service beyond the powers of a single lawyer or small firm: "It can quickly and effectively assign several lawyers to work at an urgent

189

assignment in any of several fields of law. It can furnish specialists in each of these fields. It can provide multiple skills on a basis which avoids both waste overhead and confusion to the client." Another advantage was the ability to train law graduates and help fit them for fields in which they could excel and gain professional and financial satisfactions. By testing one's aptitude in various fields, without an implication of failure that might attend a series of changes in employers, the firm offered advantages to the young lawyers. True, there were disadvantages. Communication between young lawyers and seniors might be less close; overdepartmentalization might prevail in which a member of a particular group might get no training in another; there was a risk of favoritism; there might be more difficulty in achieving a partnership if the heads of the firm were unable to judge relative capacities of aspirants as readily as through working closely with them. But these were far outweighed by the advantages. And whatever the structure of a large firm as to the partners' status and risks and internal organization, none of the few disadvantages or the variations influenced its success and value as did the abilities, attitudes, and temperaments of its principal partners. Simply stated, if those who controlled the policies were swayed by flattery or played favorites for reasons other than accomplishment or made faulty judgments based on lack of adequate information, the firm would suffer. If the senior partners were reasonably tolerant, judicial and, above all, unselfish in dealing with problems and the welfare and advancement of worthy associates, a happy and productive firm, with high morale and spirit, would result.

Austin's article won wide attention and favorable comment. It was reprinted in the *New York State Bar Bulletin* and formed the basis for a chapter Austin wrote, with the aid of James G. Archer, a newcomer from the University of Illinois College of Law, in a Prentice-Hall book, *Lawyer's Encyclopedia*, on "Choosing Between Sole and Group Practice." And beyond these responses the article was especially noteworthy because it solidly expressed the principles and practices that characterized the firm then and would do so in the years ahead.

2

Not long after publication of Austin's magazine article the unselfish character cited by him as an essential attribute of senior partners in well-run and successful large law firms assumed greater reality. This happened following the deaths in the first half of 1958 of William Sidley, John Dern, and Merritt Bragdon.

Bragdon was the first, succumbing to cancer January 30 in Presbyterian Hospital. He was sixty-six and, in his thirty-eight years with the firm, he had achieved a deserved reputation as one of its scholarly lawyers. Calm, careful, and cautious, he had specialized in probate law and affiliated fields in which he had benefitted from Charles Cutting's tutelage and whose principles and concepts he had conveyed to many younger lawyers in the years that followed.

For a decade before he died on April 25 in Evanston Hospital at the age of ninety-one, Sidley had been progressively afflicted with arteriosclerosis and had already passed on responsibility for the firm's management functions, as has been noted, to Austin and Burgess. His innumerable contributions to the firm over the years since 1892 had been unparalleled. More than anyone else in those decades, he set the tone of the firm and advocated progressive personnel practices, chief among them promotion to partnership from within the ranks. Later, Austin, chief among those who adhered to Sidley's example, paid deserved tribute: "William Pratt Sidley was a man of outstanding mentality; a keen power of analysis; a more than adequate speaker; one of the most respected figures at the Bar; blessed with an extraordinary talent for forming and exercising that rare quality called 'judgment' that led clients to want his views in any crisis."

Midway in 1957, Dern was operated on for stomach cancer. Despite a gradually weakening condition and recurring pain in the following months, he went regularly to the Detroit offices of American Natural Gas Company to carry on his duties as general counsel and attended its board meetings. Characteristically, as a diligent mentor, he made special efforts to involve Arthur Seder in all phases of the company's activities and to instill confidence in him among its top management. "Never did he bemoan his fate or complain, and never did he give up," Seder later remembered feelingly. Increasingly, Dern shifted more and more responsibility, so that when he died, at fifty-five, on May 23 in his Winnetka home, Seder was accepted as his designated successor. In the memories of all who had known Dern in his twenty-nine years with the firm, he remained vivid not only as a brilliant lawyer, open-minded and adept in dealing with matters of great complexity, but as a man of warmth and good humor, with ever-present consideration of those who worked with him and of other associates and lay personnel, "always," in Seder's words, "generous and helpful."

Dern's espousal of Seder bore lasting results. In 1967, after handling matters for the utility company and other clients, Seder was appointed general counsel, in 1973 its president and three years later was chairman and chief executive officer of American Natural Resources Company. The parent company's name had been changed to reflect widespread expansion in constructing many thousands of miles of gas pipelines and in acquiring new businesses in energy and transportation. Two other members of the firm attained high posts: Stanton K. Smith, who came from the University of Wisconsin Law School in 1956 and was named a partner in 1964, became general counsel for American Natural Resources Company; and Gary L. Cowan, an associate from the University of Chicago Law School in 1960 and a partner in 1969, was similarly appointed for Michigan Consolidated Gas Company.

The passing of Sidley, Dern, and Bragdon occasioned an important decision that broadened the number of participating partners. In the past, when a senior partner died his percentage of participation in income usually had been spread only among other senior partners, with the allocation having been determined mainly by respective ability, the amount of work done and, to a substantial extent, the quantity of business brought into the firm. Austin was vacationing with Burgess in Baden-Baden when Dern's funeral was held and could not return in time. In discussions with Burgess, he proposed that the total percentages of income that had become available be dispersed among deserving junior partners, who were then receiving guaranteed compensation plus a small percentage of participation. Burgess agreed to the plan, and half a dozen junior partners were selected by them to receive portions of the percentages on hand, joining the contingent of senior partners. Besides its obvious financial rewards, the new system marked a step forward in the internal relationships at the firm then and later, when it would be enhanced by other percentage modifications.

At this time, too, the firm's executive committee, which had been fairly casually devised earlier, took on a more structured form. Its members, meeting each month instead of at irregular intervals to discuss problems and policies, were Austin and Burgess—whose views invariably predominated—and Douglas Smith, Ray Garrett, Howard Neitzert, and, doubling as secretary, William Avery. One of its first actions was to retain Sidley's

Ray Garrett   Howard Neitzert   William H. Avery

They joined Edwin C. Austin, Kenneth F. Burgess and Douglas F. Smith on the executive committee in 1959.

name in recognition of his many years of service to the firm. In addition, a number of administrative committees were established to help with functions ranging from assignment of new associates and determination of their salaries to supervision of lay help and insurance.

In this year, a number of physical changes were made in the office in what the firm's historian, Robert Diller, later called "a violent upheaval." The entire twenty-first floor of the Roanoke Building was taken over, and it and the two floors below were remodeled to provide more offices. The "bull pen" on the nineteenth floor was broken up to furnish more offices. The library was moved to the twenty-first floor, remaining under Eugene Dupee's supervision until his retirement early in 1960. Alongside the twentieth floor offices, a permanent file room remained. Receptionists were now placed on all three floors, and the docket clerk acquired the first of many future additional assistants. In the past, the offices had a uniform decor of red mahogany woodwork, yellow calcimined walls, and mulberry red carpeting except in the case of Avery, who had secured permission from Austin and Burgess to have his walls and woodwork done in a grayish-blue pastel with pebbled gray carpet, a move that prompted a skit at the Christmas luncheon about his facing possible dismissal because of his "bordello blue" office. Now, in an overall redecorating project, each

193

member of the firm was given the choice of four soft pastels in covering the walls and woodwork, while the floors were carpeted in an attractive gray. And gone forever from the windows were awnings and the need for the seasonal distribution of electric fans. The offices and other rooms on all three floors now had air-conditioning that did away not only with the discomforts of summer humidity but also with soot that wafted through open windows to permeate the air and make it hard to keep clean books on office shelves and desks and in the library.

3

The growing necessity for dealing on a first-hand basis with the federal government—especially the proliferation of matters issuing from regulatory agencies and commissions—led to a decision by the firm to open an office in Washington on August 15, 1963.

Chosen to head it was Edward Day, most recently in the capital as United States Postmaster General. In his first years with the firm since 1938 and after naval service in World War II, he had built a fine record. Following Adlai Stevenson's election as Illinois' governor in 1948, Day left to serve as his legal and legislative assistant and, in the last two years of Stevenson's term, as state commissioner of insurance. There followed eight years with the Prudential Insurance Company of America as a member of its legal department and then as senior vice-president in charge of western operations. President John F. Kennedy offered Day the cabinet post in a telephone call to him while he was at an insurance companies' convention in Los Angeles, and Day set about to attempt the attainment of such goals stipulated by the new President as reduction of the postal department's deficit, improvement of its service, and raising the morale of its 600,000 employees.* During his administration, the use of postal "Zip code" numbers was introduced throughout the country.

When he heard reports about a possible Washington office, Day called Avery with a bid to rejoin the firm and set up the office. Avery expressed enthusiasm, but told Day he would have to confer with Austin and Burgess. Because his daughter, Mary Louise, had been married to Day in

*In 1965, Day's book, *My Appointed Round: 929 Days as Postmaster General,* received favorable critical response. Willard Edwards, a veteran *Chicago Tribune* Washington correspondent, described it as "short, breezy and anecdotal, with a chuckle on every second page to flavor acute observations of antics in the Washington jungle."

1941, Burgess had always been careful not to influence any decisions affecting Day lest the issue of nepotism be raised, and he remained non-committal now. But Austin, emphasizing Day's previous good work in the firm and his excellent contacts and reputation in the insurance industry, supported Day's proposal.

An office was selected at 1625 Eye Street Northwest. Day, named a partner on its first day, was joined there by two men from the Chicago office, Richard J. Flynn and Jules M. Perlberg. Flynn, a Northwestern University Law School graduate recruited in 1954 by Burgess after clerking for Chief Justices Fred M. Vinson and Earl Warren, had been a partner since the previous January. Perlberg, an associate since 1958 who became a partner in 1966, had built impressive records in the University of Michigan's School of Business Administration and in its law school and as a certified public accountant with Arthur Andersen & Company. Flynn was especially pleased to be in the new office because in the previous year he had made twenty-six trips of varying lengths from Chicago to Washington and back.

As anticipated, Day started to develop business, including postal matters for such clients as the Association of Third Class Mail Users and consumer products divisions of several electronic industries. Flynn and Perlberg were soon involved in railroad matters that required full-scale collaboration between the Washington and Chicago offices. The first of them was with the aid of John Schwemm, a 1959 University of Michigan Law School alumnus, and James J. Brennan, a newcomer from Harvard Law School. As clients' needs grew in connection with federal legal matters, the size of the Washington force and the amount of services—non-litigated as well as litigated—would increase considerably in the years ahead.*

4

In 1964, Austin reached the fiftieth anniversary of the day he had first gone to work for Holt, Cutting & Sidley while still a senior in the Northwestern University Law School. Appropriately, a reception and dinner was held for the firm's lawyers and their wives that August 14 in the Mid-America Club. It was a time for paying fit tribute and looking

*See Chapters XIII and XIV.

back—and ahead. Kenneth Burgess spoke of partners of the past and of his own thirty-three years as one. He recalled the trying period of the Great Depression and the start of the intensive recruitment of law graduates of unusual merit and dedication to the legal profession. And he spoke about clients brought in by Austin, such men as Dr. Claude and John Searle and Arthur Nielsen, who had relied on Austin's advice and guidance and now contributed substantially to the firm's revenues: "His industry and willingness to undertake hard jobs and always do them well has helped to make him the outstanding success that has inured so much to the benefit of all of us." Howard Neitzert wittily recalled his first meeting with Austin at the firm's offices during Easter vacation in 1929 after seeking employment at no fewer than forty-seven firms and being hired later that year to work with him: "He taught me where and how to live and, more important, why to live. He taught me how to practice law, how to recognize, meet and deal with the many problems that confront every young lawyer. He was always patient, always kind, always helpful, always available to see me, talk to me, answer my questions, discuss my problems and to help me find their solutions." And he underscored a crucial contribution to the firm's morale and basic inner strength: "My association with Mr. Austin has been typical, and I cite it because it is typical. He has helped us all, the only difference being the greater the need for his help the greater the help that he has given. In a sense Mr. Austin has whittled us all out. We have all reaped where he has sown, and wherever we walk we find that he has marked the way." Letters came from former partners, including James Oates ("You taught me that nothing in which human beings are interested is trivial and that human rights must be respected and that a legal contention can be presented both with vigor and fairness") and Bouton McDougal ("You have been a wonderful teacher as well as a counselor and an exciting and stimulating example") and Edward McDougal ("You were unfailingly kind and helpful as a guide and friend") and George Ranney ("To a large degree the firm's professional attainments are the product of your own standards and objectives and its success reflects the contentment of clients who have relied upon—and paid for—your professional advice") and from Adlai Stevenson ("I remember with what charity you often asked us 'younger men' for our opinion, and the solemn panic with which I occasionally uttered something. . . . I am becoming so maudlin that I am even forgiving you for being such a good Republican. And, by the way, thanks for letting me be such a good New Deal Democrat!").

Kenneth F. Burgess
in mid-1960s

Austin's response to such warm and appreciative expressions was typically unassuming and stressed the important qualities for the long life of the firm: "It has lived up to the highest ethical standards in its dealings with clients, the courts and its opponents. It has established and maintained a tradition of the highest excellence in the standard of its work. To do this, it has sought law school graduates whose records suggest fine mentality, fine character, and qualities of leadership. It has followed a policy of trying to keep its charges moderate rather than to take all the traffic will bear. It has maintained a consistently harmonious relationship among its members for substantially all its years of existence because the men at the head of the firm have been genuinely interested in and concerned about the professional careers of their juniors." The future? "I hope and believe that the firm will adhere to its traditions. If it does, it should live for generations, its volume of work should increase, and it will continue to grow."

5

After a brief illness, Kenneth Burgess died on May 24, 1965. He was seventy-seven and had been a lawyer for fifty-three years, thirty-four of them with the firm. During that time, he had lived by a philosophy that,

Further additions to
executive committee
in 1965:
Harlowe E. Bowes (*left*)
and Stuart S. Ball.

as he had recalled a few years earlier in a talk at the Chicago Sunday
Evening Club, his father had laid down for him: "A code of moral
precepts—stability of character, strict integrity and steadfast loyalty." A
memorial tribute drawn up for the Commercial Club by Edwin Austin,
Daggett Harvey, and Northwestern University's president, J. Roscoe
Miller, stressed such qualities in his commercial and professional life as
foresight, energy, untiring industry, and an active humanitarianism, traits
re-emphasized by Austin at the dedication in 1971 of the Burgess Plaza
on the campus of Northwestern University, whose board president
Burgess had been for twenty-two years. As a partner in the firm he was, in
Austin's words, "an asset beyond comparison, most crucial to our growth
and development," and he left his substantial mark on the firm and set
standards for its future.

Following Burgess' death, Harlowe Bowes and Stuart Ball were named
to the executive committee. Ball, elder brother of George Ball, had come
to the firm in 1951 as a partner, one of a handful in the firm's history to
enter at that level, because of his wide experience; for the preceding three
years he had been president of Montgomery Ward & Company, which he
had joined in 1932 as manager of its law department after several years'
practice upon graduating in 1927 from the Northwestern University Law
School.

On July 14, less than two months after Burgess died, Adlai Stevenson,
then United States ambassador to the United Nations, was stricken with a

fatal heart attack while walking on a London street. He had long since been out of the firm, but he retained friendships with Austin and others of earlier days. Only a few months before, at a dinner in New York's Hotel Pierre to celebrate his sixty-fifth birthday, in a playlet humorously recalling Stevenson's periodic departures from the firm starting in 1933, Edward McDougal portrayed Sidley and Steve Allen was Stevenson saying each time as he asked for a leave of absence, "I will gain valuable experience which, on my return, will enable me to represent with greater competence the firm's distinguished clients."* A day after Stevenson's death, amid hundreds of tributes from many lands Austin wrote to Adlai Stevenson III: "All of us in the office who were here during his many years as an associate and partner of the firm hold him in affectionate regard and we all take deep pride in his remarkable career. He will be sorely missed not only by his family and close friends but by the millions of people in this country and elsewhere who had faith in him."

6

On October 12, 1966, the 100th anniversary of the firm's founding was marked by a dinner held in the Mid-America Club. In attendance were the forty partners and all but two of thirty-three associates and most of their spouses, several ex-partners and widows of those who had died, and from among the lay staff of seventy-two William Jensen, the office manager, head-bookkeeper Edith M. Miller, and legal secretaries Sylvia Nelsen, Mildred Roser, Eleanor Wilson, and Bernice Schweiger, all with twenty or more years of service. Once more, Austin recalled traditions established in the early years and maintained and the challenges met then and later and delineated the special standards that had contributed to the firm's growth and accomplishments. Toasts were offered by Avery to the lawyers' wives ("We appreciate your patience, understanding, encouragement, companionship, and above all your love"), by Garrett to the associates ("We have confidence that they will carry on the traditions of the illustrious past that we celebrate this evening"), by Ned Saunders to the clerical staff ("Without the loyalty of the staff, past and present, we

*A similar skit had been staged on Stevenson's fiftieth birthday in Springfield with Edward Day as Stevenson and James Oates as Sidley.

Head table at firm's 100th anniversary party: (*Clockwise from lower left*) Mrs. Edward D. McDougal, Jr., Mrs. John Dern, Edward D. McDougal, Jr., Mrs. James F. Oates, Jr., Edwin C. Austin, Mrs. Kenneth F. Burgess, James F. Oates, Jr., Mrs. Edwin C. Austin, Mrs. Paul V. Harper, George A. Ranney.

would not be celebrating on this 100th anniversary''), by Neitzert to deceased partners (''To these men a monument has been set up—our firm and the promise of the future''), and by Ball to clients (''Without them we would be nothing—may they continue to multiply''). As principal speaker, Oates told many amusing anecdotes about his first years at the firm and about the hi-jinks of fellow associates and the respect he and his young colleagues felt for the older men and about friendships formed and the true rewards of service, and the satisfaction of achievement. ''Each of you,'' he concluded, ''has a right to rejoice because this institution with its ideals and its qualities and its personality has become one of the great institutions of the land.''

For the occasion, a handsome souvenir brochure had been prepared, with a historical sketch by Robert Diller and reproductions of interesting items from the early years that ranged from the very first listing of clients and their fees in 1866 and a letter from Mary Todd Lincoln to Norman Williams in 1872 to the 1873 lease for the Reaper Block offices signed by

Williams and John Leverett Thompson and Cyrus McCormick. Included, too, were illustrations of that structure, the Marine Bank Building before and after the Great Fire of 1871, and the Tacoma, site of the offices from 1889 to 1920, and a listing of partners present and past and current associates. Austin reminded those assembled that because public circulation of the booklets might violate the American Bar Association's canons of ethics, they were strictly for their retention. He did fill the request of Margaret A. Flint of the Illinois State Historical Library for a copy. But he advised her that while he disagreed with an earlier opinion of a subcommittee of the ABA committee on professional ethics that a mere announcement of a New York firm's fiftieth anniversary smacked of self-touting and implications that because of its age it was superior to younger ones, he warned her against any reproduction of the brochure. Austin's scrupulous heed to ethical principles in question had earlier prompted him to refuse to give details of the forthcoming anniversary observance to Eleanor Page, a popular *Chicago Tribune* columnist, after meeting her at a cocktail party in the Tavern Club to honor Walter Cummings' appointment to the United States Court of Appeals. He even sent her a letter telling about the New York Supreme Court's censure of four attorneys who had cooperated with *Life* magazine on an article about certain legal practices. From this exchange, Miss Page derived an amusing column in the form of a memorandum to one of the newspaper's editors, William Clark. In it she told of her fruitless efforts to obtain information about the centennial and a copy of the brochure from "unnamed persons" and poked gentle fun at the strictures in the canons. Beneath her column, Clark appended a paragraph reading, "Women are funny, too. They just can't keep a secret. We wormed it out of Miss Page that the law firm is Sidley, Austin, Burgess & Smith. . . ."

7

Interestingly, that name was about to undergo a change.

For its first ninety-two years, the firm had adhered to the established practice of including in its name only active members. Indeed, in one of the ABA canons of ethics were suggestions to the effect that the names of deceased or retired partners were not to be used. Some firms in New York and in Chicago—Isham, Lincoln & Beale, for one—had departed, however, from that custom. Upon Sidley's death, the firm had also broken with tradition. Because he had been so closely identified with the firm for so many years to the extent that it had come to be referred to by many as "the Sidley firm," it was decided that his name be retained. For a year after Burgess died there was scant discussion, informally or formally, about altering the name. Then the question began percolating within the firm, especially after Smith, during 1966, cut down his activities considerably, leaving Austin as the primary partner among those whose names the firm bore.

The issue began to come to a head when Avery, after talking to several consenting partners, made the initial proposal for a new name: Sidley & Austin. The reception by most members of the executive committee was decidedly cool, with Austin objecting out of innate modesty and a feeling of respect for Burgess and others espousing adherence to the habitual method. Avery received support from friends in firms outside Chicago who assured him unanimously that they and others invariably knew the firm as "the Sidley firm" or as "Sidley, Austin" and urged adoption of a permanent—and short—name. When that made no impact, Avery asked his secretary, Bernice Schweiger, to draw up a list of twenty of the city's largest law firms bearing five or more names. At the next meeting of the executive committee in the Union League Club, he distributed sheets of paper on which appeared only the first name of each firm and said, "Let's play a game. Fill out as many names as you can." Austin scored best, yet he could complete only three. Smith, who had already indicated a desire to become counsel to the firm, smiled and said, "You win, Bill," and followed with a motion to adopt the name of Sidley & Austin. There followed general assent, the alteration won approval of other senior partners and on March 20, 1967, official announcement was made of the new name and Smith's status.

Reaction was enthusiastic, but especially pleasing to Austin was a letter from Burgess' widow, Geraldine, in response to his in which he related how the change had come about ("I went along, but with mixed emotions"). Expressing gratitude for his "thoughtful note," Mrs. Burgess wrote, "It must give you tremendous satisfaction to be head of one of the most distinguished law firms in the country and to know that you arrived there by your great ability and many years of hard work. . . . May you continue for many years to come."

That June 13, at the annual summer outing of the Law Club of Chicago, the change was marked in jocular style. A trio, with lyrics set to the tune of George M. Cohan's "Mary's A Grand Old Name," warbled:

Our name is Sidley Austin,
Plain as any name can be.
We like it so much more
Than Cutting, Moore and Sidley.
We don't like all those long names
That our former partners did.
But there's still something there
That sounds so square—So
Won't you call us Sid?
Ed would like it if you did!

8

Two more changes were in the offing.

In the first, in the year after the firm's name became Sidley & Austin, Middleton Miller, Robert Thomas, Robert Foote, Edward Saunders, and Howard Trienens were added to the executive committee.

The second involved a move to the forty-eighth and most of the forty-seventh floors of a towering building under construction along Madison Street between Clark and Dearborn Streets. The structure—its official address One First National Plaza—was to house The First National Bank and its various departments and offices on twenty-four of its fifty-seven floors, with many of the upper floors filled by leading Chicago law firms. The decision to move there was prompted by the growing need for more space than could be acquired in the Roanoke Building and by a general wish to be in an impressive building that complemented the firm's character and stature. Edward Saunders, the firm's real estate specialist, handled negotiations for leasing the space in addition to arranging for selecting art works from his own collection to grace the reception and conference rooms and corridors. Plans for layout, design, and utilities were handled by a committee headed by Avery, with Edward Saunders and two lawyers in his real estate group—Harry T. Baumann, a 1952 University of Michigan Law School graduate and 1963 partner, and Donald J. Gralen, a 1957 graduate of Loyola University and a 1966 partner—as members, and a professional consultant. On December 29, 1969, the firm was settled in the new quarters, by far the most sumptuous in its history.

New members of executive committee in 1968

Middleton Miller

D. Robert Thomas

Robert L. Foote

Edward W. Saunders

Howard J. Trienens

9

Shortly after the start of the 1970s came an opportunity to fill the requirements of clients for help in foreign countries.

The precedent for doing so effectively had been set earlier by the Philadelphia firm of Dechert Price & Rhoads. When some of that firm's corporate clients needed legal services in Europe, its chairman, Kenneth Gemmill, interviewed bankers, accountants, lawyers, and corporate executives to determine their views of the best type of legal representation for American corporations in Europe. The consensus, he found, was that they would be best served by the leading firm in each country. Gemmill then invited a partner from that kind of firm in the chief business cities of France, Germany, The Netherlands, Switzerland, Italy, and England to meet in Rotterdam to discuss his plan for a loose affiliation for serving clients. The proposal met with strong approval and the affiliated firms took on the name of "Le Club." Thereafter, semi-annual meetings of a few partners from each member firm were held in the city of one of the firms. The sessions were designed to enable members to learn about laws, customs, politics, and legal developments in the members' countries and to present papers on phases of legal practice that ranged from problems of the Common Market to those of international taxation. More importantly, lawyers in each firm could call on experts in the other firms by telephone, Telex, or letter for instant advice about laws in their respective countries and to arrange for clients' more extensive services, if needed.

By late 1971, six European firms were in "Le Club:" Gide Loyrette Nouel in Paris; Bruckhaus, Kreifels, Winkhaus, Lieberknecht in Düsseldorf; Dutilh, van der Hoeven & Slager in Rotterdam—each the largest in its country—and Morera & Minoli (soon replaced by Studio Legale Bisconti) of Rome and Milan; Bär & Karrer in Zurich; and Linklater & Paines in London. Progressively, the arrangement yielded excellent results in affording mutual aid and counsel. But European members with clients who had business dealings in the Midwest urged that a major firm in that area be invited to join "Le Club." Gemmill called Bowes, whom he had met earlier, and then came to Chicago, where he explained to Bowes and Avery the workings of "Le Club" and told of its successes. With the approval of the executive committee, Avery and Bowes flew to a meeting of "Le Club" representatives in Paris. Avery, accepting the invitation to join, addressed the gathering in colloquial French—in which he had been coached by a French friend the previous evening—and added that he hoped future discussions would be held in English, as they have been ever since.

Client Matters
Sidley, Austin, Burgess & Smith
1957–1967
Sidley & Austin
1967–1972

THE 1950s and 1960s involved the firm's lawyers in a variety of services, ranging from anti-trust and railroad labor cases and mergers to corporate, real estate, and estate matters.

One of the biggest and long-lasting anti-trust cases began in the summer of 1949 with the government's suit against mighty E. I. duPont deNemours & Company, General Motors Corporation, United States Rubber Company, three duPont affiliates—Christiana Securities Company, Delaware Realty and Investment Corporation, and Wilmington Trust Company—and scores of members of the large duPont family. All were charged with conspiring in a monopoly cartel to restrain trade; General Motors and United States Rubber were, according to the suit, forced by the cartel to buy only duPont products. As the case moved to trial before a veteran jurist, Judge Walter J. LaBuy in the United States District Court in Chicago, scores of lawyers prepared to represent the various defendants. To help determine policies, tactics, and court procedures, a three-man *ad hoc* committee was established. It consisted of John M. Harlan, the future United States Supreme Court Justice, for all the duPont family members, their investment and holding companies and other related family interests, Hugh B. Cox, a former high-level government lawyer, for the duPont Corporation, and the firm's able trial lawyer, Howard Neitzert, to serve as local counsel.* In the trial that began in November 1952, each of them made opening statements, presented

*The firm did not take part in the Supreme Court proceedings, in which Cox and his colleagues at Covington & Burling were the main representatives of the defendants.

exhibits and witnesses, and delivered final arguments. Assisting Neitzert was a corps including George Ragland and several associates. The defense countered specific charges and generally maintained that the government was attacking "bigness in business."

When final arguments were concluded toward the end of 1953, Judge LaBuy took the case under advisement for a full year. On December 3, 1954, in a 220-page opinion brought to the courtroom from a printing firm under armed guard, he ruled that the government had failed to prove its case. When the government appealed, the Supreme Court reversed Judge LaBuy on June 3, 1957. It held that the duPont Corporation had violated the Clayton Act through its ownership of 23 percent of General Motors—63 million shares worth $2.5 billion—and that Judge LaBuy, who had devoted most of his lengthy opinion to Sherman Act issues which the government had emphasized at the trial, "had ignored the realities of intercorporate relations" in dismissing the Clayton Act charge. The case was remanded to Judge LaBuy to hold further hearings on "the equitable relief necessary and appropriate in the public interest." In the interim before the new trial began early in 1959, government attorneys filed a proposed decree before Judge LaBuy for duPont to dispose of its General Motors stock over a ten-year period. The second trial lasted seven weeks. On that October 3, Judge LaBuy allowed duPont to retain the General Motors stock but directed that it pass on voting rights to its individual stockholders. The divestiture sought by the government he called "unnecessarily harsh and punitive."

Again, the government took the case to the Supreme Court. Once more, the high court—with Justices Harlan and Tom Clark abstaining—returned it to Judge LaBuy in May 1961, this time with a directive for duPont to divest itself within three years of the General Motors stock, whose value had by now risen to $3.5 billion. The following March, Judge LaBuy entered "final judgment" to that effect and distribution began in June with duPont shareholders receiving one share of General Motors stock for each two shares of duPont common. The order also applied to Christiana Securities Company, owner of half a million shares of duPont stock, and to forty members of the duPont clan who were directed to sell any shares received from distribution by duPont and Christiana. General Motors was barred from hiring duPont officers and directors elected since 1959 and contracts between duPont and General Motors were ordered cancelled. This final action was regarded as a victory for the duPonts because it followed the chief provisions of recommendations made to the court during the long battle by its lawyers, one of whom, Irving Shapiro, was elected chairman and chief executive officer of the giant chemical firm in 1974.

Another anti-trust case was brought by the government early in 1951 against a group of Chicago dairies charging them with fixing prices and conspiring to monopolize the sale of fluid milk to wholesalers, various public institutions, and others in the Chicago area. Originally there were ten defendants, but by the time the case went to trial two years later before United States District Court Judge William J. Campbell, five of them signed a consent decree.* The remaining defendants were Borden Company and a subsidiary, Belmont Dairy Company, Bowman Dairy Company and a subsidiary, Ridgeview Farms Dairy, Incorporated, and Beloit Dairy Company.

The trial, which started on March 1, 1953, and was expected to last several months, was relatively—and gratifyingly—brief. After attorneys directed by Earl A. Jinkenson, who became chief of the government's anti-trust office in Chicago, called on grocers and others to testify that the defendant dairies had offered gifts, cash, and loans to lure them from competitors, Ball, heading the four-man team representing Borden, moved to dismiss the suit for lack of sufficient evidence. On the last day of the month, Judge Campbell granted his motion, asserting in an hour-long opinion that a defense would be "a useless task" because the evidence already presented showed, as Ball contended, that the companies' operations "were consistent with competition rather than consistent with any conspiracy to violate the laws." He sternly criticized the government for bringing a case to an already congested court calendar without amassing substantial proof despite, as in this instance, a six-year investigation of the Chicago milk industry.

When the government appealed directly to the Supreme Court, a unanimous decision affirmed Judge Campbell's dismissal of the charges of conspiracy to monopolize fluid milk sales but returned to the lower court for further consideration allegations of price discrimination. For a second time, Judge Campbell, after more extensive hearings, ruled for the

*A suit brought earlier by the rival Dean Milk Company against the defendant dairies was settled late in 1952 with a payment of $1.2 million to avoid, in the words of the head of Borden's Chicago Milk Division, W. N. Waterstreet, "a long trial with its great expense" but without admission of illegal acts or guilt.

defendants, and again the Supreme Court upset the part of his decision pertaining to prices. The case came to a close in April 1963—a dozen years after the anti-trust suit had been filed—when Judge Campbell, without objections by the defendants, enjoined Borden and Bowman from selling milk to independent and chain groceries at varying prices unless the price differential represented allowances made for actual cost savings. He also decreed that grocers be given their choice of the methods used by the dairies in delivering milk. During this lengthy case, Ball demonstrated his exceptional ability to teach young lawyers such as Blair White the craft of handling complex litigation.

At the time the anti-trust suit had been filed, Walter Cummings secured from the Supreme Court a vital decision stemming from similar action in 1948 against Borden and Bowman and six other Chicago area dairies. In preliminary hearings before United States District Judge John P. Barnes, Cummings, a member of Howard Neitzert's team representing Borden, sought to have made available for inspection by the defense certain documents and objects obtained by government attorneys that had been presented to the grand jury or were to be offered as evidence at the trial and were relevant to charges in the indictment. Willis L. Hotchkiss, the government lawyer, refused to accede to the request or respond to a subpoena issued by Judge Barnes for production of the requested materials; he maintained that the materials sought had been voluntarily furnished by "confidential informants" and that to give them up would impede government prosecution. Judge Barnes held Hotchkiss in contempt of court but was reversed in a 2-1 decision by the Court of Appeals. Cummings, with Burgess joining him, then took the case to the Supreme Court. There, the contempt order was vacated but the government was directed to produce the specific "evidentiary materials" asked for by Cummings. It was a significant ruling that helped establish rules that have since aided corporations and individuals prosecuted by the government.

Another big case in which Ball led the firm's defense team began on September 22, 1954, when Riss & Company of Kansas City, Missouri, the nation's largest trucking company, filed a $90 million anti-trust suit in Washington against eighty-five of the country's railroads along with the Association of American Railroads, the Association of Western Railways, the Eastern Railroads Presidents' Conference, and the Traffic Executives Association-Eastern Railroads, and Carl Byoir and Associates, a foremost public relations firm. The complaint charged all had conspired to "restrict, restrain, impede, harass and eliminate" competition by Riss in hauling ammunition and explosives for the government in various states on whose highways its fleet of 800 trucks traveled. The Byoir firm was singled out for allegedly influencing the Ohio Public Utilities Commission, at the behest of its client, the Pennsylvania Railroad, to institute proceedings before the Interstate Commerce Commission to cancel Riss' operating authority.

Rejoinders came promptly. From William T. Faricy, president of the Association of American Railroads: "The charges are utterly without foundation and will be so demonstrated if the case ever comes to court." From David I. Mackie, chairman of the Eastern Railroads Presidents' Conference: "The allegations with respect to the Conference will prove to be wholly unfounded if the plaintiff ever brings the matter to trial." From Gerry Swinehart, head of the publicity firm: "We deny the charges. They are false and baseless. Riss brought this suit for propaganda purposes and we will be glad to prove it in court." Ohio officials said that Riss trucks had accumulated almost 700 traffic violations in three years. And that December, Ball filed, in behalf of the twenty-three members of the Association of Western Railways, a counter-suit against Riss & Company for $100 million which the railroads had allegedly been deprived of in freight revenues because the trucker had been hauling explosives over the preceding twelve years without legal authority. Cited in the railroads' complaint, too, was a ruling by the United States Supreme Court in November 1953, that Riss had engaged in certain illegal operations of its trucks.

In February 1960, the battle finally landed in the Washington court-room of United States District Court Judge John J. Sirica, who would come to regard the case as his most important until he presided over hearings arising from the Watergate scandals in the administration of President Richard M. Nixon a dozen years later. By this time, the number of individual railroad defendants had been reduced to twenty-eight, but the four associations and the Byoir firm remained. Ball and his colleagues represented fifteen of the railroads and the Association of Western Railways; seven other law firms represented the balance.

As a jury was selected and the Riss attorneys then proceeded with their witnesses and introduction of voluminous exhibits to support the charges, Ball made sustained use during the sessions of Richard Flynn. Even before the trial got under way, Flynn had conducted depositions and directed discovery and now, being called on to prepare motions and to cross-examine and later present more witnesses than any other lawyers in the case, the responsibility given him by the firm made a vivid, lasting impression on him. He recalled later: "An associate in one of the other law firms later quit. I asked him why and he said because of the contrast between the firm he was with and the firm I was with. 'In mine,' he said, 'the junior partner wasn't allowed to participate, to ever do anything. In your firm you were allowed to do so many things, to take a real part. The contrast is too much. I could see myself sitting there for another fifteen years before I would get to stand up in a courtroom.' A lot of that was Stuart Ball, but that wasn't unique to him. That's been pretty well the pattern in this firm."

In the trial's fifth month, the defense lawyers asked for a directed verdict of acquittal or dismissal of the suit after Riss completed its presentation of evidence and testimony which filled nearly 12,000 pages of transcript. Judge Sirica denied the motions, asserting that there was enough evidence of a conspiracy to warrant continuing. Each defendant, he asserted, "had knowledge and approved of its illegal objective and the general means of carrying it out." To the defense's contention that anonymous publicity engendered against the Riss company by the railroads was protected by the constitutional right of free speech, Judge Sirica responded that an earlier Supreme Court ruling establishing minority groups' rights to distribute material anonymously because of fear of reprisals and intimidation did not apply in this case: "The railroad defendants are among the largest corporations in the country. It certainly cannot be contended that they will be in danger of intimidation or reprisal if their identities in connection with publicity are revealed."

On that November 5, the jury returned a verdict against five of the defendants—the Association of Western Railways, the Pennsylvania Railroad, the Traffic Executives Association-Eastern Railroads, the Eastern Railroad Presidents' Conference, and the Carl Byoir firm—but assessed no damages. Judge Sirica sent the jury back to re-consider imposition of damages. The jury then returned with a judgment of $75,000 which Judge Sirica, under the Sherman Anti-Trust Act, tripled to $225,000. That ruling was challenged; early in 1962, the United States Court of Appeals, in reversing Judge Sirica, asserted that the Supreme Court in another matter the previous year had decreed that anti-trust laws were not violated in such cases "even if deceitful propaganda is used" and, further, that the jury's initial finding of no damages was proper. The fact that Flynn had borne the task of preparing the appeals brief and in devising effective arguments that led to a successful resolution of the case was influential in his being named a partner shortly thereafter.

2

To a larger extent than before, the firm in the late 1950s and beyond was concerned with matters affecting the railroad industry, especially labor union disputes, rates, and mergers.

Howard Neitzert was engaged in representation of a group formed out of individual Carriers' Conference Committees and comprising nearly all of the country's 142 major railroads. His principal aide, in addition to associates in the firm and lawyers for the various lines, was Martin M. Lucente, who had come a decade earlier upon graduating from the University of Wisconsin Law School and was a partner since 1956. Actually, Neitzert's work in this area had started back in 1942, when Burgess and Smith assigned him to serve as the outside lawyer for western railroad clients confronted with demands by the Brotherhood of Locomotive Firemen and Enginemen for additional engineers and firemen on diesel-powered locomotives. In the next several years, numerous hearings before Presidential boards and other tribunals were held on this matter and similar ones—in which the union demands were invariably characterized by Neitzert as "indefensible featherbedding"—and others centering on bids for salary increases for hundreds of thousands of operating and non-operating railroad employees. As the result of his endeavors—in an important instance, he succeeded in obtaining an order setting new work rules that called for only one engineer on a single locomotive unit and no more than an engineer and a fireman on units of five and above—he won approbation from not only executives of the western railroads but from presidents of southern and eastern lines whom he had called as witnesses. Consequently, in 1948 he was asked to be the counsel for the three groups for whatever new predicaments they faced.

Soon Neitzert was leading his team—amplified from time to time by many lawyers, personnel and traffic specialists, economists, and technical experts to help select witnesses and prepare data and testimony—into a long series of contests, in the course of which he made cogent arguments against what he, speaking for the carriers, deemed to be obsolete and inefficient work practices and excessive expenses in an industry already weakened by fierce competition from airlines and trucking firms.

The most crucial and often dramatic of these—again concerned with featherbedding—was touched off in November 1959. Notice served by the nation's railroads on operating employees represented by five unions—the Brotherhood of Locomotive Engineers, the Brotherhood of Locomotive Firemen and Enginemen, the Order of Railway Conductors and Brakemen, the Brotherhood of Railroad Trainmen, and the Switchmen's Union of North America—proposed, among other things, that firemen no longer be used on non-steam locomotives except in passenger service and that train crews made up of conductors and brakemen in road service and foremen and helpers in yard service be staffed according to the discretion of railroad managements. The unions vigorously opposed this action and, by terms of the Railway Labor Act, the dispute was submitted to a fifteen-man commission created by President Dwight Eisenhower a week before the 1960 Presidential elections and headed by former Labor Secretary James P. Mitchell; the first of its kind in its makeup, it had equal membership representing management, unions, and the general public. Throughout 1961, there were many heated sessions in Chicago. Outmoded work rules, Neitzert charged, caused costs of $600 million a year, a sum equal to the prevailing annual net income of all Class 1 railroads. Unless those rules were substantially altered, he warned, the railroads could face bankruptcy. He cited, among many examples, the case of Chicago and North Western's "Twin Cities 400," for whose Chicago-to-Minneapolis run of eight-and-one-half hours three engine crews, under existing rules, were required; each crew received one and one-third day's pay for a little less than three hours' working time, thereby resulting in payment of four days' wages for the trip. Taking note of this and the inability of that train, even with boosts in fares, to meet expenses—indeed, its annual loss was put at $1 million—the *Chicago Daily News* commented editorially: "We don't deny that the unions have their own valid concerns in the matter. They have. . . . But there is no room in today's and tomorrow's hotly competitive transportation picture for antiquated work rules and practices that artificially inflate the costs of operation. Featherbedding is the most flagrant of such practices."

The following February, the commission issued its report granting the carriers substantial relief with respect to the use of firemen on the non-steam locomotives and the size of crews in freight and yard service. These decisions affected the status of some 40,000 men whose total annual wages amounted to half of the financial losses attributed by the railroads to featherbedding. The unions refused to abide by the commission's decree. When the carriers announced they would put the new rules into effect on August 16, the unions threatened to strike. But they withheld action so they could seek an injunction to prevent the railroads from carrying out their job-reduction plans. That move was successfully contested by Neitzert and Lucente before United States District Court Judge Joseph Sam Perry. On November 28, the Seventh Circuit Court of Appeals upheld Judge Perry and, in addition, declared that the threat of a strike was ill-advised because it would "amount to a nationwide transportation paralysis." The unions then sought a reversal of that decision in the United States Supreme Court on the ground that the carriers had violated the Railway Labor Act by proceeding with plans for initiating job-reducing work-rules changes without further negotiations. Neitzert charged the unions were carrying on stalling tactics to put off appointment of an emergency board by President Kennedy. The delays, according to him and James E. Wolfe, chairman of the railroad group, were costing the lines more than $1.6 million a day. On the following March 4, the high court upheld the appeals court ruling unanimously, minus the participation of Justice Arthur J. Goldberg because he had been in the protracted contest as Secretary of Labor in the Kennedy cabinet in 1961 and 1962. Acting on a suggestion by the high court that both parties had exhausted procedures under the Railway Labor Act and were "relegated to self-help in adjusting this dispute," President Kennedy gained Congressional approval for appointment of an arbitration board which began hearings in Washington on the two issues—whether firemen were needed on non-steam locomotives and the proper size of train crews—on September 24. Emergency legislation passed a month earlier by Congress to prevent a strike required both sides to accept the board's findings. At the initial hearing, Neitzert emphasized anew that the money which could be used to take advantage of technological improvements was being wasted by work not needed or not performed. Union attorneys maintained that elimination of firemen and other train crewmen on non-steam freights and in yard trains would jeopardize safe operations.

The board, after six weeks of hearings, issued an award that the railroads considered a partial victory. It provided for no hiring of replacements for firemen who died or retired, thereby reducing that work force by 90 percent, and cutting by similar means 30 percent of the ranks of other crewmen, chiefly brakemen and switchmen. That award was binding for only two years, by which time neither Neitzert nor any others in the firm represented the railroads in national labor matters.* In 1964, when the National Railway Labor Conference moved its headquarters to Washington, Wolfe preferred to have lawyers close at hand because he anticipated that new problems might come before more boards and commissions there. When the award expired, the unions sought to re-establish the crews that had been reduced by the 1963 arbitration board. Because some railroads were contemplating mergers, they were inclined to yield to these pressures so as to avoid renewed hearings and possibly to facilitate the mergers. Not until the 1970s was a national agreement reached that eliminated the use of firemen on non-steam locomotives except for 10 percent retained to train locomotive engineers, and in other pacts the size of crews in freight and yard services was appreciably reduced.

3

A railroad labor case successfully argued by Walter J. Cummings in the United States Supreme Court in 1957 had significance because it was one of the few of that nature in which the court rendered a unanimous decision, and it would often be cited in the future. Its origins lay in a disagreement between the Brotherhood of Railroad Trainmen and Chicago River & Indiana Railroad Company, operator of the switching and yard facilities of the Union Stockyards. Despite the existence of a collective bargaining agreement, a strike was called after efforts by a federal mediator and the National Railroad Adjustment Board failed to resolve the union's claims for additional compensation and for reinstatement of a discharged worker. Because the work stoppage threatened irreparable harm to it, other employees, and some 600 industries and some two dozen railroads it served, the carrier sought and obtained an injunction in United States District Court. This action was affirmed by the Seventh Circuit Court of Appeals, whereupon the case landed in the Supreme Court on the union's appeal. Cummings' chief argument against the union's contention that the

*In the same period, Neitzert and Lucente also represented the National Railroad Industry Group in cases—some successfully resolved, others less so—involving salaries, fringe benefits, and related issues before a number of emergency and arbitration boards.

1932 Norris-La Guardia Act had negated the power of federal courts to issue injunctions in labor disputes was that this was not applicable to "minor disputes" (namely, disputes over the meaning of contracts) as spelled out by the Railway Labor Act—and the issues in the union-railroad controversy were admittedly of such a nature. The high court ruled for the railroad, stressing that the Norris-La Guardia Act could not be "read alone in matters dealing with railway labor disputes" and that a railroad labor union had no lawful right to resort to a strike while a dispute was pending before the National Railroad Adjustment Board, whose decision, as specified in the Railway Labor Act, was final and binding on both sides.

Also in the 1950s, Howard Trienens and Martin Lucente were assigned to Thomas to join lawyers for most of the country's railroads in the "Productivity Wage Case," so-called because union demands for salary boosts were based on increased productivity per employee. The unions' claim was for an additional eighteen cents an hour—seemingly small but in the aggregate, considering the many thousands of workers, could come to well over $15 million a year. After lengthy hearings in New York before an arbitration board, evidence presented by Thomas, plus testimony from witnesses including prominent economists and briefs prepared by Trienens and Lucente, emphasized that the productivity at issue had resulted primarily from higher capital investments and technological improvements. The ultimate ruling granted an increase of only four cents an hour.

In September 1962, the Order of Railroad Telegraphers climaxed a five-year controversy with the Chicago and North Western over a reduction of personnel by calling a strike that ended after thirty days upon President Kennedy's appointment of a three-man arbitration board. The strike had been called when the union refused to accept the recommendation of a Presidential Emergency Board favorable to the railroad after hearings in which Carl McGowan, the line's general counsel (and later a judge in the United States Court of Appeals for the District of Columbia) and Trienens represented Chicago and North Western and the Association of Western Railroads. Trienens argued the railroad's case before the arbitration panel headed by Sylvester Garrett, a veteran arbitrator, as the neutral member with Ben W. Heineman, the line's chairman, and George Leighty, the union's president, as respective representatives of management and labor. Foremost among Trienens' points was that it was financially imperative that the road reduce the number of employees whenever such action was necessary for efficient and economic operations. Automation and technological advances, he noted, had pared the work load of some telegraphers to only twelve minutes a day, with a daily average of an hour. Garrett's decision supported the railroad's position.

4

Trienens' primary concerns in his neophyte period with the firm had been rate cases for Illinois Bell Telephone Company and later, as he headed toward a partnership in 1956, rate cases for the western railroads and anti-trust matters. While thus engaged, Trienens was brought by Douglas Smith into "divisions cases" in which railroad groups vigorously vied for adequate shares of joint revenues derived mostly from freight traffic across the country. Determination of percentages of revenues—often totaling many millions of dollars—was initially made by the Interstate Commerce Commission after hearings replete with masses of technical data and cost studies drawn up by both sides. ICC decisions could be appealed in the courts, and often were. Two hotly contested decisions in the 1960s constituted what were designated as the "Transcontinental Divisions Case," in which the firm represented railroads in the Far West against those in the East and Midwest, and the "North-South Divisions Case," in which the firm's clients, an aggregation of southern lines, opposed the claims of northeastern railroads. Both before the ICC and later in the lower courts and the United States Supreme Court, Trienens proved himself unusually adept in preparing and presenting cost studies to support his case. At one ICC hearing, his study was so detailed and thorough that his opponents filed for a two-year extension in which to draw up replies. Smith took special note of this by observing in a copy of the request for extension by opponents who had previously pressed for expedition: "Man bites dog!" Trienens continued to be involved in divisions cases, his chief aides being George L. Saunders, Jr., a 1959 graduate of University of Chicago Law School who came in 1962 after clerking for two years for Supreme Court Justice Hugo L. Black and was named a partner in 1966, R. Eden Martin, an arrival from Harvard Law School in 1967, and Theodore N. Miller, a 1967 Yale Law School graduate who came in 1968 from a clerkship with Chief Judge Luther Swygert of the Seventh Circuit Court of Appeals. Martin and Miller achieved partnerships in 1973.

217

In the last half of the 1960s Trienens assumed a major role in what was called an "Inclusion Case" that affected Norfolk and Western Railway, whose origins lay in the formative years of the American rail industry early in the nineteenth century. On a Saturday in 1964, he received a telephone call at his home from Robert Claytor, the NW general counsel he had come to know as an opponent during the North-South divisions litigation. Would the firm, Claytor asked, help in opposing the petitions before the Interstate Commerce Commission of three small roads—Erie Lackawanna, Delaware & Hudson, and Boston & Maine—to become part of NW and also represent NW in a proposed merger with Chesapeake & Ohio Railway? Each of these proceedings was the result of fears engendered by action then pending for a union of New York Central Railroad with the Pennsylvania Railroad into a gigantic Penn Central and consequent domination of freight traffic in the northeastern part of the country. Trienens assented, and soon he was the lead counsel in a prolonged legal battle.

The Penn Central merger was approved by the ICC in 1966 before deciding either the inclusion case or the NW-C&O merger case. Trienens and NW lawyers went to court to prevent the formation of the Penn Central until the NW-C&O merger was sanctioned. On March 27, 1967, the Supreme Court gave the objectors to the Penn Central merger cause for fleeting satisfaction by referring the case back to the ICC for reconsideration until the inclusion petitions of the three small roads could be decided. The commission thereafter ordered the NW to acquire the three lines and again gave approval to the Penn Central merger. After litigation before three-judge courts in New York, Philadelphia, and Richmond, the high court on the following January 15 ended all debate by unanimously sustaining the ICC's ruling. Two weeks later the Penn Central merger became a reality and its new board of directors met in Philadelphia to express optimism about the future. But the roseate feelings were to be relatively short-lived. Woes—financial, operational, and managerial—piled upon woes, and losses rose to as much as $1 million a day. In a special Sunday session on June 21, 1970, the line's board voted to file for bankruptcy, and the merger that authoritative commentators called the "most miserable fiasco in American business" came to an end.*

*The Penn Central and five other insolvent northeastern carriers were taken over on April 1, 1976, by the quasi-governmental Consolidated Rail Corporation—familiarly known as Conrail—that had been set up by the United States Railway Association under terms of the 1973 Regional Rail Reorganization Act.

Trienens meanwhile had obtained in the fall of 1969 an ICC examiner's report favoring the NW-C&O merger, but in the aftermath of the Penn Central's collapse there was scant enthusiasm for any merger and NW and C&O dropped their plans. The firm's relationship with the Norfolk and Western road continued, however. When the Erie Lackawanna went bankrupt in June, 1972, shortly after 135 miles of its mainline tracks in upstate New York, along with eleven bridges, were destroyed by a devastating hurricane, the firm worked with NW in handling tax problems arising from having a bankrupt railroad in a consolidated NW tax return. And well into the present the Norfolk and Western remains a steady client.

5

In virtually everything relating to railroads in these years as in the past, Burgess either participated directly or supervised preparation of briefs and other pertinent documents in cases before the Interstate Commerce Commission and in the courts. In 1960, the firm served as chief counsel for the merger of three carriers—Minneapolis, St. Paul & Sault Ste. Marie, familiar for years as the Soo, Wisconsin Central, and Duluth, South Shore & Atlantic—into a new Soo Line Railroad Company, based in Minneapolis and operating with an anticipated annual saving of $1.2 million on 4,800 miles of track in Minnesota, Wisconsin, Michigan, Montana, and North and South Dakota. A diligent aide in bringing about this merger was Ray Garrett. To solve intricate mortgage questions, he locked himself in a room in Evanston's Orrington Hotel for several days to study details and work out basic elements. He then moved his deliberations to the attic of his home, refusing to take telephone calls while he moved pieces of paper denoting various aspects of the puzzle around on the floor so that he could fix in his mind the diverse steps to be taken and the results that would follow. Burgess accepted Garrett's ultimate suggestion that the Soo and the Wisconsin Central be consolidated with the Duluth, South Shore & Atlantic.

Within a few months, Burgess was a dominant figure in a much larger consolidation, one of the biggest in railroad history.

Early in 1955, John Budd, then president of the Great Northern Railroad Company, and Robert S. Macfarlane, president of Northern Pacific Railway, met informally to talk of many things. Foremost among them was the prospect of combining their carriers, which had parallel lines from

219

Minneapolis and St. Paul to the Northwest coast, and their mutually-owned affiliate, Chicago, Burlington & Quincy Railroad, whose lines ran from the Twin Cities to Chicago and from Chicago as far west as Montana. Each was well aware that previous endeavors had failed. The first had occurred in 1896 when James J. Hill, the mogul who had organized the Great Northern in 1890 and had acquired the Northern Pacific during the national financial panic of 1893, brought about a union of the two roads, a move that was held unlawful in a Supreme Court ruling that it would "unavoidably result in a monopoly against which public regulation would be but a feeble protection." In 1901, shortly after he gained control of the Burlington with the aid of the mighty J. Pierpont Morgan, Hill tried again by forming the Northern Securities holding company with Morgan to contain the roads' stock and thereby bring about the merger. That venture was declared in a 5-4 Supreme Court landmark decision in 1904 to be in violation of the Sherman Anti-Trust Act because it constituted an "illegal combination" in restraint of interstate commerce; one of the dissenters was the newest justice, Oliver Wendell Holmes, who pleaded for the "rule of reason," a stand that prompted President Theodore Roosevelt, then on his vigorous foray against trusts and combines, to say—most unjustifiably—of his appointee, "Holmes has the backbone of a ripe banana." A further merger attempt came to naught in the late 1920s because of rejection by the roads of the Interstate Commerce Commission's order approving the union only if the Burlington were divested.

Budd and Macfarlane authorized a comprehensive study that presented impressive evidence that combining the lines would improve service to shippers, stabilize employment, and produce sorely-needed growth capital and yearly pre-tax cost reductions of more than $40 million by the fifth year of the merger. After many months of discussion and negotiations in which Burgess, as chief counsel for the three carriers, offered cogent wisdom derived from his years of experience in the railroad industry, a formal application for approval of the consolidation was filed with the Interstate Commerce Commission on February 17, 1961. This touched off a long and often dramatic sequence of events in which Burgess and others in the firm figured prominently.

Nearly 450 parties intervened in the proceedings. More than half—shippers or others interested in transportation rates and services—backed the merger, although some sought to impose certain conditions on an approval order. Several western railroads, worried about a merger's possible effects on their traffic and revenues, wanted protective conditions. The merging lines made satisfactory stipulations with several such railroads, but the Milwaukee and the Chicago and North Western adamantly sought conditions which the applicants opposed. This became one of the major issues. Labor union leaders were anti-merger for fear of reductions in jobs. Some municipalities and local shopkeepers were apprehensive about economic distress in their communities that layoffs would cause, but other cities, port districts, chambers of commerce, and civic groups were pro-merger. Federal and state authorities and agencies interposed objections or support. The Justice Department maintained that the merger would negate benefits for shippers and the public. At first, the Department of Agriculture also came out against consolidation, but later changed its position if the ultimate approval order were to "open gateways to competing railroads, thus creating more vigorous competition." State agencies that intervened were nearly equally divided in reactions to the merger, with opponents' resistance based mostly on potential reduction in employment.

In July 1961, the matter was referred to ICC Examiner Robert H. Murphy and that October hearings started in the old Federal Courts Building in St. Paul. During the next nine months, Murphy, a retired Army officer, held eighty-two sessions in fifteen other cities and towns along the routes of the applicants' lines; by the end of those hearings the following July, testimony of 623 witnesses for and against the amalgamation filled over 15,000 pages and 243 exhibits had been introduced.

Burgess took the leading role on behalf of the applicant railroads, attending most of the hearings, examining and cross-examining witnesses and arguing many issues as they arose. His aides from the firm, augmenting the railroads' attorneys, were Robert Thomas, who helped prepare the merger application and, accompanied by John Schwemm, traveled with railroad officials over the Northern Lines to aid them in getting ready for the hearings; Ray Garrett, who figured in preliminary phases and later concentrated on all the complex corporate aspects; and Martin Lucente, who questioned witnesses on labor issues. In later phases of the proceedings, Garrett was assisted by associates who later became partners, including Robert T. Beam, at the firm since 1957 after graduating from the University of Illinois College of Law, earning a master's degree from New York University, and practicing with a Manhattan firm for four years, and Thomas J. Gregg, a 1964 Northwestern Law School alumnus.

221

Early in 1963, twenty-nine separate briefs were filed with Murphy. Justice Department lawyers and those for Washington, Minnesota, and Oregon claimed that the merger's opponents had been deprived of a fair hearing and argued for dismissal of the merger application or a complete rehearing of evidence. After thorough study of the briefs and the massive record, Murphy wrote a report comprising 456 single-spaced legal-length pages, exclusive of extensive appendices, and submitted it to all parties on August 24, 1964. He found no merit in claims of lack of fair hearing and, on the substantive issues, he approved the merger, finding that it would be in the public interest and that a unified company could provide better service and achieve substantial economies. Responding to the report, the Justice Department not only repeated the charges of unfair hearing but also accused Murphy of what they called ''a shocking, extreme and undisciplined'' bias in favor of the merger. Affidavits from two union officials who strongly opposed the merger were introduced that purported to describe an informal conversation with Murphy in 1961 in which he allegedly had said, among other things, that so-called public witnesses, because they lacked knowledge of transportation, could not contradict the applicants' witnesses and that the lines should merge to avoid financial difficulties that other railroads had encountered.

Burgess and his team were certain that the allegations against Murphy were baseless. But because of the possibility, however distant, of an ICC order for retrial, a brief was filed on the following March 15 in which 35 of its 174 pages were devoted to countering the issue of bias and partiality. Included in it were statements from shippers that they had been treated fairly and with dispatch and from the Milwaukee road that Murphy had acted without prejudice. The ICC scheduled oral arguments on all issues for June 16 in its ornate hearing room in Washington.

6

At the time of his death on May 24, 1965, Burgess had been preparing for the June 16 hearing. In his absence, Garrett, who now shared with Thomas all of Burgess' tasks, read a brief statement about Burgess' death and added, ''If he were here today, he would mention with pride that he argued his first case before this commission just fifty years ago this spring. In the succeeding years he achieved national fame and will long be remembered for his accomplishments and leadership in the field of railroad transportation. He had planned to make this hearing his last major appearance before the commission." Thomas then argued mostly about the merger's many substantive issues, including the applicants' opposition to conditions sought by the Milwaukee and C&NW which Murphy had not recommended for adoption. He also discussed at length the issue of Murphy's alleged bias and answered the commissioners' many questions.

Nearly a year passed before the next development. At noon on April 27, 1966, Thomas and others active in the merger effort lined up inside the ICC building to which they had been summoned to receive copies of the fateful decision. Also present was another group awaiting word on the application to combine New York Central and Pennsylvania. Ironically, in view of future events, the latter was unanimously approved. But the first was denied by a 6-5 vote; the five dissenters filed extensive vigorous opinions noting that the "majority's points of departure misapplied the law and fumbled the facts." The commission's unanimous ruling that the charges of bias against Murphy were lacking in merit did little to assuage the applicants' lawyers' disappointment. But, although shocked and depressed over the rejection of the merger, Thomas and his colleagues and the applicants' officers were gratified to learn after close study of the decision that the denial was based mainly on the anticipated effects of the merger on the Milwaukee and the Chicago and North Western and on employees of the merging lines. Negotiations with the two railroads and unions resulted in contracts and agreements for imposition of conditions satisfactory to those lines and the unions. There were further briefs and further hearings and negotiations with contending parties that occupied Thomas and his associates for the rest of the year. By that summer, such objecting states as Oregon, South Dakota, and Iowa switched their stands, the Milwaukee and the C&NW withdrew their opposition, and the unions expressed satisfaction with attrition pacts that had been worked out. Thomas presented a petition to the ICC for reconsideration of its negative ruling, and on November 30 the commission issued its lengthy "Report on Reconsideration and Further Hearing" and authorized the merger.

But troubles developed.

The following April, shortly before the May 10 deadline for the merger to go into effect unless appeals of the ICC decision were taken to United States District Court, action was renewed on three fronts—in Seattle by officials of a nearby small town who claimed that their rail service would be wiped out, in New York by a group of holders of Northern Pacific securities thwarted earlier in a hard-fought proxy battle when the revised merger agreement had been submitted to all stockholders for approval, and in Washington by Justice Department lawyers traditionally adamant against large combines they maintained would stifle competition. Thomas sped to Seattle to contest the latest move there. George Saunders did likewise in New York and Richard Flynn in Washington. On May 9, all three achieved success when the judges refused to interfere. Saunders, who would later recall the day as "one of the most exciting in my career," gathered that evening with colleagues in the Sky Club atop the Pan-American Building to celebrate the victories, and Thomas and Frank Farrell, Northern Pacific's general solicitor, did likewise in Seattle.

Their glee was premature. Late that night, government attorneys made a last-minute visit to the Wardman Park Hotel apartment of Chief Justice Earl Warren with an application for a restraining order. Apprised of this move, Flynn, Warren's former law clerk, hurried to the apartment at midnight with a sheaf of written reasons for denying the request. Early the next morning, Flynn received a phone call from the clerk of the Supreme Court to the effect that the chief justice wanted the carriers to postpone the merger voluntarily. Flynn replied that such a move would have an adverse financial effect on the roads' stockholders but that the carriers obviously would abide by the court's order. Within five minutes, the clerk called again to say, "The chief justice said to tell you, 'If Flynn wants an order, tell him he's damn well got one!' " And later that morning Warren issued an order for a temporary injunction until a three-judge court could hold a hearing. At these, Thomas argued that a stay would harm shippers and the general public. In a 125-page brief, he cited figures to show that competition would be eliminated at only 3 percent of the proposed merged lines' total number of stations. But the panel, by a 2-1 vote, continued the stay, and arguments on the merits of the appeal lasted through July. On that November 20, the judges unanimously affirmed the ICC order authorizing the merger and dismissed the complaints. Three months later, the Supreme Court agreed to hear appeals from the government and other foes of the merger. Efforts to expedite the matter were fruitless. By the time the high court heard the arguments presented by Covington & Burling's Hugh Cox for the railroads, Warren had resigned and had been succeeded by Warren E. Burger.

On February 2, 1970, in a unanimous ruling, the high court, with Justice William O. Douglas abstaining, approved the merger. In a thirty-seven-page opinion, the chief justice rejected the contention that unification of the strong, prospering railroads would reduce competition, and stressed that benefits to be gained by the public and by shippers who would get an improved car supply, wider routing, better loading and unloading privileges, and enhanced claims service outweighed the loss of competition between the merging lines. Emphasized, too, was the fact that federal law directed the ICC to approve mergers aimed at promoting efficiency of operation as well as those in which a financially sound line absorbed a weaker one: "Rail mergers should not be restricted to combinations by which the strong rescue the halt and the lame." A month later the merger was a reality, and on the next day John Budd, chairman of the new line, wrote a congratulatory letter to Thomas: "Your people have done a magnificent job all the way through, climaxed by the splendid performance yesterday, which represented so much and such careful preparatory work." Of Beam, who had taken on many of Ray Garrett's duties after Garrett died on November 23, 1969, and was in charge of the multitude of corporate and other steps necessary for the consummation, Budd wrote, "Bob Beam really did himself proud."

The merger, including the jointly-owned smaller Spokane, Portland & Seattle road, created the world's largest rail system, covering 26,500 miles of track in eighteen states between the Great Lakes and the Pacific Coast and from Canada to the Gulf of Mexico. The name affixed to this imposing entity upon its formalization on that March 2 was Burlington Northern, Incorporated, with a combined worth of $2.8 billion and a fleet of 2,000 diesel units, 122,000 freight cars, 1,230 passenger cars, and 48,000 employees, in addition to such long-held assets as tracts of timber lands, coal fields, and mineral and oil rights to extensive properties. The firm, which had fulfilled so indispensable a function in nine years of legal strife, continued to represent the new company over the next decade. Beam dealt with financing, a government inquiry, and other matters. In 1977, after Thomas retired, an application was filed with the ICC for union with St. Louis-San Francisco Railway, a plan that, with Lucente handling proceedings before the commission, reached fruition three years later with the sanction of the Supreme Court.* Thereby, another 1,800 miles of track were added to make the big Burlington Northern even bigger and, more significantly, uppermost among the few healthy and prospering railroads in the country.

*See Chapter XIV.

In 1963, the firm became involved in another proposed merger, that of the mighty Union Pacific with the faltering Chicago, Rock Island & Pacific, no longer the "mighty fine line" sung about by balladeers.

Stuart Ball was counsel for Union Pacific as the plan wound its way though the next twelve years, with innumerable ICC hearings in several cities amid opposition from other railroads, chiefly Chicago and North Western, which put in its bid for Rock Island with testimony by Ben Heineman that a Union Pacific-Rock Island consolidation would make impossible the creation of a strong rail system—"much needed and deserved"—in the Middle West. Among Ball's arguments was that the merger would bring about "competitive, long-haul rail systems" while any other, especially with Heineman's road, would decrease competition through a "single-carrier dominance" of the region—a view supported in a Department of Justice brief filed with the commission early in 1969. Another four years passed before a ruling was made. In a massive three-volume report, Nathan Klitenic, an ICC examiner, recommended approval of the Union Pacific-Rock Island merger if there were also a restructuring of western railroads into four major systems with inclusion of numerous weaker systems into stronger ones. This was rejected by Union Pacific as, in Ball's words, "utterly unworkable and unacceptable."

By this time, Rock Island's 7,500 miles of trackage and its equipment were in deplorable condition because its management, starting in 1963, had deferred maintenance in the expectation that Union Pacific would assume all upkeep costs. Consequently, despite the ICC's endorsement of the merger in accord with Klitenic's report, Union Pacific withdrew its original merger offer on March 30, 1975. After its request for a $100 million government loan was rejected, Rock Island declared bankruptcy.*

A merger of another sort was that of Pure Oil Company with Union Oil Company of California in 1965. It climaxed several years of Pure Oil's search for consolidation because, although it ranked fifteenth among the nation's oil companies, its profits remained fairly static. After rejecting

*In the course of subsequent reorganization, its trackage was sold to other carriers or abandoned. A portion of blame for its fate was ascribed by David Young, transportation editor of the *Chicago Tribune*, to the unduly long time it took for the ICC to reach a decision. His detailed account was headed: "Rock Island story: How to regulate a railroad to death."

bids from several other companies, its management opened discussions early in 1965 with Union Oil. By July, after objections from some stockholders were overcome, the merger was effected under a plan worked out by Harlowe Bowes and Pure Oil's regular law firm, Vinson & Elkins of Houston, with Union Oil's attorneys, that called for Pure Oil stockholders to receive one share of a new Union Oil convertible preferred stock for each share of Pure Oil common stock. The merger combined the two regional companies into a nationwide organization with total assets of almost $1.5 billion. By 1970, the Union Oil symbol supplanted Pure Oil's on its refineries and stations in a twenty-four-state area in the Midwest, South, and Southeast.

8

An Illinois company, in whose expansion and diversification the firm assisted, had been organized in 1912 by a dozen farmers led by Thomas Roberts. This was the DeKalb County Soil Improvement Association, whose original aim was to seek out better methods of soil conservation.

In the early 1920s it started experimenting and producing hybrid corn, a new kind of hardy corn seed about which Roberts had been told at a company picnic by Henry A. Wallace, the agricultural expert and future Secretary of Agriculture and vice-president in the Roosevelt administration. By 1961, the company, then known as DEKALB AgResearch Incorporated with annual worldwide sales of $30 million primarily in seed corn, had need of expert counsel in matters relating to possible Federal Trade Commission action. Its young president, Thomas Roberts, Jr., consulted with Stuart Ball after the firm—and Ball particularly—had been one of several recommended to him by his bankers and accountants. Ball brought Blair White into the discussions. The problem was handily resolved and Roberts asked that the firm take on all subsequent tasks.

Henceforth, as DEKALB experienced a phenomenal growth, considerable attention was required in myriad matters, from arranging for long-term loans to purchasing additional companies. Before DEKALB went public in 1969, White and others supervised the recapitalization of the company by splitting the common stock into voting and non-voting stock and the subsequent sale of non-voting stock to the public. Agricultural research continued to be the main concern, but other companies were acquired, with the firm as catalyst, that included a major manufacturer of electrically-powered agricultural sprinklers, another that made photo detectors, a third in controlled release drugs and food preservatives. Its entry into the commodities brokerage field eventually made several in the firm experts in commodities futures. It marketed hogs and cattle and increased its quest for copper and gas and oil in the Aegean Sea and on land purchased shortly before World War II. So extensive have been DEKALB's continuing activities that often as many as two dozen of the firm's lawyers worked with it at the same time on assorted matters. DEKALB's management group now includes Vice-president Bruce P. Bickner and John H. Witmer, Jr., vice-president and general counsel, both formerly associated with the firm.

9

From the firm's earliest years, its partners engaged extensively in furnishing legal advice and representation to clients in a wide variety of real estate matters.

Norman Williams and John Leverett Thompson were thus involved almost from the very start of their affiliation in 1866, and they set the precedent and pattern followed by others as Chicago and surrounding areas expanded decade by decade. In the years preceding World War II, Nathan Moore, Dwight Dickerson, Edward McDougal, and Philip Schofield were most prominently occupied with this work. When the latter two entered military service, Avery carried principal responsibility in this field, and after war's end he was loaded with work for Illinois Bell Telephone Company and other clients who undertook acquisition and construction programs that had been deferred in the war years. To assist him he asked the senior partners for the assistance of Edward Saunders when Saunders returned from the Navy. Upon Avery's recommendation, Saunders was made a partner in 1952 and head of the real estate group, and before long he became recognized in Chicago and elsewhere as one of the leading real estate lawyers in the Middle West.

A major part of real estate practice in the post-war period dealt with regional shopping centers, a growth industry of the time. In these endeavors, the firm represented major department stores seeking to expand into the burgeoning suburban areas, as well as certain individual shopping center developers. These included such longtime clients as Carson Pirie Scott & Company—on whose board Dern, Avery, and Edward Saunders successively served—Wieboldt Stores, and Montgomery Ward.

An initial project—indeed, one of the earliest major North Shore suburban shopping centers—was Edens Plaza, a twenty-acre tract in Wilmette, with a Carson's department store as its centerpiece. To obtain zoning approval for the development, Avery and an associate, John King, persuaded Wilmette officials to amend their zoning ordinance to permit a new type of shopping center modeled on similar zoning in New York and Los Angeles suburbs. The center opened in May 1956. Five years later in Mount Prospect, the $20 million, 100-acre Randhurst shopping center opened with one million square feet of floor space, the end result of a consortium of three Chicago merchandisers whose complex details had been worked out by Edward Saunders and Donald Gralen. Randhurst then was the largest enclosed mall center in the United States and the first of its kind in Illinois. In 1963, Gralen represented Carson's and Wieboldt's in creating the Yorktown shopping center in Lombard; it was the first major center in Illinois to utilize an easement and operating concept in which the major department stores and the mall's owner owned the land under their respective establishments and a portion of the parking lot and agreed to build, operate, and maintain the stores amid a bewildering and diverse array of cross easements, restrictions, and agreements. The complicated transaction served as a model for many future major shopping centers in the Chicago metropolitan area.

More than shopping center business was handled by the firm in this period. In 1964–65 it represented Jones & Laughlin Steel Corporation in acquiring 6,000 acres of contiguous farmland in downstate Illinois for an integrated steel mill facility. Involved was the procurement of thirty-four separate parcels but it was necessary to effect sixty transactions because many of the landowners chose to exchange farmland for their properties in lieu of cash. Gralen soon was concerned with elements of infinite variety including, among other things, barnyard auctions at which he bid and purchased exchange property. By the time the effort ended, the firm also handled a suit to perfect title to underlying mineral estates and a specific performance suit when one of the landowners refused, at the last minute, to close the transaction.

Over an eighteen-month period in 1963–64 Harry Baumann handled the acquisition of Bell Laboratories' Indian Hill office and research site of approximately 170 acres at Warrenville and Naperville Roads in DuPage County. The property was acquired through a nominee under contracts for purchase conditioned upon rezoning. Land owned by Daniel F. Rice, a Chicago commodities dealer and nationally-famed racehorse breeder, abutted the property to the north. Other neighbors were single family homeowners. A carefully planned sales program involving personal calls on the neighbors with explanatory materials, frequent presentations at luncheons for civic groups, and closely timed news releases preceded the zoning proceedings. Since the property spanned two townships, two overflow hearings were held by the DuPage County zoning authorities in Wheaton and in Lisle. After successful rezoning and closing, intense negotiations were undertaken with the Sanitary District for the construction of a trunk sewer at the company's cost. Subsequently, in 1973–74 Baumann represented Western Electric Company in acquiring, annexing, and rezoning of a sister facility on 125 acres immediately east of the Bell Laboratories site. Later, the company participated in the construction of a temporary sewage treatment plant on adjacent lands, which was completed and ready for service on the day the new facility was opened.

In 1967, the firm served as local counsel for New York investors in purchasing the Insurance Exchange Building—then the city's largest structure composed entirely of offices—in a downtown Chicago block bounded by Jackson, Wells, VanBuren, and Sherman Streets. An especially complex deal in which ownership of the ground had to be separated from ownership of the building, it marked the first time in half a century that an entire block in that area had changed hands.

10

A case in which the sum in question was relatively slight but would have legal import had arisen out of imposition in 1957 of a federal tax lien of $7,912 against a Frank Cacciatore, beneficiary of a land trust that had been set up by Chicago Title and Trust Company, the firm's client. In behalf of the company, the originator and major trustee of Illinois land trusts, Avery and Cummings sought resolution of the central issue of whether the land trust in the complex matter was lawfully protected from such a lien and other claims. Cook County Circuit Judge Harold P. O'Connell ruled that it was.

In 1961, the Appellate Court rejected the government's contention that its lien took precedence over the rights of the trustee and beneficiary of the land trust, the trustee under a second mortgage, and other claimants. Its decision, written by Judge Robert E. English, held that because the interest of a beneficiary of an Illinois land trust is not an interest in real property, a tax lien filed against the beneficiary does not attach to the real estate held in trust and is subordinate to mortgages of the property recorded both before and after filing of the lien. A year later, affirmation by the state supreme court of Judge English's well-stated opinion attested further to the validity of such trusts, and this particular case became the country's leading one on land trusts, to be cited often in similar ones in other states.

11

Establishment of new state law stemmed from a suit filed by James A. Dooley, a veteran personal injury lawyer, in Cook County Circuit Court in 1963 for damages against Illinois Bell Telephone Company in behalf of the widow of a man killed when an automobile, swerving out of the path of one of the company's unlighted sawhorse barricades on a DuPage County road, crashed head-on into his.

Representing the phone company was James Kissel, who had been raised to a partnership in 1956. The woman had since remarried, a fact Kissel wanted to impress on the jury, although no authority existed in state law that allowed this. Before jury selection began, Kissel informed the presiding judge that he intended to mention the remarriage only during the questioning of jury candidates. He was granted permission to do so. After Kissel won the case, Dooley appealed to the Illinois Appelate Court because of Kissel's second-marriage references during jury selection and, when he lost there, to the Supreme Court where, again, the ruling went in favor of the telephone company.

These decisions established a lawyer's right during the selection process to bring up a remarriage so that any possible prior contact might be determined between potential jurors and a widow or her late or current husband, an important element in the proper use of peremptory challenges.

12

Among the many estates handled by the firm from 1950 to 1970 were four which were especially interesting.

In 1960, Austin, aided by Loren E. Juhl, an associate since graduating from Harvard Law School in 1948 and a 1956 partner, and James Archer, undertook the representation of the families of Stanley G. Harris and Hayden Harris in connection with the construction of the will of their

231

father, Norman Wait Harris, founder of one of the city's major financial institutions. A year after arriving in Chicago from his native Massachusetts in 1881 at the age of thirty-four, he had established the investment banking firm of N.W. Harris & Company with a capital of $30,000, an enterprise that was incorporated in 1907 as the Harris Trust & Savings Bank.

In addition to Stanley and Hayden, both officials of the bank at various times, there were three other children—Albert W., who succeeded to the bank's chairmanship when his father died in 1916; Norman Dwight, a Northwestern University political scientist; and Mrs. Pearl Harris MacLean.

The Harris will, drawn by another firm, was unique in several respects. It provided that the residue of Harris' estate was to be held and managed as a single trust, without any initial division between the children. Each son, if he accumulated property with a net cash value of $4 million, over and above his liabilities, was granted the right to withdraw "his equal share" of the trust. In 1918, Albert satisfied the trustees that he met the requirements and withdrew his one-fifth share. The other sons refrained from withdrawing their shares, although they could have qualified.

In 1958, Norman Dwight Harris died, leaving no descendants, and the question was whether the share he might have been entitled to withdraw would remain in the trust for the benefit of the other children and their descendants, or whether Albert's "share" would be augmented by one-fourth of Norman's share. On behalf of the families of the other children, the firm argued that since Albert had withdrawn completely from the trust he and his family had no further interest in it and that only the other children should benefit from Norman's share.

The case was argued by Juhl in 1961 before Master in Chancery Arthur A. Sullivan, later a judge of the Illinois Appellate Court, and next before Circuit Judge Cornelius J. Harrington, both of whom held in favor of the position advocated by the firm. By agreement of the family, Judge Harrington's decision was accepted, and no appeal was taken.

13

Robert Allerton, scion of a pioneer Chicago family and a multimillionaire art collector and philanthropist, was assisted by the firm in many matters, three of them unusual: his adoption of an adult, his estate planning, and the administration of his estate.

In 1922, Allerton had been invited to a "Dads Day" football game in the University of Illinois stadium at Champaign and a dinner in the Zeta Psi fraternity house. Because Allerton was a childless bachelor and the parents of John Wyatt Gregg, an undergraduate architectural student, were dead, the two were paired for the festivities and thereafter became close friends. Upon graduation, Gregg worked a few years for a Chicago architectural firm and then on various projects at Allerton's art-filled Georgian mansion on his 12,000-acre farm at Monticello in central Illinois. From 1938 on, the two spent part of each year in Monticello and part on Allerton's Hawaiian estate on the island of Kauai. When, in 1959, the Illinois legislature amended the Adoption Act to permit, for the first time, the adoption of an adult, Frank L. Bixby, a 1953 associate from the University of Wisconsin Law School and a 1963 partner, called the amendment to the attention of Avery, who had handled Allerton's legal affairs for some years. Avery advised Allerton of the change in the law and, with the permission of his client and Gregg, filed a petition for Gregg's adoption by Allerton. Early in 1960, Judge Henry Timmons Dighton in Piatt County Court in Monticello entered a decree for the adoption.

Allerton died in 1964 after a fall in his Hawaiian home and in his will, drawn by Avery and Bixby, who had been named a partner the previous year, Gregg was bequeathed the Kauai house and personal effects that included paintings and sculpture. The Art Institute, which Allerton had served as a trustee for many years and where he had supplemented his gifts of works by Van Gogh, Ingres, Rodin, Daumier, and Picasso by establishing in 1928 the Agnes Allerton Wing—later renamed the Agnes Allerton Gallery—to honor his mother and to exhibit his and others' collections of textiles, was designated to receive two-thirds of the income from millions left in perpetual trust, with the other third to the Honolulu Academy of Art. The estate plan conceived by Bixby and carried out by him and Avery gave Gregg a large outright bequest instead of a life income in the entire estate. This greatly reduced death taxes on the estate and Gregg's income taxes. Gregg thereby benefitted substantially and the art museums started to receive income immediately instead of upon Gregg's ultimate death. In recognition of Allerton's services and gifts, the Art Institute's main building was renamed for him.

The principal problem in administering Allerton's estate was the valuation of his ninety-three-acre valley, Lauai-Kai, once owned by Hawaii's last ruler, Queen Emma. The government attempted to impose an estate tax on the theory that the property's "highest and best use" would be for constructing an elaborate high-rise hotel complex. But the court sustained the estate's contention for a much lower valuation based on residential use.

14

A client then acknowledged to be the largest landowner in Illinois was Thomas A. Scully. His father, William, had migrated from Ireland in 1850 and proceeded to buy up land in central Illinois—mostly from Mexican War veterans who had been given parcels by the government in lieu of cash bonuses—for as low as $1.25 an acre. Each year he added more land, leasing much of what he acquired to tenant farmers. With his British-born son, trained at England's Royal College of Agriculture, he developed advanced soil conservation and farming techniques. By the time the elder Scully died in 1906, he had built a virtual empire that consisted of 246,000 acres of rich farmland scattered throughout Illinois and four other midwestern states. Thomas Scully inherited a substantial portion of the vast holdings. He sold several thousand Missouri acres in 1941 for $1.1 million to the government for a munitions plant site, but retained some 46,000 around Lincoln, the seat of Logan County where the estate offices were situated in a red sandstone building.

In 1952, Scully, then eighty, came to Austin for counsel about his will. In preceding years, he had spent much time in England, where an early marriage produced three daughters and a son. After he and his wife, Isabel, were divorced in London in 1921, he married again and fathered two more sons, Michael and Peter. As discussions progressed with Austin and Loren Juhl, it became clear that Scully intended to disinherit his first wife and children. Austin sought to persuade him to discard that notion, but Scully was stubborn in his belief that no trouble would result because of his decision. So a will was drawn and trusts established in accord with Scully's wishes. When he died in the summer of 1961, he left most of his estate of $7.5 million in land and securities in trust for his widow, Violet, and their sons.

Before long, James Dooley, in his first major will contest, filed suit in Logan County Circuit Court at the direction of the first marriage's children challenging the will and trusts. The main charge in his bill was that Scully had been mentally incompetent and "unduly influenced" when the will and trusts had been made. There followed nearly seven years of legal conflict. As potential witnesses, neither Austin nor Juhl nor anyone else in the firm could appear as attorneys of record, so the services of Peter Fitzpatrick, an experienced trial lawyer, were secured. In addition to court proceedings, depositions were taken in this country and in Europe from some 200 persons, including a grandson of the Aga Khan. After a copious accumulation of testimony and frequent lawyers' conferences, the outcome was a settlement in May 1968 for $950,000 and an affirmation of Austin's view that, as he later recorded in his memoirs, "it is unwise, however strong the emotions, to completely disinherit an heir."

15

In contrast to the battle over the Scully estate was the firm's involvement in that of Lyle M. Spencer. Back in 1938, Spencer, then in his mid-twenties, was a founder, in a one-room office on Chicago's Near North Side, of Science Research Associates, a firm to develop educational and psychological tests. Acclaim and success came soon; two years later he was named by the United States Chamber of Commerce as one of the country's ten outstanding young men. After World War II, in which he served as an officer in the Army's Information and Education Division and was instrumental in developing research and analysis techniques and the point system by which millions of servicemen returned to civilian life, his enterprise expanded swiftly. To the tests were added various systems and scores of publications and teaching devices designed to give vocational, academic, and personal guidance and to improve training and learning methods in classrooms on all grade levels and assorted industries.

The firm's representation of Spencer's ingenious company began with its complete reorganization and the subsequent sale of securities by which it became publicly-held. By 1964, with SRA materials in use at some 20,000 public and parochial schools and in 5,000 business and industrial corporations and government agencies, Spencer received a bid from International Business Machines Corporation to acquire his company. Under Harlowe Bowes' direction, the assets of the company were transferred to a newly formed IBM subsidiary in exchange for 239,000 shares of IBM stock. Two years later, Spencer went on the IBM board of directors while continuing to be president of the new SRA subsidiary. He also was active in many civic and professional affairs ranging from the chairmanship of the city's Roosevelt University to membership on the board of the

Young Presidents' Organization. Early in 1968, the firm—with Bowes and Bixby in central roles—helped to establish the non-profit Spencer Foundation whose stated purpose was "to propagate the development of the educational processes, wherever learning occurs." On that August 21, Spencer died at fifty-seven in Passavant Hospital. When his will, drawn by Bixby, was filed in Cook County Probate Court, the accompanying inventory set the worth of Spencer's holdings in IBM stocks and other securities and property at $88 million. Substantial bequests, directly and in trusts, were made to Spencer's widow, Catherine, and each of their four sons, along with cash gifts to many business aides and employees. The bulk of the estate was left to the Spencer Foundation, whose board Bowes and later Bixby served as chairman in subsequent years when the foundation made grants of more than $37 million and its assets rose to $120 million.

NEVER IN its long lifetime had the firm found reason for consolidating with another. But in 1972 consideration was given to such a move, and it was soon followed by action toward that end.

The progenitor of the firm that was to merge with Sidley & Austin was started by Robert F. Carney in 1937. In his undergraduate days at the University of Wisconsin, Carney excelled scholastically and as a football tackle, then went to Harvard Law School. Upon graduation in 1930 in the same class with, among others, William Avery, he was hired as an associate by the Milwaukee firm of Lines, Spooner & Quarles. A major client was International Cellucotton Products Company, the sole distributor of Kleenex tissues and Kotex sanitary napkins and other commodities manufactured by the Kimberly-Clark Corporation centered in Neenah, Wisconsin. Gradually, Carney came to spend most of his time on this company's matters, so much so that he was in Chicago far more often than in Milwaukee. By agreement with the law firm, he moved to Chicago where, early in 1937, he opened an office at 231 South LaSalle Street; its outer door, despite the relatively limited space for himself, a secretary, and a rudimentary library, bore the rather grand appellation of "The Law Offices of Robert F. Carney."

One of the vexing problems that had long confronted International Cellucotton and its president, Charles Sumner Pearce, arose from the widespread practice by some merchants of cutting prices for Kotex and Kleenex, which they used as "loss leaders" to attract customers. Respond-

Robert F. Carney

ing to the need to maintain control of such prices, Carney devised a plan at whose core was the retention of title to the trademarked products. He well knew that there was no difficulty in consigning merchandise to wholesalers for eventual sale in the market place but that the very word *consignment* if coupled with other activities in a particular state, might result in the consignor being held resident there for tax purposes, whereas the word *factor* described a less close relationship between the consignor and consignee. So Carney applied the phrase *del credere factor* to denote an International Cellucotton wholesaler-customer who guaranteed the credit of its product-purchasers. The trademark-owner could then control the merchandise in the hands of the factors, but could not extend that control beyond that point. To avoid any charges of collusion or conspiracy, International Cellucotton held no discussions of the price-cutters' activities with the factor or, for that matter, with any price-cutters. Its main recourse when a dealer cut prices repeatedly was to direct the factor not to make any future sales of Kleenex and Kotex to the offending merchant. The concept actually was not new but its application to trademarked products was. The outcome was virtual elimination of price-cutting of International Cellucotton's products.

Another company benefitted from Carney's idea. In 1935, Charles

Luckman, an architect turned innovative salesman, had come to the Pepsodent Company after scoring remarkable sales records for the Colgate-Palmolive-Peet Company. As Pepsodent's sales manager, he was faced with the same kind of problem that had beset International Cellucotton. Scores of cut-rate merchants and chain stores were selling the company's dentifrice products far below cost—in trade terms, *footballing*. Independent dealers, mainly drug store owners who constituted Pepsodent's mainstay, complained loudly and steadily. Control was imperative.

Carney's other principal client in his first Chicago months was the Sherman-Marquette advertising agency whose president, Stuart Sherman, knew Luckman well. He referred Luckman to Carney, and Carney set up for Pepsodent a factor-consignment system similar to International Cellucotton's by which it kept title to its toothpaste and allied products until druggists and other dealers sold them. This prevented the price-cutters from continuing their practices. Carney became Pepsodent's counsel, and, as sales rose and the company prospered, Luckman was soon on his way to new executive and managerial feats. Carney and the lawyers who joined him in ensuing months and years would be on hand to deal with legal matters along that way and in other areas.

Among those who came into Carney's firm were two other Harvard Law School alumni. G. Kenneth Crowell was hired in early 1940 after eight years of practice in Milwaukee and as Wisconsin's deputy director of

G. Kenneth Crowell

securities and Russell M. Baird shortly after his graduation in June 1941. All were deep into labors—general corporate work, litigation, copyright matters, and specialized contract work relating to arrangements between national advertisers and radio personalities—when the Japanese attacked Pearl Harbor. Before long, Carney and Baird were headed for Navy commissions and Crowell for the Army Counter Intelligence Corps.

Before leaving, Carney, having notified all his clients, arranged with the highly-regarded Taylor, Miller, Busch & Boyden firm, then in the same building, to take over all pending matters. He asked especially that Morris I. Leibman, one of its ablest associates, be used extensively. Carney had come to know Leibman well, often asking him for assistance in some matters because of his own relative unfamiliarity with Illinois law. As class president of the 1927 graduating class of Waller High School in Chicago's Lincoln Park district, Leibman had been undecided about his future, although he had gained considerable distinction as a speaker and champion debater. A former fellow-student, Kathryn Busch, enlisted the aid of her father, Francis X. Busch, a senior partner at the firm, in getting Leibman a part-time job there as office boy and assistant switchboard operator while attending the University of Chicago. The association with Busch, in earlier years a colleague of Clarence Darrow's and recently the city's corporation counsel, and another partner, Laurens G. Hastings, motivated him to become a lawyer. But by the time he was ready to start his legal education, his funds were low, and his father was unable to help with tuition because of financial reverses brought on by the depression. He intended to work days and go to night classes at DePaul University Law School, which Busch had once headed. But Busch urged him to attend University of Chicago Law School, and the firm paid for his tuition. When Leibman graduated in 1933, he became a fulltime associate, working mostly with Busch ("I carried his briefcase") and soon was amassing wide and varied experience in everything from divorce suits to mail fraud cases and developing a reputation as a knowledgeable and resourceful lawyer.

2

As World War II drew to an end, Carney and Crowell were the first in their firm to return to Chicago. Leibman was now the senior associate at Taylor, Miller, Busch & Boyden. When Carney asked him to join in forming a new firm with Crowell and him as partners, Leibman readily agreed. On November 1, 1945, the Carney, Crowell and Leibman three-room office opened on the seventh floor of 208 South LaSalle Street, with the elevated trains rumbling past its rear windows. Before long, Baird was back from Navy service that included months on a submarine chaser. From the war, too, came two more Harvard men: D. Benjamin Williams, whose specialties were probate and real estate law, and Russell O. Bennett, a colleague of Leibman's at Taylor, Miller, Busch & Boyden. Bennett was well-versed in tax and corporate law and had been a fellow-officer of Crowell's in Army intelligence.

With these and others hired as associates and with clients increasing, larger quarters were soon needed. In 1947, a new suite of offices with innovative design and decor was inaugurated on the twelfth floor. Luckman, risen by that time to the presidency of Lever Brothers after that giant soap manufacturing conglomerate purchased the Pepsodent Company in 1944, reverted temporarily to an architect's role and planned the layout. He secured Raymond Loewy, pre-eminent in the field of industrial design, to fashion and outfit the offices. In decided contrast to the traditionally somber decor of most law offices, the new quarters featured bleached woods, glass partitions, pastel carpeting, modern furniture, white raw silk draperies, fresh-cut floral arrangements in the reception area, an occasional coffee table of antique Chinese carved panels, and leather chairs throughout in a variety of colors. Carney's office was especially striking. Among distinctive features were an enormous lightwood desk covered with red Spanish leather and containing a side drawer in which a telephone was concealed, and two sofas with dark brown fabric coverings, elaborately styled gold metal lamps, pieces of Chinese sculpture, and reproductions of Picasso paintings encased in lightwood frames. The modern decor attracted visitors and compliments from members of the business and legal communities.

At the outset, the new firm's clients included mainly those Carney served in the pre-war years and several that Leibman brought with him. Initially, most work was devoted to the preparation of contracts, real estate transactions, wills, anti-trust questions, litigation, and other customary matters. Of importance then and for the future was the establishment of its basic philosophy. A key ingredient was to carry on a practice oriented to business clients, serving them not case by case but totally and maintaining so close a relationship and becoming an integral part of their operations that errors and consequent litigation could be avoided and

241

efficiency achieved. "Preventive medicine" was the term applied by the partners to this central component of the firm's endeavors. "We were trained in those days," Bennett recalled later, "to spend as much time as possible in the clients' offices, with the intention of making them realize the importance of the legal element in the business equation. We used to stop sometimes in their offices even before we got down to our own. That was unusual then and maybe the fact that we were a small firm was what made it acceptable for us to do that. We were younger and newer and more ready to try a different kind of approach, to do things differently from the established firms."

One such client was Foote, Cone & Belding, created in 1943 by three of Albert D. Lasker's executives in his mighty Lord & Thomas advertising agency. For four decades, Lasker had been a titan in his field, hailed as "the father of modern advertising" because of pioneering methods and techniques he introduced while developing Lord & Thomas into one of the country's largest and wealthiest agencies. In 1942, Lasker decided to liquidate his firm so he could devote himself to philanthropic enterprises and public service. At year's end, he turned over his clients to the new firm bearing the names of Emerson Foote, Fairfax M. Cone, and Don Belding, who had been executive vice-presidents in charge, respectively, of the Lord & Thomas offices in New York, Chicago, and Los Angeles. The trio took up where Lasker had left off, continuing top-flight services with attention to a company maxim that had long prevailed: "Honest advertising is good business."

Early in 1946, the new agency sought legal services in connection with World War II excess profits taxes that represented a threat to its financial stability. For years, Lord & Thomas had represented the Pepsodent Company, with Lasker taking the lead in devising effective advertising campaigns that helped to produce excellent results. Luckman had continued the association after formation of Foote, Cone & Belding and he now recommended to Cone that Carney, Crowell and Leibman be employed to deal with the matter of the excess profits taxes.

The effect of this levy, originally legislated by Congress to increase needed governmental revenues for expanded national defense programs in pre-World War II years, was to tax at confiscatory rates—90 percent and more—that portion of a corporation's income that exceeded its excess profits credit. In general, the taxed corporation could use as that credit either the amount of its average income in a 1936–39 base period or an

242

amount equal to 8 percent of its invested capital. The amount assessed against the agency for the first three years of its existence came to $2 million, of which it paid $1.38 million and was allowed to defer the remaining liability of $625,000. In the excess profits tax law, however, was a relief provision that seemed applicable to the agency because the taxes imposed on it were based on income from 1936 to 1939, a period before it started in business. So, in this very first of many functions for the agency, the firm, early in 1946, filed with the Internal Revenue Service a claim for relief. Carney was in charge, with Bennett, summoned from terminal military leave, assisting in the collection of data, preparation of memoranda and briefs, and in the hearings and conferences. A central point in their presentation was that inasmuch as the agency was not in existence in the 1936–39 base period and its invested capital was not a relevant standard on which to base its normal earnings, there could be established "a fair and just amount representing normal earnings to be used as a constructive average base period net income" in determining the excess profits credit.

There followed more than four years of conferences in Chicago and Washington, during which the agency claimed a constructive average 1944–46 income of $1.6 million, which would have resulted in no excess profits tax. The welcome outcome, in 1951, was approval of the agency's claim by the Commissioner of Internal Revenue and then by a joint congressional committee, with cancellation of its $625,000 deferred liability and, in addition, a cash refund of $115,000. The action brought about a 70 percent increase in the agency's worth. Thus began a long-lasting relationship in which, in addition to dealing with legal problems, the firm acted as an adviser on language and product claims in every piece of advertising copy. The agency was now the first in its field to use a law firm on a steady, intimate basis—virtually as its general counsel—rather than for sporadic purposes, an association later duplicated by others.

The law firm's advice on advertising claims and content was not always heeded by an agency client. In one important instance, Vincent Riggio, president of American Tobacco Company since the death of George Washington Hill in 1946, balked at counsel about claims in advertisements for its Lucky Strike cigarettes. The agency had prepared a series of ads, the first of which was "Among tobacco men it's Lucky Strike two to one!" The text of another read, "Among agricultural department inspectors it's Lucky Strike four to one!" Although the agency had done its research carefully, Foote had reservations about its format because it involved government functionaries. He conferred with Leibman, who warned firmly against use of this ad. "It's bad because the government won't like it," he said, "and if the government won't like it you'll have lots of problems. Don't do it. It'll be bad for the agency." Foote agreed, but Riggio was convinced that there would be no governmental complaints. Within months, however, the ads were abruptly canceled. As Leibman had predicted, high officials from the Department of Agriculture called Riggio to ask that the references to the inspectors be eliminated. This experience and other disagreements with Riggio led to an event that shocked the nation's advertising community. In March 1948, Foote, as president of the agency, announced that it was resigning the $12 million-a-year account it had handled for the American Tobacco Company since its very first days. "We do so neither in anger nor in rancor," he said. "But if an agency can't do the kind of advertising it believes in, it ought to stop taking commissions."

3

Through its representation of Foote, Cone & Belding, the firm, in another of what Baird called "growth events," came to represent Gillette Safety Razor Company after its acquisition of a St. Paul company making the phenomenally successful Toni home permanent-wave kits for America's women.

The Toni Company's beginnings in 1944 were quite modest. Its president, R. Neison Harris, had gone into the beauty-shop supplies business in his native St. Paul after graduating from Yale University in 1936. Then he conceived an idea for an inexpensive way for women to do permanent waves in their homes. Harris created a kit comprising fiber hair curlers, a gentle waving lotion, and a neutralizer for setting the curls. At a friend's suggestion, Harris called his new product Toni—to denote its stylish character—and embarked on a store-to-store canvass to urge druggists in the Twin Cities to stock it. After some early disappointments, distribution expanded in the Midwest and elsewhere and within a year Harris's fledgling company had 35 percent of the market. His older brother, Irving, left the aircraft parts business in 1946 to handle Toni's administration and advertising, with Foote, Cone & Belding as its agency. The company's sales spurted not only because of the excellence of its product but because of the widespread publicity engendered by its advertisements bearing a photograph of two pretty twin sisters—one with a Toni permanent, the other with a beauty-parlor wave—and the catchy slogan, "Which twin has the Toni?" The firm, with Leibman and Baird taking the lead, successfully protected the all-important slogan against an attack by the Federal Trade Commission. Throughout 1947, Toni kits sold at the rate of one million a month, and annual sales headed toward a mark of $20 million.

In that year, the Harrises realized that it would be wise to sell their prospering company to a big, well-established concern. Officials of The Gillette Company, then engaged in a survey of home-permanent makers, were impressed with Toni's sales figures and with the Harris brothers. After a number of conferences, the Gillette directors on that December 12 authorized the purchase for $12 million, with an assured $8 million more as a share of future Toni profits. By terms of the agreement, the Harrises were elected to the Gillette board, and a decision was made to move the Toni division, with Neison as president and Irving as vice-president, to Chicago. Carl J. Gilbert, of the parent company's Boston law firm, had played a vital part in the negotiations, and when the shift was pending, he asked Cone to recommend a good local law firm. When Cone suggested Carney, Crowell and Leibman, Gilbert was delighted, for he was a Harvard Law School friend of Carney's and Crowell's. The law firm arranged for the lease for the Toni division, and soon it was embarked on other work for it as annual sales continued to rise—in the first year after the move from $60 million to $86 million—and new hair-care products were launched with advertising and publicity campaigns that required the close attention of lawyers. As time went on, and with Gilbert appointed a Gillette vice-president in charge of subsidiaries, the relationship with Toni advanced and flourished and extended to Gillette itself, with Leibman and Baird in main roles.

A client whose many years of representation by the firm started in the late 1940s was Commerce Clearing House, the world's largest tax and business law reporting service. Ever since 1913, shortly after enactment of the first federal income tax law, this company had been publishing voluminous loose-leaf reports on law, taxes, and trade regulations. It employed in its Michigan Avenue headquarters a staff of several hundred lawyers and assorted experts and maintained reporters with legal training and experience at state legislatures and Congress and governmental

245

agencies dealing with tax, trade, and banking laws. Its reports, crammed with all kinds of information and data, were of great value to lawyers and business executives who needed to be kept aware of all aspects of legislation that might affect their clients or their companies. In addition to these loose-leaf volumes, annual summaries based on the amount of federal excise taxes collected were issued to inform the general public about drops or boosts in the consumption of liquor, beer, wine, and tobacco and purchase of tickets for plays, concerts, and sports events.

One morning, a salesman with whom the firm had dealt in ordering CCH publications for its library called on Leibman to say he had recommended the firm to his president, Justus L. Schlichting, to help resolve a copyright problem. Schlichting summoned Leibman to his office to tell him that a competitor in Indiana had violated CCH's rights in some of its publications and that he wanted to sue to protect its copyrights. Leibman explained that the firm had no copyright specialist and that out-of-state litigation was expensive and time-consuming. But he added that the firm would be pleased to handle the matter if given the opportunity. Leibman was making progress toward a settlement with the Indiana lawyers when the competitor decided to refer the issue to New York lawyers with whom Leibman now resumed negotiations.

After several trips to New York, Leibman worked out a settlement with the lawyers there and assured Schlichting that litigation could be avoided. He drew up a contract with details of the settlement and sent it to New York. It was returned with a letter so filled with contradictions and ambiguities pertaining to the settlement that had been agreed upon in discussions that litigation seemed inevitable. At this point, Schlichting was out of patience, but he reluctantly agreed to Leibman's suggestion that the solution was to write an equally ambiguous letter to the opposing lawyers. In a few days, he received a signed contract and a check that disposed of the matter. Schlichting was astounded and impressed with what had been accomplished.

Other assignments from him came to the firm, and in ensuing years it served, in effect, as CCH's general counsel in varied matters such as expansion of its range and diversity of reports beyond 150 in a new $4 million plant, after 1957, on Chicago's far Northwest Side in which a staff of over 1,000 turned out as many as seven million pages each day. In 1959, when Robert C. Bartlett became CCH's new and innovative president, he sought a broader range of services. Working with Baird and others in the firm, he acquired a controlling interest in the Computax Corporation, then a fledgling computer tax-processing company that provided a system enabling accountants and tax lawyers to process federal and state income tax returns on computers; the company has since become a major and growing part of the CCH family. Foremost among acquisitions of other specialty concerns was Facts on File, Incorporated, whose output includes a weekly news digest, yearbooks, and indices of current events and periodic summaries of major happenings in continuing news areas.

The firm's relationship with Charles Luckman had continued after he was made president of Lever Brothers in 1946. An interesting matter in the summer of 1949 concerned the desire of Bob Hope to tape his Pepsodent-sponsored weekly radio shows instead of doing them live. Luckman was adamant against the idea because he felt that Hope's witty commentaries on current events might be outdated and lack their usual spontaneity. When Hope's lawyers sought to bring the issue to arbitration in Los Angeles, Luckman dispatched Leibman to the West Coast with the order: "Win—or don't come home!" Leibman was well aware that similar conflicts with other performers before boards of arbitration composed mainly of men from the entertainment industry had been decided in favor of the performers. He argued vigorously before the American Arbitration Association that the hearing be held elsewhere, either in Boston, Chicago, or New York. Moreover, he discovered that Hope's original contract with Pepsodent, drawn in 1939, had been superseded by a new one with Lever in 1943, which gave the company the right to determine how the programs were to be produced. Subsequently, Leibman's request to remove the case from Los Angeles was granted and later that year a three-man board in New York rendered a 2-1 decision in Lever's favor, the crucial vote being cast by Eugene Breitenbach, a notable corporation lawyer and future judge. That ruling came without any witnesses being presented but on Leibman's motion to dismiss Hope's petition on strict legal grounds. "The intent of the contract," Breitenbach declared, "clearly was for live broadcasting inasmuch as there was no legal verbiage that could be interpreted otherwise." In its report, *Variety* noted Luckman's reluctance to have shows, especially those at military installations, taped, and added, "The no-tape ruling will not curtail peregrinations materially and Hope will continue to bat around the country and keep pouring gold into his bulging coffers."

247

In that same year, plans were drawn for the erection of a $6 million, twenty-story building on New York's elegant Park Avenue, into which the Lever headquarters would move from Cambridge, Massachusetts. At one point, when Crowell and Williams were making frequent trips on the overnight Twentieth Century passenger train to supervise legal details connected with the project, a bid was made by Luckman for Carney, Crowell and Leibman to become Lever Brothers' main counsel. The compliment was appreciated—"heady wine," Leibman called it—but the invitation was not accepted.

With the development of Lever House well under way, Luckman resumed the career for which he had been educated two decades earlier at the University of Illinois and in which he could find no work in the depression year of 1931—architecture. The law firm retained him as a client when he and William Pereira, a friend and architectural classmate at the university, organized an architectural-engineering company in Los Angeles only a few months after he left Lever Brothers. In the next eight years, their firm was responsible for over $1 billion worth of construction before dissolving amicably. Luckman's next step was to form Charles Luckman Associates, which by 1968 had a corps of 300 architects and four offices across the country. He sold this company to the Ogden Corporation, which then formed the Ogden Development Corporation, with Luckman as president, to offer clients a combination of architecture, engineering, leasing, management, consultation, and research services. In all phases of these varied ventures, he frequently availed himself of the services of the law firm whose founding partner had helped to ease his marketing woes at Pepsodent years before.

4

That partner, Robert Carney, was no longer a member of the firm he had created in 1937. He had left in August 1951 to be chairman of Foote, Cone & Belding. Earlier that year, Emerson Foote had departed to assume the presidency of the much larger McCann-Erickson advertising agency.*

---

*Foote's tenure at McCann-Erickson ended in 1964 when, as chairman, he resigned to avoid "a conflict of interest" between the firm's profits from overseas tobacco accounts and his own strong views about the perils of cigarette smoking, about which he announced he wanted to be free to take a public position. He did so vigorously in subsequent years.

Foote's departure left a major gap in the executive structure. Cone proposed to Carney and Leibman that Carney come over as president. Carney was receptive to the offer, but he opted for the chairmanship, which represented a corporate policy position whereas the presidency as an operating function ought to be held by an experienced executive from the advertising industry. Cone and Belding agreed and announcements of the shift were duly issued to the press and the agency's 1,000 employees. There followed a realignment of responsibilities among top-level management, but the relationship remained unchanged between the agency and the law firm, which now took on the name of Crowell and Leibman.

The law firm had been steadily strengthened by the addition of young lawyers with sterling academic records. Foremost among them were members of the Harvard Law School class of 1948 led by Gale A. Christopher and including Jack D. Voss, Kendall M. Cole, Donald S. MacLeod, and Thomas O'Boyle. And by now the firm had achieved further experience and a reputation in matters relating to marketing and advertising, trademarks and fair trade regulations, and for maintaining a kind of close relationship with clients. "We spent a lot of time in their offices," Leibman later recalled. "We liked to say that we lived with them. And we took a very active part in helping them reach various decisions and drawing up plans even for non-legal purposes."

XII

Crowell and Leibman 1951–1962
Leibman, Williams, Bennett and Baird 1962–1964
Leibman, Williams, Bennett, Baird and Minow 1965–1972

IN THE first half of the 1950s, Crowell and Leibman remained comparatively small—by 1955 it had thirteen lawyers—and its roster of clients included mainly those from the preceding decade. Among several new ones were the Simoniz Company, whose new executive vice-president, W. Gardner Barker, had dealt with the firm when he was a Lever Brothers executive in charge of its Pepsodent division in the late 1940s, the Kimberly-Clark Corporation, and the Nelson Brothers furniture chain.

Soon there was a top-level change. At the start of 1955, Crowell accepted a vice-presidency at Kimberly-Clark shortly after it acquired International Cellucotton Products Company, whose affairs Crowell had handled after Carney's departure. Because he was not certain that he would remain there permanently or return to his law practice, Crowell's name was retained in the firm. Leibman now was the senior managing partner, sharing responsibility for running the firm with Williams, Bennett, and Baird, who had been elevated to partnerships three years earlier. They also continued to hold regular discussions with associates about pending matters, cases won or lost, and weaknesses in the firm's structure and organization ("The holes in the Swiss cheese," Leibman called them).

At about this time, Leibman was asked to write an article for the *Illinois Bar Journal* embodying his central thoughts about legal practice. Titled significantly "The Changed Order of the Client-Lawyer Relationship," it appeared in that February's issue.

At once, Leibman made clear that he was always interested in every

Morris I. Leibman

aspect of a client company's activities, even personal and domestic problems of its employees. He emphasized the need to meet fresh challenges confronting him and the client. Increasingly, a business decision, he maintained, required a legal decision at virtually every step, from the hiring of employees and raising or lowering salaries to the pricing of products or establishing discounts. More than before, lawyers old and young alike, he asserted, needed to be social scientists, legislators, historians, and philosophers.

Delineating the mechanics of such lawyer-client relationships, Leibman stressed broader training of young lawyers, almost precisely typifying that which prevailed at Crowell and Leibman. Continuing legal education was, of course, essential but, wrote Leibman, "We should simultaneously be training them to the new dimensions of the day." This meant their development as counselors able to detect legal problems and work out techniques for prompt group solution, ready service—"whether it be answering mail the same day, returning calls or all the important courtesies of protocol"—and emphasis on a firm's function as an added, integrated, yet anonymous, department of a corporation and a de-emphasis of the lawyer's "technical personality and the pseudo-professional trappings."

As he persistently encouraged his associates and partners to do, he counseled frequent visits to clients. And his concluding view of the future was challenging: "The greatest days of legal practice are still ahead of us.

251

The creative opportunities are far beyond any we have ever experienced in the past. The client's growing needs are here. Each of us has to develop a breadth of vision and depth of perspective geared to these new and growing opportunities. . . . If we can serve our clients on a superior level of general counselling, then recognition and respect for the law and the lawyer is certain.''

No opportunity was lost by Leibman, in his role as paterfamilias, to impress the message of that article on associates. Thomas H. Morsch, an enthusiastic newcomer that year from Northwestern University Law School, later recalled Leibman's ''true life lessons in the form of one liners.'' Among these were ''You have to learn the violin before you can lead the orchestra'' and ''Stop over at the client's office and have a cup of coffee with him'' and ''Don't be afraid to call the client at his club on a weekend, he'll love it'' and ''Keep notes like the accountants keep notes'' and ''Never ask the client to come see you, go see him.''

2

While Leibman continued as a generalist, there was a sharpening of the firm's overall structure in 1956 by the organization of three primary sections covering specialized areas of practice. Heading each was a senior partner—Williams on wills, trusts, real estate, labor, and litigation, Bennett on taxation and corporate and securities matters, and Baird on anti-trust, advertising, fair trade, radio, and television. Present and future associates would concentrate on specialties but were advised to keep in mind Leibman's admonitions, whether expressed orally or in his magazine article and memos, to maintain sustained relationships with clients, no matter what their needs might be at a specific time. With the trend toward specialization and the growth in the ranks of associates—in 1957, to join Morsch, came two Northwestern University Law School graduates, Franklin A. Chanen and Robert E. Mason, and John E. Robson from Harvard Law School and two years in the Army, and in 1960 Neil Flanagin from University of Michigan Law School—and the ascent in 1956 of the ''Harvard Group'' of 1948 to partnerships, there was an apparent call for senior partners to assume expanded roles. Bennett expressed this in a memorandum to Williams and Baird: ''If we are to keep up with the changing character of the expanding firm, we must devote less time to the spade work ourselves and more time to consulting with the other men, training the newer men, and with the clients.''

The prevailing philosophy that every client was the firm's rather than one belonging to an individual lawyer contributed to development of a strong fraternal feeling and a collegial atmosphere and warmth, camaraderie, and loyalty. This sense of fellowship was reflected at annual Christmas season dinners. In the firm's earliest days these had started in the Racquet Club, and at each, in the memory of one member, "The linen, silver and glassware were impeccable, the food exquisite and the offerings of Bacchus outstanding and plentiful." For one of the early dinners, Baird proposed a program format in which each lawyer was called on for a three-minute talk on whatever subject pleased him, whether in jest or serious contemplation. In the 1950s, especially at the instigation of the 1948 Harvard Group, there began the rite of offering skits that aimed genial barbs at the senior partners in much the same way that the Chicago Bar Association's yearly "Christmas Spirits" frolics made satirical assaults on local, national, and international figures and events in the legal profession and in government, politics, entertainment, and other fields. Baird created most of these amusingly irreverent playlets as he did many of the "Christmas Spirits" shows for a decade and more starting in 1954.

3

One of the matters in the decade in which the firm performed key services was the purchase by Gillette of Paper Mate Pen Company, whose founder was Patrick J. Frawley, Jr.

Frawley was a remarkably energetic entrepreneur who had gone into the ball-point pen business in 1949 at twenty-six. This kind of pen, invented in the late 1930s by a Parisian newspaper proofreader named Laszlo Biro, fed ink around a tiny ball encased in a miniscule socket. During World War II and for a while thereafter, it gained revolutionary popularity. One of its earliest manufacturers, Reynolds International Pen Company, advertised it as "the fantastic, atomic era, miraculous pen" that was guaranteed to write under water, and in a single week a New York department store sold 30,000 of them at $12.50 each. By 1948, there were dozens of other manufacturers whose pen prices ranged as low as twenty-five cents and as high as $25—and provoked customer complaints that none, whatever the cost, performed well; banks, for one, refused to accept checks written with them because it was possible for a forger to lift ball-pointed signatures and transfer them to other checks. Within months, the ball-point pen business appeared to be headed for extinction. Frawley, then a successful import-exporter in San Francisco, had lent money to a failing company that supplied parts for the pens. He took over that firm and, with the aid of a chemist whose formula made possible a non-fading ink, turned out excellent pens. A master salesman, Frawley overcame initial resistance from customers with unhappy experiences with inferior pens of similar design; in one instance he persuaded two San Francisco banks to honor checks written with one of the pens he called "Paper Mate" and thereupon was able to advertise that his product was bank-approved. By 1951, sales of Frawley's pens amounted to $9 million annually and attracted the interest of Neison Harris, then heading Gillette's Toni division. Early in 1955, Frawley received a bid from Eversharp, Incorporated, to sell his firm for $8 million in cash and stock, with an annual $1 million for the next decade. Instead, he invited Harris, whom he admired for his accomplishments with Toni, to buy a half-interest in Paper Mate for $1.5 million and become its chief executive officer. When Harris notified Carl Gilbert of his intention to accept Frawley's offer, Gilbert surprised him by proposing that Gillette buy Paper Mate.

To effect the purchase, Crowell and Leibman, as counsel for Gillette, became deeply engrossed in preparing sales contracts and other pertinent documents. Gale Christopher headed a six-man team that settled into rooms in Chicago's Midland Hotel to work on an around-the-clock basis, with meals at the famous Staley's steakhouse nearby and changes of white shirts furnished by the client. The team did its work well. After an all-night final negotiating meeting, with Leibman presiding at the session with the principals, announcement on that November 21 told of the purchase for $15.1 million in cash of the Paper Mate companies.

Frawley served briefly as president of Gillette's Paper Mate division before departing for other ventures. Harris succeeded him, while Stuart K. Hensley became Toni's new president and organized a management board, on which, as evidence of the law firm's involvement in its affairs, he placed Baird. One of the terms in Frawley's non-competition agreement drawn up by Christopher's team had stipulated that he would not market any writing instruments. After he joined Eversharp in 1958 as president, Frawley found it easy to abide by the pact; indeed, shortly before his arrival, Eversharp sold its pen-making subsidiary. Before long, however, he was engaging Gillette in harsh competition through Eversharp's Schick safety-razor division. Under Harris, Paper Mate continued to prosper.

254

Russell O. Bennett   Russell M. Baird

Foote, Cone & Belding remained for a time its advertising agency and
Crowell and Leibman its law firm. In 1966, in addition to its ball-point
pens Paper Mate introduced the Flair line of porous pens. Foote, Cone &
Belding's representation ended later that year and was succeeded by North
Advertising, Incorporated, another of the law firm's clients.

4

In 1962, Crowell decided to stay with Kimberly-Clark as its executive
vice-president. His decision made logical altering the firm name to
Leibman, Williams, Bennett and Baird that May.

There had been changes in the firm's legal personnel, which now had
thirteen partners and thirteen associates. Several of the members of the
1948 Harvard Group left to take executive posts with major business
firms: Kendall Cole to Scott Paper Company and later to Eastman Kodak
Company as general counsel, Donald MacLeod to American Photocopy

Equipment Corporation and then to North American Rockwell Corporation, Jack Voss to Anchor Hocking Glass Corporation, Thomas O'Boyle to Union Tank Car Company. A four-man general practice firm on the floor below that came as partners was headed by Laurens G. Hastings, who had been so helpful to Leibman in his early days at Taylor, Miller, Busch & Boyden, and David P. List, a Harvard University Law School alumnus and an experienced litigator.

Now with the firm as counsel was the brilliant Max Swiren, whom Leibman had known in his University of Chicago days. In the early 1950s, Swiren had been a law partner of Ben Heineman's, gaining control with him in 1954 of the faltering Minneapolis & St. Louis Railway through stock purchases. When Heineman became chairman of Chicago and North Western two years later, he resigned from the line as chairman of its executive committee and was succeeded by Swiren. Subsequently, the Chicago and North Western acquired the smaller carrier's assets with $3.9 million in cash, assumption of its $13.4 million in liabilities and $17.5 million of new 6 percent bonds. Left in 1960 with a shell corporation, the $3.9 million in cash and a $30 million tax loss carry forward on the sale of its physical properties, Swiren altered its nature, changed its name to MSL Industries, and set out to buy companies. Among the first were two of the law firm's clients, Heads & Threads and Universal Screw Company, leaders in making and distributing bolts, screws, washers, and fasteners to industrial users. Soon, with Leibman and Bennett chiefly involved, there were other additions, particularly of concerns manufacturing horsepower motors, blowers, fans, and steel tubing. By 1962, MSL had six companies and Swiren was chairman and majority stockholder. He then became affiliated with the law firm, maintaining an office there and enlisting the aid of Leibman and various associates in matters concerning his affluent conglomerate. Few doubted Swiren's legal acumen and ability as an entrepreneur, but lawyers who worked with him quailed at his brusque ways and temperament. In 1963, when Swiren was in failing health, Joseph T. Zoline, a corporate specialist who was of counsel to the firm, was named MSL's president to succeed Arnold Meyer, who became chairman of a newly-formed executive committee. Shortly thereafter, with his health continuing to decline, Swiren retired and moved to Honolulu, where he died in 1969. The firm's representation, with Bennett the primary lawyer, continued for several years thereafter and ended with a change in management.

5

In 1962, Erwin S. Wolfson, a London-born real estate developer whose projects in New York included construction of the Pan-American Building over the Grand Central station, called Leibman and said he was interested in real estate in Chicago. He explained that he wanted to acquire the air rights over a city block bounded by the Chicago River and Madison, Monroe, and Canal Streets for the construction of a twenty-story office building, a novel development concept for that time. Leibman and Williams were in the midst of negotiations with the city and the land owners when Wolfson died suddenly.

Ultimately, his option to lease the air space from Chicago Union Station Company, Pennsylvania Railroad, and Pittsburgh, Fort Wayne & Chicago Railway was taken over by the Tishman Realty and Construction Company, for some sixty-five years a foremost New York-based real estate firm with a deserved reputation as the world's largest builder of office and apartment buildings. Williams and several associates including James L. Marovitz, freshly arrived from Northwestern University Law School, continued to work with Tishman executives and their New York counsel in carrying forward plans for the skyscraper to be built at a cost of $20 million and for acquiring air rights to additional blocks extending along the river's west bank to Van Buren Street as sites for two more office and transportation buildings. The entire complex, at an estimated cost of $200 million, was designated as the Gateway Center and there was general agreement with Edwin Darby, the *Sun-Times* financial editor, that the development was "splendiferous . . . a pioneering boon to the city" and the catalyst in the rebirth of the Near West Side.

By 1965, the first of the skyscrapers was up, fully rented, and the second followed suit in early 1968. Construction in 1970 of the third Gateway structure, at thirty-five stories the largest of the three, necessitated remodeling of the old Romanesque Union Station and the building of an entirely new, streamlined concourse below the glassed-walled lobby of the skyscraper while passengers for trains entering or leaving were rerouted over temporary walkways. The firm handled all legal aspects of these undertakings, from the preparation of leases and contracts with the architectural firm of Skidmore, Owings and Merrill to hearings before the Illinois Commerce Commission and dealings with major Chicago banks in financing construction, and would continue to represent the Tishman real estate empire in a host of subsequent building projects.*

6

In the summer of 1963, the firm aided a long-time client in breaking precedent. That August, Foote, Cone & Belding filed a registration statement with the Securities and Exchange Commission for the sale to the public of 500,000 common shares of its stock at seventeen dollars each. It thus became first of the nation's major advertising agencies to make a public offering of its stock. The decision to do so had been reached after extended discussions on the part of the principal agency officers, including Carney as chairman, with Bennett on the corporate and securities aspects and Baird on the marketing aspects. The action was considered unusual—although others would come to duplicate it—because investment analysts were accustomed to dealing with companies that held real estate and inventories rather than one whose assets, in Cone's words, "went up and down in the elevator each day."

In an unusual and impressive appearance before the New York Society of Security Analysts, Carney not only talked frankly about the agency's prospects but about the general nature of advertising. He cited the failure of the Ford Motor Company's efforts to stimulate sales of the ill-fated Edsel automobile despite a multi-million dollar advertising campaign from 1957 to 1959 as an example of the "myth of advertising's Svengali-like control over the buying habits of the public." Generally, he said, the advertising business had grown by 5 percent annually and predicted that, barring negative economic conditions, advertising billings could reach an $18 billion mark by 1970. As for his agency, he admitted that although its growth rate had lagged behind that of total advertising volume earlier, it was now gaining at a faster pace, with $155 million in billings in 1963 and an anticipated $170 million the next year. In his favorable report on the unusual presentation, Peter Bart in the *New York Times* paid Carney and his colleagues a compliment: "The depth and candor with which they discussed their business will go far in removing the veil of mystery from what is, after all, an industry that is very much in the public eye."

*See Chapter XIV.

Leibman firm in 1962, including (*extreme left*) D. Benjamin Williams, who died in 1969, and those who later became Sidley & Austin partners: Morris I. Leibman in center; *Kneeling (second and third from left)* Thomas H. Morsch and Russell M. Baird; *Front row*: (*third from left*) Russell O. Bennett, (*fourth from left*) John H. Rockwell, (*sixth from left*) David P. List; *Back row*: (*left*) Robert E. Mason, (*third from left*) Donald A. Mackay, (*seventh from left*) Gale A. Christopher, (*eighth from left*) Neil Flanigan.

The firm continued to lay emphasis on service to its advertising agency clients. Under Baird's direction, lawyers concerned with them wholly or in part met regularly to discuss a wide range of matters, from the intensification of governmental actions—especially after the 1959–60 "payola" scandals in highly rated television quiz shows—and paying heed to the dangers inherent in false or misleading claims for products in print or electronic advertising that could spur governmental censure to keeping abreast of shifting policies in network programming. Each was advised to be persistently aware of advertising agencies' legal liability under the Federal Trade Commission Act and of potential problems stemming from such sales boosters as trading stamps, prize offers, premiums, "cents-off" coupons, and box top discounts and, in the broadest sense, the firm's responsibilities to these clients. From Commerce Clearing House came all kinds of materials on state and federal legislation pertaining to drugs and cosmetics, cosmeticians and beauticians, the dispensing and sale of drugs and "hazardous substances," advertisements on radio and television and in newspapers and periodicals, and advertising contests and promotional campaigns. Late in 1963, the advertising and anti-trust sections were   *259* merged into a single unit thereafter referred to as the "Section on Marketing and Anti-trust Law" and encompassing matters relating to advertising, trademarks, unfair competition, literary properties, statutes affecting monopolistic practices, fair trade, and marketing programs.

Morsch, elevated to a partnership the previous year, was put in charge of this section. He would soon be cited by Baird as being responsible for the vigor with which those in it tackled problems then and later, particularly as this type of practice gradually moved from one that was primarily advisory to one marked by heightened litigation that arose either from faulty advertisements that had not been submitted to the lawyers for scrutiny or claims by a company that questionable statements in a rival's commercial touting a specific product constituted unfair competition and caused financial losses. Morsch was ably assisted by Quincy White, a 1960 Harvard Law School graduate who, as Morsch became increasingly involved in litigation, assumed a growing role in the management of the firm's marketing practice.

7

Early in 1965, the firm's reputation and strength were considerably enhanced by the arrival of Newton N. Minow.

Minow had aimed for a career either in journalism or law ever since, laden with scholastic honors, he had graduated from high school in his native Milwaukee in 1944. After two years in the Army Signal Corps in the China-Burma-India theater of operations, he enrolled at Northwestern University and upon graduation entered its law school, where his instructors included Howard Trienens in criminal law and Arthur Seder in contracts and where he edited the *Illinois Law Review*, stood first in his class, and received the coveted Wigmore Award. After graduation, he was an associate for a few months with the distinguished Chicago firm of Mayer, Meyer, Austrian & Platt, when, in 1951, he was asked to join Trienens as a law clerk for United States Supreme Court Chief Justice Fred M. Vinson, replacing another Northwestern Law School alumnus, Daniel Walker, a future Illinois governor. After this service, he joined Adlai Stevenson in Springfield as an administrative assistant and worked in Stevenson's behalf in the unsuccessful 1952 Presidential race. Another stint for two years with Mayer, Meyer, Austrian & Platt followed and

Newton N. Minow

Minow then accepted a bid to join Stevenson in practice with Willard Wirtz and William McCormick Blair, Jr. When Stevenson lost his second try for the Presidency in 1956, his firm merged with the New York firm of Paul, Weiss, Rifkind, Wharton & Garrison, but retained offices in Chicago; Minow, at thirty, became its youngest partner.

In 1961, Minow was appointed chairman of the Federal Communications Commission in President Kennedy's administration at the suggestion of Robert Kennedy and the Kennedys' brother-in-law, R. Sargent Shriver. He brought with him ample knowledge and experience in communications that ranged from helping to string the first telephone line between India and China in his Army days to representing the Midwest Council for Airborne Television Instruction designed to transmit lessons from airplanes to classrooms, Encyclopaedia Britannica Films, and various television performers and executives. But for all Minow's abilities, what produced nationwide attention was his address that May to the National Association of Broadcasters in which he characterized television programming as "a vast wasteland." That speech served to touch off a sustained dialogue and comment inside and outside the television world. In addition, Minow was largely responsible for instituting, by congressional action, all-channel receivers which led to creation of hundreds of ultra-high frequency

Chief Justice Fred M. Vinson flanked by his 1951 law clerks (*right to left*)
Howard J. Trienens, James Paul and Newton N. Minow

stations, initiating appropriations for educational stations, and stimulating the initiation of dollar telephone calls anywhere in the United States after 9 p.m.

Early in 1963, Minow departed Washington for the Chicago headquarters of Encyclopaedia Britannica, Incorporated, as executive vice-president and general counsel. He had come to know Leibman during the Stevenson campaigns and the friendship had been maintained. Several times—especially after the second Stevenson loss and during Minow's tenure with the encyclopaedia company—Leibman had broached the possibility that Minow might join his firm, but these informal discussions came to naught. But one day in 1965, Minow telephoned Leibman: "I'd like to talk." They did, Minow expressing willingness to become affiliated. Leibman informed Bennett and Baird, who displayed enthusiasm over the prospect but wondered how well Minow, with his national reputation and interests, would adapt to a relatively small firm of fourteen partners and fourteen associates. More discussions followed and an agreement was drawn—until then there had never been a formal partnership agreement —reflecting Minow's insistence that whatever percentage of firm income would accrue to him would have to be covered by service to clients he brought with him. Leibman asked Bennett to prepare an agreement. When Bennett delivered the first draft, he warned that it might not reflect all that had been discussed. After Baird read it, he advised Leibman that he thought it was unfair to Minow—and fifteen minutes later Minow called to tell Leibman he thought it was unfair to Baird and Bennett. At this, Leibman summoned all three and proposed that since each thought it was unfair to the other the first draft be accepted as the ultimate document. The agreement was never referred to again. On May 1, announcement was made of the new senior partner and the firm's name was changed to Leibman, Williams, Bennett, Baird and Minow.

On his very first morning as he resumed general practice, Minow received a telephone call from an old friend, Philip M. Klutznick, a leading Chicago citizen and real estate developer with a history of innovative projects starting with Park Forest that bordered on the city's southern rim as the first of the country's "new towns" that were brought into being after World War II. "I want to be your first client," said Klutznick, thereby initiating Minow's long association with him and his company as it originated and maintained scores of enterprises throughout the nation. In addition to this new client, Minow continued to serve as special counsel for Curtis Publishing Company and Encyclopaedia Britannica and also handled special assignments for American Telephone and Telegraph, in the latter working in conjunction with Howard Trienens. Within months, he was representing fresh clients ranging from Commonwealth Edison Company and the family of Marshall Field IV, publisher of the *Sun-Times* and *Daily News* at the time of his death late that year, to Salomon Brothers and the Columbia Broadcasting System, whose chief executives he had known since his days as FCC chairman. For CBS, with Morsch assisting, he would, among other things, lead the defense of CBS's Chicago television outlet, WBBM-TV, against charges in 1967 that one of its reporters had staged a marijuana party telecast at a student rooming house on the edge of the Northwestern University campus. And as time went on he represented other important clients, always as a generalist rather than, as was increasingly the tendency in Chicago and elsewhere in the nation, concentrating on a specialty.

8

Gradually, the number of lawyers in the firm increased, from thirty-two in 1966 to forty-one in 1970, forty-two in 1971 and forty-eight early in 1972. Among the newcomers was an experienced practitioner in the specialized field of commercial law. Before joining as a partner in March 1966, A. Bruce Schimberg had spent most of his fourteen years after graduating from the University of Chicago Law School in concentrating mainly on commercial financial transactions and litigation as a member of a Chicago firm founded by his father, Archie. He brought to Leibman, Williams, Bennett, Baird and Minow a specialized kind of practice for clients engaged in the risky business of providing short term funding for growing companies with inadequate capital or companies that had been or were in trouble.

Commercial Discount Corporation had made loans totaling $8 million to Westec Corporation, a Houston geophysical instruments and electronics concern formed in 1964 through a merger of Geo Space Corporation, a maker of seismic instruments, and Western Equities, a uranium producer. Westec's stock, of which the commercial finance company held 250,000 shares, was one of the "high-flyers" of the times, soaring in two years from two dollars a share to a high of sixty-seven dollars. When an $8 million order by insiders for 160,000 shares could not be paid for, investigations began that led to criminal charges of market-rigging of Westec stock and false financial reporting of earnings. Trading in the stock on the American Stock Exchange was suspended while creditors—Commercial Discount Corporation foremost among them—converged. Westec filed for bankruptcy and a trustee was designated to attempt a complete financial reorganization. Several high company officials went to prison, and by 1969 Commercial Discount Corporation, represented by Schimberg for the firm, and other creditors had received partial settlement of claims and resumption of trading in the stock was allowed.

Another disaster had roseate origins in 1964 when Cortes W. Randell gave up his engineering job to form National Student Marketing Corporation, specializing in selling assorted products to college and high school students. Randell scored remarkable successes with the widespread sale of items ranging from beer mugs and desk pads to youth-discount air fares, low-cost insurance, and computerized horoscopes. He acquired company after company until, at its height, NSM's acquisitions numbered forty-nine and its total market value was set at $350 million. When NSM went public in 1966, a share of its stock sold for six dollars; by the end of 1969, the price was $144. But only two months later, the bubble burst. Announcement was made that the corporation had sustained a quarterly loss of $1.2 million. Investigations soon revealed that earlier reports of annual sales and earnings had been inflated and that the company's growth had been based on fraud and financial manipulations. Criminal action and a flock of lawsuits were instituted against Randell and several officers of his company and all subsequently served jail terms. The value of the stock suffered a swift and precipitous decline and ultimately it was estimated that some 4,000 stockholders lost over $100 million in the collapse.

Schimberg became involved in May 1970, at the behest of the corporation's directors. The NSM headquarters were moved from lavish Park Avenue offices in New York to Spartan accommodations on Michigan Avenue. Schimberg and several associates, principally H. Bruce Bernstein and Stephen P. Thomas, two recent Harvard Law School graduates, proceeded to try to stave off bankruptcy and to rehabilitate the company. Early in 1972, Joseph Cottrell, whose Buffalo, New York, bus company had been bought by NSM before catastrophe struck, was named by the directors to be president. Faced with an inordinate number of problems legal and financial, Cottrell, a low-keyed man in contrast to his super-kinetic predecessor, set about streamlining the corporation, with the law firm to advise and counsel, and within a few years there were beneficial results for the creditors.

9

By 1969, the firm had become more widely known to lawyers, government agencies, and businessmen outside its own circle of clients. It still was paramount in the representation of companies engaged in marketing and advertising, but its widening range of clientele now included such others of national scope as The First National Bank of Chicago, Sony Corporation, Montgomery Ward, the *Louisville Courier-Journal*, Arthur Andersen & Company—also served by Sidley & Austin for some years—and Trans-Union Corporation. When J. Arthur Friedlund, a veteran Chicago attorney, decided to reduce the time he was devoting to his practice and approached Leibman with the advance approval of his clients, the firm undertook to assist in handling his various clients, which included Canteen Corporation, of which Commercial Discount Corporation was a subsidiary, and W. F. Hall Printing Company.

Reflecting its expanding nature, the firm made two important moves that year.

To fill more effectively requirements of clients dealing with government agencies, it was decided to open an office in Washington. John Robson, having taken a leave earlier, was serving in the capital as the first general counsel and then deputy secretary of the newly-created Department of Transportation after having spent a year as a consultant on economic matters for the Bureau of the Budget. He was designated to head the Washington office, and as he made plans he invited Elroy H. Wolff, his senior trial attorney and a 1963 alumnus of Columbia University Law School experienced in Federal Trade Commission matters, to join him. They leased space at 1156 Fifteenth Street, but for six weeks before it was ready for occupancy they worked out of the Sidley & Austin quarters at 1625 Eye Street. Upon the opening of the office in late April, the principal client was REA Express, which was involved in air rate and surface cases before the Civil Aeronautics Board and the Interstate Commerce Commission. Associates were soon added, among them Lee M. Mitchell, who came to the firm in Chicago in 1968 after graduating from University of Chicago Law School and was now starting to specialize in communications law practice that would grow to substantial size, and in time more clients, and their needs, multiplied.*

And in Chicago, the firm was one of the first to lease space in the gleaming new skyscraper at One First National Plaza. Charles Luckman designed the offices on the thirty-second floor, with one of its unusual features a reflecting pool in the center of the floor.

*See Chapters XIII and XIV. In 1975, Robson left to become chairman of the Civil Aeronautics Board, a position he held until 1977, when he was named executive vice-president of G. D. Searle & Company.

Mergers and Internal Development 1972–1983

FOR SOME time, Leibman had become increasingly convinced that, with depths of service required by clients in an increasingly complex society, a growth in the number of large law firms was inevitable. He felt that his firm had come to a crossroads; if it were to grow, the greater would be its requirements for additional legal personnel, and the pressures of time would not enable a careful selection of the kinds of people that future development of the firm would demand. He also hoped to be able to shed some of his managerial duties and administrative chores as he grew older. The notion of combining with Sidley & Austin, for which he had great respect, especially attracted him. He and Minow had close relationships with various senior partners. Minow's friendship with Howard Trienens had endured since their clerkships for United States Supreme Court Chief Justice Fred M. Vinson, and they had joined in handling several AT&T matters. Leibman had worked on problems with William Avery in addition to consulting with him from time to time in past years about the development and management of law firms. Indeed, it was of Avery during informal luncheon meetings at the Mid-Day Club in 1966 and 1967 that Leibman had asked, "Wouldn't it be fun to practice law together?" To this, Avery had replied affirmatively but without any realization that Leibman was in earnest.

The likelihood of consolidating with Sidley & Austin gained impetus early in 1972. While riding in a taxicab with Trienens on the way to a dinner of the Economic Club honoring Akio Morita, founder and president of Sony Corporation, Leibman again suggested that a merger

267

would be fun, adding that he had a great idea for a name for the merged firm: Sidley & Austin. Trienens took this as a signal that Leibman was serious. Although he held scant hope for fulfillment of Leibman's suggestion, he told Avery and Bowes about the conversation. At the next meeting of the firm's executive committee, they brought up the matter, which was briefly discussed. Trienens was asked to confirm that Leibman was serious—as indeed he was. Avery and Bowes then suggested that to determine if the idea had any merit, three younger partners be chosen to meet with their counterparts in Leibman's firm for further parleys. Those so appointed were Trienens, Robert Foote, and Ned Saunders. On that May 16, they met with Minow, Robson, and Baird for dinner in the Chicago Club. With them, the Sidley & Austin lawyers carried the tacit approval of Edwin Austin of the idea of merger. When Avery and Bowes had visited him earlier during his winter vacation in Naples, Florida, to inform him of Leibman's proposition and selection of the younger men to explore it, Austin had replied, "I think you're going about it in the right way. Maybe it will work out and maybe it won't. I'll defer to the rest of you to decide the question and I'm not going to stand in the way." At their session, the conferees agreed generally that successful law firms were certain to grow larger and that, in principle, a firm with over 150 lawyers —Sidley & Austin then numbered 100 and Leibman, Williams, Bennett, Baird and Minow fifty-three—would probably have some advantages over smaller firms and, more specifically, that while there might be too many problems to warrant going ahead with the merger, the matter was worth further consideration if both firms' executive committees would agree to an exchange of information about possible client conflicts, compensation, and principal sources of fee income.

Subsequently, at executive committee meetings, transmission of the requested data in generalized form was authorized, and at a June 26 meeting of the six men in the Chicago Club the information was reviewed, with the finding that there was very little in the way of client conflicts, that compensation levels appeared to be compatible, and that the sources of income did not present serious problems. Most importantly, awareness developed that each firm had special strengths not possessed by the other. Sidley & Austin was well-known especially for its experience, developed in 105 years of practice, in the fields of utilities, railroads, corporate financing, real estate, tax, probate, and trust matters. Leibman, Williams, Bennett, Baird and Minow, in far less time, had come to be recognized particularly in matters relating to marketing, bankruptcy, and commercial law.* Both firms engaged extensively in general corporate matters and in litigation. Out of a merger could evolve a firm possessing well-balanced personnel in substantially all fields of the law. It would combine one of the oldest, most eminent firms in the city with possibly the fastest-growing local firm.

The move toward consolidation advanced. Once again, Austin made his views known, this time to Foote over that July 4 weekend at his summer home at Wausaukee, Wisconsin. While he might well be content, he said, to continue as in the past, the issue ought to be decided by the partners who would be living with the outcome over the next many years and added that he had no objection to going ahead with the merger if it appeared to be in the overall interest of the firm. On July 10, the executive committee considered the matter further. After extensive discussion of the subject it was agreed that the proposal of the special committee should be pursued in whatever manner the executive committee determined, with the understanding that any final detailed plan would be presented to all of the senior partners for their consideration and action. This was done on July 17 at the Chicago Club, with Howard Neitzert presiding. Foote submitted a comprehensively detailed report on all discussions held to date and his group's findings on the feasibility of the merger. Various partners spoke their views, queries were propounded, and answers given. Then a vote was taken on the question of whether the firm should go ahead with fashioning a specific merger agreement. It won unanimous approval.

2

The next important step, after Avery and Bowes joined the negotiating committee, was to establish an appropriate financial basis for the merger. Foote and Bennett had been working on the comparative data; they and Trienens met with three senior partners of the firms' mutual accountants, Arthur Andersen & Company—Leonard Spacek, Harvey Kapnick, and Donald Erickson. It was then decided that the Sidley & Austin negotiating team would take the lead in working out details of the merger so that it could be consummated before the end of the year. In a number of sessions

*The firm's partner most experienced in probate and trust matters, D. Benjamin Williams, had died six months after the move to One First National Plaza in 1969, but the firm name remained unaltered.

during the summer, discussion centered on the relative evaluations of each firm and the structuring of the combined firm. By September 22, a "Memorandum of Understanding" had been drafted under which all the partners and associates of Leibman, Williams, Bennett, Baird and Minow would become partners and associates of Sidley & Austin under its amended partnership agreement. Both the memorandum and the revised agreement were approved on that day by the senior partners, subject to review with all partners. At meetings later that week, each partner expressed approval and on September 28 a detailed statement was issued by the executive committee to associates about "an event of major importance to our firm" and stressing that "this matter be held in strictest confidence within the office until October 15."

The statement was meticulous in its embodiment of all the motives, details, advantages, benefits, and possible problems in the consolidation. One of its most vital sections emphasized that the new firm of 150 and more lawyers would be "stronger than the sum of its former parts," that the primary objective was "the best professional service to the combined clientele," and that the merger was "a marriage of two well-known and highly regarded firms who have worked out the arrangement in an atmosphere of mutual trust, confidence and respect, a free and voluntary act on the part of each group." There was this assurance: "It is not intended that any partner, associate or lay employee will be any worse, or immediately better, off financially, solely as a result of the consolidation, than he or she was before the event." And another: "The professional capabilities and talents of the new organization will be greater, not only numerically, but richer and more diverse in character than those which either firm formerly possessed alone. The consolidation will qualify the new firm to serve its clients in an unusually wider range of specialized knowledge and experience." And yet another: "The public interest will be correspondingly served since the nation and the community depend on the availability of highly qualified and reliable professional services to implement economic growth and prosperity and to assure advancement in the general quality of public and private life." And there were details about shifts of office locations, about the new letterhead that would carry no names of partners ("a manifest impossibility with a total of 70 partners") but in any required listing all partners would be recorded alphabetically, and about the retention of Sidley & Austin as the consolidated firm's name ("The Sidley & Austin people. . . are highly gratified and feel complimented that their colleagues from the Leibman firm are willing to help carry on the Sidley & Austin name and tradition during a second century of progress and accomplishment'').

Initial reaction among associates at Leibman, Williams, Bennett, Baird and Minow was not universally enthusiastic. Some preferred to work in a small, less structured firm and made their complaints known to Leibman. He offered counter-arguments, emphasizing that the merger idea had been developed for their benefit and citing the basic reality that each firm had professional capacity and expertise in certain areas that the other lacked and that combining the two eventuated in what he termed ''a perfect mix.'' He accentuated, too, another major gain for their firm: ''It would take us another twenty-five years to achieve the maturity Sidley & Austin offers.'' All decided to remain, whatever momentary problems might present themselves. To stimulate a spirit of comradeship, members of the executive committees of both firms and their wives were entertained at the Winnetka homes of Avery and Middleton Miller on October 9 and two days later a dinner was held for all the lawyers at the Mid-Day Club. Avery made introductory remarks, after which Leibman and two men from his firm, Quincy White and Henry L. Mason III, another 1967 Harvard Law School graduate, spoke briefly, and, following Minow's remarks, Austin and two of his lawyers, George Saunders and John McDonough, an 1969 Yale Law School alumnus, made brief comments. ''Good fellowship and enthusiasm were evident,'' Avery later remembered.

The consolidation was to become official on October 16. In the preceding days, all major clients had been apprised of the impending event. In preparing official announcements for mailing without arousing undue curiosity at the respective offices, Bowes made available the recreation room in the basement of his house in suburban Golf. There, William Jensen, Sidley & Austin's office manager, joined with Joan Till, his counterpart at Leibman, Williams, Bennett, Baird and Minow, in supervising a corps of four assistants working with lists from each office to avoid duplication of recipients. Typewriters used in addressing envelopes had been rented from outside the offices. Secrecy was preserved until news of the merger leaked out to the *Tribune*, which published its story two days before it technically went into effect. Other newspapers carried their stories on October 16, all noting that the consolidation ''creates one of the largest law firms in the country'' and that retaining the name of Sidley & Austin ''reflects a trend away from the traditional practice among law firms of changing names as senior partners change.''

271

3

In the immediate aftermath, partners of both firms received congratulatory calls. Some fellow-lawyers expressed surprise at this joining of a relatively youthful firm with one of the city's legal giants. But it seemed generally recognized that the prospects for success and progressive gains for all concerned were good and that as a result of the merger's synergistic effect there would be further growth and an even greater range of services for clients.

Shifts of office locations at One First National Plaza were instituted so that lawyers and their assistants doing the same types of work would be physically situated as close to one another as possible. All of the Sidley & Austin tax and corporate lawyers moved to the thirty-second floor, and the Leibman firm's trial, real estate, and probate people were transferred to the forty-seventh and forty-eighth floors, with its marketing group assigned to a section of the forty-seventh floor formerly occupied by Bowes' financial group. These physical changes, effected once telephone numbers were transposed, had been planned in the weeks before announcement was made of the consolidation, as had significant organizational changes.

The executive committee was now expanded to eighteen members, consisting primarily of a combination of both firms' executive committees. To Sidley & Austin's committee, whose members were Austin, Avery, Ball, Bowes, Foote, Middleton Miller, Neitzert, Edward Saunders, Thomas, and Trienens were added Blair White and Loren Juhl, and from Leibman, Williams, Bennett, Baird and Minow, were Baird, Bennett, Christopher, Leibman, Minow, and Robson. Avery was elected chairman and Bennett was made secretary. This committee had general authority over the firm's affairs, including determination of policies and the admission and participation of partners. For the first time, a management committee was created; its members were Avery, Baird, Foote, Minow, Edward Saunders, and Trienens, the latter as secretary. It was given responsibility for day-to-day operations of the firm and general supervision over its administrative committees.

It is significant that men in their forties and fifties constituted a majority of the executive committee (eleven of eighteen) and of the management committee (five of six). And in the next year the ratio of younger partners on the executive committee was increased further by the addition of Beam, Flynn, Frei, Lucente, and Schimberg, so that sixteen of the twenty-three members were under sixty.

William H. Avery
as firm chairman in 1973

As in the pre-merger days of Sidley & Austin, there continued to be two main groupings of all the firm's lawyers, both destined to increase in numbers and diversity in the future.*

One involved the various areas of law in which the lawyers concentrated their efforts. Its basic purpose, according to the firm manual, was "to facilitate the assignment of work and is not intended to departmentalize the work of the office or inhibit assignments crossing over group lines. The partners of each have the responsibility for equitable and efficient assignments of work to associates and legal assistants within each." In this assemblage were fourteen functional groups: general; corporate and securities; creditors' rights, banking, commercial law, and bankruptcy; estate, trust, state and local taxes, and legislation; federal tax; labor and miscellaneous; litigation (anti-trust and special); litigation (utility, product liability, and special); litigation (general); marketing; real estate; Washington office; Detroit; and Brussels.

The second major grouping was for administrative purposes. It was composed of ten committees, under direction of the management committee: finance and accounting; lay personnel, space, and equipment; employment of associates; assignment and compensation of associates and legal assistants; retirement plans; insurance; personnel relations; library; summer program; and Washington office.

*See Chapter XVI.

273

Members of post-merger management committee

William H. Avery

Howard J. Trienens

Robert L. Foote

Russell M. Baird

Newton N. Minow

274

Edward W. Saunders

4

The Washington arrangement led to trouble.

The new executive committee's decision was to unite the two firms' offices there and establish the combined one the following spring in a building nearing completion at 1730 Pennsylvania Avenue. Edward Day and John Robson, formerly each office's chief, were to be co-chairmen, with Day as resident head and Robson as liaison between Washington and Chicago. Day was offended by having to share the chairmanship and by the move. Although he had been informed about negotiations in the three months preceding the merger and had approved and signed the merger agreement and the amended partnership agreement, he told the firm after the merger had been consummated that he intended to resign and did so, effective the last day of 1972.

On July 1, 1974, Day filed suit in the Superior Court of the District of Columbia against Sidley & Austin and the pre-merger members of its executive committee, seeking $2.23 million in compensatory and "exemplary" damages. Neitzert acted as "inside counsel" and James J. Bierbower of the Washington firm of Bierbower & Rockefeller was retained as "outside counsel" to represent the firm in the case. The suit was removed to the United States District Court and assigned to Judge Barrington D. Parker. On the basis of extensive answers by members of the executive committee to Day's interrogatories, a motion was made for a summary judgment. The motion was argued by Bierbower and granted by Judge Parker on May 29, 1975, dismissing the suit.

The court held that Day had no vested right in the sole chairmanship of the Washington office nor in the continued maintenance of an office at the original location. Moreover, the court expressly stated that the partnership agreement to which Day had freely consented "clearly provided for management authority in the executive committee and for majority approval of the merger with the Leibman firm. Even if plaintiff had voted against the merger he could not have stopped it." Day's petition for rehearing, his appeal to the United States Court of Appeals, and his petition to the Supreme Court for a writ of *certiorari* were all denied.

5

The traditional practice of promotion from within the firm continued. In the three years after the merger, thirty-three associates were elevated to partnerships. An exception to this procedure was the admission of Charles E. Lomax at that level in March 1975, after twenty-five years of notable service in the offices of the chief counsel and the Chicago regional counsel of the Internal Revenue Service. Lomax was the firm's first black partner. Although he attracted considerable attention for his representation of the Nation of Islam and Wallace and Herbert Muhammad, the sons of its founder, Elijah, and of Muhammad Ali during and after his reign as world's heavyweight boxing champion, his governmental experience made him an effective addition to the firm's thriving corporate income tax group.

The latter had grown substantially since the late 1940s, when Middleton Miller and J. Dean Vail were the main lawyers doing corporate tax work. Robert R. Frei joined them in 1949 and, as related earlier, dealt with many cases in this field. In succeeding years, the department grew in expertise and scope, with eight partners and as many associates, all with practical experience or academic backgrounds in taxation, accounting, and allied fields.*

Changes in the firm's foreign operations were made at the end of 1973. When Richard G. Clemens, a 1965 graduate from the University of Virginia Law School, had been assigned to a newly-established office in Brussels at the start of the preceding year, he had received a temporary work permit with the expectation that he would soon be issued a "professional card." But the Belgian bar and government altered that policy and refused to give any new cards to foreign lawyers. The office was shut down and Clemens returned to Chicago for other assignments and membership on a newly-formed committee on foreign operations to assist clients with foreign and international matters. The continuing association with firms in "Le Club" enabled Sidley & Austin to provide legal services in Western Europe. Additionally, an arrangement was made with Robert A. Albert, a Harvard University alumnus and Columbia University Law School graduate practicing in London, to provide services, other than the practice of local law, there and elsewhere in Europe for the firm's clients

*See Chapter XIV.

referred to him. This relationship was solidified in 1977 when Albert was named a partner, and his office officially became the firm's London office, its staff then comprising Albert and an associate, Lisa Spry-Leverton, a London barrister who would attain partnership six years later.

6

Augmenting the legal force was a group of men and women technically known as "legal assistants" or "paralegals."

In the 1950s, before these terms were in general use, Sidley & Austin became one of the nation's first law firms to use such personnel. The firm's trial lawyers found that qualified college graduates, with training and supervision, could perform many tasks that otherwise would have required their time. In the early 1960s the probate and trust group decided that it would operate more efficiently if similar lay personnel were hired to assist in the area of estate planning and administration, preparation of drafts of income, gift, estate and inheritance tax returns, inventories and accounts for probate estates, and tax projections for estate-planning clients and independently handling transfer of securities in probate matters.

The first person engaged for such services in the estate field was Nellie H. Olk, who had previously been employed in a bank. So successful was the experiment that additional legal assistants were hired, with Mrs. Olk as coordinator. Among them were two members of the initial class of the newly-formed Institute for Paralegal Training in Philadelphia, which admitted only college graduates and granted certificates upon successful completion of an intensive six-months' course. At first there was concern that use of legal assistants might constitute unauthorized practice of law. The firm adopted a policy to prevent this. Legal assistants worked under a lawyer's active supervision and were not to proffer legal advice or make statements orally or in correspondence that could be construed by clients or others to connote the giving of legal advice, nor appear in court unless court rules permitted this on routine matters such as obtaining an agreed continuance. The system has worked well and has since been extended to the real estate and corporate groups. With one legal assistant to about every six lawyers, the quality of service to clients has been decidedly improved and so has the work by young lawyers, who have been freed from routine labors of the kind performed by earlier counterparts.

7

Other men and women perform essential duties as secretaries to individual lawyers and administrative officers and as typists, secretarial coordinators, receptionists, librarians, proofreaders, accounting, time systems, reservations and insurance personnel, docket, file and mailroom clerks, messengers, duplicating technicians, and word processing specialists. The latter are in a vital sector of a highly automated communications and information-processing system that accelerates transmission and reception of diverse legal documents between cities in minutes instead of days and reduces turnaround time, even for complex and detailed ones, to two or three hours. Sidley & Austin was one of the first law firms in the country, in 1967, to institute word processing technology with the use of then-new magnetic tape. In the early 1970s, it switched to magnetic card equipment and began the operation of two small word processing centers with eight International Business Machines Mag Card II typewriters in each. Later these centers were combined into one under supervision of Lela Whitted, one of the earliest operators in Chicago trained to use such equipment. Constant improvement and expansion of word processing facilities have continued as advanced and complex equipment has been devised to heighten capabilities. Lawyers not only communicate with each other by these means but with clients who have communicating typewriters, specialized printers, and other innovative devices, and an electronic hookup by wire in the United States and by satellite to London also affords direct communication with R. R. Donnelley, which does most of the firm's printing.

The lay staff is now headed by Edward J. Kernan, who had come in 1973 when William Jensen took full retirement after nearly four decades as office manager. As the firm's administrative director, Kernan had wide experience as a college athletic director and the administrative and personnel manager for Price, Waterhouse in Cleveland. With frequent assistance from Homer Mattingly, the firm's veteran comptroller, Kernan centralized administrative services in a smooth-running operation and supervised the expansion and advancement of the firm's electronic communications techniques and the word processing system.

8

The years since the 1972 merger have brought successes, benefits, and growth in personnel and clients beyond the expectations of its most optimistic proponents.

There were, as anticipated, problems of varied sorts. But in the main they were minimal. Within months, even those who had been tepid about prospects to be afforded by the consolidation had their apprehensions assuaged and were heartened by the effective melding of personalities and practices later aptly characterized by Leibman as "our getting-to-know-you period."

Gradually, the merger continued to be appreciated as an event that had created a complementary aggregation in which the whole became of greater significance than its prior parts.

Avery's summation of the merger's effects was apt: "Financial results were increasingly remarkable. But the best and lasting achievements were in other areas that nourished development into a firm of increased stature and a greater ability to provide clients with all types of service and one more widely known nationally and locally than ever before, with the biggest bonus from our firm's standpoint being the acquisition of a wonderful group of partners and associates as friends as well as partners and associates and we derived increased pleasure from the practice of law."

9

At a meeting of the executive committee in November 1974, Avery proposed a further step in shifting leadership of the firm to younger partners by urging the selection of another lawyer to succeed him as chairman of the committee, to become effective at the end of the year. But his recommendation was unanimously rejected and he continued in the post.

The following spring, before departing for a trip to Europe, Avery renewed his proposal and also suggested that two partners be selected, one to head the executive committee and another to lead the management committee; he hoped, he said, that the choices would be made before he came back from Europe so that the chairmanships could be filled by July 16, when he would turn seventy.

Upon his return, he was delighted to learn that Howard Trienens had been elected chairman of the executive committee and Robert Foote as chairman of the management committee, each taking over his duties in July. Trienens has served ever since, but in line with his long-standing desire to retire at sixty-five, Foote did retire at the end of 1979 and was succeeded as management committee chairman by Blair White, who had replaced Avery on that committee.

10

In the last half of the 1970s, thought was given by the executive committee to having an additional office on the West Coast to strengthen the firm's ability to serve clients more efficiently on a national basis. Discussion led to the conclusion that consolidation with a firm there—especially one that was relatively small but highly specialized—was preferable to opening a new office. Blair White, as chairman of the management committee, took the lead in finding that kind of firm. At the suggestion of Schimberg, who knew one of the managing partners, he checked into Shutan & Trost.

Shutan & Trost was an eleven-lawyer firm whose practice concentrated on corporate reorganizations, insolvency, and commercial transactions, and White found ample reason to proceed with consideration of it as a highly likely candidate for consolidation. Chicago-born Robert Shutan had graduated in 1942 from the University of California School of Jurisprudence (Boalt Hall), Berkeley, where he had been a member of the law review. He started to practice shortly after his discharge from the Navy in 1946. Initially, he handled only a few bankruptcy cases, but he rapidly became actively involved in that practice. By the end of 1950, he had opened his own law office in Beverly Hills, specializing in bankruptcy and reorganization matters. J. Ronald Trost, born in Fresno, California, but raised in the Sacramento area and schooled at Rice University and the University of Texas Law School, returned to California from government service in 1962. He had scant experience in bankruptcy matters, but through a self-imposed regimen he became facile in that complex body of statutory and case law and was soon recognized as a specialist.

In 1970, Shutan and Trost started talking about forming a partnership. They knew each other well from mutual involvement in several cases and were also aware of each other's solid reputations for skill and maintenance of high ethical standards. In a series of discussions about a partnership, each meeting was pleasant in a business sense, but neither seemed ready to

Robert H. Shutan and J. Ronald Trost

take such a step. At breakfast one morning in Nibbler's Restaurant in Beverly Hills, they once again hashed and rehashed the advantages and disadvantages of becoming partners. The discussion was friendly, but at one point it became loud enough to attract the attention of other patrons. Finally, a man in an adjoining booth leaned over and said, "Do it!" That sensible advice from a disinterested third party broke the deadlock.

On the first day of 1971, the firm of Shutan & Trost opened its office in Beverly Hills, its personnel consisting of the name partners and a single associate who had worked for Shutan. From the outset, the practice was limited to bankruptcy, insolvency, and corporate reorganization matters, and the firm became involved in large and small bankruptcy cases primarily on behalf of debtors but also on behalf of creditors, trustees in bankruptcy, and assignees for the benefit of creditors. A few years earlier Trost had begun to lecture to groups of lawyers on bankruptcy problems and had written law review articles on insolvency matters. He now increased this activity and his renown as a bankruptcy scholar spread, as did that of Shutan & Trost. The young firm grew and prospered. The first associate left in 1972 but new associates were hired from law schools, judicial clerkships, and other Los Angeles law firms. At the time the merger was being considered, the firm's partners were Thomas E. Garcin, an experienced trial lawyer, and five younger attorneys—Richard W. Havel, a 1971 alumnus of University of California Law School; Marc A.

281

Levinson, a 1973 graduate from the same school and former law clerk to Chief Justice Donald R. Wright of the California Supreme Court; Sally S. Neely, a 1971 graduate of Stanford University Law School; and J. Robert Nelson and Richard T. Peters, both of the 1971 class of University of California Law School.

Illustrative of the breadth of practice was Shutan's retention in a Chapter XI proceeding involving Los Angeles Airways, a helicopter commuter service that had financial problems intensified by two crashes within three months. Trost's clients included Doris Day in her various lawsuits against her former husband and business manager, Martin Melcher; this case took Trost all over the country and was resolved favorably for the movie star. In 1973 the firm began representation of United States Financial, a San Diego-based real estate conglomerate that developed and owned resorts, office buildings, and apartments. A virtual empire built on extremely large loans from American and foreign lenders, it began to shake in the real estate recession of the early 1970s. Together with the New York firm of Fried, Frank, Harris, Shriver & Jacobson, Shutan & Trost initiated Chapter XI action for the San Diego conglomerate. In the several years it took to complete the case, an associate maintained a residence in San Diego part of that time, and for all intents and purposes Trost lived there as well. Among other clients were a large alfalfa farming and pelletizing operation on the Colorado River in Blythe, California, and the trustee in bankruptcy of Goldstein, Samuelson, Incorporated, a multi-million dollar commodities fraud that resulted in the jailing of the company's founder and loss to investors of over $20 million.

As the firm grew and its expertise developed, its practice expanded from a local to a nationwide one and began to attract clients among institutional lenders, with a shift in emphasis on creditors rather than debtors: among such clients were Crocker National Bank, Travelers Insurance Company, and The First National Bank of Chicago. Its most important client in the insolvency area was the ailing Chrysler Corporation. At the invitation of Senator Donald Riegle of Michigan in mid-1979, Trost had addressed Congress about the proposed federal bailout of the automobile manufacturer. So compelling was his testimony on the ramifications of a Chrysler bankruptcy that Chrysler executives thereafter retained Shutan & Trost as the company's special insolvency counsel.

The more White learned about Shutan & Trost the more interested he became in the firm's members and its kind of practice. It was evident that practice in bankruptcy law was on the verge of a boom because of depressed economic conditions and the new bankruptcy code of 1979 that encouraged reorganization rather than liquidation, enabling a debtor to stay in business instead of being placed in receivership. And the complexities of such legal action needed the expertise of a law firm which a client's in-house counsel might not possess.

After a weekend meeting early in 1980 with Trost in Miami, White was greatly impressed with prospects for a fruitful merger and so informed his partners. Other meetings followed between Shutan & Trost and senior Sidley & Austin partners in the next few months in Chicago and Los Angeles. At one, Leibman delineated to Shutan the boons of the 1972 merger. At another in April, White, Minow, Trienens, and Maurice J. Miller, a 1955 graduate of University of Wisconsin Law School and a 1963 partner, met with the Shutan & Trost lawyers in an all-day session in Garcin's home in Encino and engaged in a frank examination of every aspect of the merger. White offered assurances of a profitable and professionally gratifying future and emphasized the flexibility of the Sidley & Austin structure and the opportunities for entering additional areas of practice. Shutan, Trost, Garcin, and the Sidley & Austin partners had dinner that night at Trost's house and an agreement to merge was reached.

One problem with conflict-of-interest potential was Shutan & Trost's affiliation with the New York firm of Debevoise, Plimpton, Lyons & Gates in aiding Chrysler to secure government funding to relieve its massive financial woes while Sidley & Austin represented a consortium of seven Japanese banks that were among Chrysler's many creditors. To ease this apparent complication, White and Trost agreed that the consolidation would not take place until the government loan went through. Schimberg and Bernstein informed representatives of the Mitsubishi bank, chief of the Japanese lenders, and Trost told the Debevoise firm of the merger discussions. No objections were raised. All prospects were increasingly favorable for consummation of the merger, and formal agreements were drawn to cover all phases to mutual satisfaction.

At a fiftieth anniversary party early that June for William Avery in the Casino Club, when Trienens, during a speech lauding Avery's many legal accomplishments and contributions to the firm, referred to the Shutan & Trost lawyers present as "someday hoped-to-be partners," there was a burst of applause. Within a few weeks, the first check for $497 million of

Chrysler's $1.5 billion federal loan guarantee was processed. On June 24, the way was clear for the consolidation whereby all eight Shutan & Trost partners became Sidley & Austin partners and the Los Angeles office took on the Sidley & Austin name. "We plan," said White, "to expand the Los Angeles office to provide a greater range of legal services on the West Coast to our clients."

In the months ahead, after Edward Kernan and his staff had set up all clerical and administrative systems, this was borne out. By 1983 the Los Angeles legal personnel had grown considerably and was housed in expanded offices in Century Park East, considered the most prized office buildings in the new Century City area of Los Angeles. Newcomers were typified by Melville B. Nimmer, professor at the University of California, Los Angeles Law School and one of the world's foremost scholars in national and international copyright, as counsel, and as partners Charles S. Vogel, former Los Angeles Superior Court judge, and Gary O. Concoff, who formed and headed an entertainment law group.

11

When the firm began thinking seriously of broadening into fields that would be burgeoning in the future and in due course consolidated with Shutan & Trost, the idea was also to be on the lookout for ways to become more deeply involved in growth opportunities beyond national boundaries such as international trade. Since 1974, clients had been well served in Europe by the London office; and membership since 1972 in "Le Club" had afforded information on legal developments of international interest and facilitated the handling of international matters, especially in Western Europe. In addition, the international business transactions group headed by Russell Bennett had worked on many international matters, such as the multi-million-dollar financing of the purchase by Peru and Brazil of seed through DEKALB AgResearch. But it became apparent that international practice was a fertile field with great growth possibilities that would be enhanced by opening several offices.

In seeking to enlarge this practice, the firm learned of three men with expertise in the Middle East. One was Thomas W. Hill, Jr., who maintained offices in Muscat, the capital of the Sultanate of Oman on the Arabian peninsula, and in Dubai, one of the United Arab Emirates. In ten years' practice in the area, Hill had been legal adviser to the Sultan of

Oman and had drafted its banking and commercial laws. Another was Marshall W. Wiley, a career diplomat of twenty years' service in Yemen, Lebanon, Egypt, Jordan, Iraq, and Saudi Arabia, with a period as United States Ambassador to Oman. The third was Edmund Wise, a Washington lawyer experienced in dealing with Saudi Arabia. Negotiations with all three climaxed with an announcement early in October 1981, that Hill's offices, employing eight associates, had consolidated with the firm and would be the Sidley & Austin offices in the Arabian Gulf and that Wiley, like Hill named a partner, would be based in the Washington office to coordinate and concentrate on efforts to expand further the firm's international and Middle East practice. Wise moved from Washington to London and, as counsel, works out of the office there for clients on Middle Eastern matters.

And the move toward establishment of additional relationships in that part of the world continued, with the opening of offices in Cairo and Singapore. The first is operated jointly by Nels J. Ackerson, a 1972 Harvard Law School graduate and 1983 partner who had practiced in Washington and Indianapolis, and Gamal N. Naguib, an experienced Egyptian lawyer who had been an adviser to various Egyptian presidents; its legal personnel includes two Americans, one Swede, and eight other Egyptians, among the latter former judges in local courts and ex-ambassadors to the United Nations, Zambia, Mexico, and Norway. The second, to co-ordinate Far Eastern practice, was established by George McBurney, a graduate of State University of Iowa Law School and a 1964 partner, who is assisted by Mark Angelson, an experienced financial lawyer.

At the same time, an office was established in New York under Andrew C. Quale, Jr., a 1966 Harvard Law School alumnus who had been a summer associate with the firm but had declined permanent employment upon graduation because he wanted to engage immediately in international practice. He did so as counsel to the Colombian government and later taught at the law school of William & Mary College and was a partner with Coudert Brothers in New York before returning in 1982 to Sidley & Austin as a partner. Also in this office is David A. Richards, a 1972 graduate of Yale Law School with wide experience in international law prior to joining the firm as a partner in 1982.

The New York office's practice is oriented toward serving domestic and foreign clients not only in the United States but elsewhere in the world. Its lawyers are experienced in European, Latin American, and Middle and Far East matters. Some have lived and practiced law in Great Britain, Belgium, France, Italy, Germany, Norway, Switzerland, Egypt, Colombia, and Indonesia; among the languages spoken by them are French, Spanish, German, Italian, Norwegian, Hebrew, Chinese, and Arabic. They have negotiated and documented hundreds of millions of dollars of financings by foreign governments and private borrowers and foreign investors' real estate acquisitions and have advised sovereign governments or their agencies on assorted matters.

The London office was moved to new and larger quarters in the building which housed General Dwight Eisenhower's headquarters in the Second World War and, under Rob Albert's direction, joined with those in the United States and the other countries in a wide variety of international transactions and other matters.

The Washington office, with fifty lawyers led by Eden Martin, also moved. It now occupies three floors in a new building on Eye Street leased by the firm, adjacent to property where the home of United States Supreme Court Justice Oliver Wendell Holmes once stood. This office has expanded not only in size but in the scope of its practice. In addition to rate and anti-trust litigation for AT&T and railroads, it serves the oil pipeline industry in regulatory litigation, the District of Columbia in municipal financing, and a wide variety of other clients in their relations with the government.

Client Matters
1972–1983

ONE OF the new clients of national scope after the 1972 merger was the American Bar Association. This representation began after Chesterfield Smith, ABA's president, came to confer with Avery in 1974 about having the firm represent the association in various matters, particularly constitutional and anti-trust issues. Avery proposed Blair White to handle the association's legal problems. Before long, White —assisted by Robert D. McLean, a graduate of Yale Law School and a clerk with United States Supreme Court Justice Thurgood Marshall before becoming an associate in 1972 and a partner in 1975, and David T. Pritikin, a 1974 Harvard Law School graduate named a partner in 1981—was acting as an adviser to the association about changes in its code relating to group legal services.

On June 25, 1976, the long-discussed question, perennially debated at ABA sectional and annual meetings, of whether lawyers could advertise came to a head when the Department of Justice filed an anti-trust suit in United States District Court in Washington that charged the association with conspiracy to restrain trade through the ABA ethics code's ban on advertising. At the time, the association actually was liberalizing that code through a resolution adopted at its convention earlier that year that permitted advertising of initial consultation fees, specialties, office hours, and credit terms in telephone books and "reputable law lists." Lawrence E. Walsh, ABA's president, decried the government's action as "bizarre" and emphasized that lawyer advertising was controlled by federal and state courts and agencies to which the anti-trust statutes were inapplicable.

287

Walsh's assertions were enlarged upon by White after obtaining a change of venue to Chicago. "The ABA does not enforce the code," he said. "There is no ABA disciplinary procedure related to the code and ABA membership doesn't turn on the code. In essence, the ABA position is that all it is doing is recommending action in its code. Individual states and their courts, which regulate advertising, have chosen to adopt the code." He pointed out that although various consumer groups and others had termed the ABA resolution inadequate, he knew of no state that had yet gone so far as to sanction even that relaxation of strictures governing advertisements. "In effect," he added, "the Justice Department is attacking a recommendation that has not been adopted anywhere. We are considering seeking dismissal of the suit as improperly filed."

White was amply prepared to go to trial on that basis. But even as he amassed an array of evidence and witnesses, there was a surprising development. In 1977, in a case against the State Bar of Arizona, the United States Supreme Court ruled that newspaper advertisements of fees for certain routine legal services were protected by the First Amendment. The firm prepared an *amicus curiae* brief on behalf of the ABA, urging the high court to give the states flexibility in experimenting with advertising. That summer, the ABA's 360-member House of Delegates endorsed rules allowing newspaper and magazine advertising with listing of fees and the airing of radio commercials. A year later, only six weeks before trial, White received a telephone call from a Justice Department attorney that the anti-trust action was going to be voluntarily dismissed. The detailed memorandum in support of the government's motion to dismiss the suit without prejudice was published in the *American Bar Association Journal* that October. The tenor of that document was that dismissal of the case had been prompted primarily by the Supreme Court's ruling and also by significant changes in the ABA's activities relating to lawyer advertising.

Asked by the ABA president, S. Shepherd Tate, to comment on the memorandum, White, in that November's issue of the *Journal*, made a forceful rejoinder in which he re-emphasized earlier arguments against existence of the alleged conspiracy and urged that "the action was without merit from the beginning." In bringing a lawsuit that even if won, he wrote, would not have changed the advertising rules of courts and governmental agencies and that could only have curbed advocacy by the association of model rules it believed to be in the public interest, the anti-trust division's actions had dangerous implications for the First Amendment. "If the division quarreled with restrictions on advertising imposed by states and agencies, then it should simply have urged its own views directly . . . rather than seek to coerce the ABA into modifying its recommendations. The First Amendment broadly protects efforts to propose ethical standards for adoption by governmental agencies. With this unfortunate lawsuit now over, any doubts about the rights of private bar associations to make collective recommendations for governmental action should be laid to rest."

In the months that followed the Supreme Court's decision, advertisements by individual lawyers and firms began to appear in print and on television and radio. With rare exceptions, these were low-keyed and reasonably dignified, describing the kinds of services offered. Neither Sidley & Austin nor other firms of substantial size and stature advertised, and, indeed, two years after the Supreme Court's ruling, only 6 percent of the nation's firms were doing any kind of price advertising, according to a survey by two University of Miami professors, Timothy J. Murris and Fred S. McChesney.

The firm's representation of the ABA continued. Of national interest and controversy was the association's consideration in 1981 of the application for accreditation of the Oral Roberts University Law School in Oklahoma City. The association's accreditation committee and section on legal education and admissions to the bar had declined to recommend approval because the institution required incoming students to sign a "Code of Honor Pledge" recognizing Jesus Christ as their savior and vowing to accept a fundamentalist Christian philosophy. Charging that the association had violated the school's First Amendment right to the free exercise of religion, Roberts filed suit in June 1981, in United States District Court in Chicago. White and Pritikin, recently named a partner, were joined by William H. Baumgartner, Jr., a 1979 Harvard Law School alumnus, in arguing that the ABA's action did not infringe on any religious practices or rights. Nevertheless, Judge James B. Moran granted a preliminary injunction against using religious discrimination as the basis for denying accreditation. But he stayed the injunction until after the 1981 summer meeting of the ABA's House of Delegates. At that meeting, there was sustained and vigorous discussion as efforts were made to reach a decision that would neither limit the school's constitutional rights nor appear to sanction religious discrimination. An amendment to existing accreditation rules was drawn by the association's section on legal education and admissions to the bar. It exempted from ABA's non-discrimination standards any school with a religious affiliation or purpose if the school furnished written notice of its discriminatory enrollment and hiring policies. Division over its adoption was exemplified by a former president, Whitney North Seymour, who saw it as the lesser of two evils ("It may be necessary to take a deep gulp and accept some things that we might prefer not to accept"), and Erwin N. Griswold, former dean of Harvard Law School and United States Solicitor General, who said, "This proposed change is contrary to the whole history of this country in the realm of religious liberty. Under this proposal, any institution that wants to can put up the sign saying, 'No Jews Admitted'." By the narrow vote of 147 to 127 the amendment was approved and a resolution was adopted granting provisional accreditation to the school. Oral Roberts then dismissed its Chicago lawsuit as moot. Arguments for and against the rules changes resounded again the following January when the House of Delegates met in Chicago and a resolution to repeal changes was defeated, 176 to 138.

2

Another national organization that became a client was the American Medical Association, which came to Newton Minow in 1973 with a dispute involving a controversial National Broadcasting Company television program. After the problem was solved to the AMA's satisfaction, the firm became its regular outside counsel and won several major cases for it in various federal courts. Interestingly, a major matter handled by Minow and Jack R. Bierig, a 1972 Harvard Law School alumnus and a 1978 partner, had to do with a problem with which the American Bar Association was concerned: advertising.

The case began at the end of 1975 when the Federal Trade Commission formally charged that certain AMA rules, instituted at the turn of the century to stamp out widespread medical quackery, violated the FTC statute pertaining to restraint of trade and anti-competitive practices. In reply, Minow stressed that the AMA was not subject to FTC jurisdiction, and, moreover, member physicians were not prevented from advertising but only prohibited from using false or misleading promotional practices.

From Labor Day in 1977 until the following Memorial Day, extensive hearings were held throughout the country. In California, the AMA produced witnesses who had been lured by deceptive advertising to un-scrupulous physicians with tragic results. Nevertheless, Ernest G. Barnes, an FTC administrative law judge, held that the AMA was subject to FTC jurisdiction and had violated the Federal Trade Commission Act. He also ordered that the AMA would not be permitted to set any ethical guidelines for doctors' advertising for two years and after that only with FTC approval. This was denounced by the association's board chairman, Robert S. Hunter, as "the most shocking and pervasive attack on profes-sionalism." In a speech to AMA delegates at a four-day meeting in the Palmer House in Chicago, Minow announced that Barnes' decision would be appealed, and the association's executive vice-president Dr. James H. Sammons said, "The FTC is in for a hell of a fight."

That fight took on new vigor when, on October 25, 1979, the full commission upheld Barnes' basic ruling but overruled his recommenda-tion to keep the AMA from setting ethical advertising guidelines. The association expressed apprehension that deceptive advertising could in-crease, inasmuch as only 53 percent of the country's 400,000 doctors were AMA members. Doctors and medical societies around the country gen-erally disapproved of the FTC order as a stimulus to a return to "the day of snake oil" while various consumer organizations welcomed it as a means of increasing competition and lowering medical costs. On appeal, the commission's order was upheld in a 2-1 decision, the dissenting opinion agreeing with the AMA's contention that the entire proceeding was "unjustified, unnecessary and a waste of administrative and judicial resources."

In 1982 the conflict reached the United States Supreme Court. In strong arguments against the FTC order, Minow contended that the commission was "stretching to establish a precedent that it has jurisdiction over not-for-profit associations." And he declared, "If Hippocrates were alive today, he would need the FTC's permission before he could write the Hippocratic oath!" In bringing the action despite the AMA's recent revisions in its ethical standards, the FTC, he asserted, "has been obsessed with the past, unconcerned with the present and blind to the future." Minow's argument was characterized by *The American Lawyer* as one of the liveliest of the term. But on the following March 23, the high court, with Justice Harry Blackmun not participating, affirmed the appeals court with a 4-4 tie, and so the seven-year-old dispute was left simmering in Congress, where the issues were still being debated in 1983.

Important as were the ABA and AMA cases, the biggest and most complex of anti-trust cases in the country's history began on November 20, 1974, when the Department of Justice filed in the United States District Court in Washington a civil suit against American Telephone and Telegraph Company, with Western Electric Company and Bell Telephone Laboratories as co-defendants. In its fifteen-page complaint, the government charged AT&T with monopolization of the nation's telecommunications service and equipment and asked for the divestiture of Western Electric, part or all of the long-distance telephone network and the twenty-two domestic companies comprising the Bell System.

AT&T was then the world's largest corporate entity, with $67 billion in assets, one million employees and more stockholders—three million—than any other American company. Western Electric, employing 180,000 workers, was the country's twelfth largest industrial corporation, with yearly sales of $7 billion. There had been similar actions in the past against "Ma Bell," as it was familiarly known in financial and communications circles. Back in 1913, it had faced the threat of governmental anti-trust prosecution by disposing of its telegraph stock and promising to grant long-distance connection of Bell System lines to independent companies. An anti-trust suit instituted in 1949 had ended in 1956 with a consent decree that limited the Bell System to common carrier communications and government projects but preserved the long-standing relationships between its operating, manufacturing, and research arms.

The law firm's representation of the huge company and its components and predecessors went back many decades when Norman Williams served as counsel and first president of the Chicago Telephone Company in 1881, Arthur Wheeler as its president and chairman in the early 1900s, William Sidley as Western Electric's vice-president and general counsel for twenty-five years after 1908 and William Bangs in the 1920s and Kenneth Burgess for two decades after 1931 as general counsel for Illinois Bell Telephone Company. In more recent times, the firm had been retained for varied matters, particularly for those relating to rates. In 1961, Douglas Smith and Arthur Seder participated in hearings before the Federal Communications Commission for eventual approval of the institution of Telpak, a new service designed to create "electronic highways" between specified points, over which many types of communications could be transmitted. In 1966, a United States Court of Appeals decision upheld an FCC ruling that AT&T should eliminate the low-volume offering of Telpak but might continue its high-volume Telpak service. A decade later, AT&T recognized that it had become economically necessary to end its Telpak service and the FCC permitted it to do so. Such customer groups as the airline industry, various newspapers, large industrial users such as General Electric, and federal executive agencies appealed that decision, arguing that AT&T should be required to continue to give them Telpak bulk rate discounts. Jules Perlberg and David J. Lewis, a 1980 partner who had graduated from the University of Illinois College of Law in 1974, prevailed in the United States Court of Appeals in Washington, and in 1981 the United States Supreme Court cleared the way for abandonment of Telpak by declining to hear the customers' appeals. And in the next two years, the two won decisions in appeals courts affirming AT&T's costing procedures and its right to hike private line rates.

In the mid-1970s and early 1980s, spiraling rates of inflation, high interest rates, and high costs of raising equity capital prompted AT&T to seek further increases in its allowed level of earnings. In 1975–76, Trienens and Perlberg secured an FCC decision permitting AT&T's rate of return to go up to a range of 9½ to 10 percent. In 1981, they obtained an FCC ruling allowing the company's interstate rate of return to increase to 12¾ percent, the highest level ever granted the Bell System; it was a decision that resulted in an annual rise in AT&T revenues of more than $1 billion. Although these rate increases were far below the inflation rate—from 1976 to 1980 the nation's Consumer Price Index rose by over 53 percent in contrast with a 5 percent boost in AT&T's interstate long distance rates—various special customer groups challenged the FCC's decision in the courts. A group of large communications users, including the three major radio-television broadcasting networks and the Department of Justice, representing federal executive agencies as communications users, sought to block the 1981 rate increase by appealing to the United States Court of Appeals in New York. Perlberg and Lewis succeeded in having the court affirm the FCC's order.

During the same period, Henry Mason and David W. Carpenter, a 1975 graduate of Boston University, law clerk to United States Supreme Court Justice William J. Brennan, Jr., and a 1982 partner, successfully briefed and argued in the Illinois Appellate Court an Illinois Bell Telephone case in which the state sought to impose nearly $1 billion of back taxes on the Bell System's interstate revenues. In December 1982, the Illinois Supreme Court upheld IBT's position.

4

Of greatest concern to Trienens starting toward the end of 1974 was the renewed governmental assault on the Bell System. In a heated press conference after the suit was filed, John DeButts, AT&T's chairman and chief executive officer, vowed not to seek a consent decree but to "fight to the end." A sustained conflict was in the offing.

One of the first moves, early the next February, was to file a twenty-seven page answer which also asked for dismissal of the government's suit. Main points in it were that primary jurisdiction over issues raised by the Justice Department rested with the Federal Communications Commission rather than with the courts, that the 1956 consent order deciding the monopoly questions precluded raising them anew, and that the Bell System's basic aim was not to maximize profits but to provide "quality service at reasonable rates." That July 23, George Saunders offered these and other arguments in support of a motion for dismissal before Judge Joseph C. Waddy. Using no written notes, Saunders laid emphasis on the FCC's "exclusive jurisdiction" over actions cited in the government's complaint. After Judge Waddy denied the motion, an unusual step was taken with an appeal directly to the United States Supreme Court in which was cited the potential tremendous expense of a long trial; the cost of producing over one billion pages of documents already requested by the government would amount to $300 million. When the high court declined to consider the jurisdictional question, the way was clear for the case to go to trial.

5

While both sides were preparing for trial, another attack on AT&T was heading for determination in the courts.

In 1971, the Federal Communications Commission had enabled independent carriers to offer inexpensive long-distance service through links with Bell's local systems. One outcome was the creation of several small companies, among them William G. McGowan's MCI Communications Corporation, which operated a system of microwave transmitters to send telephone messages between two dozen cities in the United States. On

April 3, 1974, MCI climaxed a series of allegations that the Bell System had hindered its efforts to expand its long-distance phone business by filing in the United States District Court in Chicago an anti-trust suit accusing AT&T and some of its telephone units of monopolization and conspiracy in restraint of trade and seeking $900 million in damages it claimed to have incurred. After preliminary legal skirmishes—MCI was represented by Robert Hanley and Chester Kamin of Jenner & Block—the case went to trial before a jury in the courtroom of Judge John F. Grady early in February 1980. After four months of examining over 1,000 exhibits and hearing seventy witnesses, the jury of seven women and five men returned a verdict in favor of MCI, with an award of $600 million that was automatically trebled under the anti-trust statutes to $1.8 billion, considered the largest sum ever awarded in civil anti-trust history. George Saunders, lead attorney in the case, announced that action to set aside the verdict would be taken within a month. "The award," he added, "is based on a terribly confusing damage study prepared by MCI and it bears no relationship to the specific charges on which MCI prevailed." Charles L. Brown, DeButts' successor as AT&T chairman, termed the award "grotesquely disproportionate to any conceivable damages MCI may have experienced as a result of the matters on which the jury supported its allegations" and predicted that after a "full judicial review we will be found to have been fair competitors."

Shortly before the MCI trial began, Trienens had been named AT&T's general counsel and vice-president in the wake of the retirement of F. Mark Garlinghouse. He now undertook not only overall supervision of the company's 900 lawyers in addition to carrying on duties for such other clients as Northwest Industries and G. D. Searle but also took the lead in appealing the MCI verdict. In an hour-long argument on April 30, 1981, before the United States Court of Appeals, he excoriated the damage award as improper, unsubstantiated by evidence, and based on erroneous instructions to the jury. He also asserted anew that AT&T was a public utility regulated by the FCC: "This case is all snarled in with the regulatory process. It shouldn't have been in the court in the first place. This is really a regulatory fight." The MCI lost-profits study that claimed AT&T's activities had cost MCI $900 million was, he said, "barely admissible evidence" that compelled the jurors to "speculate on damages." For MCI, Kamin described the case as an issue of "classic market exclusion" in which AT&T "used its power to deny a competitor access to the market place."

6

Meanwhile, there were significant developments in the government's anti-trust case on trial during 1981 before Judge Harold H. Greene, who had replaced Judge Waddy.

Late that July, reports emanated from Washington that the suit might be dropped if a legislative solution could be achieved by means of amendments to a telephone deregulation bill then pending in the Senate. A spokesman for Assistant Attorney General William Baxter, who had initially threatened to litigate the case "to the eyeballs," said that the amendments "would afford substantially all the relief objectives sought by the government." Judge Greene, however, refused the government's request to recess the trial until the following June to give Congress time to act on the legislation. After the Justice Department's chief trial attorney, Gerald A. Connell, concluded his presentation with a forty-five minute clarification of previous testimony and introduction of 1,000 documents as evidence, Saunders made a motion for dismissal, which Judge Greene granted as to some but denied as to most issues. Saunders was in the process of calling 400 witnesses when, early in October, the Senate passed, by a vote of 90 to 4, Senator Bob Packwood's bill that—duplicating the FCC's action of the preceding year—would enable AT&T, through a new subsidiary referred to informally as "Baby Bell," to enter such unregulated fields as information processing, computer-to-computer data transmission, and the sale of sophisticated telephones, switchboards, and other terminal equipment. Basic telephone service would continue to be regulated by state utility boards and the Federal Communications Commission.

While the House of Representatives went to work on its version of the bill as drafted by Representative Timothy E. Wirth, discussions were proceeding between Trienens and Baxter about the possibility of a settlement that would negate prolonged litigation whose costs had already amounted to $360 million for AT&T and many millions for the government. These reached the point where, on New Year's Eve, the Justice Department made formal disclosure that the talks about a settlement were under way. Baxter flew to Utah for a skiing vacation, but he spoke by telephone with his aides and with Trienens. No less than twenty drafts of the proposed settlement agreement were prepared before completion of a final draft which was flown to Baxter by Loren Hershey, one of his staff attorneys. Baxter approved the document, flew back to Washington with it, and on the morning of January 8, 1982, he and Trienens signed it. At noon, they joined AT&T Chairman Brown at the National Press Club for a public announcement of the pact that editorialists were quick to call "historic" and "dramatic" and "monumental"—and the day on which the government also voluntarily gave up its thirteen-year anti-trust legal battle with the International Business Machines Corporation, as "epochal."

Basically, the agreement completely eliminated the restrictions of the 1956 decree and called for AT&T to divest itself of the local exchange assets of its operating companies over the following eighteen months while retaining its nationwide long distance and intercity telephone service and Western Electric and Bell Telephone Laboratories. There were still hurdles in the path toward consummation: the need for a finding by Judge Greene that the proposed modification of the 1956 order was in the public interest; opposition from state commissions to certain sections dealing with the operating companies; clamor from competitors and suppliers of telecommunication equipment; statements from consumer groups about prospects of rate increases; apprehension of stockholders over undue delays in actual realization of the settlement; and the possibility of congressional weakening of the agreement through passage of restrictive legislation. But Charles Brown envisioned a future with many benefits. By removing the restrictions of the 1956 decree, the settlement would facilitate AT&T's entry into the information age, in which computer and telephone technologies overlapped. In a full-page statement in many major newspapers addressed to share owners and Bell System employees, Brown emphasized that the company had not sought divestiture but had agreed to the consent order "because we believed it expresses the consensus that, in the main, has been reached on the framework for a new national telecommunications policy." The course chosen, he added, was "one that best serves the public interest by enabling the telecommunications industry to move ahead into a new age, with your company serving in a major and proper role."

On August 11—after a summer of public comment on the January agreement and abandonment of the bill designed by Representative Wirth to stiffen its terms—Judge Greene, in a 178-page opinion, accepted the settlement with certain modifications. It was, he stated, "in the public interest" for AT&T to give up ownership of its twenty-two local operating companies while retaining its long distance division, its Western Electric

297

manufacturing subsidiary, and its innovative Bell Laboratories. He approved a provision in the settlement that would enable AT&T to provide a wide range of data processing services. But he modified the decree in several respects, including permitting the individual companies to continue to market telephone terminal equipment and publish the Yellow Pages advertising. Two weeks later, Judge Greene formally entered the consent decree. At the end of the year, AT&T submitted to Judge Greene a 471-page plan detailing how divestiture would be carried out by the end of 1983. The team of firm lawyers working with AT&T in preparing the plan, as well as the briefs defending it, was led by John D. Zeglis, a 1972 graduate of Harvard Law School and 1978 partner. After submission of the plan and, in addition, the upholding of the decree by the United States Supreme Court the following March, Brown once more expressed optimism. In nation-wide public advertisements headed "We're Managing Divestiture, Not Demolition," he acknowledged how complicated the process would be but added, "Both AT&T and the local phone companies have a bright future. We're at the heart of the fastest growing, most promising industry in the country. The new AT&T—with its long distance network and its new subsidiary, American Bell, plus Western Electric and Bell Labs—is in league with the future."

On July 8, 1983, Judge Greene, in giving final approval to the divestiture plan, required six modifications out of some 500 issues contested before him; one was that the Bell name and symbol should belong only to the 22 phone companies after divestiture.

Earlier, almost a year to the day after announcement of the basic agreement between AT&T and the Justice Department in the anti-trust case and after a reargument in April 1982, the United States Court of Appeals in Chicago overturned the $1.8 billion award to MCI made in the summer of 1980. It absolved AT&T of predatory pricing practices alleged by MCI while upholding some other findings by the jury and ordered a new trial limited to damages. In addition, that May the Sidley & Austin team that had been on trial for over 170 days in the MCI and government cases had gone to trial in a third major anti-trust case, that of Southern Pacific Communication Company against AT&T. This was virtually a carbon copy of the MCI case. SPCC was a firm that had come into being to do what MCI had done and consequently had been in similar disputes with AT&T. Unlike the MCI trial, this one was tried without a jury before Charles E. Richey, one of the country's outstanding federal judges. After proceedings that lasted little more than two months, Judge Richey issued a 600-page opinion in which he found for AT&T on every single issue—an outcome that afforded the Sidley & Austin team considerable satisfaction and a kind of vindication for many of the involved AT&T officers and employees.

7

Among various other developments in the post-merger decade were cases stemming from new environmental regulation and a growing trend toward litigating conflicts in the area of product advertising.

Creation in 1970 of the Environmental Protection Agency to consolidate existing programs to combat pollution resulted in establishment of environmental law as a legal specialty. A well-qualified member of the firm in this field was Thomas M. McMahon, who had worked for it as a clerk between his junior and senior years at the Law School of Northwestern University, from which he graduated—*magna cum laude*, law review editor and Order of the Coif—in 1970. In that year, he helped to start the Illinois Environmental Protection Agency and for the next eighteen months took part in the drafting of the state's environmental regulations and then headed the agency's legal division. McMahon returned to the firm early in 1972 as the full brunt of the environmental movement was beginning to be felt by many clients. Before that time, environmental matters had been handled by James Kissel. On the verge of election to the presidency of the Chicago Bar Association, Kissel welcomed McMahon's arrival to aid in a Procter & Gamble water pollution case, which they won against one of the city's most aggressive groups, Citizens for a Better Environment, and the Borden odor pollution case, which they lost at trial but eventually won with precedent-setting opinions in the Illinois Appellate and Supreme Courts.

During this period, as McMahon advanced to a partnership in 1975, he began to work with a long-time client, R. R. Donnelley & Sons Company. Illinois' recently-adopted pollution regulations would have required a capital investment of millions of dollars in air pollution control equipment for its *Life* magazine presses. Because *Life* was then nearing the end of its publication as a weekly, McMahon and the printing company's general counsel, John Schwemm, the Sidley & Austin alumnus who would become Donnelley's chairman and president in 1983, devised a strategy by which the magazine was allowed a natural death while providing equivalent environmental protection by the use of superior control technology elsewhere in Donnelley's massive Chicago facility. *Life* later resumed publication as a monthly, using different presses.

Increasingly stringent environmental regulations through the mid-1970s and failure in some areas in the country to meet Clean Air Act deadlines caused a virtual prohibition against new construction in such sectors in 1977. PreFinish Metals wanted to build a plant of considerable size in one such area in Ohio and sought the firm's help. The company had already developed a state-of-the-art process which reduced emissions by 99 percent. The remaining 1 percent, so that the plant generated no net increase in air pollution, was attained through a unique pact in which the Ohio Transportation Department agreed to use a less-polluting road resurfacing material in the affected county. Because the agreement was viewed as an example of how cooperation between industry and federal, state, and local agencies could influence continued industrial growth and environmental protection, a ceremony was set in Governor James Rhodes office in Columbus. Although a blizzard paralyzed mid-Ohio, the scheduled formalities proceeded, and McMahon, who had come with a contingent of PreFinish executives, would remember well the scene in the governor's office, which had been turned into a virtual war room to coordinate the state's disaster services.

The most time-consuming and important environmental work by McMahon and his group was for Velsicol Chemical Corporation, a subsidiary of Northwest Industries, which had become a client in the early summer of 1978. The firm represents NWI as general counsel, including litigation, financing, and corporate transactions, such as the sale of its beverage business (Coca-Cola of Los Angeles and the Buckingham Corporation) to Beatrice Foods for $600 million. Thomas A. Cole, an associate from the University of Chicago since 1975 and a 1981 partner, is NWI's vice-president-law, and Trienens works closely with him in coordinating services to NWI. Most of NWI's operating subsidiaries, with headquarters in various parts of the country, are represented by other outside counsel. Velsicol, whose headquarters are in Chicago, is represented by Sidley & Austin.

At the time the firm began its representation of NWI, Velsicol had been charged with creating one of the worst agricultural disasters in United States history. In the early 1970s, a flame retardant—

polybrominated biphenyls, known as PBB—had been substituted for an animal-feed supplement, which allegedly caused the deaths of millions of farm animals in Michigan. This and other cases prompted NWI's president, Ben Heineman, to direct the company and the law firm to put environmental security ahead of all other corporate priorities and capital spending. James Archer and McMahon, aided by others, undertook the assignment to assist new Velsicol officials in negotiating amicable and fair settlements of several environmental disputes with federal and state authorities.

The first of these, after some eighteen months of such negotiations, resulted in a consent judgment to shut down operation of a plant in Memphis, Tennessee. The second was more complex and drawn-out, for it concerned the Michigan plant and involved dealing with representatives of the state's Department of Natural Resources and attorney general, the federal EPA, and the Department of Justice. Negotiations began in June 1979 and finally ended with entry of a consent judgment in December 1982, which, among other things, called for cash payments of $14 million to the government and $6 million of remedial action by Velsicol in return for a release of the chemical corporation from further liability to state and federal governments. In addition, McMahon's group gave valuable counsel on governmental matters. With changed attitudes of Velsicol management and determination to fulfill Heineman's order to make its plants and its products environmentally safe and secure, Velsicol succeeded in turning its environmental image around effectively.

In the early 1980s, with the environmental group grown to seven attorneys, there emerged a new and immensely controversial environmental problem—hazardous waste dumps such as the Love Canal. Robert M. Olian, a 1977 Harvard Law School graduate, became one of the country's authorities on the complex body of laws and regulations that proliferated to deal with that problem. He was also given responsibility for environmental matters of the 1992 Chicago World's Fair, to be built on a proposed landfill in Lake Michigan, and he and McMahon, along with Henry Mason and Douglas F. Fuson, a University of Chicago Law School 1968 graduate and a partner since 1974, also represented SCA Services, Incorporated, a waste disposal company, in a pending dispute over its operation of a hazardous waste disposal site in downstate Illinois.

An interesting case, indicating the broad scope of environmental regulation, dealt with the Dr. Scholl Company, which had incorporated an anti-bacterial agent into the fabric of an insole product without registering it with the EPA. After the company had initiated its marketing, the EPA took the position that the bacterial agent made the insole a pesticide subject to EPA regulations. Tomas M. Russell, a 1967 graduate of University of Wisconsin Law School and a partner since 1973, resolved the conflict by relying on a little-known exception in the massive EPA regulations that recognized a distinction between the bacteriacides for treatment of materials as distinguished from treatment of the human body.

As for court battles over advertising claims, a typical case resulted from a television commercial for Tame, a hair-conditioning product made by the firm's long-time client, Gillette. In it, Tame was displayed side by side with Alberto Balsam, a similar conditioner manufactured by Alberto-Culver Company. A model deposited drops from each bottle on a plastic sheet, which was then dipped into a container of water. When a film remained on the sheet holding the Alberto Balsam, a voice was heard to say, "The difference is, Tame rinses clean . . . like it does on your hair." In this first case to challenge comparative brand advertising that identified a rival product by name instead of by the traditional "Brand X," Alberto-Culver filed suit in the United States District Court in Chicago against Gillette and its advertising agency, J. Walter Thompson, for up to $8.4 million in damages for profits allegedly lost because of the commercial and for another $16 million for anticipated future losses. In the trial that started in early March 1979, before Judge Joseph Sam Perry, Alberto-Culver witnesses testified that the Gillette campaign produced a devastating effect on the company's sales, reducing them by 50 percent in the year the commercial was telecast. By the trial's tenth day, a satisfactory settlement was reached. Russell Baird subsequently presented the case to summer associates in a session on advertising and marketing law as an example not only of the importance of checking claims in print and electronic advertising but of the movement from the firm's earlier role as primarily an adviser in the advertising field to one in litigation.

8

The firm's real estate practice, traditionally strong, expanded during the 1970s and beyond under the leadership of Edward Saunders until his death in 1976 and thereafter under Donald Gralen, with the support of a substantial number of partners, associates, and legal assistants. The services varied greatly in nature, size, and types of individual and corporate clients. Some transactions involved only straight real estate work. Others extended into diverse fields of law, requiring the collaboration of lawyers in other functional groups, such as those in the fields of estates and trusts, the environment, taxes, bankruptcies, and litigation.

Among specific transactions exemplifying the variety of real estate matters was the representation of the Hyatt Regency Hotel in erecting a second thirty-three-story hotel tower adjoining the original on Wacker Drive east of Michigan Avenue. This was complicated by, among other things, the presence of an easement for a future Chicago subway line running eastward to Navy Pier; because it traversed the site, some of the hotel's caissons had to be constructed in the median strip of the subway. The firm also represented The First National Bank and other lenders in several large mortgage transactions. One was the $184 million financing of the construction of the Chicago Mercantile Exchange Center on Wacker Drive, a structure consisting of a new trading floor and an adjoining forty-story office tower. Another was the $264 million financing of a new 1800-room Marriott Hotel in downtown Atlanta.

Earlier, the firm had been engaged by Philip Klutznick's Urban Investment and Development Company as lead counsel in the annexation and rezoning by Aurora of 3,900 acres of land owned or controlled by a joint venture comprising Klutznick's company, Metropolitan Structures, and Henry Crown & Company. The annexation, one of the largest in Illinois history, increased Aurora's land area by 50 percent. A planned unit development was created, with Gale Christopher and city attorneys cooperating in detailing transformation of the land into a site, over the next two decades, for a multitude of uses ranging from an enclosed shopping mall and an office building to residential housing, schools, roads, and parks. Christopher's concept was considered unique in providing flexibility to a developer for a long-term project while municipal authorities continued to retain control. In connection with the Aurora project, there were environmental obstacles that required the services of McMahon and others engaged in the broadening field of environmental law.

Work for the Tishman interests that had started in the 1960s continued. In 1980, a decisive point was reached in a plan of Tishman Midwest Management Corporation, the new corporate entity into which the Tishman realty and construction operations had been consolidated in

1973. It called for TNS Associates, a partnership made up of the company's employees, to acquire the seventy-year-old Italian Renaissance-styled Chicago and North Western passenger terminal at Madison and Canal Streets and, after its demolition, to build a 1.4-million-square-foot, $240 million, forty-one-story terminal. Various individuals and groups devoted to the preservation of what they considered an architectural landmark entered objections which were answered by a team headed by Jack Guthman, a 1963 Yale University Law School graduate who specialized in representing the private sector in governmental matters and had achieved a reputation as a "trouble-shooter" as a partner with Leibman, Williams, Bennett, Baird, and Minow and was, among other things, chairman of the city's zoning board of appeals. The staff report issued by the Commission on Chicago Historical and Architectural Landmarks supported designation of the station as a landmark. But Martin Murphy, city planning commissioner, agreed with Guthman that retention of the station would constrict contemporary modifications needed for effective rail passenger movement and that the Tishman purchase and proposed action were essential to expansion of the central business district to the north and west of the Loop. At the commission's hearing, architectural historians emphasized that not only was the station considered unremarkable as an architectural creation but that, in the years since its completion in 1911, it had lost its architectural integrity. Subsequently, the City Council, with final say in all landmark issues, affirmed the commission's decision not to give landmark status to the station and its sale for $21.5 million was closed.

Two other projects designed to bear benefits to Chicagoans were also represented by the firm.

In 1973, the Chicago 21 Plan was unveiled as one of the most massive undertakings in Chicago history. So called because its aim was to fashion a bigger and better city by the advent of the twenty-first century, its key element, at a contemplated cost approaching $1.5 billion, was nothing less than the creation of a South Loop New Town in an area which was then fifty-one acres of unused railroad yards south of the city's central business and shopping district. Three dozen leading institutions joined in forming Dearborn Park Corporation to act as a catalyst in attracting private developers to participate in a project which, as a whole, envisaged 13,000 housing units for 30,000 persons, ranging from single-family townhouses to apartment complexes to high-rises, and including areas of open space for recreation, public transit facilities, diverse kinds of schools from the traditional to the Montessori, and first-rate police and fire protection.

Minow, aided by Guthman and James L. Marovitz, assisted the corporation in fulfilling the first phase of the overall project: Dearborn Park, a $150 million residential development of fifty-one acres bounded by Polk, State, Clark, and 15th Streets in which, ultimately, some 3,000 housing units of varied sorts were to be built. Myriad details required services of the firm, from the acquisition of the rectangular site from a railroad consortium for $7.3 million to preparing certificates for the development's shareholders, including financial institutions, retail establishments, industrial giants, and the Catholic Archdiocese of Chicago. At hearings before the Chicago Plan Commission and the City Council, witnesses to testify in Dearborn Park's behalf were called by Guthman. They emphasized the advantages—addition of nearly $3 million annually to the city's tax income, 800 construction jobs and a payroll of $80 million during the five-year building period, and the injection of new life into the Loop shopping area—and countered claims of opponents that the development would be "an enclave for wealthy whites" with predictions that families with incomes of $15,000 would be able to afford to live there, a promise dimmed because of drastic rises in inflation, mortgage rates, and rents by the time the first units were ready for occupancy in 1979. To Guthman and Marovitz later fell the task of drafting and securing the City Council's approval of essential ordinances and the city's agreement to sustain costs for streets, sewers, schools, and recreational facilities.

Work progressed on more units as time passed. The second phase was launched in mid-1982 to fill out the original intentions and to join in a virtual "housing Renaissance" such other nearby developments as Printing House Row, a two-block stretch along South Dearborn Street to be transformed from an area of printing, industrial, transportation, and shipping facilities into a $50 million complex of 1,000 apartments, shops, and restaurants. These and others in prospect held hopes for attainment of what Philip Klutznick, as chairman, said when he announced the Chicago 21 Plan: "This is an idea whose time has come. I definitely believe it is time to bring people back to our central urban area. The vitality of Chicagoland depends on a city that is not a 5 o'clock city."

Toward the close of planning the creation of Dearborn Park, Guthman instigated action that led to cut-rate mortgages for middle-income home buyers. This came about as the result of an idea proposed to him in the

305

summer of 1977 by a close friend, Robert Kutak, an Omaha lawyer and the outside counsel on revenue bond matters for E. F. Hutton. That idea, developed by Kutak and W. James Lopp II, a Hutton executive vice-president, was to use for residential purposes a section of the Internal Revenue Code that historically allowed tax-free bonds to be issued for industrial developments, wharves, airports, and the like. Chicago could do this under its home rule powers. Guthman and Kutak drew up position papers and won the backing of Thomas Donovan, top aide to Mayor Michael Bilandic, who had been named successor to Mayor Richard J. Daley after the latter's death late in 1976, and City Comptroller Clark Burrus. By summer of the next year, Guthman gained the support of E. Stanley Enlund for his First Federal Savings and Loan Association—a client of the firm in assorted matters—to handle the lending of money to potential home-purchasers with annual incomes of up to $40,000 at an interest rate of 7.99 percent, two percentage points lower than prevailing rates. The result was the city's first-in-the-nation $100 million low-interest mortgage revenue bond program. The bonds, marketed through a Hutton-organized underwriters' syndicate, sold out in a single day. Moreover, city after city followed the Chicago example so that by June 1979, fifty throughout the nation were employing the basic plan or an adaptation. Despite enthusiastic response to the innovative idea, opposition to it arose in Washington. The Treasury Department contended that proliferation of the mortgage bonds would lead to considerable reductions in federal revenues. Other critics charged that the tax-free bonds competed with general obligation bonds and would force up interest costs to municipalities. In April 1979, Representative Al Ullman, chairman of the House Ways and Means Committee, introduced a bill to limit cities in issuing the bonds, and shortly before his defeat in the 1980 elections, a bill embodying the essence of his proposed legislation was passed by Congress.

Ancillary to the firm's real estate projects yet calling for cooperation with members of other groups was the task of clearing up one of the nation's largest real estate bankruptcy cases on record. As lead counsel for secured creditors, the firm participated in bankruptcy proceedings, numerous mortgage foreclosures, renegotiation of first mortgage loans, and appellate work. The central figure in this disaster that received nationwide attention was Walter Judd Kassuba, who was called by many in the early 1970s "America's biggest apartment landlord" because of his $500 million empire of motels, condominiums, and 34,000 moderate rental apartment units he had built or acquired mainly in Illinois, Wisconsin, and Florida and scattered in fourteen other states, plus hundreds of acres of undeveloped land. By 1973, Kassuba was in deep financial trouble. The nation was in the midst of an economic recession. A wage-price freeze instituted by the Nixon administration barred rent increases. Apartment vacancies multiplied, as did operating costs and interest rates on new projects. As his problems mounted, Kassuba found himself unable to pay his debts when they came due. When a Chicago-area creditor sued him in DuPage Circuit Court for recovery of a $900,000 debt, Kassuba was urged by his lawyers to file for reorganization under Chapter 11 of the federal bankruptcy code. This was done at the close of the year. The amount owed by Kassuba was set at about $450 million, mostly to such secured creditors as banks, insurance companies, and savings and loan institutions. Some of these creditors were Sidley & Austin clients, so a team of its lawyers experienced in real estate and creditors' rights matters—Edward Saunders and Bruce Schimberg, along with Howard Haynie, a 1959 Loyola Law School alumnus and 1969 partner, Robert A. Downing, a 1956 University of Wisconsin graduate and 1964 partner, and Mark E. MacDonald, a 1967 Northwestern University Law School graduate and partner since 1973— undertook to enforce over $125 million in 119 separate first mortgages in twenty states. Gradually, through many negotiations, conferences, and court sessions, the details of reorganization and repayment of available funds were worked out, but Kassuba's reputation as one of the country's real estate moguls had faded.

9

The post-merger years were busy ones for estate planners. Major changes in the federal estate tax law were enacted as part of the 1976 Tax Reform Act and as part of the Economic Recovery Tax Act of 1981. As a result of these changes, hundreds of clients' estate plans became obsolete and needed rewriting. Shortly after the merger, the firm reviewed all of its estate planning files and prepared a computerized list of clients and significant features of their wills and trust documents, which proved to be invaluable in identifying clients to be contacted because of tax law changes. Review and revision of client estate plans consumed a substantial part of the probate group's time in the years following each of the major tax changes. This work was similar to that done in prior years, as, for example, when the marital deduction was enacted in 1948.

Due partly to better estate planning and draftsmanship by most law firms, there has been substantially less litigation involving will and trust construction and contests in recent years, but the valuation of assets and the economic and tax problems faced by estates with illiquid assets or substantial liabilities, require careful attention. An example of the former was the valuation of Wrigley Company and Cubs stock in the estate of Philip Wrigley, while the latter problems were encountered in the estate of Carl G. Klehm, a nursery man who, at the time of his death in 1973, owned valuable tracts of land adjacent to the Northwest Tollway near O'Hare Airport. The family assets were encumbered with mortgages and assignments securing millions of dollars of Klehm's obligations. Not only did the estate have virtually no cash to meet these obligations, but there were also its tax liability, the numerous claims filed against it, and administration expenses. After eight years of effort, a "fire sale" of the real estate was avoided while orderly liquidation of a substantial portion of it was accomplished. The most pressing debts and death taxes were paid, and a settlement made among the family members. The nursery business still is intact, operated by Klehm's sons.

In 1980, the firm was retained by a wealthy Western European family which had invested a substantial portion of its wealth in United States real estate as a hedge against the potential loss of its European assets through foreign invasion of the family homeland or a radical change in its government. The family and its lawyers—a member of "Le Club" had referred the client to the firm—feared that in the event of a takeover by unfriendly forces, either the government would force the family to repatriate its assets in this country or the United States would seize them as owned by an enemy. John C. Williams, a 1954 Yale Law School alumnus and partner in 1964, devised an emergency trust designed to settle the assets and the beneficiaries in the United States in case of such an emergency. In addition, the firm provided extensive tax, corporate, and real estate counseling to the family with respect to these assets. Other clients came to the firm since then in connection with similar problems, and it appears that work with foreign nationals owning United States property is a potentially fast growing area of practice.

The estates of John Searle and his wife, Frances, and of Arthur Nielsen also were probated during the decade; they provided substantial benefits to charities in the Chicago area, their families having been provided for through other arrangements devised by the firm. On behalf of several Chicago area charities, Larry D. Berning, a 1968 Indiana University graduate and 1974 partner, was instrumental in securing enactment by Congress of legislation to remedy the unintended effect of a tax law that would have seriously impaired the integrity of charitable trusts created by the Searles and other clients.

In addition to serving individual clients and estates, lawyers in the estate group work with others to improve estate and tax law and practice, especially to reduce taxes. Williams, as co-chairman of a joint committee of the Chicago and Illinois State bar associations, drafted and helped to secure passage of a bill to simplify and speed up Illinois probate procedures. In 1982, Avery and Thomas E. Swaney, a 1968 associate from the University of Michigan Law School and a 1973 partner, worked closely with counsel for the Corporate Fiduciaries Association in securing repeal of the Illinois inheritance tax.

10

The firm's corporate and securities practice, a vital and growing element of its overall activities, continued to thrive and expand.

Of its three major corporate areas—financing; mergers and acquisitions, and dispositions; and counseling—the first, as in the past, occupies the greatest share of time, accounting for somewhat less than half of the total work of the corporate group. Financings include public offerings, private placements, and project financings. In recent years as market needs have changed and tax advantages have become significant, the types of investment instruments have greatly expanded from classic common stock and bond offerings to complicated leveraged lease transactions and a wide variety of investment vehicles.

Among clients engaged in registered offerings of stocks and bonds or government-guaranteed securities to the public are such prominent investment banking firms as Smith Barney, Harris Upham & Company; Merrill Lynch, Pierce, Fenner & Smith Incorporated-Merrill Lynch White Weld Capital Markets Group; Salomon Brothers; Morgan Stanley & Company; Goldman, Sachs & Company; and Kidder Peabody & Company. An important aspect of the corporate group's duties is functioning as bond counsel for various public utility systems whose securities are often offered with competitive bidding procedures; underwriters of Commonwealth

Edison Company have thus been represented for over forty years. Among other clients for whom such services have been performed are Central & Southwest Power, Iowa-Illinois Gas and Electric, Kansas City Power & Light, Ottertail Power, and Indiana Public Service. Private placements have been handled for Equitable Life Assurance Society of the United States, Aetna Life Insurance Company, Metropolitan Life Insurance Company, and others in lending to many private corporations.

Project financing increased greatly in scope and importance during the post-merger years, providing an example of the variety and innovation in the group's practice.

One of the largest in project financing with which the firm has ever been involved is the $2.1 billion Great Plains Coal Gasification Project, the nation's first commercial-scale facility to convert lignite coal into pipeline-quality natural gas. It was conceived early in the 1970s with American Natural Resources Company's plan to construct such a plant, and the firm's initial assignment was to help an ANR subsidiary acquire rights to lignite coal reserves in North Dakota. John O'Hare, a 1971 Harvard Law School graduate and a 1977 partner, and Robert Beam performed this service, and O'Hare also negotiated agreements on behalf of it and another ANR subsidiary with utility and coal companies to facilitate preliminary steps in the operation. As time passed and unanticipated delays developed and costs mounted unduly, ANR and other interested companies, notably a subsidiary of Chicago's Peoples Gas Light and Coke Company, joined with subsidiaries of the Columbia Gas System, Incorporated, Tenneco, Incorporated, and Transco Corporation in forming a partnership called Great Plains Gasification Associates.

In 1970, upon graduating *cum laude* from Northwestern University Law School after a career as a Navy fighter pilot, restaurant owner, and stock broker, R. Todd Vieregg joined the firm, achieving partnership in 1973. He represented the ANR system in preparing the partnership agreement and the partners' related contracts, and he also represented Great Plains in negotiations with a consortium of banks for debt financing for the project. Such financing hinged on whether the project could obtain approval from the Federal Energy Regulatory Commission for a plan to have potential consumers of the natural gas finance the project through increased rates. The commission sanctioned the rate hike but when various consumer groups appealed that ruling, the United States Court of Appeals in Washington reversed the order. Richard Flynn and Frederic G. Berner, Jr., a 1973 George Washington Law School graduate and a 1980 partner, both of the firm's Washington office, then worked out a settlement with the appellant groups and the FERC, which approved the price at which any gas produced by the plant would be sold to consumers. Simultaneously, the Columbia Gas System withdrew from the project, to be replaced later by a Pacific Lighting Corporation subsidiary. Shortly, the Department of Energy, with whom Vieregg had been negotiating along with underwriters and banks for federal guarantee of loans if the FERC order were overturned, determined that a $250 million guaranteed loan should be obtained from the federal financing bank and not from commercial banks or from the public through underwriters. Vieregg and Andrew H. Shaw, a 1979 Cornell University Law School graduate who came to the firm in 1981 after clerking for United States District Court Judge Newell Bedenfield in Savannah, Georgia, drew up the basic guarantee agreement with the DOE and most of twenty other major financing documents. To provide the government with rights to the project if it had to pay on its guarantee of the loan and take over the project, Jon M. Gregg, a 1968 Harvard Law School alumnus and 1974 partner, arranged numerous pacts concerning technology and proprietary data with contractors and advisors on the project in Washington, New York, Johannesburg, South Africa, and Frankfurt, West Germany.

Culmination of the complex transaction came on January 29, 1982, in the firm's Washington office with the delivery of hundreds of executed documents related to construction of the huge plant set to be completed outside Beulah, North Dakota, by the end of 1983 and capable of producing 125 million cubic feet of gas a day, the equivalent of 20,000 barrels of oil. A year and a half earlier, in a Cabinet Room ceremony, President Jimmy Carter had presented the loan guarantee commitment to Arthur Seder, Jr., the former Sidley & Austin partner who headed American Natural Resources, and to O. C. Davis, the Peoples Gas Light and Coke chairman. It had been a long and difficult time since the project had been conceived and in that time between ten and twenty of the firm's lawyers had worked on it.

Later in 1982, The First National Bank of Chicago engaged the firm to represent it in a $140 million loan guaranteed in part by the Department of Energy to enable the New Energy Company of Indiana to build an ethanol fuel plant in South Bend. Vieregg and Shaw were responsible for basic elements in the transaction which, in some respects, was even more complicated than the Great Plains Gasification financing.

In the early 1970s, International Minerals & Chemical Corporation, a long time client of the firm, conceived a plan for the financing of a new phosphate fertilizer plant in New Wales, Florida. Maurice Miller spent approximately a year on in negotiating take-or-pay fertilizer contracts with six major customers, then negotiating financing arrangements with New York lenders using such contracts as security, with proceeds of loans used to construct the plant to purchase the fertilizer.

An early example of the synergistic effect of the 1972 merger was the dramatic growth in so-called Title XI financing. On the very day the merger was announced, President Nixon signed into law amendments to Title XI of the Merchant Marine Act of 1936 making possible 100 percent government-guaranteed construction and permanent financing of United States vessels. Roy Bowman, a former Maritime Administration official then in the Washington office of Leibman, Williams, Bennett, Baird, and Minow, represented Marine Fruit Carriers in the proposed financing of three 165,000-ton crude oil carriers being built at the Bethlehem Steel yards with financing by leveraged lease. Upon consolidation, several experienced Sidley & Austin corporate lawyers joined in drafting many of the original documents under Title XI, James Archer prime among them. At the same time, the firm had begun to represent the new corporate financing group of First Chicago Corporation, which was highly interested in ship financing. Two years later, Archer and Richard Clemens led the organization of a thriving practice to represent institutional purchasers of Title XI securities. In 1980, such financings amounted to $280 million in thirteen transactions that ranged from $2 million to $5 million gulf coast oil tug and supply vessels to $100 million to $150 million oil and bulk product carriers and including even the *Mississippi Queen*, the replacement for the famous cruise ship, the *Delta Queen*. This expertise in government-guaranteed ship financing has led to such other guaranteed financings as that for aircraft, the Economic Development Administration, the International Trade Administration, and the Federal Housing Administration.

The practice of acting as bond counsel in municipal financings had long been the province of a relatively few firms that specialized in that field.

Newton Minow, foreseeing the growing role of state and local governments in society and the increasing financing needed to support such activities, suggested this as an area of expansion. The problem the firm faced was that it was not listed in the "red book," the directory of municipal bond lawyers. To be so listed, the firm needed to have its opinion as bond counsel accepted by bond purchasers, but for these purchasers to do so it needed that important listing. To solve this dilemma, Minow, drawing on experience gained in advising The First National Bank of Chicago in the Chicago public school financial crisis of 1979–80, convinced that bank and Continental Illinois National Bank and Trust Company to accept the firm's opinion as bond counsel for the city.

Those who worked with Minow on this important task included Richard Clemens, Maurice Miller, Martin F. Robinson, a 1964 associate from the University of Pennsylvania and a 1972 partner, and Lee Schwartz, a 1966 Harvard Law School graduate who came to the firm in 1980 after a dozen and more years as a legislative aide in Springfield and Chicago and achieved partnership in 1983. As a result, new assignments came from the Chicago Park District, the District of Columbia—where James W. Dyke, Jr., a 1971 Howard University Law School graduate and a 1982 partner, was especially helpful—and other local and state agencies, and the firm was recognized by financial institutions and governmental bodies as an acknowledged expert in the legal issues and problems of municipal finance.

Robert Beam, a veteran of scores of corporate matters in his many years with the firm, joined a member of the tax group—Frank V. Battle, Jr., a 1969 graduate of the DePaul University Law School and a 1974 partner —in helping to carry through the construction and complex financing of a major Burlington Northern dock facility at Allouez, Wisconsin. To be built there at a cost of $70 million, it was to be an important link in transporting iron pellets from plants in Minnesota's Mesabi Range by three-and-a-half-mile conveyer belt through Allouez to blast furnaces operated by two large steel companies at various locations on the Great Lakes. To get the lowest possible cost for money to finance the project, an innovative and extremely intricate plan was devised by Burlington Northern's financial department and participating investment bankers. Beam and Battle represented Burlington Northern in the multitude of problems associated with the plan which, in essence, called for creation of a trust for the benefit of the financial institutions providing the equity capital and which were to be the facility's owners. The trust acquired the property and built the dock, which was then leased to a Burlington Northern subsidiary. Construction initially was financed by interim borrowing, repaid by the trust's owners to the extent of about 30 percent of the dock's cost; the

313

rest was obtained by the trust's borrowing the proceeds from the sale of tax-exempt municipal bonds. Payment of the facility's cost was secured by assignment to the trustee for the owner participants of long-term transportation contracts by the steel plants and net lease proceeds by the Burlington Northern subsidiary. The bonds were secured by assignment to the bondholders' trustee of certain proceeds of the transportation contracts and of the net lease, together with a first mortgage on the premises. These complicated transactions took over a year to complete and involved, apart from ultimate purchasers of the bonds, eleven principals and their respective lawyers. But the effort proved worthwhile, for Burlington Northern's after-tax cost of capital to build the dock was less than 5.5 percent.

As a corporate financing expert, Beam was no stranger to work on unique projects. In the early 1960s, he had succeeded Ray Garrett and George Ranney as the lawyer for Peabody Coal Company, a valued client for many years. Services for Peabody were highly varied, ranging from acquisitions of other coal producers and coal lands to a complete reorganization of the company. Probably the most complicated, interesting project was a joint venture to produce coal from an Australian mine for nine great steel companies of Japan. Begun in 1962, it involved building a huge mine in Queensland and a 200-mile railroad through a mountain range to the port of Gladstone. Australian interests were to own the mine that would be operated by Peabody as a consortium of American, Australian, and Japanese interests, and the Queensland government would build, own, and operate the rail line. As chief legal advisor and a principal negotiator for Peabody, Beam traveled extensively—from Chicago to Tokyo, to Brisbane and Pittsburgh and back to Chicago. A take-or-pay coal sales agreement with one of the large Japanese trading companies had to be approved by each of the nine ultimate buyers of the coal. An agreement with Queensland officials for construction of the railroad required approbation by that government's Parliament, and a financing agreement needed confirmation by the lending bank in Pittsburgh. Accordingly, Beam's frequent peregrinations over nearly five years were necessary to negotiate nearly every principal document and inevitable changes in an approved draft. The final piece of the labyrinthine process fell into place when the contract with Queensland was approved by its Parliament at a marathon session that began early on one day and did not end until 4:30 o'clock the next morning with a vote in favor of an enabling bill related to the railroad's construction. Furthermore, the contract drafted and negotiated by Beam was incorporated into the bill and became part of Queensland's statutory law.

During the late 1960s and 1970s, mergers and acquisitions and dispositions became an increasingly important part of the corporate group's practice. International Minerals & Chemical Corporation, interested in diversifying from its historical dependence on the agricultural fertilizer business, was very active and Maurice J. Miller, James D. Johnson, a 1970 graduate of the University of Iowa and a 1973 partner, and George E. Crapple, a 1969 Harvard Law School graduate and a 1974 partner, represented IMC in the acquisition and dispositions of businesses ranging from barrel cleaning operations to coal mines. Miller and Johnson also handled two large real estate dispositions for Kimberly-Clark Corporation, which owned vast acreages of timberlands in Northern Wisconsin, Upper Michigan, and Northern California. They represented the company in a complex option-sale transaction with Champion International, Incorporated, for some 385,000 acres of woodlands in Northern Wisconsin and Upper Michigan, and a few years later in the sale of approximately 325,000 acres of California woodlands and two sawmills to Roseburg Lumber Company.

As in the Great Plains Gasification and Title XI projects, combinations and dispositions of businesses have required the cooperation of various functional groups in the firm.

In representing The First National Bank of Chicago in the sale of $150 million worth of real estate properties to a purchasing syndicate organized by the Victor Palmieri Company, Donald Gralen led a team of twelve from the corporate and securities, real estate and banking, and commercial groups. Another example of joint group work was the representation of the firm's long-standing client, Carson Pirie Scott & Company, in acquiring Dobbs Houses, Incorporated, and related entities from the Squibb Corporation, a move that doubled the company's size. For four months, a team composed of Joseph S. Ehrman, a 1957 Harvard Law School graduate and 1966 partner, John O'Hare, Jon Gregg, and Michael S. Sigal, a 1967 University of Chicago Law School graduate and 1973 partner, labored to work out an acceptable contract with Squibb representatives who periodically suggested they were also negotiating with a large British concern. Difficult tax and pension problems were resolved by Robert Frei and Robert A. Ferencz, a 1973 *magna cum laude* graduate of University of

Michigan Law School and a 1981 partner, and real estate associates aided by analyzing Dobbs' extensive holdings. During the negotiations, Ehrman and O'Hare also assisted Carson Pirie Scott & Company in securing a $100 million term loan agreement with three major banks and another to sell $20 million in its preferred stock to Squibb.

<h1 style="text-align:center">11</h1>

There were other matters of importance or interest in the decade after the merger.

Starting in 1973, the firm's banking and commercial law group, headed by Schimberg and increasingly active in behalf of creditors' rights, worked for a client affected by the nationwide scandal touched off by Equity Funding Corporation of America's multi-million-dollar deceptions in fake insurance policies and in stock rigging. In behalf of Ranger National Life Insurance Company of Houston, Schimberg and Bruce Bernstein and other members of the group pursued various claims against the Illinois-based Equity Funding Life Insurance Company, a wholly-owned EFCA subsidiary involved in a liquidation proceeding under the Illinois Insurance Code. The claims arose out of re-insurance and co-insurance agreements under which Ranger had paid nearly $3 million in commissions and death claims for policies that were either invalid or non-existent. Through conferences and negotiations and hearings before Judge Alfred Woodward in the DuPage County Circuit Court in Wheaton, a plan of liquidation was worked out that provided for payment to Ranger of 55 percent of the amount due and a settlement also was made of claims against the subsidiary by defrauded security holders.

In an epilogue to the earlier misfortunes of National Student Marketing Corporation, Schimberg aided its new chairman, Joseph Cottrell, in getting its complicated affairs in order. Many businesses acquired in the "go-go 1960s" were sold off. By 1977, Schimberg had helped Cottrell accomplish a reasonable resuscitation by reorganizing the suit-ridden firm into four divisions, including Interstate National Insurance Corporation and the popular Arthur Frommer Company that specialized in charter air travel. In 1980, although its assets were at a record $85 million, liquidation was agreed upon by its directors because of inflation, shrinking earnings, and increased competition. The Interstate subsidiary was sold to American Insurance Company for a reported $54 million and its bus company to Charterways Transportation for $11 million, making possible a return to its stockholders of $6.50 a share, a gratifying contrast to the seventeen-cent price at the low point in the company's precipitous decline a decade earlier.

Following congressional passage in 1976 of the Railroad Revitalization and Regulatory Reform Act—popularized as the "4 R Act"—to encourage and expedite mergers as a way to improve the railroad industry's economic health, the firm resumed its work in the railroad merger movement.

The first to be presented to the Interstate Commerce Commission for approval late in 1977 involved the application of the Norfolk and Western and the Baltimore and Ohio for joint control of the Detroit, Toledo and Ironton Railroad, a strategically located line between Detroit and Cincinnati that had been built by Henry Ford. But the application was denied after a year and more of hearings, because the commission issued new regulations requiring total financial commitment instead of the 50-50 stock ownership proposed by the two carriers. Next was the merger of the recently-created Burlington Northern with St. Louis-San Francisco Railway Company, the firm representing both. As narrated earlier, this was successfully brought about in 1980 after nearly three years spent countering opposition from a dozen competing lines.

A proceeding of great complexity involved the Southern Pacific's application in 1979 to purchase the bankrupt Rock Island's so-called "Tucumcari Line." This was opposed by the firm's client, the Union Pacific, and by virtually all the western railroads and most of the midwestern carriers because approval would have given the Southern Pacific coveted ownership of a line to the Mississippi River, which the Union Pacific and others had also long wished for. In ninety-nine days of hearings in Washington, Kansas City, and Los Angeles, over 19,000 pages of transcript and 600 exhibits were amassed. The commission's ultimate approval of Southern Pacific's application spurred Union Pacific to merge in 1983 with the Missouri Pacific and the Western Pacific and thereby trigger more restructuring of the western railroads.

The firm represented the Norfolk and Western in consolidating, effective in early 1982, with the Southern Railway System to create in the Norfolk Southern Corporation the country's third largest rail company, with a combined income of $500 million. In another matter, a legal precedent was set after the Norfolk and Western filed a motion in 1979 with the ICC opposing formation of CSX Corporation, a holding company created by the Family Lines (Seaboard Coast Line, Louisville & Nashville, and Clinchfield) and the Chessie System (Chesapeake & Ohio, Baltimore and Ohio, and Western Maryland) to control the lines of both systems. At the start of hearings that ultimately resulted in an agreement satisfactory to the Norfolk and Western, the Chessie System moved to disqualify Sidley & Austin from representation of the Norfolk and Western in the CSX matter because the firm was representing the two applicants in other pending litigation. The objection was overruled by the commission in a decision granting the right of a law firm to assume in cases involving multiple parties the role Sidley & Austin had taken, with the consent of both clients to the representation. The firm also participated in the Rock Island and Milwaukee reorganizations in the late 1970s on behalf of line haul carriers interchanging traffic with the two railroads by successfully obtaining non-deferrable payment of accounts due all the carriers. In 1982, the firm was successful in defending the Norfolk and Western in a criminal anti-trust suit brought by the Department of Justice in which all the other original defendant railroads had pleaded *nolo contendere*.

In these various cases, counsel included Martin Lucente of the Chicago office and, from the Washington office, Richard Flynn and Michael A. Nemeroff, a 1973 alumnus of Columbia University Law School and a 1978 partner who also had developed expertise in campaign financing and Political Action Committees. They were augmented in the Detroit, Toledo and Ironton matter by Trienens and in actions related to the Milwaukee and Rock Island bankruptcies by Schimberg and Bernstein. Associates who assisted in all phases were, in Washington, Terence M. Hynes of the 1979 class of Duke University Law School, and G. Paul Moates of the 1957 University of Chicago Law School class and named a partner in 1983, and, in Chicago, Christian L. Campbell, a 1975 Harvard Law School alumnus and a 1983 partner, and Kirk Johnson, a 1975 University of Chicago Law School graduate who, in 1980, was named a partner. Since 1976, Eden Martin has been lead counsel in a large number of cases in which the railroads' rates for coal have been actively contested before the Interstate Commerce Commission, in various appellate courts and in a unanimous victory before the Supreme Court in an important phase in the protracted litigation over railroad rates in unit trains.

What he later described as "a very large case, an exotic case" occupied much of Blair White's time in 1977. The case was a criminal anti-trust suit brought by the federal government alleging that AMAX, Incorporated, Duval Corporation, and the firm's client, International Minerals and Chemical Corporation, and Freeport Minerals Company, National Potash Company, Potash Company of America, and Ideal Plastic Industries, Incorporated, had conspired from the late 1960s into the early 1970s to fix the price of potash, a basic agricultural fertilizer product, by direct agreement, and by limiting domestic potash production. The government alleged that there were more than 100 unindicted co-conspirators, including a former governor of New Mexico, a former premier of the Province of Saskatchewan, and a justice of the Supreme Court of Ontario.

White, assisted by Nathan P. Eimer, a 1973 associate from the Northwestern University Law School and a 1980 partner, participated as legal counsel in a fourteen-week jury trial before Judge Prentice Marshall. Scores of witnesses testified that following discovery of potash fields in Saskatchewan, Canada, in the early 1960s and a consequent oversupply of the substance and plummeting prices in the market, the government of Saskatchewan had imposed price and production quotas in Canada. White argued that this governmental action and not a private conspiracy caused the reduction in production and the rise in prices. After deliberating for eight days, the jury acquitted Freeport Minerals and National Potash but failed to reach a verdict on the remaining defendants. Instead of retrying the case, the parties agreed that Judge Marshall should decide it on the record already made. Judge Marshall declared that the evidence of conspiracy was insufficient with respect to Duval and AMAX. But when he turned to International Minerals and Chemical Corporation, he noted that a particular memorandum by one of its officials "read almost like a blueprint for the government's theory of the case." Then he went on to say, much to White's delight, "When I review all of the evidence, however, in light of the conclusions that I have reached with respect to all of the other defendants. . . . I am hard pressed to find where International Minerals conspired with anyone, with the possible exception of itself. I don't think that they can conspire alone and, as a consequence, I believe and find that they should not be found guilty."

12

Other areas of practice flourished in the years after the merger, among them product liability and labor.

The first had started early in the 1960s when the doctrine of strict liability in tort began to be adopted by the courts. Initially, Edwin Austin was in charge of responses to such problems, with James Baker and James Kissel as senior members of the trial group. Then William P. Richmond, a 1959 University of Chicago Law School graduate and a 1967 partner, became head of the group which, by 1983, comprised nine lawyers. With the surge in product liability litigation, the group's practice became and continues to be devoted principally to the defense of particular products for several major clients. Coordination of that defense needed to be made in such a way as to promote uniformity and avoid duplication of effort since important products are distributed nationwide and bring about litigation in many jurisdictions. Crucial to each litigated matter is the organizing and presenting at trials of scientific and medical information relating to the product, witnesses necessary to offer evidence, and cross-examination of opposing witnesses.

In so doing, Richmond and his group have defended products of Borden, Kimberly-Clark, and Velsicol. Those defended for the longest period have been the oral contraceptives manufactured by one of the firm's oldest clients, G. D. Searle & Company. The first birth control pill was Searle's Enovid, introduced in 1960. Over the years, hundreds of suits have been filed involving complex problems related to claims that the pill had caused blood clotting, in some instances fatally. The great majority of such cases have been won in the courts by Richmond's team after presentation of expert testimony of scientists and medical experts for both sides. More than two decades after Enovid became available by prescription, oral contraceptives still remain probably the most thoroughly investigated drugs ever marketed and the subject of intense scientific investigation that is still continuing.

As has been related, the firm had long been active in earlier years in the railroad labor area, with Howard Neitzert as the lines' lead counsel in controversies with unions. Like most other large firms in Chicago, it did not actively encourage an industrial labor practice, although one of its partners, Howard Robinson, advised corporate employers from 1940 until his retirement in 1971 and represented them in labor negotiations and litigation.

By the early 1970s, it became apparent that to serve its clients more fully, the firm needed to handle all sorts of labor problems. Lawrence I. Kipperman, a 1966 University of Illinois College of Law graduate and a 1973 partner who had been a clerk for a National Labor Relations Board member, was hired to work with Robinson until he retired. The labor work rapidly expanded. In 1975, Mark C. Curran, a 1950 graduate of Northwestern University's College of Law who had specialized in labor law as associate general counsel of Montgomery Ward, joined and became a partner the next year. James S. Whitehead, a 1974 graduate of the University of Chicago Law School, joined after a clerkship with United States Circuit Judge John Paul Stevens, the future United States Supreme Court Justice, and assumed partnership in 1981. By 1982, the labor group also had three associates.

Although a substantial number of traditional labor clients are served, much of the firm's labor practice since the merger has been on behalf of clients in white-collar industries which had not previously been subject to much labor regulation. Practice is diverse, ranging from representation of Commerce Clearing House in an NLRB election in which its labor law editors voted on whether they wanted to be members of the Teamsters Union—the union lost—to its successful representation of William Sexton in his charge of age discrimination against Beatrice Foods, whose vice-president he had been, and the defeat of a charge of race discrimination against American Sugar Company. Also served are Northwestern University, Beloit College, Kendall College, George Williams College, and College of St. Theresa, several banks and savings and loan associations, a school board, two large accounting firms, the A. S. Hansen actuarial firm, Zurich Insurance Company, and a number of corporations in media or related industries such as A. C. Nielsen, WFYR Radio, and Field Enterprises, Incorporated, and its Chicago newspaper, the *Sun-Times*.

13

Over the decades, the firm has represented members of the Marshall Field family in various matters.

In the mid-1960s, Katherine Fanning, the divorced wife of Marshall

Field IV, retained Minow to handle her affairs. After her former husband died late in 1965, she married Lawrence S. Fanning, former editor of the *Daily News*, the other Field Enterprises newspaper then in Chicago. Thereafter, Minow continued to represent Mrs. Fanning and also Fanning and the three children of her marriage to Field: Barbara, Katherine, and Frederick Field. When the Fannings and the children moved to Anchorage, Alaska, in 1967, Minow aided them in purchasing the *Anchorage Daily News*. Fanning died at his desk in 1971 and Mrs. Fanning assumed the editorship of the newspaper. The difficulties she encountered were alleviated by the firm—with Minow and Franklin Chanen, who had been named a partner since 1964, in charge—in obtaining the consent of the United States Attorney General to conduct a joint operation with the rival *Anchorage Times*, the first of its kind granted under the Newspaper Preservation Act. Mrs. Fanning subsequently sold majority control of the newspaper to the McClatchy chain in an arrangement by which she continued as editor and publisher.*

In addition, in the 1970s the firm's work included counseling in real estate investments for Frederick Field and in connection with family trusts for him and his sisters; Chanen played the most active role as tax and corporate advisor through complex and difficult problems. Late in the decade, the firm took part in negotiations between Frederick and Marshall Field V, then publisher of the *Sun-Times*, that led to creation of a 50-50 control arrangement of Field Enterprises, Incorporated, of which Marshall was chairman and to whose board of directors Minow was named. Lee Mitchell worked closely with the corporation, particularly in acquiring a majority interest in five UHF television stations from the Kaiser Corporation, and was named its general counsel and vice-president. Subsequently, working with Maurice Miller and James Johnson, Mitchell brought about the multi-million-dollar sale of WFLD, its Chicago television station, to Metromedia, Incorporated. The firm's close relationship with the family and corporation continued. In 1983, when the Field brothers decided to liquidate the company, Mitchell, who had become the corporation's president, worked with Minow and Miller in seeking it to sell its assets, including the *Sun-Times*.

*In 1983 she was appointed editor of the *Christian Science Monitor*.

14

In the post-merger period, the firm undertook additional matters for Commonwealth Edison Company, headed by Thomas Ayers and later by James O'Connor.

The range of this representation was wide, from a significant contractual dispute with General Electric Company and diverse regulatory questions to the organization of the electrical company's Breeder Reactor Project and complex litigation involving nuclear reprocessing. Those who worked on such tasks, most of them of a continuing nature, were Minow, Henry and Robert Mason, Vieregg, Kissel, and Shalom Kohn, a 1975 associate after graduation from the Harvard Law School with a Bachelor of Laws degree and simultaneously a Master of Business Administration degree from the Harvard Business School, and a 1980 partner.

Late in the 1970s, Ayers also sought Minow's assistance in legal work for the group he headed in carrying out an idea proposed by Harry Weese, a foremost Chicago architect, and carried forward by the prominent firm of Skidmore, Owings and Merrill to plan for a World's Fair in Chicago in 1992 to commemorate the 500th anniversary of Christopher Columbus' voyage to America and the nearly-100th anniversary of the city's famous World's Columbian Exposition of 1893. Minow enlisted Jack Guthman and others in the firm who volunteered their services as legal counsel for Ayers' group, and they and dozens more have given countless hours that the firm has contributed as a public service. Their efforts in handling scores of details helped lead to the official designation of the city in June 1983 as the site for the big event, and it is anticipated that in the next decade Sidley & Austin will play a most important part in moving plans from dreams to reality.

XV Service to the Profession and the Public

A TRADITION since the firm's first days has been fulfillment of professional responsibilities in diverse ways, from work in bar associations and kindred organizations to legal assistance to educational, cultural, charitable, and socially beneficial institutions, and *pro bono publico* service to the indigent.

When the firm was founded in 1866, it would be another eight years before the Chicago Bar Association came into being. Norman Williams and John Leverett Thompson were early members. Among CBA presidents in subsequent years were Charles Cutting, William Sidley, and James Oates, each espousing maintenance of ethical and professional standards and judicial reform. Another was James Kissel, whose membership since 1950 on assorted committees and his role in successfully pressing for establishment of the Illinois Courts Commission empowered to discipline errant judges was climaxed by his presidency in the CBA's centennial year. His term was marked not only by internal achievements but by the first call from any of the nation's large bar associations for Congress to investigate the conduct of President Nixon in actions stemming from the Watergate scandals. Over the decades, many others in the firm have filled influential positions on the CBA's board of managers as well as on so-called "bread and butter" committees that deal with such substantive fields of law as corporations, anti-trust, real estate, litigation, trusts, taxes, securities and commercial law, and others concerned with matters for the good of the profession and the administration of justice. They also are represented on similar groups of the Illinois State Bar

324

Association and other regional associations and the American Bar Association.

Members of the firm have served in the ABA's House of Delegates, and Morris Leibman's many years as the diligent chairman of ABA's Standing Committee on Law and National Security were recognized when President Ronald Reagan awarded him the prestigious Presidential Medal of Freedom late in 1981. Others have been on lawyers' disciplinary committees. Edwin Austin, who was a member of the Illinois State Board of Law Examiners in the 1920s, was appointed by the Illinois Supreme Court in 1969 to a special five-man commission that conducted an investigation that led to the resignations of Chief Justice Roy F. Solfisburg, Jr., and Justice Ray I. Klingbiel after findings that they had acted with impropriety in acquiring shares of stock in a bank of which Theodore J. Isaacs, former state revenue director then under criminal indictment, was a founder and director.

Ever since the creation in 1950 of the American College of Trial Lawyers, a select group with the primary aim of improving and enhancing standards and ethics of trial practice, Sidley & Austin has had representation among its 3,500 Fellows; in 1956, James Baker was the first from the firm to be inducted and in 1979, after serving as its secretary and regent, he was elected president. Among other innumerable professional groups in which the firm's lawyers have served as officers and members are the International Bar Association, American Bar Foundation, American Judicature Society, Bar Association of the Seventh Federal Circuit, Federal Bar Association, American Society of International Law, American College of Probate Counsel, Bar Association of the District of Columbia, Association of the Bar of the City of New York, Chicago Council of Lawyers, Cook County Bar Association, Women's Bar Association, Chicago Bar Foundation, and Chicago's Law and Legal Clubs. Many partners have spoken before these organizations on legal and historical subjects and have written for their publications. Others have taught, at universities and professional schools, courses in everything from taxation and securities law to commercial financing and probate law.

In another educational area, the firm has taken part in the formulation and maintenance of law school clinics designed to make students more responsive to community service and aware as lawyers of their public responsibility for law reform and to give them greater exposure to the realities of legal practice. These clinics were the idea of Emory Brownell, director of the National Legal Aid and Defender Association, who gained the backing of William Pincus of the Ford Foundation in 1959 in forming the National Council of Legal Clinics, of which Avery was a member. The Ford Foundation, in the early 1960s, made an $800,000 grant for the venture and the American Bar Association and Association of American Law Schools, together with NLADA, offered moral and practical support. As an officer of the council and NLADA's president, Avery wrote about the availability of grants to the deans of 137 then-accredited law schools in the United States and participated in selecting twenty for initial foundation grants. Students took part in clinics in the fields of family law, psychiatry, interviewing, counseling, city planning, prosecution, and defense of persons charged with crimes, and legal aid services. They worked in legal aid offices and with jurists, public defenders, prosecutors, and other law enforcement officers and with city planning commissions and other public bodies. Some visited prisons and mental hospitals to help deal with problems of prisoners and patients and their families, and others served as part-time clerks to trial judges and in rural law offices. In several schools, students were exposed to ethics and principles of professional responsibility through a "pervasive" approach, with the injection of such matters into regular courses in torts, criminal law, family law, corporations, bankruptcy, and taxation. In a few instances, the council financed the writing of textbooks and casebooks in the field of professional responsibility. By 1968, the program's success was so evident that many other schools joined in the project. The council was incorporated as the Council on Legal Education in Professional Responsibility and has received and disbursed more than $16 million in grants made by the Ford Foundation. Many of the firm's associates participated in these programs in their years in law schools.

2

The firm's representation of not-for-profit organizations and individuals at reduced or no cost in and out of the courts or before state and city agencies dates back to John Leverett Thompson's arduous work in the 1870s and 1880s on behalf of the civic committee that sought, as related earlier in detail, to regain for Chicago the rights to land along the Lake Michigan shore that had been ceded by the state legislature in 1869 to Illinois Central Railroad. Charles Holt and Arthur Wheeler were prominent in the firm's first half-century in legal work at minimal cost for the national and local Young Men's Christian Association. Later, their example was duplicated by William Sidley, James Oates, and William Avery; the latter two also were trustees and attorneys for YMCA College and its successor, George Williams College. Among other educational institutions variously served over the years have been Beloit College, Kendall College, Loyola University, Shimer College, and, most prominently, Northwestern University. From the latter have come a large number of the firm's partners and associates—more than a few laden with Order of the Coif and the Phi Beta Kappa honors—and its trustees have included Kenneth Burgess, Austin, Minow, Oates, Seder, and Trienens and its law school instructors or lecturers Austin, Avery, Baker, Daggett Harvey, Minow, Seder, Thomas, and Trienens.* Other firm members have taught at De Paul University, the University of California at Los Angeles, John Marshall Law School, and Kent College of Law.

Representation of Northwestern University has been especially broad, starting in 1933 when Burgess was named to its board of trustees and continuing in the years of his board presidency from 1937 to 1959. When J. Roscoe Miller became the university's president in 1949 he relied heavily on Burgess not only for legal counsel but on his ability to obtain foundation grants, one of them, for $1.5 million from the Kresge Foundation, resulting in the erection in 1954 of Kresge Centennial Hall on the Evanston campus. Although the university maintained in-house counsel, diverse matters were often turned over to Sidley & Austin or, if a conflict of interest existed, to other firms.

Throughout the decades, the university had warded off perennial legal action contesting crucial provisions in amendments to its original 1848 charter in which the state legislature gave it "perpetual freedom from taxes" on all its land holdings. In early 1971, Circuit Court Judge Helen F. McGillicuddy deemed unconstitutional the exemption granted the university and thirteen other educational and charitable institutions, a ruling that would have required Northwestern to pay some $1.3 million annually in property taxes. In appealing the decision to the Illinois Supreme Court, Trienens argued that payment of such a sum would have "a grievous effect" on the university, which, unlike the University of Illinois and state-supported institutions, received no tax support. He

*As a Northwestern University life trustee since his initial term in 1929, Austin in 1973 established the Edwin C. Austin Scholarships in the School of Law.

defended the original charter's legality by citing the precedent-setting decision of Chief Justice John Marshall in the Dartmouth College case of 1819 that a state charter was a contract that could not be revoked. His argument produced a reversal of Judge McGillicuddy's decree. (A decade later in a suit brought against businesses and persons who rented property from the university, the high court ruled that Cook County could charge real estate taxes against the lessees.)

In another crucial tax matter, the firm gave important aid. Northwestern's first audit by the Chicago office of the Internal Revenue Service was conducted in 1974; it was also the first such audit of any major university in the Chicago area. After the IRS's ten-month examination of records, a deficiency of about $2 million was imposed, and Robert Frei and William C. Golden, a 1967 Columbia Law School alumnus and partner since 1970, assisted by Robert Ferencz, were assigned to the matter. One of the interesting issues was the IRS claim that football scholarships did not qualify for tax-exemptions but were taxable wages paid to students in return for athletic services and that the school was therefore liable for the income taxes that should have been withheld from money paid them. The lawyers submitted memoranda and held conferences with IRS officials, the result of which was a decision not only in the university's favor but the basis for a published ruling that athletic scholarships were not subject to federal income taxes. The remaining issues were resolved satisfactorily for Northwestern and final settlement was for $65,000, only 3 percent of the proposed deficiency.

Trienens was instrumental in the aftermath of the campus unrest in the late 1960s in establishing procedures and a disciplinary system that dealt fairly and with due process with students involved in sit-ins and occupation of university offices. Assisting him was William Thigpen, a Northwestern alumnus who had come to the firm in 1958 after graduation from Harvard Law School. In early 1971, Thigpen, a 1966 partner, was named Northwestern's general counsel. He continued to advise and work with the law school's dean, John Ritchie III, in carrying out the purposes of the system of hearings. Thigpen also played a vital role in his initial year in drawing up an innovative affirmative action agreement. In the years since his appointment, Thigpen has continued to handle varying matters for Northwestern, in addition to his work in the firm for other clients, particularly in the fields of estates and trusts.

3

Another non-profit client of long standing has been The Chicago Community Trust, created in 1915 with a $250,000 gift from Albert W. Harris of the Harris Trust & Savings Bank as a philanthropic institution to receive gifts and bequests for benevolent purposes and to encourage private charitable organizations, in the words of its charter, "to greater efforts to effect the greatest possible good." Charles Cutting was one of the five members of its first executive committee and carried out assorted legal functions until his death in 1936. For the next eight years, Donald McPherson was its counsel and at his death in 1944, he was succeeded by Austin, who had assisted both Cutting and McPherson and now began two decades as counsel for the trust, whose assets had risen by then to $15 million and whose scope of activities had broadened markedly.

In 1949, shortly after becoming a member of the Harris Bank board, Austin brought about a vital change in the trust's structure. From the year of its origins, its sole trustee had been the Harris Bank, with full responsibility for accepting bequests and gifts. It had never been made clear which person connected with the trust was responsible for taking care of the bequests. Austin felt it was time for the bank to relinquish control and be supplanted by nine banks and trust companies as multiple trustees, with the trust's executive committee continuing to make decisions about beneficiaries of its largess. He drew up an amendment to the charter with these specifications, and Albert Harris, head of the bank, agreed to the change, later described in the trust's official publication as "one of the major developments in the history of the CCT which contributed in a great measure to its phenomenal growth."

Avery, who had assisted both McPherson and Austin, became the trust's counsel in 1964 and was aided by Loren Juhl, William Golden, and John McDonough, who is currently chiefly responsible for the trust's legal affairs. In addition, Austin's eldest daughter, Barbara (Mrs. Robert Foote), an earnest worker in community service, has filled important posts in the trust since appointment to the executive committee in 1970. In 1978, she became chairman, the first woman to hold that office. Indicative of the expansion of the trust and its range of endeavors was the distribution in that year of nearly $7 million, income derived from its total funds of $106 million, mainly for health and social needs; other grants were made to deserving cultural and fine arts organizations, educational institutions, and civic affairs groups.

In addition, the firm has taken part in establishing several funds of the trust which indicate a general substantive area of charitable interest rather than a specific agency or agencies as income recipients. One such is the William J. Cook fund, set up in 1940 by a grandson of Daniel Pope Cook, for whom Cook County was named; it created the Cook Scholarships for the education in colleges and universities of male graduates of schools in the county bearing his forebear's name. Since then, the $593,000 value of the bequest has risen to over $3 million and some 1,000 students have received scholarships totaling close to $2.5 million. Another is the Edna L. Dunning Medical Student Loan Program, whose principal is used to guarantee loans from a commercial bank to men and women attending medical schools while its income is used to subsidize the interest students must pay. The Searle Scholars Program was created, with counsel from the firm, by bequests from John Searle, grandson of the pharmaceutical firm's founder and long a client of the firm, and his wife, Frances, who were both generous contributors to the Community Trust and similar organizations in their lifetimes. Under the program, leading educational institutions are invited to recommend outstanding research scholars. A blue-ribbon panel of scientists selects the winners, each of whom receives a three-year grant totalling $150,000 for independent research in medicine, chemistry, and the biological sciences or other worthy scientific or educational activities in the health field.

Will Keith Kellogg, who founded the Kellogg Company in Battle Creek, Michigan, in 1908 to make corn flakes and later other breakfast foods, created the Kellogg Foundation and Trust in the 1930s. From their inception, each was represented by Chicago counsel who was about to retire in 1981, necessitating appointment of a replacement. That August, after a search of several months and following conferences with White, Golden, and Berning, Sidley & Austin was selected. The Kellogg Foundation is one of the few grant-making private foundations to have maintained an uninterrupted growth in the level of its charitable expenditures over the last twenty years. It is the sole beneficiary of the trust, which owns approximately 47 percent of the outstanding common stock of the Kellogg Company, and their combined assets rank the foundation and trust among the ten largest private foundations. Representation of both involves a wide range of legal matters encountered by non-profit institutions, with particular emphasis on the private foundation rules in the Tax Reform Act of 1969.*

4

Both as a firm and through the participation of individual partners and associates, Sidley & Austin has recognized the importance of making legal services available to persons who are unable to pay fees.

Since 1905, the Legal Aid Bureau of Chicago, a unit of United Charities, has provided free services to those who need but cannot afford counsel and representation. Three partners—Avery, Bouton McDougal, and Robert Thomas—served as its chairmen, and the firm has contributed annually to its support. Other partners and associates have been volunteers or especially active on American and Chicago Bar Associations legal aid committees. During his years as chairman—in 1957 he was also president of United Charities—Avery introduced what became known as the "Chicago Plan" for financing legal aid through substantial yearly contributions by law firms on a "per lawyer" basis plus voluntary assessments on dues bills of CBA members. Later, when he was president of the National Legal Aid and Defender Association, that organization achieved its goal of having legal aid offices in all cities whose populations exceeded 100,000 as well as in scores of smaller communities and extended its services to public and private defenders in criminal cases. Avery also served on ABA's seven-man Special Committee on Availability of Legal Services in 1965–68 that studied ways of reducing legal costs for people of moderate means and drew up reports that led to creation of committees and programs for legal services insurance, group legal services, law clinics, and specialization.

Another organization in which the firm and lawyers individually have taken part in behalf of legal assistance for minority and underprivileged groups has been the Lawyers' Committee for Civil Rights Under Law. It was formed in the summer of 1963 at the request of President Kennedy to provide legal representation to people in the South—mainly civil rights workers white and black—for whom it was otherwise unavailable. He had been moved to make this request in a White House meeting with some 200 lawyers after Dr. Martin Luther King had been jailed in Alabama for

*Representation of the YMCA and other not-for-profit organizations in certain litigated cases has been described in earlier chapters about client matters. Activities of individual partners in educational, charitable and professional organizations are cited in Appendix II.

leading a sit-in in a segregated restaurant and no lawyer could be found there willing to represent him. In 1968, the committee—for which lawyers from all parts of the country donated their services in civil rights cases—established its Urban Areas project, funded by the Ford Foundation and designed to mobilize the legal profession in aiding individuals and community groups striving to overcome the related problems of poverty and discrimination. When the Chicago branch of the national committee opened its office the next year, Henry A. Preston, a 1948 Harvard Law School alumnus and a Sidley & Austin partner since 1956, and Gale Christopher of Leibman, Williams, Bennett, Baird and Minow were among its twenty-three founding members. Each year attorneys from both firms and later from the merged firm volunteered for committee tasks, and financial support was given toward the cost of maintaining the local office.

An important *pro bono* case undertaken on behalf of the committee by Jules Perlberg of the Chicago office and David Tatel, an associate in Washington and later the committee's national director, concerned unfair aspects of a major Civil Service examination. In 1970, the Chicago regional office of the Department of Housing and Urban Development recruited eight black college graduates for HUD's Urban Intern Program, designed to bring qualified minority group citizens into the agency for responsible positions. A few months after the group started work, the Civil Service Commission required them to take the Federal Service Entrance Examination. Three who failed were fired solely because of that result. The scores of the others were deemed not good enough to secure permanent employment in higher positions. Yet all eight had performed their jobs satisfactorily and their HUD supervisor had declared them "extremely well qualified" for federal jobs and "highly qualified" for the jobs to which they had been assigned. After Perlberg and Tatel were unsuccessful in challenging the FSEE before the Civil Service Commission, they sued in the United States District Court in Washington to enjoin continued use of the FSEE. They lost again and appealed to the United States Court of Appeals for the District of Columbia. In his arguments in 1974 in that court, Perlberg was supported by the United States Equal Employment Opportunity Commission. This time he succeeded. The appeals court ruled that the lower court had improperly denied the injunction against the test and it noted that extensive data introduced in the lower court by Perlberg and Tatel had established that white college graduates performed better than black graduates by a margin of five to one on the FSEE, thereby showing that the test had "a racially disproportionate impact." It also held that the Civil Service Commission had failed to demonstrate that its testing procedures had been properly validated to show a positive relationship between test scores and successful performance for the federal jobs for which the tests were used. In the wake of that decision, the Civil Service Commission dropped its use of the Federal Service Entrance Examination.

By the time of the 1972 merger, other Sidley & Austin members were involved in additional matters under auspices of the committee. One was action against Chicago's Board of Education challenging the discriminatory allocation of funds to racially and economically different school districts. In that case, George Saunders headed a *pro bono* team made up of lawyers from the firm and others, the American Civil Liberties Union, the Lawyers' Committee, and the Legal Assistance Foundation of Chicago, which he and Kenneth Howell, a University of Chicago Law School classmate and a 1976 counsel and 1978 partner, had taken part in organizing and which Thomas served as chairman. Allegations in a class action suit filed in 1970 in the United States District Court were based on findings by the Urban Systems Laboratory of Massachusetts Institute of Technology of substantial disparities in the amounts of money spent for predominantly white and predominantly black schools. Working with Saunders and Howell were several associates, particularly Theodore Miller. The case dragged on until 1974, by which time corrective measures had been taken so that Judge Richard McLaren, while finding the complaint justified, saw no need to issue the injunction sought in the suit.

A *pro bono* case that received wide media attention concerned Lillian K. Ware, an elderly black woman who occasionally worked as a practical nurse. In 1967, she neglected to pay a final installment of $41.57 of a ten-year special assessment levied for repairs on the alley behind her $25,000 Evanston home in which she had lived since 1943. At the time, she lay in a hospital for treatment of a heart ailment and did not receive a notice to make the payment. Four years later, again in the hospital for installation of a pacemaker, she was not aware that a tax-buyer who specialized in acquiring tax-delinquent properties had secured title to her modest home for only $57.61 in taxes, interest, and penalties and now sought to take possession of it. Her family lawyer was unsuccessful in trying to have the tax deed set aside because the state's tax-delinquent property sales statutes sanctioned such seizures.

In August 1973, an official of Evanston's First National Bank, where

Mrs. Ware had a small savings account, told Edward Saunders of her plight, and he asked George Saunders, Theodore Miller, and Gerald A. Ambrose, a new associate from the University of Michigan Law School and a 1978 partner, to determine if a way could be found to prevent what appeared to be a miscarriage of justice. After deep research, extensive briefing, and three hearings, they obtained from Circuit Court Judge Daniel A. Covelli a preliminary injunction restraining the tax-buyer from dispossessing Mrs. Ware. But the Illinois Appellate Court, while expressing sympathy for Mrs. Ware, overturned the injunction because the purchaser had complied with all statutory provisions entitling him to the tax deed. Newton Minow joined in asking the Illinois Supreme Court to permit Mrs. Ware to appeal that ruling and to stay her eviction until it could rule on the motion, but this move failed too. The outcome, though, was a happy one for Mrs. Ware. Saunders and his colleagues persuaded the tax-buyer to agree to resell the house to Mrs. Ware for $9,000 raised through the efforts of friends, the local branch of the National Association for the Advancement of Colored People, and the Second Baptist Church of Evanston. Some $60,000 of the firm's time had been expended in Mrs. Ware's behalf but, as Saunders emphasized, he and those associated with him on the case had the satisfaction of fulfilling the firm's commitment to protecting the rights of individuals irrespective of their financial means or background with the kind of diligence devoted to affluent clients.*

Equally publicized—and watched intently by other lawyers—was Alice Bright's fervent representation of Linda Polales, an unwed mother seeking to regain custody of her infant son, Sean, whom Catholic Charities, the welfare arm of the Archdiocese of Chicago, had put up for adoption in 1977. At the insistence of the child's father, a married Californian, Sean had been placed in the care of Catholic Charities a month after his birth while Miss Polales, a former secretary in a suburban office, secured legal help to determine—and terminate—the father's parental rights. Early the next year, Miss Bright, with the aid of James Carroll, a 1972 DePaul University Law School graduate newly named a partner, began action in support of Miss Polales with a suit in the Cook County Circuit Court that charged Catholic Charities with changing its case records to make it appear that she had agreed to the adoption.

*Saunders also called on the state legislature to abolish the delinquent-tax collection system, declaring, "It harks back to unjust tax procedures that brought about the Magna Carta and the American Revolution!" Abolition did not come about, but the law was modified to afford more time for house-owners to pay taxes due.

In a forty-five day trial before Judge Nathan M. Cohen, they presented evidence that Catholic Charities destroyed the case records, allowed Miss Polales to see Sean only twice during the six weeks it had custody before turning the child over to a foster family, gave unauthorized legal advice to her, permitted the father to sign an illegal form allowing the adoption, and took advantage of Miss Polales' harassed state by persuading her to sign a form that surrendered the child for adoption. Early in May 1979, Judge Cohen handed down an unequivocal decision that restored Sean's custody to his mother. Later that year, Judge Cohen's decree was sustained by the Illinois Appellate Court.

5

Much of recent *pro bono* work has been generated by established civil rights and community organizations. Each new associate is especially encouraged to take on at least one such matter in his or her first year with the firm. Approval is readily given if there is no conflict with an existing client and as long as regular assignments are managed. In addition to organizations already mentioned, others through which aid is given include Leadership Council for Metropolitan Open Occupancy, Neighborhood Legal Assistance Center, Evanston Latin-American Association, Wilmette Youth Resources, Chicago Urban League, and the Illinois Division of the American Civil Liberties Union. Foremost among service for the latter has been Henry Mason, who was co-counsel in numerous ACLU cases in the late 1970s after attaining partnership in 1973.

Types of *pro bono* services range widely. A representative list drawn up by Thomas Morsch, who not only has engaged in specific cases but helps coordinate them, includes discrimination in housing, schooling, and employment, tax exemptions and contracts for community organizations, Vietnam and Thai refugee problems, a program for college students who intend to attend law school under a minority enrollment plan, and judicially assigned representation of defendants in criminal cases on various levels. A recent example of the last is the Federal Defendant Panel Program, in which Edna Selan Epstein, a 1975 associate from the University of Chicago Law School who became a partner in 1982, has been especially active. (An oft-recalled criminal case from an earlier time involved the appointment of Arthur Seder, with Calvin Sawyier of Winston & Strawn, to represent William Heirens in his 1954 post-conviction appeal from a sentence of three consecutive life terms in Stateville Peni-

335

tentiary for the murder of a six-year-old girl, Suzanne Degnan, and two women. Seder and Sawyier ably argued before the Illinois Supreme Court that Heirens had been unlawfully injected with a "truth serum" upon his arrest and that his lawyers had openly agreed with the prosecution that he be put away for life. But their arguments failed to win Heirens a new trial.)

Amid its wide and diverse practice, the commitment of Sidley & Austin to *pro bono* matters continues.

Sidley & Austin Today

IN ITS 117th year, Sidley & Austin is one of the country's largest law firms and among the oldest in Chicago. With the admission on July 1, 1983, of a record twenty-seven partners and the arrival of new associates, it has some 400 lawyers, nearly half of them partners.

Gone from this impressive assemblage is Edwin Austin, who died on February 10, 1983, at the age of ninety.* He had served the firm for nearly seventy years, during which he had established a reputation as an accomplished lawyer in varied fields and had guided and strengthened practices and policies which contributed to the firm's growth and its stature in the nationwide legal community. William Avery, now counsel to the firm and associated longer with him than any still-active partner, said it best in his eulogy at a memorial service in the Winnetka Congregational Church:

"To us partners and associates, he was the true leader, yet always willing to listen to the rest of us and to accept our ideas if they had merit. To his clients he gave sound advice and vigorous representation. To the cause of justice, he was dedicated and fearless. To the young men and women in the firm, he was patient, understanding, encouraging and a model of integrity, ability and fairness."

---

*Alice Bright, the first woman hired by the firm, succumbed to a long illness in 1982, and other active partners who died in recent years were Gale Christopher, Edward Saunders, and Stuart Ball.

2

Among the firm's clients—many of long duration that grew with Chicago and the nation as the firm grew—are commercial and industrial corporations, public utilities, railroads, banks, savings and loan associations, governmental units, accounting firms, advertising agencies, television and radio broadcasters, publishers, insurance companies, realtors, investment firms, professional sports teams, estates and trusts, professional and trade associations, and many hundreds of individuals.

Through the years, the Chicago office has developed specialized expertise in most areas and has one of the country's largest civil litigation practices. The Washington office concentrates on representing industries subject to federal regulation, especially anti-trust and economic regulation. In addition to a full-service general practice, the Los Angeles office has one of the largest bankruptcy practices on the West Coast. The firm's fast-growing practice in international transactions is reflected in activities of the New York office and those in Dubai, Muscat, Riyadh, and Singapore, and in the office in Cairo, which is operated jointly with Gamal Naguib, an Egyptian lawyer, and is the largest foreign office in that country. The London office, oldest of those abroad, not only represents clients in the United States and Great Britain on American and international law matters but also knows well the film, television, and entertainment industries and is a vital link between the offices in the United States and those in the Middle East and Southeast Asia. Through the firm's affiliation with leading law firms in London, Rotterdam, Dusseldorf, Paris, Zurich, Milan and Rome, which are fellow members of ''Le Club'', the needs of American clients are promptly and effectively met in Western Europe. The firm also provides services in the United States and Middle and Far East to European and other foreign clients.

3

As in the past, policy matters and key decisions such as admission to partnership and partnership participation are the responsibility of the executive committee, currently compromising twenty-one members. Its chairman is Howard Trienens,* its secretary is Robert Beam, and its

---

*Trienens' predecessors as head of the firm, following Norman Williams and John Leverett Thompson, were Charles Holt, William Sidley, Edwin Austin (with Kenneth Burgess until 1965), and William Avery. Only three persons were with the firm for more than fifty years: Sidley, Austin, and Avery.

members include lawyers of many years' service and others who are comparatively young; they range in age from 43 to 64, with the average at 55. This committee chooses the members of the six-person management committee that is in charge of operations and the nineteen administrative committees which report to the management committee. Blair White is the management committee's chairman and its other members are Eden Martin, as secretary, and Maurice Miller, Newton Minow, Howard Trienens, and Ronald Trost, all of whom are also on the executive committee; their average age is 54, varying from 43 to 59. Issues large or small have never been decided by closely contested votes in either committee. "We find a consensus in almost everything," Minow has said, "and hope to have enough sense and maturity to see that if we can't come close to agreement on something, then we should forget it. That's been part of the philosophy of this firm."

The functional groups into which the firm is loosely structured reflect fields of concentration and client responsibility. Nearly all the lawyers practice in more than a single area and often specialists from one group join with counterparts in others in carrying out especially complex projects. Groups involved in judicial and administrative litigation are concerned with anti-trust and product liability cases and utility, communications, transportation, environmental, labor, and international matters, as well as general litigation. Those in primarily non-litigated areas are concerned with corporate and securities matters, domestic and international banking and business transactions, commercial law and bankruptcies, marketing, estates and trusts, real estate, federal, state, and local taxes, legislative matters, and energy and entertainment.

4

The firm has more than doubled in size over the post-merger decade, occasioned by the demand by ever-increasing numbers of clients for ever more varied services. This increase has been met primarily by recruiting efforts and partly by consolidation with Shutan & Trost. Over the years, but especially since the 1970s, the firm's system for recruiting associates has undergone refinements and improvements. Each autumn, the work groups furnish the assignment and compensation committee with estimates of how many new people they will require the following year. This gives the lawyers doing the recruiting of summer and permanent associates, in what is sometimes called "the legal mating dance," an idea of the number of offers to make. By the time the recruiting season starts, letters have been sent to law school placement offices describing the firm, its areas

Present Executive Committee

Robert T. Beam

Richard J. Flynn

Robert R. Frei

Thomas E. Garcin

Donald J. Gralen

Loren E. Juhl

Martin M. Lucente

R. Eden Martin

Maurice J. Miller

Newton N. Minow

340

Thomas H. Morsch   Jules M. Perlberg   William P. Richmond   George L. Saunders, Jr.

A. Bruce Schimberg   Stanton K. Smith, Jr.   William H. Thigpen   Howard J. Trienens

Ronald J. Trost   Charles S. Vogel   H. Blair White

341

of practice, the backgrounds of partners and associates, its philosophy and organization, and its opportunities for young lawyers. Annually in recent years, the firm has taken in thirty to forty new associates. Students sought are invariably those with strong academic records plus an evident ability to relate well to people and a genuine interest in solving problems, qualities long deemed essential in the making of a proficient lawyer. The candidates who show a decided interest in working for the firm are invited to spend a day or two in one or more of the offices. Most of those hired have ranked high in their classes, many having been elected to Phi Beta Kappa, Order of the Coif, or similar scholarly orders and having worked on the editorial staffs of their schools' law reviews. In addition to those who come upon law school graduation are some associates who have spent a year or more clerking for judges on various levels or having worked in such occupations as accounting, banking, teaching, and tax auditing, or have held jobs in government or as legislative aides or, in a few instances, have had business experience before deciding to study law.

Once hired permanently, an associate is assigned to a functional group in which he or she is given assorted assignments. The long-standing "open door" policy of the firm encourages associates to discuss professional or personal problems with the partner in charge of the group or with any other partner. Every six months, partners for whom new associates have worked are asked to evaluate them. Their reports are transmitted to the committee on assignment and compensation, which reviews them and recommends action to the management committee. Ultimately, the committee's decisions are conveyed to the group leaders for discussion with the associates concerned. In case of a negative rating, an associate may be transferred to another area. If termination is recommended, efforts are made to help the associate find employment elsewhere before the relationship with the firm is dissolved.

Summer associates join permanently hired newcomers at the weekly survey luncheons. There, they hear senior partners discuss everything from their experiences and notable events and personages in the firm's history to pending cases and the firm's goals and basic purpose, the latter simply and frankly stated by such a major partner as Trienens as "All we're here for is to serve clients and if we have clients who have fascinating problems that pay well, that's fine, and if we get fascinating problems in the *pro bono* area, that's fine, too." Summer associates' ratings of the firm are generally high. In a survey conducted in 1980 by *The American Lawyer*, which a

Howard J. Trienens,   H. Blair White,

year earlier had dubbed the firm "the talk of the town" in a complimentary cover story by James B. Stewart, Jr., its executive editor, Sidley & Austin was accorded top honors in Chicago and among the ten major firms nationally whose summer associates were asked to pronounce judgment on their experiences. "Unmitigated raves from one of the most enthusiastic groups of summer interns we encountered anywhere," the publication's article began, and then went on to recount satisfaction with the training, client contact, salaries, working hours, and social events and, in one instance, sending out for an associate who was an orthodox Jew for kosher lunches in outlying neighborhoods because there were no kosher restaurants nearby.

Turnovers of legal personnel do occur, as elsewhere in the profession, for various reasons. But an underlying morale strength at Sidley & Austin is its partner-to-associate ratio approaching one-to-one, unlike other large firms, principally in the East, where associates far outnumber partners, thereby reducing the prospect of participation in revenues by younger lawyers. Associates who show potential for partnerships have recently averaged six to seven years before attaining them. The strong tradition still prevails of promoting from within, with exceptions alluded to earlier and

343

in the case of Samuel K. Skinner, who entered as a partner in 1977 after distinguished service as United States Attorney in Chicago. Basic factors in selection of partners are proven ability in one or more areas of practice, demonstrated integrity and character, and a high degree of maturity. Austin, who saw many dozens attain that rank, expressed it well: "As he or she reaches the point where the firm can, with confidence, consider they are responsible and mature, that they can go into situations with clients and others and speak for the firm so there will be no question about the fact that they will adequately and properly represent the firm—that is perhaps the best single test of whether an associate is ready to become a partner."

5

As the firm looks to the future, its leaders are aware of traditions that remain steadfast and challenges to be met.

They know of the need, beyond the avowed aim of providing high-grade services for all clients, for improved organization and internal communications, coordination of efforts, quality control, maintenance of morale, continuing legal education, and avoidance of conflicts of interest. Some of the lawyers find nostalgic satisfaction in recollecting earlier times when the firm was smaller and relationships, both professional and personal, were more close-knit. Others, recognizing overall changes in society and in the profession itself, are concerned that the practice of law in America has become more a business than a vocation. But most of these join with the majority in expressing gratification in meeting continual intellectual challenges posed by complex legal matters, in individual development of skills through working with some of the nation's best lawyers, in development of strong friendships, and in contributing to what many consider the principal distinguishing characteristic of the firm—a commitment to superior work, whether for a mighty corporation or an indigent individual represented without a fee, coupled with a pledge of integrity in doing the very best job within the bounds of professional, moral, and personal concepts of propriety and fair play. Younger lawyers especially relish their association with top practitioners and appreciate the lack of cut-throat internal competition prevalent in some firms.

The firm is hardly monolithic in nature. Diversity is encouraged. There are Democrats, Republicans, and independents, conservatives and liberals, men and women of varied religions and social or economic classes and differing degrees of participation in professional and civic activities.* Whatever their personal backgrounds or preferences, the ultimate test is the extent of their devotion to duty and the results they achieve for clients, an element of the firm's philosophy inculcated early in new associates, as in this advice from Trienens at a summer luncheon: "Far beyond the nice space and adequate salary and participations is challenging legal work and you get that not by socializing and not by the way you may hear about how people get and keep clients but by doing good work."

The firm's growth has been accomplished, as perceived by the *Legal Times* recently in a long and laudatory article, with "an absence of internal strife" and it "has positioned itself as well as any firm in the country to deal with changing legal practice." It is not intent on growing for growth's sake but, as White emphasized in the course of a recent partners' meeting, in response to developing needs: "We intend to grow where it is necessary to protect the high quality and interesting aspects of our practice. We must stay flexible to respond to our clients' needs. There is plenty of room for this firm to grow, in the Chicago area and elsewhere. If we open additional offices in this country or elsewhere in the world, our aim will be simple—to protect the kind of exciting and interesting practice that we have today." And in his view of the future, Minow, at another partners' meeting, cited four factors affecting the legal profession: The tendency to seek business more aggressively, the proliferation of branch offices, the growth and quality of in-house counsel, and the need to develop techniques to respond to the increasing costs of legal services. "In the last analysis," he said, "the quality of our work is our best asset—and our best way of marketing our services. We serve our clients not as individual lawyers and practitioners but as an institution. The reason our firm has succeeded and is successful is that its partners have been more devoted to the firm than to themselves. I'm optimistic about Sidley & Austin in the new world because we have everything needed—a great reputation, great talent, a willingness to work hard, an enthusiastic firm spirit and commitment to quality performance."

The reputation that Sidley & Austin enjoys in the community of lawyers and the general public is of a stature exemplified by a tribute from United States District Judge Prentice Marshall at an annual firm dinner to "your

*See the autobiographical appendix for details of the latter endeavors.

many contributions to our profession and our society." And never lost sight of is the credo so often enunciated by Edwin Austin and inscribed on the frontispiece of the office manual:

"The goal of the firm has always been the pursuit of excellence, especially in three particulars: performance of the highest quality of professional work, adherence to the highest ethical standards and avoidance of charging all the traffic will bear."

That tradition, initiated in the small law firm that Norman Williams and John Leverett Thompson started on an October morning in Chicago in 1866, endures to this day.

APPENDIX I

Firm Names

WILLIAMS & THOMPSON	1866–1889
WILLIAMS, HOLT & WHEELER	1889–1899
HOLT, WHEELER & SIDLEY	1900–1913
HOLT, CUTTING & SIDLEY	1913–1919
CUTTING, MOORE & SIDLEY	1919–1936
SIDLEY, McPHERSON, AUSTIN & BURGESS	1937–1944
SIDLEY, AUSTIN, BURGESS & HARPER	1944–1949
SIDLEY, AUSTIN, BURGESS & SMITH	1950–1967
SIDLEY & AUSTIN	1967—

APPENDIX II

Partners

(As of December 31, 1982, adjusted to August 1, 1983 for partners admitted or withdrawn)

NELS J. ACKERSON

Partner 1983

Born April 12, 1944, Indianapolis, Indiana. B.S. with distinction 1967 Purdue University, Master in public policy 1971 and J.D. *cum laude* 1971 Harvard University (board of editors law review 1968–71). Chief counsel and executive director United States Senate subcommittee on the Constitution, Committee on the judiciary 1976–79. Nominee United States Congress 1980. Member Bilateral Fulbright Commission of the United States of America and Egypt, Egyptian Society of International Law, American Bar Association, International Bar Association. Principal area of specialization: International law, particularly Middle East.

ROBERT A. ALBERT

London representative 1973–76; partner 1976

Born May 29, 1933, Boston, Massachusetts. LL.B. 1960 Columbia University. First lieutenant United States Army Artillery 1955–57. Practice New York 1960–62. Trustee International Youth Foundation (London), Globe Theatre Trust (London), Benjamin Franklin Foundation (London). Member American Bar Association, International Bar Association, Association of the Bar of the City of New York, Phillips Exeter Alumni Council. Founder American Lawyer Luncheon Group (London). Clubs: Harvard, American (London), Garrick (London), Queens (London), Hurlingham (London). Principal areas of specialization: General and international.

GERALDINE M. ALEXIS

Associate 1977–1979, 1981–1983; partner 1983

Born November 3, 1948, Flushing, New York. A.B. *magna cum*

laude 1971 University of Rochester, J.D. *cum laude* 1976 Northwestern University School of Law, (notes and comments editor law review 1975–76). M.M. with distinction 1976 Kellogg Graduate School of Management, Northwestern University. Law Clerk to Judge John F. Grady, United States District Court for the Northern District of Illinois 1976–77. Attorney-advisor Office of Legal Counsel United States Department of Justice 1979–81. Member American Bar Association, Chicago Bar Association. Principal area of specialization: Litigation.

GERALD A. AMBROSE
> Associate 1972–78; partner 1978
> Born August 18, 1947, Charleston, Illinois. B.A. 1969 DePauw University, J.D. 1972 University of Michigan. Member American Bar Association, Chicago Bar Association, Phi Beta Kappa, Chicago Council on Foreign Relations. Clubs: East Bank, Michigan Law. Principal areas of specialization: Anti-trust litigation and utility regulation.

GERALD L. ANGST
> Associate 1975–81; partner 1982
> Born December 29, 1950, Chicago, Illinois. B.S. *magna cum laude* 1972 and J.D. *cum laude* 1975 Loyola University of Chicago (executive editor law journal 1974–75). Member American Bar Association, Illinois State Bar Association, Chicago Bar Association (lecturer), Delta Sigma Rho, Phi Sigma Tau, Alpha Sigma Nu. Principal area of specialization: Commercial litigation.

JAMES G. ARCHER
> Associate 1960–65; partner 1965
> Born January 16, 1936, San Antonio, Texas. B.A. 1957 and LL.B. 1959 University of Illinois. Member Chicago Bar Association, Order of the Coif, Phi Beta Kappa, Illinois State Board of Accounting Examiners, board of High School District 225 1973–76, board of North Shore Mental Health Association 1976–79, board of Christian Laity of Chicago 1973–79. Clubs: Monroe, Omicron Alumni Association (past president), Psi Upsilon. Principal area of specialization: Corporate and securities.

VIRGINIA L. ARONSON
> Associate 1975–83; partner 1983
> Born June 4, 1947, Bremerton, Washington. B.A. 1969, M.A. 1973

and J.D. 1975 University of Chicago. Member Chicago Bar Association (real property committee, condominium subcommittee), Illinois State Bar Association, Chicago Mortgage Attorneys Association. Member Park West Community Association. Principal area of specialization: Real estate.

FREDERIC J. ARTWICK

Associate 1971–75; partner 1975

Born June 4, 1944, Chicago, Illinois. A.B. 1966 Harvard University, M.A. 1967 University of Reading (England). J.D. 1970 University of Chicago. Law clerk United States District Judge Bernard M. Decker 1970–71. Member American Bar Association, Illinois State Bar Association, Chicago Bar Association, Chicago Council of Lawyers, Evanston Mental Health Board 1982—, Evanston United Way/Community Services Board 1978— (president 1980–82), Dewey Community Conference Board 1977—. Instructor John Marshall Law School 1975–77. President Neighborhood Legal Assistance Center 1973–75. Club: University (Chicago). Principal area of specialization: Litigation.

EDWIN C. AUSTIN

Associate 1915–20; partner 1920–83

Born March 28, 1892, Barrington, Illinois. B.A. 1912 University of Wisconsin, LL.B. and M.A. 1917 Northwestern University. Lieutenant United States Navy 1917–19. Member American Bar Association, Illinois State Bar Association, Chicago Bar Association, Order of the Coif, Delta Sigma Rho, Sigma Phi, Phi Delta Phi. Fellow American Bar Foundation. Member Illinois State Bar Examiners 1925–27, Illinois State Board of Examiners in Accountancy 1934–37. Director Brooks-Scanlon, Incorporated, Harris Trust and Savings Bank, The Hoover Company, International Minerals and Chemical Corporation, MacMillan Bloedell and Powell River Limited, Leath and Company, A. C. Nielsen Company, G. D. Searle & Company. Counsel Chicago Community Trust 1944–64. Member New Trier High School Board 1919–20, Glencoe School Board 1927–31 (president 1929–31). Past trustee Vassar College. Governing member Chicago Orchestral Association, Art Institute of Chicago. Director Lyric Opera of Chicago. Trustee American Library Association, Old People's Home, Evanston Hospital. Past president Roycemore School, Cook County School of Nursing. Clubs: Chicago, Commercial, Commonwealth, Law (president 1966–67), Legal (president 1944–45), Mid-Day, Old Elm, Union League (president 1935), University (Chicago), Executives, Indian Hill, Wausaukee, Army and Navy. Principal areas of specialization: Corporate and securities, federal tax, probate and trusts. Died February 10, 1983.

WILLIAM H. AVERY

Associate 1930–44; partner 1944–82; counsel 1983–

Born July 16, 1905, Jacksonville, Florida. B.S. with high honors 1927 Princeton University, J.D. 1930 Harvard University. Member American Bar Association (House of Delegates), Illinois State Bar Association, Chicago Bar Association, International Bar Association, International Legal Aid Association (co-founder), American Judicature Society, American Law Institute, Chicago Estate Planning Council, Fellow American Bar Foundation. Lecturer National Trust School 1947–64. Director Acme Printing Ink Company, Carson Pirie Scott & Company, Chicago Musical Instrument Company, Chicago Title & Trust Company, Equitable Life Assurance Society of the United States. Member Advisory Council Illinois Department of Public Welfare 1948–52, Kenilworth School Board 1950–53 (president), Citizens Board University of Chicago, Northwestern University Associates. Trustee or director Civic Federation of Chicago (past vice-president), George Williams College, Legal Aid Bureau of Chicago (past chairman), National Legal Aid and Defender Association (past president), United Charities (past president), Young Men's Christian Association (past president), Council Legal Education for Professional Responsibility, Chicago Sunday Evening Club, Presbyterian Home of Evanston, Ravinia Festival Association, Chicago Association of Commerce and Industry. Counsel Chicago Community Trust 1964–75. Clubs: Commercial (past president), Commonwealth (past president), Economic (past president), Tax (past president), Mid-Day, University (Chicago), Indian Hill (Winnetka), Old Elm (Lake Forest). Principal areas of concentration: Estate planning, estates and trusts, local, state and federal taxes, real estate, and general.

RUSSELL M. BAIRD*

Associate 1941–45; partner 1945

Born August 4, 1916, Chicago, Illinois. A.B. 1938 University of Chicago, LL.B. 1941 Harvard University. Officer United States Navy 1942–45. Director Chicago Crime Commission 1960—. Member University of Chicago Citizens Board 1958—. Visiting Committee University of Chicago Divinity School 1963—, Lyric Opera of Chicago board. President Mental Health Association of Greater Chicago 1962–64. Fellow American Bar Association (standing committees on communications, anti-trust and patents, trademark and copyright sections), Illinois State Bar Association, Chicago Bar Association. Author Chicago Bar Association "Christmas Spirits" shows 1954–64. President Legal Club of Chicago 1962–63, Law Club of Chicago 1972–73. Governor International Food & Wine Society of Chicago. Clubs: University (Chicago), Racquet, Wayfarers', Bagatelle, Sky-Line, River Forest

Tennis, Oak Park Country, Crystal Downs Country. Principal area of specialization: Marketing.

STUART S. BALL
Partner 1953

Born September 5, 1904, Marshalltown, Iowa. B.A. 1924, M.A. 1927 and J.D. 1927, Northwestern University. Practice Des Moines 1927–32. Official Montgomery Ward & Company (assistant secretary 1932–33, secretary 1933–49, vice-president 1949, president 1949–52, director 1950–52). Chairman selection committee Cook County Hospitals, governing commission 1969–73, 1978–79, Northwestern University Library Council 1974–83. Director Cook County School of Nursing 1955–73 (also vice-president), Northwestern Memorial Hospital 1972–75. Trustee Orchestra Association of Chicago 1952–83 (president 1971–75, chairman 1976–78), Wesley Memorial Hospital 1953–72. Citizen Fellow Chicago Institute of Medicine. Fellow American College of Trial Lawyers. Member American Bar Association, Illinois State Bar Association, Chicago Bar Association, Order of the Coif, Delta Sigma Rho, Chicago Association of Commerce and Industry (director 1946–70, member senior council 1971–83), Associated Stationers (director 1956–64, chairman 1957–58). Clubs: Chicago, Commercial, Economic (past president), Law, Legal, Glen View, Mid-Day. Principal areas of specialization: Litigation and anti-trust. Died January 19, 1983.

J. ROBERT BARR
Associate 1960–69; partner 1970

Born April 10, 1936, Gary, Indiana. A.B. 1957 Grinnell College, LL.B. *cum laude* 1960 Harvard University. Member Illinois House of Representatives 1981–83. Chairman Illinois Board of Regents 1971–77. Member Commission on Presidential Scholars 1975–77. Chairman Republican Central Committee of Cook County 1978—. Member Evanston Zoning Board of Appeals 1965–74. Trustee Taxpayers Federation of Illinois. Member American Bar Association, Illinois State Bar Association, Chicago Bar Association (chairman committee on state and local taxation 1974–75), Selden Society, International Association of Assessing Officers, Chicago Area Public Affairs Group, Phi Beta Kappa. Clubs: Chicago, Law, Legal, Monroe. Principal areas of specialization: State and local taxes, marketing and legislative.

FRANK V. BATTLE, JR.
Associate 1969–73; partner 1974

Born July 19, 1942, Chicago, Illinois. B.S. 1960 Loyola University (Chicago), J.D. 1968 De Paul University. LL.M. 1969 New York University.

Attorney-advisor Office of Tax Legislative Counsel, United States Department of the Treasury 1973–74. Director North Shore Mental Health Association. Member American Bar Association, Illinois State Bar Association, Chicago Bar Association. Clubs: Mid-Day, Skokie Country. Principal areas of specialization: Federal tax and corporate.

HARRY T. BAUMANN*
  Associate 1952–63; partner 1963
  Born April 11, 1927, Chicago, Illinois. B.S. 1950 Northwestern University, J.D. 1952 University of Michigan. United States Army Infantry 1945–46. Member Wilmette School Board District 39 1969–76 (president 1973–76), American Bar Association, Chicago Bar Association, American Judicature Society, Phi Eta Sigma, Phi Delta Theta, Phi Delta Phi. Clubs: Legal, Union League. Principal area of specialization: Real estate.

ROBERT T. BEAM*
  Associate 1957–63; partner 1963
  Born October 27, 1919, What Cheer, Iowa. B. Sc. 1951 University of Illinois, J.D. 1954 University of Illinois, LL.M. 1956 New York University. Served to major United States Army Air Force 1941–47, to lieutenant-colonel 1950–52. Practice New York 1954–57. Member American Bar Association, Illinois State Bar Association, Chicago Bar Association, Phi Delta Phi. Clubs: University (Chicago), Mid-Day. Principal area of specialization: Corporate and securities.

RUSSELL O. BENNETT*
  Associate 1946–52; partner 1952
  Born July 11, 1915, Dexter, Missouri. A.B. 1936 University of Oklahoma, LL.B. 1939 Harvard University. Served to major United States Army 1941–46. Director Lawrence Hall School for Boys 1949–, president 1960–63. Northwestern University Settlement. Trustee Seabury-Western Theological Seminary. Member American Bar Association, Illinois State Bar Association, Chicago Bar Association, American Law Institute, Chicago Council on Foreign Relations, Phi Beta Kappa, Phi Gamma Delta. Clubs: Economic, Law, Legal, Attic, Tavern, Mid-Day. Principal area of specialization: Corporate and securities.

FREDERIC G. BERNER, JR.
  Associate 1973–80; partner 1980
  Born May 7, 1943, Washington, D.C. 1965 B.A. Middlebury College, M.B.A. 1970 American University, J.D. 1973 George Washington University. Economist Central Intelligence Agency 1965–67, 1970. Lieutenant

United States Army 1967–70. Director Washington D.C. Chapter American Hemophilia Foundation 1977–80. Member American Bar Association, District of Columbia Bar Association, Federal Energy Bar Association, Order of the Coif. Principal area of specialization: Energy litigation.

LARRY D. BERNING

Associate 1978–1974; partner 1974

Born October 21, 1940, Kendallville, Indiana. A.B. 1963 and J.D. *cum laude* 1968 Indiana University. United States Army 1963–65. Trustee Old People's Home of Chicago (secretary), Georgian, William H. Miner Foundation, Medic Alert Records Trust. Member American Bar Association, Illinois State Bar Association, Chicago Bar Association, Indiana State Bar Association, Order of the Coif, Chicago Estate Planning Council, Sigma Nu, Phi Delta Phi. Clubs: Legal, Law. Principal areas of specialization: Estate and trust and federal taxes.

H. BRUCE BERNSTEIN

Associate 1968–74; partner 1974

Born December 9, 1943, Omaha, Nebraska. A.B. 1965 Cornell University, J.D. 1968 Harvard University. Member American Bar Association, Illinois Bar Association (chairman commercial, banking and bankruptcy section 1974–75, editor commercial, banking and bankruptcy newsletter 1972–74), Chicago Bar Association (co-chairman Uniform Commercial Code committee 1975–76, chairman 1976–77). Author and editor numerous articles on various aspects of commercial and bankruptcy law. Lecturer Practicing Law Institute 1977–79, American Law Institute 1983. Member National Bankruptcy Conference. Clubs: Monroe, Northmoor Country. Principal area of specialization: Commercial and bankruptcy law.

JACK R. BIERIG

Associate 1972–78; partner 1978

Born April 10, 1947, Chicago, Illinois. A.B. *cum laude* 1968 Brandeis University, J.D. 1972 Harvard University. Adjunct professor Illinois Institute of Technology-Chicago Kent College of Law 1974—. President Neighborhood Justice of Chicago. Member American Bar Association, Illinois State Bar Association, Chicago Bar Association (board of managers), Phi Beta Kappa. Club: Standard. Principal area of specialization: Representation of medical and other professional associations.

FRANK L. BIXBY*

Associate 1953–63; partner 1963

Born May 25, 1928, New Richmond, Wisconsin. A.B. 1950   *355*

Harvard College, LL.B. 1953 University of Wisconsin (editor-in-chief law review 1952–53). Director Illinois Bar Automated Research Fund for Justice, Chicago Urban League 1962— (general counsel 1972—), Community Renewal Society 1973—, Spencer Foundation 1967— (chairman 1975—), Board member Evanston Township District 202 High School 1975–81. Trustee MacMurray College 1975—, Unitarian Church of Evanston 1962–63 (chairman). Editorial board *Chicago Reporter* 1973—. Member American Bar Association, Illinois State Bar Association, Chicago Bar Association, Wisconsin Bar Association, Florida Bar Association, Chicago Council of Lawyers, Chicago Council on Foreign Relations, Chicago Committee, Order of the Coif, Phi Beta Kappa. Clubs: Harvard (president 1962–63), Mid-Day. Principal area of specialization: Estate and trust.

STEWART A. BLOCK
Associate 1979–1983; partner 1983

Born July 29, 1946, Astoria, New York. B.A., *magna cum laude* 1968 University of Maryland, J.D., *cum laude* 1971 University of Pennsylvania. Member American Bar Association, District of Columbia Bar, Phi Beta Kappa. Staff Attorney Federal Trade Commission, Division of National Advertising (1972–75), Adjunct Assistant Professor Delaware Law School, Evening Division (1975). Principal areas of specialization: Anti-trust and administrative agency litigation.

DAVID J. BOYD
Associate 1964–71; partner 1972

Born December 16, 1939, Mount Vernon, Illinois. B.A. 1961 Wabash College, LL.B. 1964 Duke University. Member American Bar Association, Illinois State Bar Association, Chicago Bar Association, Order of the Coif. Principal area of specialization: Corporate and securities.

JAMES J. BRENNAN*
Associate 1963–69; partner 1970

Born April 13, 1936, San Francisco, California. B.S. 1957 Marquette University, LL.B. *magna cum laude* 1963 Harvard University. United States Navy 1957–60. Member Chicago Bar Association. Clubs: Legal, Tavern. Principal areas of specialization: Corporate and securities.

RICHARD F. BROUDE
Partner 1980

Born June 6, 1936, Los Angeles, California. B.S. 1957 Washington University, J.D. with honors 1961 University of Chicago. Law clerk to Illinois Supreme Court Justice Walter Schaefer 1961–62. Practice Chicago 1962–66,

Los Angeles 1971—. Associate professor of law University of Nebraska 1966–69, professor of law Georgetown University Law Center 1969–71, adjunct professor of law University of Southern California Law School. Member American Bar Association, National Bankruptcy Conference, State Bar of California, Los Angeles Bar Association, Order of the Coif, Co-author *Cases and Materials on Land Financing,* contributing editor *Collier on Bankruptcy* 14th and 15th editions. Principal Areas of specialization: Bankruptcy and secured transactions.

C. JOHN BURESH

Associate 1970–71, 1973–78; partner 1978

Born January 28, 1945, New York City. B.A. with highest distinction 1967 and M.A. 1967 Northwestern University, J.D. *cum laude* 1970 University of Chicago (comments editor law review 1969–70). Lieutenant United States Navy Judge Advocate Generals Corps 1971–72. Instructor Boalt School of Law, University of California at Berkeley 1972–73. Member of the American Bar Association, District of Columbia Bar Association, California Bar Association, Phi Beta Kappa, Order of the Coif. Principal areas of specialization: Utility, anti-trust and litigation.

CHRISTIAN L. CAMPBELL

Associate 1975–1983; partner 1983

Born November 21, 1950, Chicago, Illinois. B.A. *summa cum laude* 1972 M.A. (economics) with honors 1972 Northwestern University, J.D. *cum laude* 1975 Harvard Law School. Member American Bar Association, Illinois State Bar Association, Chicago Bar Association, Phi Beta Kappa. Lecturer on anti-trust, American Management Association (1976—). Principal area of specialization: Anti-trust.

STEPHEN C. CARLSON

Associate 1976–83; partner 1983

Born March 22, 1951, Minneapolis, Minnesota. A.B. *magna cum laude* 1973 Princeton University, J.D. 1976 Yale University. Law clerk to Justice James C. Otis, Minnesota Supreme Court 1976–77. Member American Bar Association, Illinois State Bar Association, Chicago Bar Association, Phi Beta Kappa. Clubs: Princeton (Chicago), Yale (Chicago), Yale Law School Association of Chicago. Principal area of specialization: Litigation.

DAVID W. CARPENTER

Associate 1978–82; partner 1982

Born August 26, 1950, Chicago, Illinois. B.A. 1972 Yale University,

J.D. 1975 Boston University. Law clerk to Chief Judge Frank M.Coffin, United States Court of Appeals for First Circuit 1975–77, United States Supreme Court Justice William J. Brennan, Jr. 1977–78. Lecturer Illinois Institute of Technology-Chicago Kent College of Law (1980–82). Member American Bar Association, Illinois State Bar Association, Chicago Bar Association. Principal areas of specialization: Anti-trust and regulated industries.

JAMES J. CARROLL
Associate 1972–78; partner 1978

Born January 10, 1948, Chicago, Illinois. B.S. *magna cum laude* 1969 and J.D. *summa cum laude* 1972 DePaul University (editor-in-chief law review 1971–72). Director David and Ruth Barnow Foundation. Principal area of specialization: Estate and trust.

FRANKLIN A. CHANEN*
Associate 1957–64; partner 1965

Born March 12, 1933, Burlington, Iowa. B.B.A. 1954 and J.D. 1957 Northwestern University. Director, president Illinois Society for the Prevention of Blindness. Member Chicago Bar Association, Order of the Coif. Club: Birchwood. Principal areas of specialization: Federal tax and corporate.

JAMES E. CLARK
Associate 1976–83; partner 1983

Born September 2, 1948, Washington, D.C. A.B. *magna cum laude* 1970 Brown University, J.D. 1976 University of Chicago Law School. United States Navy 1970–72. Member American Bar Association, Illinois State Bar Association (member section council on commercial, banking and bankruptcy law 1981—), Chicago Bar Association (chairman commercial law committee 1982–83), Phi Beta Kappa. Editor Illinois State Bar Association Commercial, Banking and Bankruptcy Law Newsletter 1981—. Contributing author *New York Law Journal, National Commercial Finance Journal, The Journal of Commercial Bank Lending*, Illinois Institute for Continuing Legal Education. First vice-president North Avenue Day Nursery Auxiliary Board 1981–82. Clubs: University (Chicago). Principal area of specialization: Commercial, banking and bankruptcy law.

RICHARD G. CLEMENS
Associate 1968–73; partner 1973

Born October 8, 1940, Chicago, Illinois. B.A. with honors 1962 and

J.D. 1965 University of Virginia. Member American Bar Association, Illinois State Bar Association, Chicago Bar Association, Chicago Council on Foreign Relations, International Business Council, Order of the Coif, Phi Beta Kappa, Phi Delta Phi. Clubs: Legal, Monroe. Principal areas of specialization: Corporate, securities and international.

THOMAS A. COLE
Associate 1975–81; partner 1981

Born November 2, 1948, Philadelphia, Pennsylvania. A.B. with honors John Hopkins University, J.D. with honors 1975 University of Chicago. Corporate counsel 1980–82 and vice president-law 1982 Northwest Industries, Incorporated. Director Southern School (Chicago). Member American Bar Association, Chicago Bar Association, Chicago Crime Commission, Phi Beta Kappa, Order of the Coif. Clubs: University (Chicago), Metropolitan (Chicago). Principal areas of specialization: Corporate and securities.

GARY O. CONCOFF
Partner 1982

Born June 28, 1936, Los Angeles, California. B.S. 1958 University of California, Los Angeles, LL.B. 1962 Harvard University. Lecturer UCLA Law School 1979–82. Co-chairman UCLA Entertainment Law Symposium 1977–79. Numerous articles in legal journals on entertainment law. Trustee Los Angeles Copyright Society 1976–77. Principal area of specialization: Entertainment law.

WILLIAM F. CONLON
Associate 1979–80; partner 1980

Born January 14, 1945, Chicago, Illinois; A.B. 1967 Indiana University, J.D. 1970 University of Illinois (board of editors law review 1968–70). First Lieutenant United States Army 1970–72, Practice Des Moines, Iowa 1972–74. Assistant United States Attorney Northern District of Illinois 1974–1979, chief civil division 1977–79. Member American Bar Association, Illinois State Bar Association, Chicago Bar Association, Illinois State Board of Ethics 1982—, District Court Performance Assistance Committee, Northern District of Illinois 1982—, District 35 Board of Education Glencoe Elementary School District 1981—. Recipient Director's Award United States Department of Justice 1979. Co-author articles on legal subjects. Adjunct professor John Marshall Law School 1976—. Principal areas of specialization: Federal court commercial and business litigation.

GARY L. COWAN
>Associate 1960–68; partner 1969
>
>Born October 19, 1934, Livingston, Montana. B.A. 1956 and M.A. 1957 University of Montana, J.D. 1960 University of Chicago. General counsel Michigan Consolidated Gas Company 1973–81, Wisconsin Pipe Line Company 1981—. Clubs: Detroit, Grosse Point Hunt. Principal area of specialization: Corporate.

PHILIP J. CRIHFIELD
>Associate 1971–77; partner 1977
>
>Born October 3, 1945, Chicago, Illinois. B.S. with highest distinction 1967 Purdue University, J.D. with honors 1971 John Marshall Law School. Amoco Oil Company 1967–70, Standard Oil Company 1970–71. Chairman administrative board First United Methodist Church of Evanston. Member American Bar Association, Chicago Bar Association. Principal areas of specialization: Intellectual property, advertising and marketing.

MARK C. CURRAN*
>Counsel 1976–78; partner 1978
>
>Born September 11, 1924, Chicago, Illinois. B.S. 1947 St. Ambrose College, J.D. 1950 Northwestern University. Lieutenant United States Naval Reserve 1943–46. Trial attorney National Labor Relations Board Washington 1950–52, Chicago 1952–55. Assistant Counsel P.P.G. Industries (Pittsburgh) 1956–67. Associate General Counsel Montgomery Ward & Company 1967–76. Lecturer American Management Association 1975–81. Director United Way 1970–78. Member American Bar Association, Chicago Bar Association. Club: Mid-Day. Principal areas of specialization: Litigation and labor.

JOHN DAMES
>Associate 1971–78; partner 1978
>
>Born May 19, 1946, Chicago, Illinois. B.A. 1966 Washington University (St. Louis), M.A. 1968 Indiana University, J.D. 1971 Loyola University of Chicago. Member American Bar Association, Chicago Bar Association. Principal area of specialization: Product liability litigation.

MICHAEL W. DAVIS
>Associate 1975–83; partner 1983
>
>Born November 12, 1950, New York, New York. B.A. *magna cum laude* 1972, S.U.N.Y. Binghamton, J.D. *cum laude* 1975 Northwestern University School of Law (law review 1973–75). Member American Bar Association,

Illinois State Bar Association, Chicago Bar Association. Principal area of specialization: Litigation.

SYLVIA O. DECKER
Associate 1964–71; partner 1972

Born February 18, 1939, Canton, Illinois. B.A. 1960, Wellesley College, J.D. 1963 Yale University. Law clerk to Judge Robert E. English, Illinois Appellate Court 1963–64. Trustee Federal Defender Program, Incorporated 1980—. Member American Bar Association, Illinois State Bar Association Chicago Bar Association (chair operations of Circuit Court committee, probate practice committee, various subcommittees), Chicago Estate Planning Council. Past president Yale Law School Association of Illinois. Past director Better Government Association. Counsel Vietnamese Association, Lao Association, Hmong Association, Lecturer Wellesley College Clubs, Francis W. Parker School, Rotary Club, Juvenile Court. Clubs: Law, Legal, University (Chicago), East Bank. Principal areas of specialization: Estate and trust.

WILBUR C. DELP, JR.*
Associate 1960–68; partner 1968

Born October 26, 1934, Cedar Rapids, Iowa. B.A. 1956 Coe College, J.D. 1959 New York University. Root-Tilden Scholar. Member American Bar Association, Chicago Bar Association, Phi Beta Kappa, Phi Delta Phi. Clubs: Law, Legal, Mid-Day. Principal area of specialization: Corporate and securities.

J. DOUGLAS DONENFELD
Associate 1970–77; partner 1977

Born September 6, 1945, Indianapolis, Indiana. B.A. 1967 Northwestern University, J.D. 1970 Ohio State University. Parliamentarian Illinois General Assembly 1971. Member Illinois Property Tax Reform Commission 1979. Trustee Adler Planetarium. Governing member Chicago Symphony Orchestra. Member President's Council of Museum of Science and Industry. Member Chicago Bar Association, American Association of Immigration and Naturalization Lawyers. Principal areas of specialization: State and local taxation, immigration, administrative, and legislative.

CHARLES W. DOUGLAS
Associate 1974–80; partner 1980

Born April 1, 1948, Chicago, Illinois. B.A. 1970 Northwestern University, J.D. 1974 Harvard University. Principal areas of specialization: Litigation and anti-trust.

ROBERT A. DOWNING*

Associate 1956–64; partner 1964

Born January 6, 1928, Kenosha, Wisconsin. B.S. 1950 and LL.B. 1956 University of Wisconsin. Member American Bar Association, Illinois State Bar Association, Chicago Bar Association, Wisconsin Bar Association, Seventh Circuit Bar Association. Clubs: Law, Legal, Mid-Day, Society of Trial Lawyers, Union League, W-Club. Principal area of specialization: Litigation.

STEPHEN P. DURCHSLAG

Associate 1966–73; partner 1973

Born May 20, 1940, Chicago, Illinois. B.S. 1962 University of Wisconsin. Student 1962–63 Hebrew University of Jerusalem. LL.B. 1966 Harvard University. Member American Bar Association (corporate section), Chicago Bar Association (chairman food and drug committee 1977), Chicago Council on Foreign Relations (chairman Forum 1970–73, director 1973–79), Spertus College of Judaica 1976—, Anshe Emet Synagogue 1976—, secretary 1982—. Director Chicago Symphony Orchestra Junior Board 1967–69, Chicago chapter National Academy of Television Arts and Sciences 1974—. Numerous articles on legal aspects of advertising. Clubs: Legal, Standard, East Bank, Mid-Town Tennis. Principal area of specialization: Marketing.

JAMES W. DYKE, JR.

Counsel 1981–82; partner 1982

Born November 25, 1946, Washington, D.C. B.A. 1968 and J.D. 1971 Howard University. Law clerk to Judge Spottswood W. Robinson III, United States Court of Appeals District of Columbia Circuit 1971–72. Practice Washington 1972–77. Chairman District of Columbia Neighborhood Legal Services Program 1974–75. President Washington Council of Lawyers 1973–74. Adjunct professor Howard Law School 1975–76. Visiting professor University of Virginia Law school 1977—. General counsel Democratic party 1976 platform committee. Political advisor Vice-presidential candidate Walter F. Mondale 1976, domestic policy advisor 1977–81. Trustee District of Columbia Public Defender Service 1981—. Member District of Columbia Bar's Board of Governors 1981—, Legislative/Fiscal steering committee Greater Metropolitan Washington Board of Trade 1982, Federal City Council Board of Trustees 1982. Chairman Lawyers Committee for Mayor Barry 1982. Principal areas of specialization: Commercial, municipal finance, legislative, and real estate.

JOSEPH S. EHRMAN*

Associate 1957–66; partner 1966

Born March 28, 1931, Milwaukee, Wisconsin. B.S. with highest distinction 1953 University of Minnesota. J.D. 1956 and LL.M. 1957 Harvard University. Director Montessori School of Lake Forest. Past director, vice-president Chicago Commons Association. Member American Bar Association, Chicago Bar Association, Phi Beta Kappa, Delta Gamma Sigma. Clubs: Law, Legal, Mid-Day, Union League. Principal area of specialization: Corporate and securities.

NATHAN P. EIMER

Associate 1973–80; Partner 1980

Born June 26, 1949, Chicago, Illinois. A.B. *magna cum laude* with highest distinction in economics 1970 University of Illinois, J.D. *cum laude* 1973 Northwestern University (notes and comments editor law review 1972–73). Member Trial Bar of the United States District Court for the Northern District of Illinois, American Bar Association, Chicago Bar Association, Seventh Circuit Bar Association, Omicron Delta Epsilon. Principal areas of specialization: Litigation and anti-trust.

EUGENE R. ELROD

Associate 1977–80; partner 1981

Born May 14, 1949, Roanoke, Alabama. A.B. 1971 Dartmouth College, J.D. 1974 Emory University. Trial attorney Federal Power Commission 1974–77. Member American Bar Association, Georgia Bar Association, District of Columbia Bar Association, Federal Energy Bar Association (chairman tax developments committee 1980–81, oil pipeline committee 1982–83). Principal area of specialization: Energy and transportation.

EDNA S. EPSTEIN

Associate 1975–82; partner 1982

Born July 26, 1938, Yugoslavia. A.B. *cum laude* 1960 Barnard College, M.A. 1961 Johns Hopkins University, Ph. D. 1967 Harvard University, J.D. *cum laude* 1973 University of Chicago. Assistant professor French 1967–70 University of Illinois at Chicago. With Cook County state's attorney 1973–75. Member faculty Michigan Institute of Continuing Legal Education 1977, National Institute of Trial Advocacy 1979–81, Illinois institute of Continuing Legal Education 1981. Visiting lecturer University of Chicago Law School 1980–81. Director Hyde Park-Kenwood Development Corporation 1980–83, Friends of Parks 1978—, Music of the Baroque 1981–82. Member Citizens Committee for Victim Assistance 1976–78, Mayor Byrne's Transition Task Force 1979, State's Attorney's professional advisory committee 1980–83. Delegate Democratic National Convention 1980 (member rules committee). Member American Bar Association (chairman trial evidence committee 1979–83), Chicago Bar Association, Chicago Council of Lawyers (board of governors 1975–77), Phi Beta Kappa, Order of the Coif. Contributor of articles to professional journals, author *Attorney/Client Privilege and Work Product Doctrine and Motions to Disqualify Attorneys for Conflicts of Interest*. Principal area of specialization: General litigation.

ARLENE C. ERLEBACHER

Associate 1974–80; partner 1980

Born October 3, 1946, Cicero, Illinois. B.A. 1967 and J.D. 1973 Northwestern University. Director Northwestern University Law Alumni Association 1976—. Member American Bar Association, Illinois State Bar Association, Chicago Bar Association, Chicago Council of Lawyers, Wigmore Club, Order of the Coif. Principal areas of specialization: General trial and appellate litigation.

DONALD ETRA

Associate 1981–83; partner 1983

Born July 23, 1947, New York City. B.A. 1968 Yale University, J.D. 1971 Columbia University, M.B.A. 1971 Columbia University. Associate of Ralph Nader 1971–73. Trial attorney Civil Division, United States Department of Justice, 1973–78. Assistant United States Attorney, Central District of California, 1978–81. Author *Citibank*, the Nader report on First National City Bank 1974. Member American Bar Association, Los Angeles County Bar Association, Century City Bar Association, Los Angeles County Bar Association, Century City Bar Association. Chairman Jewish National Fund, Leadership Council 1981—. Pro tem judge Beverly Hills Small Claims Court. Member Federal Indigent Defense Panel, Central District of California. Principal areas of specialization: Product liability, litigation and criminal law.

ROBERT A. FERENCZ

Associate 1973–81; partner 1981

Born September 10, 1946, Chicago, Illinois B.S. 1968 University of Illinois, J.D. *magna cum laude* 1973 University of Michigan (assistant editor law review 1971–73). Director Old Town School of Folk Music 1981—, The Savoy-Aires 1980—. Member American Bar Association, Chicago Bar Association, Order of the Coif. Principal area of specialization: Federal income tax, employee benefits, and corporate taxation.

WILLIAM O. FIFIELD

Associate 1971–77; partner 1977

Born May 25, 1946, Crown Point, Indiana. B.S. with honors and distinction 1968 Purdue University, J.D. *cum laude* 1971 Harvard University. Member American Bar Association, Chicago Bar Association, Chicago Crime Commission. Principal areas of specialization: Litigation, joint ventures, and international transactions.

NEIL FLANAGIN*

Associate 1960–66; partner 1966

Born December 2, 1930, Chicago, Illinois. B.A. 1953 Yale University, J.D. 1956 University of Michigan. United States Army 1956–59. Attorney-examiner Securities Exchange Commission 1959–60. Fellow American College of Investment Counsel. Member American Bar Association, Chicago Bar Association, Zeta Psi, Phi Delta Phi. Director Dr. Scholl Foundation. Clubs: Law, Indian Hill (Winnetka), University (Chicago). Principal area of specialization: Corporate and securities.

RICHARD J. FLYNN*

Associate 1954–63; partner 1963

Born December 6, 1928, Omaha, Nebraska. Student Cornell University 1944–46, B.S. 1950 and J.D. 1953 Northwestern University. Law clerk to United States Supreme Court Chief Justices Fred Vinson and Earl Warren 1953–54. United States Navy 1946–48. Member American Bar Association, Chicago Bar Association, District of Columbia Bar Association, Federal Energy Bar Association, Association of ICC Practitioners, Order of the Coif, Phi Beta Kappa, Phi Delta Phi, Sigma Chi. Clubs: Economic, Kenwood Golf and Country, Legal, Metropolitan (Washington), National Lawyers. Principal areas of specialization: Regulated industries, anti-trust and other business litigation and appellate matters.

ROBERT R. FREI*

Associate 1949–57; partner 1957

Born March 23, 1923, Evanston, Illinois. A.B. 1947 Princeton University, J.D. *cum laude* 1949 Harvard University (editor law review 1947–48). First lieutenant United States Army 1943–46. Trustee Winnetka Congregational Church 1974–77. Member priorities committee of United Way of Metropolitan Chicago 1975–80 (vice-chairman 1978–80), Chicago Association of Commerce and Industry 1974—, American Bar Association, Illinois State Bar Association, Chicago Bar Association, American College of Tax Counsel. Contributor tax articles to various publications, speaker University of Chicago Tax Conference, American Law Institute and American Bar Association programs. Clubs: Law, Legal, Mayflower Society of Illinois, Mid-Day, Skokie Country. Principal areas of specialization: Federal tax, employee benefits and corporate.

DOUGLAS F. FUSON

Associate 1968–74; partner 1974

Born January 19, 1944, Ann Arbor, Michigan. B.A. *magna cum laude* 1965 Oberlin College, J.D. 1968 University of Chicago. Member American Bar Association, Illinois State Bar Association, Chicago Bar Association, Seventh Circuit Bar Association, Chicago Council of Lawyers, Phi Beta Kappa. Director Legal Assistance Foundation of Chicago 1979—. Principal area of specialization: Litigation.

THOMAS E. GARCIN*

Partner 1979

Born August 1, 1925, Boston, Massachusetts. LL.B. 1952 Loyola University (Los Angeles). United States Army 1943–46. Practice 1952–80 Los Angeles. Lecturer-panelist California Continuing Education of Bar, Board of Visitors Loyola University School of Law. Principal area of specialization: Trial practice.

DAVID R. GINSBURG

Counsel 1981–82; partner 1982

Born January 20, 1951, Los Angeles, California. A.B. 1972 and J.D. 1976 University of California, Los Angeles (editor-in-chief law review 1975–76). First National Prize, Nathan Burkan Memorial Copyright Competition 1975. Clerk to Judge Herbert Y. C. Choy, United States Ninth Circuit Court of Appeals 1976–77. Member State Bar of California, Hawaii State Bar Association, United States Supreme Court Bar, American Bar Association (forum Committee on entertainment and sports industries), Los Angeles Copyright Society, UCLA Entertainment Symposium Advisory Committee, Phi Beta Kappa. Municipal court judge *pro tem*. Lecturer-in-law, UCLA School of Law. Principal area of specialization: Entertainment law.

WILLIAM C. GOLDEN

Associate 1967–69; partner 1970

Born October 27, 1936, New York City, B.S. 1957 Wharton School of Finance and Commerce, University of Pennsylvania, LL.B. 1960 Columbia University. United States Department of Justice 1960–61, Office of Tax Legislative Counsel, United States Treasury Department 1962–65. Associate Professor Indiana University Law School 1965–67. Member Chicago Bar Association (chairman federal tax committee 1977–78). Principal areas of specialization: Federal tax and corporate.

DONALD J. GRALEN*

Associate 1959–66; partner 1967

Born March 18, 1933, Oak Park, Illinois. B.S.C. 1956 and J.D. with honors 1957 Loyola University of Chicago. Member American Bar Association, Chicago Bar Association (chairman land trust committee 1976–77), Illinois State Bar Association. Lecturer Continuing Legal Education Institute 1969–77. Director Carson Pirie Scott Foundation, Junior Achievement of Chicago, Metropolitan Housing and Planning Council, La Grange Community Family and Mental Health Center. Trustee Village of La Grange 1973–77, chairman La Grange Zoning Board 1971–73, La Grange Economic Development Committee 1982. Clubs: La Grange Country, Law, Legal, University (Chicago). Principal area of specialization: Real estate.

JON M. GREGG

Associate 1968–74; partner 1974

Born October 22, 1943, Louisville, Kentucky. B.S. with honors 1965 University of Illinois, LL.B. 1968 Harvard University. Member American Bar Association, Chicago Bar Association, Alpha Delta Phi. Principal area of specialization: Corporate and securities.

THOMAS J. GREGG

Associate 1964–71; partner 1972

Born March 24, 1939, Bloomington, Illinois. A.B. 1961 Harvard University, J.D. *cum laude* 1964 Northwestern University. Member American Bar Association, Illinois State Bar Association, Chicago Bar Association, Order of the Coif. Club: Monroe. Principal areas of specialization: Corporate and securities.

JACK GUTHMAN

Associate 1970; partner 1971

Born April 19, 1938, Cologne, Germany. B.A. 1960 Northwestern University, LL.B. 1963 Yale University. Law clerk to Judge Hubert L. Will, United States District Court for Northern District of Illinois 1963–65. Member Chicago Zoning Board of Appeals 1970—, chairman 1975—. Lecturer various law schools on zoning law and practice and the law of professional sports. Member visiting committee Northwestern University College of Arts and Sciences. Trustee Michael Reese Hospital and Medical Center, National executive committee Yale Law School Association. Clubs: Economic, Legal. Aide to various national political candidates. Principal areas of specialization: Government regulation (including zoning) and legislation.

RONALD W. HANSON

Associate 1975–83; partner 1983

Born August 3, 1950, LaCrosse, Wisconsin. B.A. *summa cum laude* 1972 St. Olaf College, J.D. *cum laude* 1975 University of Chicago. Member American Bar Association, Illinois State Bar Association, Chicago Bar Association, Phi Beta Kappa, Order of the Coif. Lecturer and author Illinois Institute for Continuing Legal Education. Club: Monroe. Principal areas of specialization: Insolvency and commercial litigation.

JAMES A. HARDGROVE

Associate 1971–76; partner 1977

Born February 20, 1945, Chicago, Illinois. B.A. 1967 and J.D. 1970 University of Notre Dame, (editor law review 1969–70), certificate in English law 1969 University of London. Law clerk to Judge Roger J. Kiley, United States Court of Appeals for Seventh Circuit 1970–71. Member American Bar Association, Illinois State Bar Association, Chicago Bar Association. Club: Legal. Principal area of specialization: Litigation.

JAMES M. HARRIS

Associate 1981–83; partner 1983

Born August 13, 1951, Evanston, Illinois. A.B. with honors 1973 Brown University, J.D. *cum laude* 1976 University of Chicago (editor-in-chief law review 1975–76). Law Clerk to David L. Bazelon, Chief Judge United States Court of Appeals for District of Columbia Circuit. Lecturer University of Virginia Law School 1978–79. Member American Bar Association, California State Bar Association, Los Angeles County Bar Association, Order of the Coif. Principal areas of specialization: Litigation, labor and health.

RICHARD W. HAVEL

Associate 1971–77; partner 1977

Born September 20, 1946, Fairmont, Minnesota. B.A. 1968 University of Notre Dame, J.D. 1971 University of California, Los Angeles (note editor law review 1971–72). Member Order of the Coif. Adjunct professor of law Loyola University at Los Angeles 1975–80. Lecturer-panelist California Continuing Education of the Bar. Principal areas of specialization: Corporate reorganization, bankruptcy and debtors-creditors rights.

HOWARD E. HAYNIE*

Associate 1959–69; partner 1969

Born May 30, 1928, Chicago, Illinois. B.S. and B.A. with highest distinction 1951 Northwestern University, J.D. *cum laude* 1959 Loyola University at Chicago. First lieutenant United States Marine Corps 1951–57. Member Wilmette Zoning Board 1970–80 (chairman 1975–80). Director Chicago Association for Retarded Citizens, numerous other charitable organizations. Instructor Loyola Law School 1961–64. Member American Bar Association, Illinois State Bar Association, Chicago Bar Association, Phi Alpha Delta, Beta Gamma Sigma, Blue Key. Clubs: Law, Legal, Union League, Westmoreland Country, Sheridan Shores Yacht. Principal area of specialization: Real estate.

BENJAMIN W. HEINEMAN, JR.

Partner 1983

Born January 25, 1944, Chicago, Illinois. B.A. 1965 Harvard University, B. Litt. 1967 Oxford University (Rhodes Scholar), J.D. 1971 Yale University (editor-in-chief law journal 1970–71). Law clerk to United States Supreme Court Justice Potter Stewart 1971–72. Staff attorney Center for Law and Social Policy 1973–74. Practice Washington 1975–76, 1980–82. Executive assistant to Secretary of Health, Education and Welfare 1977–78, assistant secretary for planning and evaluation HEW 1978–79. Member District of Columbia Bar Association. Reporter *Chicago Sun-Times* 1968. Author *The Politics of the Powerless: A Study of the Campaign Against Racial Discrimination* 1972, *Memorandum for the President: A Strategic Approach to Domestic Affairs in the 1980s* 1981. Principal area of specialization: Litigation.

STEPHEN S. HILL

Associate 1976–83; partner 1983

Born October 27, 1951, Washington, D.C. A.B. *magna cum laude* 1973 and J.D. 1976 Harvard University. Member American Bar Association, District of Columbia Bar Association, Massachusetts Bar Association. Director Washington Parent Child Center, Incorporated. Principal area of specialization: Litigation.

THOMAS W. HILL, JR.

Partner 1981

Born December 25, 1924, New York City. B.S. 1948 University of Pennsylvania, M.B.A. 1950 New York University, J.D. 1953 Columbia University (editor law review 1952–53). Assistant United States Attorney Southern District of New York 1953–54. Practice New York 1954–75. President Belco Petroleum Corporation 1962–63. Trustee International College of Beirut 1978. Legal advisor Sultan Qaboos bin Said, Sultanate of Oman 1972–76. Member American Bar Association, Association of the Bar of the City of New York, New

369

York State Bar Association, New York County Lawyers Association, American Institute of Certified Public Accountants, New York State Society of Certified Public Accountants. Clubs: Dubai Gold, Racquet & Tennis, Pinnacle, Winged Foot Golf, Woburn Golf (England). Contributor articles to legal publications. Principal area of specialization: International banking and commercial law.

KENNETH K. HOWELL
　　　Counsel 1976–78; partner 1978
　　　Born December 30, 1931, San Pedro, California. A.B. 1956 University of Alabama, J.D. 1959 University of Chicago. Executive director Legal Assistance Foundation of Chicago 1968–76. Associate professor University of Alabama 1961–63. Bigelow Fellow University of Chicago Law School 1969–70. Principal areas of specialization: Litigation and utility.

LAWRENCE H. HUNT, JR.
　　　Associate 1970–75; partner 1975.
　　　Born July 15, 1943, Chicago, Illinois. A.B. 1965 Dartmouth College (Senior Fellow, Reynolds Scholar to Institut D'Etudes Politiques 1966), J.D. 1969 University of Chicago (comment editor law review 1968–69). Member American Bar Association (member committee on commodities regulation, chairman subcommittee on futures commission merchants, Illinois State Bar Association (securities advisory committee 1978—). Principal area of specialization: Commodity futures law and regulation.

DeVERILLE A. HUSTON
　　　Associate 1977–83; partner 1983
　　　Born March 2, 1947, Great Falls, Montana. B.A. 1969 University of Minnesota, J.D. 1975 William Mitchell College of Law. Member American Bar Association, Illinois State Bar Association (commercial, banking and bankruptcy section council 1978–83), Chicago Bar Association (chairperson consumer credit committee 1979–80). Clubs: Monroe, River. Principal area of specialization: Commercial, banking, and bankruptcy.

JAMES D. JOHNSON
　　　Associate 1970–73; partner 1973
　　　Born April 12, 1943, LeMars, Iowa. B.S. 1965 and J.D. 1967 University of Iowa. Law clerk to Circuit Judge George C. Edwards, Jr. 1967–68. Professor University of Toledo Law School 1968–70. Consultant St. Louis Metropolitan Area Airport Authority 1975–77. President trustees First Presbyterian Church of Evanston 1980–82. Member American Bar Association, Chicago Bar

Association, Phi Delta Phi. Clubs: Monroe, Saddle & Cycle. Principal area of specialization: Corporate and securities.

KIRK B. JOHNSON

Associate 1973–80; partner 1980

Born December 13, 1947, Camden, New Jersey. B.A. with distinction 1969 Dartmouth College, J.D. 1973 University of Chicago. Member American Bar Association, Chicago Bar Association, Association of Interstate Commerce Practitioners. Director Scholarship and Guidance Association, Metropolitan Housing and Planning Council. Club: Economic (Chicago). Principal areas of specialization: Regulatory and labor litigation.

LOREN E. JUHL*

Associate 1948–56; partner 1956.

Born November 19, 1918, New Holland, Illinois. B.S. 1940 University of Illinois, LL.B. 1948 Harvard University. Served to major United States Army 1941–45. Member American Bar Association, Illinois State Bar Association, Chicago Bar Association, American College of Probate Counsel, Chicago Estate Planning Council. Director Northwestern Memorial Foundation, Chicago Maternity Center (counsel), The Thresholds (former president). Clubs: Illini of Chicago (former president), Law (former secretary and treasurer), Legal, Mid-Day, University (Chicago), Westmoreland Country. Author articles in various legal and tax journals. Speaker at estate planning programs University of Chicago and city and state bar associations. Principal areas of specialization: Estate and trust.

ALBERT R. KAREL

Associate 1979–82; partner 1982

Born November 10, 1942, Bemidji, Minnesota. B.B.A. 1964 and J.D. 1971 University of Wisconsin. Captain United States Army 1964–68. Member American Bar Association, Illinois State Bar Association, California Bar Association. Principal areas of specialization: Bankruptcy, insolvency, and bank liquidation.

LAWRENCE I. KIPPERMAN

Associate 1971–73; partner 1973

Born November 22, 1941, Chicago, Illinois. B.A. 1963 and J.D. 1966 University of Illinois, LL. M. 1970 George Washington University. Attorney National Labor Relations Board 1966–70. Member Chicago Bar Association. Clubs: Legal, Monroe, American Judicature Society. Principal areas of specialization: Labor and litigation.

JAMES W. KISSEL*

Associate 1942–56; partner 1956

Born December 5, 1915, Hartford, Wisconsin. B.A. 1938 University of Wisconsin, J.D. 1942 John Marshall Law School, postgraduate 1943–44 Harvard Graduate School of Business Administration. Lieutenant United States Naval Reserve 1942–45. Lecturer Northwestern School of Law, Illinois Institute of Continuing Legal Education. Recipient Distinguished Service Award John Marshall Law School. Member Chicago Bar Association (president 1973–74), American College of Trial Lawyers, Society of Trial Lawyers, National Association of Railroad Trial Counsel, American Bar Foundation (fellow), Chicago Bar Foundation (director). Contributor articles to professional journals. Principal area of specialization: Litigation.

SHALOM L. KOHN

Associate 1975–80; partner 1980

Born November 18, 1949, New York City. B.S. 1970 Brooklyn (CUNY), rabbinic ordination 1970, J.D. and M.B.A. 1974 Harvard University. Law clerk to Chief Judge Irving R. Kaufman, United States Court of Appeals for Second Circuit 1974–75. Principal area of specialization: Complex financial litigation.

MORRIS I. LEIBMAN

Partner 1945

Born February 8, 1911, Chicago, Illinois. Ph.B 1931 and J.D. 1933 University of Chicago, honorary LL.D 1978 Loyola University of Chicago. Founding partner Carney, Crowell and Leibman 1945 (later Leibman, Williams, Bennett, Baird and Minow). Lecturer University of Chicago, University of Illinois, DePaul, Northwestern. Member Illinois State Bar Association, Chicago Bar Association, American Bar Association (chairman committee on law and national security 1962–67, 1975–82), Chicago Law Institute, American Judicature Society, American Bar Foundation, Association of the Bar of City of New York, Selden Society. President Law Club 1975–76. Recipient Presidential Medal of Freedom from President Reagan 1981. Member Presidential panel of consultants on international affairs and national security 1964–68, Secretary of Defense advisory committee on non-military instruction 1962, director National Strategy Information Center, New York, Georgetown University's Center for Strategic and International Studies, Freedoms Foundation at Valley Forge; participant strategy seminars National War College, Army War College, and Naval War College. Chairman national advisory council on Economic Opportunity 1967–70. Trustee Loyola University of Chicago, Michael Reese Medical Center, USO of Chicago, United Cerebral Palsy and Ethics Resource Center (Washington).

Clubs: Army/Navy Club (Washington), Carlton, Mid-Day, Standard, Sky (New York). Principal areas of specialization: General, corporate and litigation.

JOHN G. LEVI

Associate 1973–83; partner 1983

Born October 9, 1948, Chicago, Illinois. A.B. with honors 1969 University of Rochester, J.D. 1972 and LL.M.1973 Harvard Law School. Member American Bar Association, Illinois State Bar Association, Chicago Bar Association. Director Chicago Child Care Society (vice-president 1979—), Chicago Opera Theater. Trustee Chicago Institute for Psychoanalysis, Chicago Sinai Congregation. Member University of Chicago Visiting Committee for Student Affairs. Clubs: Monroe, East Bank. Principal area of specialization: Labor and employment.

MARC A. LEVINSON

Associate 1971–80; partner 1980

Born August 12, 1948, Brooklyn, New York. B.A. 1970 University of California, Los Angeles, J.D. 1973 University of California, Davis (editor-in-chief law review). Law clerk to Chief Justice Donald R. Wright, California Supreme Court 1973–74, Judge William H. Orrick, Jr., United States District Court, Northern District of California 1974–75. Member American Bar Association (business bankruptcy committee 1981—), Los Angeles County Bar Association (law schools committee 1981—), Order of the Coif. Member University of California Davis Alumni Association, director 1978–81 (president 1980–81). Principal areas of specialization: Bankruptcy, insolvency and corporate reorganization.

DAVID J. LEWIS

Associate 1974–80; partner 1980

Born February 4, 1948, Zanesville, Ohio. B.S. 1970 and J.D. 1973 University of Illinois (editor-in-chief law forum 1972–73). Member American Bar Association, Order of the Coif. Club: Bethesda Country (Maryland). Principal areas of specialization: Anti-trust and public utility regulation.

DAVID P. LIST*

Partner 1955

Born February 4, 1920, Belvidere, Illinois. A.B. 1942 Dartmouth College, LL.B. 1948 Harvard University. Eighth Air Force Army of the United States 1942–45. Fellow American College of Trial Lawyers. Member American Bar Association, Illinois State Bar Association, Chicago Bar Association. Clubs: Law, Legal, University (Chicago), Westmoreland Country. Principal area of specialization: Litigation.

WILLIAM F. LLOYD

Associate 1975–82; partner 1982

Born December 27, 1947, Youngstown, Ohio. A.B. *magna cum laude* 1969 Brown University, J.D. *cum laude* 1975 University of Chicago. United States Army 1970–73. Member American Bar Association, Illinois State Bar Association, Chicago Bar Association, Order of the Coif, Phi Beta Kappa. Principal areas of specialization: Commercial securities and anti-trust litigation.

CHARLES E. LOMAX*

Partner 1975

Born March 24, 1924, Wilkesboro, North Carolina. B.A. 1948 and LL.B. 1951 Howard University. Staff assistant regional counsel Internal Revenue Service 1952–74. Member American Bar Association, Illinois State Bar Association, District of Columbia Bar Association, North Carolina Bar Association, Chicago Community Trust. Club: Law. Principal areas of specialization: Federal tax and corporate.

MARTIN M. LUCENTE

Associate 1948–55; partner 1956

Born September 15, 1919, Cumberland, Wisconsin. LL.B. 1948 University of Wisconsin (executive editor law review 1947–48). United States Army Air Force 1941–45 (air medal with two Oak Leaf clusters, two Presidential Unit Citations, seven battle stars, Bronze Arrowhead). Research assistant University of Wisconsin Law School 1947. Member American Bar Association, Chicago Bar Association, American Judicature Society, Order of the Coif. Clubs: Benchers Society of University of Wisconsin Law School, Lake Geneva Country, Legal, Skokie Country, Union League. Advancement committee Troop 20 Boy Scouts of America, past attorney Winnetka Board of Education, Winnetka caucus Committee. Principal areas of specialization: Litigation and labor.

CHESTER J. MACIOROWSKI

Associate 1972–78; partner 1978

Born August 8, 1946, Chicago, Illinois. B.A. 1968 and J.D. *cum laude* 1971 DePaul University. Club: Union League. Principal areas of specialization: Railroad and products liability litigation.

DONALD A. MACKAY*

Associate 1961–68; partner 1968

Born May 16, 1933, New York City. B.A. 1957 Dartmouth College,

J.D. 1961 University of Chicago. Associate general counsel Council for Periodical Distributors Association. Member Order of the Coif. Club: Monroe. Principal area of specialization: Marketing.

ROBERT J. MAGANUCO
Associate 1975–82; partner 1982

Born April 22, 1950, Chicago, Illinois. A.B. 1972 Boston College, J.D. 1975 University of Illinois. Member American Bar Association, Illinois State Bar Association, Chicago Bar Association, Order of the Coif. Principal area of specialization: Real estate.

ROBERT A. MALSTROM
Associate 1973–80; partner 1980

Born May 28, 1946, Ancon, Panama Canal Zone. B.S. 1969 University of Illinois, J.D. 1973 University of Michigan. United States Army 1969–71. Trustee and member T. Lloyd Kelly Foundation 1978—. Member American Bar Association, Illinois State Bar Association, Chicago Bar Association, Chicago Estate Planning Council. Principal areas of specialization: Estate and trust.

JAMES L. MAROVITZ
Associate 1963–70; partner 1970

Born February 21, 1939, Chicago, Illinois. B.S. 1960 and J.D. 1963 Northwestern University. Lecturer-panelist Illinois Continuing Legal Education, Kent State University. Director Deerfield United Fund 1969–71, Village of Deerfield Planning Commission 1973–80. Member American Bar Association, Illinois State Bar Association, Chicago Bar Association, Order of the Coif. Clubs: Law, Legal, University (Chicago). Principal area of specialization: Real estate.

R. EDEN MARTIN
Associate 1967–73; partner 1973

Born May 17, 1940, Sullivan, Illinois. B.A. 1962 University of Illinois, M.A. 1964 and LL.B. 1967 Harvard University. House counsel Arthur Andersen & Company 1973–75. Member American Bar Association, Chicago Bar Association. Clubs: Chicago, Mid–Day, University (Washington). Principal areas of specialization: Administrative agency litigation, anti-trust and appellate.

HENRY L. MASON III
Associate 1967–72; partner 1973

Born February 10, 1941, Boston, Massachusetts. A.B. 1963 and

LL.B. 1967 Harvard University. Director Illinois Division American Civil Liberties Union 1977–79. Member American Bar Association (advisory committee to standing committee on education about communism 1976–79), Illinois State Bar Association, Chicago Bar Association. Principal area of specialization: litigation.

ROBERT E. MASON*

Associate 1957–64; partner 1964

Born June 9, 1932, Los Angeles, California. B.A. 1954 and J.D. 1957 Northwestern University (law review 1956–57). Member American Bar Association, Seventh Circuit Bar Association, Chicago Bar Association, Order of the Coif. Clubs: Law, University (Chicago). Principal areas of specialization: Anti-trust and litigation.

W. STIRLING MAXWELL*

Associate 1949–61; partner 1962

Born May 2, 1922, Chicago, Illinois. A.B. with distinction 1947 and J.D. 1949 University of Michigan. United States Army 1944–46 and 1951–52. Senior legislative counsel United States Secretary of the Treasury 1960–61. Director Arizona Biltmore Estates 1967–73, Santa Catalina Island Company 1974—. Member Delta Upsilon, Phi Beta Kappa, Order of the Coif. Clubs: Law, Legal. Principal areas of specialization: Federal tax and estate.

GEORGE W. McBURNEY

Associate 1953–64; partner 1964

Born February 17, 1926, Ames, Iowa. B.A. 1950 and J.D. 1953 State University of Iowa (editor law review 1952–53). United States Army 1944–46. Member American Bar Association, Illinois State Bar Association, Chicago Bar Association, International Bar Association, Seventh Circuit Federal Bar Association, American Arbitration Association (panelist), American Judicature Society, Phi Kappa Psi, Omicron Delta Kappa, Delta Sigma Rho, Phi Delta Phi, Chicago Crime Commission 1966—. Trustee Old People's Home (secretary 1967–69), executive vice–president 1969–74, president 1975–82), The Georgian (honorary life, counsel 1976–82, vice-president 1980–82). Clubs: Union League, Executives (Singapore), Mid-Day. Principal areas of specialization: Litigation and utility.

JOHN M. McDONOUGH

Associate 1969–75; partner 1975

Born December 30, 1944, Evanston, Illinois. A.B. *magna cum laude*

1966 Princeton University, LL.B. 1969 Yale University. United States Army Reserve 1969–75. Director Chicago Alliance for the Performing Arts (past president), Chicago Child Care Society, Sarah Hackett Stevenson Memorial, Metropolitan Housing and Planning Council (president 1982—), Center for American Archeology (chairman 1982–83), Lakefront Gardens, Incorporated (secretary-treasurer 1979—), Brain Research Foundation. Recipient Princeton Club of Chicago Award for Distinguished Community Service 1983. Member American Bar Association, Illinois State Bar Association, Chicago Bar Association, Chicago Council on Foreign Relations, Phi Beta Kappa. Clubs: Chicago, Chikaming (Michigan), Law, Racquet, University (past president). Principal areas of specialization: Estate and trust.

ROBERT D. McLEAN
> Associate 1972–75; partner 1975
> Born March 1, 1945, Mankato, Minnesota. B.S. 1967 Northwestern University, J.D. 1970 Yale University. Law clerk to United States Supreme Court Justice Thurgood Marshall 1970–71. Trustee Latin School of Chicago. Member American Bar Association, District of Columbia Bar Association, Illinois State Bar Association, Chicago Bar Association. Clubs: Chikaming (Michigan), Legal, Racquet, Saddle & Cycle. Principal areas of specialization: Anti-trust, securities, and financial litigation.

THOMAS M. McMAHON
> Associate 1972–75; partner 1975
> Born May 11, 1941, Evanston, Illinois. University of Notre Dame 1959–61, B.A. 1963 Marquette University, J.D. *magna cum laude* 1970 Northwestern University (board of editors *Law Review*). Lieutenant United States Navy 1963–67, Republic of Vietnam campaign and National Defense Service medals. Manager Legal Advisory Section Illinois Environmental Protection Agency (Springfield) 1970–72. Member American Bar Association, Illinois State Bar Association, Chicago Bar Association, Order of the Coif, Chicago Association of Commerce and Industry, Evanston Environmental Control Board. Director Evanston Community Coordinated Child Care and Chiaravelle Montessori School. Club: Union League. Principal areas of specialization: Environmental and regulatory.

LAWRENCE A. MILLER
> Associate 1976–83; partner 1983
> Born December 3, 1946, Cleveland, Ohio. B.A. with highest distinction 1969 Northwestern University, J.D. 1976 Yale Law School. Research

student 1969–73 New College and Institute of Social Anthropology, University of Oxford. Member American Bar Association. Principal area of specialization: Federal administrative litigation.

MAURICE J. MILLER*

Associate 1955–62; partner 1963

Born May 14, 1926, Barron, Wisconsin. B.B.A. 1951 and J.D. 1955 University of Wisconsin. United States Army 1944–46. Member American Bar Association, Illinois State Bar Association, Chicago Bar Association, Wisconsin Bar Association, Phi Alpha Delta, Phi Kappa Phi. Clubs: Chicago, Law, Monroe. Principal areas of specialization: Federal tax, corporate and securities.

MIDDLETON MILLER*

Associate 1935–42; 1945–48; Partner 1948

Born August 16, 1906, Lexington, Kentucky. A.B. 1929 Princeton University, LL.B. 1932 Harvard University. Private to captain United States Army Air Corps 1942–45. Trustee William H. Miner Foundation. Director Gaylord Donnelley Foundation. Past director Miehle-Goss-Dexter, Incorporated, Moline Corporation, American Foundation for Biological Research. Member planning committee University of Chicago Tax Conference, American Bar Association, Illinois State Bar Association, Chicago Bar Association. Clubs: Law, Legal, Mid-Day, University (Chicago) Indian Hill (Winnetka). Principal areas of specialization: Estate, trust and federal taxes.

THEODORE N. MILLER

Associate 1967–73; partner 1973

Born October 9, 1942, Chicago, Illinois. B.A. 1964 University of Michigan, LL.B. 1967 Yale University. Member American Bar Association, Chicago Bar Association, Chicago Council of Lawyers, Order of the Coif, Phi Beta Kappa. Principal areas of specialization: Litigation and utility.

NEWTON N. MINOW*

Partner 1965

Born January 17, 1926, Milwaukee, Wisconsin. B.A. 1949, J.D. 1950 and LL.D. 1965 Northwestern University. Honorary LL.D. 1963 University of Wisconsin, Brandeis University, 1972 Columbia College. United States Army 1944–46. Law clerk to United States Supreme Court Chief Justice Fred M. Vinson 1951–52. Administrative assistant Governor Adlai E. Stevenson 1952–53, special assistant Stevenson Presidential campaigns 1952, 1956. Prac-

378

tice in Chicago since 1953. Chairman Federal Communications Commission 1961–63. Executive vice–president and general counsel *Encyclopaedia Britannica* 1963–65. Director and general counsel Aetna Casualty and Surety Company of Illinois and Aetna Life Insurance Company of Illinois, director CBS, Incorporated, Foote, Cone & Belding Communications, Incorporated. Trustee and former board chairman The Rand Corporation, trustee University of Notre Dame 1964–77, 1983—. Mayo Foundation 1973–81, Northwestern University, William Benton Foundation 1980—, Chicago Orchestral Association. Co–chairman Presidential debates for League of Women Voters 1976, 1980, Governor Public Broadcasting Service 1973–80 (chairman 1978–80). Chairman board of overseers Jewish Theological Seminary 1974–77. Recipient George Foster Peabody broadcasting award 1961, Ralph Lowell award 1982. Fellow American Bar Foundation, Member American Bar Association, Illinois State Bar Association, Chicago Bar Association, Northwestern University Alumni Association (alumni medal 1978). Clubs: Carlton, Casino, Chicago, Century (New York), Commercial, Economic, Federal City (Washington), Law, Legal, Northmoor Country, Standard. Author *Equal Time: The Private Broadcasters and the Public Interest* 1964, co–author *Presidential Television* 1973, *Tomorrow's American: Electronics and the Future* 1977, contributor *As We Knew Adlai*. Principal area of specialization: Communications law.

LEE M. MITCHELL
     Associate 1968–72; partner 1972
     Born April 16, 1943, Albany, New York. A.B. 1965 Wesleyan University, J.D. 1968 University of Chicago. Executive vice–president and general counsel Field Enterprises, Incorporated 1981–83, president and chief executive officer 1983. Director Westview Press, various Field Enterprises subsidiaries. Member American Bar Association, Federal Bar Association, Federal Communications Bar Association, Chicago Bar Association, National Panel of American Arbitration Association, Association of American Law Schools (section on mass communication law), Northwestern University Associates, National Academy of Arts and Sciences. Participant seminars and conferences Aspen Institute, Brookings Institution, Twentieth Century Fund, Ditchley Foundation, League of Women Voters. Clubs: Economic, Federal City (Washington), National Press (Washington). Co–author *Presidential Television* 1973, author *Openly Arrived At* 1974, *With the Nation Watching* 1979, contributor *Aspen Notebook on Government & the Media* 1973, *Annals of American Academy of Political and Social Science* 1976, *Journal of Communications* 1978, *American Bar Foundation Research Journal* 1980. Principal area of specialization: Communications.

G. PAUL MOATES

Associate 1975–82; partner 1982

Born May 26, 1947, Los Angeles, California. B.A. Amherst College, J.D. 1975 University of Chicago. United States Army 1970–73, White House Communications Agency, recipient Presidential Service Badge and Joint Service Commendation Medal. Member American Bar Association, Illinois State Bar Association, District of Columbia Bar Association. Principal areas of specialization: Commerce and anti-trust.

LEE A. MONROE*

Associate 1960–68; partner 1969

Born February 20, 1932, Detroit, Michigan. B.A. 1954 Williams College, J.D. 1960 Northwestern University. United States Navy 1954–57. Member American Bar Association, Illinois State Bar Association, District of Columbia Bar Association. Clubs: Bethesda Country, Legal, National Lawyers. Principal areas of specialization: Public utility and anti-trust.

ALAN L. MORRISON

Associate 1978–82; partner 1982

Born November 27, 1947, Raleigh, North Carolina. B.S. 1970 North Carolina State University, J.D. *cum laude* 1974 Harvard University. Practice 1975–78 Washington. Principal area of specialization: International law, especially Middle East.

THOMAS H. MORSCH*

Associate 1955–62; partner 1962

Born September 5, 1931, Oak Park, Illinois. University of Notre Dame 1949–52, B.S.L. 1953 and J.D. 1955 Northwestern University. Fellow American College of Trial Lawyers. Member American Bar Association, Illinois State Bar Association, Chicago Bar Association (board of managers 1979–81), Chicago Council of Lawyers. President Republican Workshops of Illinois 1962–63. Chairman Chicago Lawyers Committee for Civil Rights Under Law 1981—, LaGrange, Illinois police & fire commission 1969–72, plan commission 1972–80. Clubs: LaGrange Field, Legal, Notre Dame (director 1965–68), University (Chicago). Principal areas of specialization: Litigation and general.

GAMAL M. NAGUIB

Partner 1982

Born March 7, 1920, Cairo, Egypt. Licence en Droit 1942 Faculty of Law, University of Cairo. Director general cabinet of Prime Minister of Egypt

1970. Egyptian Foreign Service 1946–80. Ambassador to Zambia 1971–73, Norway 1973–80. Member Bar Association of Egypt, Egyptian Society of International Law (vice–president 1965–71, board member 1982—). Principal areas of specialization: International and Egyptian law.

SALLY S. NEELY

Associate 1977–79; partner 1979

Born March 2, 1948, Los Angeles, California. B.A. 1970 and J.D. 1971 Stanford University. Law clerk to Judge Ozell M. Trask, Ninth Circuit Court of Appeals 1971–72. Practice Phoenix, Arizona, 1973–75. Assistant professor Harvard Law School 1975–79. Practice Los Angeles 1977–80. Member American Bar Association, California Bar Association, Arizona Bar Association, Financial Lawyers Conference, Order of the Coif, Phi Beta Kappa, Organization of Women Executives. Principal area of specialization: Corporate reorganizations.

J. ROBERT NELSON

Associate 1975–79; partner 1979

Born April 3, 1944, Santa Monica, California. B.S. 1968 and J.D. 1971 University of California, Los Angeles (associate editor *Law Review* 1970–71). Lieutenant United States Naval Reserve 1972–75. Member American Bar Association, California Bar Association, Los Angeles County Bar Association, Center for Prisoner of War Studies. Principal areas of specialization: Bankruptcy and debtor-creditor rights.

MICHAEL A. NEMEROFF

Associate 1973–78; partner 1978

Born February 16, 1946, New York City. B.A. with honors and special honors 1968 University of Chicago, J.D. 1971 Columbia University (Stone Scholar 1971, articles editor *Journal of Law and Social Problems*). Assistant counsel Senate Committee on the Judiciary 1971–73, Subcommittee to Investigate Juvenile Delinquency. Treasurer Friends of Jim Stasser, Committee to elect Congressman Robert Garcia, Educators Political Action Committee. Staff liaison Governor Michael S. Dukakis for 1976 Action Committee. Democratic Platform Committee, 1974 Campaign Committee of Democratic National Committee. Member American Bar Association, Federal Bar Association (vice-chairman water transportation committee). Principal areas of specialization: General administrative and legislative, with special emphasis on telecommunications, international trade, and campaign finance.

WILLIAM J. NISSEN

Associate 1976–83; partner 1983

Born July 28, 1947, Chicago, Illinois. B.A. with highest distinction 1969 Northwestern University, J.D. *magna cum laude* 1976 Harvard Law School. Officer United States Navy, 1969–73. Member American Bar Association, Illinois State Bar Association, Chicago Bar Association. General Counsel Heinold Commodities, Incorporated 1982–83. Principal areas of specialization: Commodities law and litigation.

JOHN M. O'HARE

Associate 1971–76; partner 1977

Born April 9, 1946, Oak Park, Illinois. A. B. 1967 and M.S. 1969 University of Illinois, J.D. 1971 Harvard University. Member American Bar Association, Chicago Bar Association, Phi Beta Kappa. Principal areas of specialization: Corporate and securities.

DENNIS V. OSIMITZ

Associate 1976–83; partner 1983

Born May 28, 1951, Racine, Wisconsin. B.A. 1973, J.D. 1976 University of Wisconsin-Madison (law review 1974–75, editor 1975–76). Member American Bar Association, Illinois State Bar Association, Chicago Bar Association, Phi Beta Kappa, Order of the Coif. Principal areas of specialization: Corporate and securities.

PETER I. OSTROFF

Partner 1980

Born December 15, 1942, Washington, D.C. A.B. 1964 Washington University, J.D. 1967 University of Chicago. Law clerk to Judge Shirley N. Hufstedler, United States Court of Appeals Ninth Circuit 1969–70. Practice in Chicago 1967–68. Teaching fellow Monash University, Victoria, Australia 1968–69. District representative Malibu, California Township Council. Member American Bar Association (chairman commercial transactions litigation committee, council member litigation section 1980—), Los Angeles County Bar Association (trustee, chairman section on human rights). Visiting professor of law Monash University 1982. Principal area of specialization: Commercial business litigation.

JULES M. PERLBERG*

Associate 1958–66; partner 1966

Born January 28, 1931, Chicago, Illinois. B.B.A. 1952 and J.D.

1957 University of Michigan (editor law review 1956–57). First lieutenant United States Army 1952–54. Certified Public Accountant Chicago 1954–55. Recipient Gold Medal Illinois Society of Certified Public Accountants 1955. Faculty University of Michigan Law School 1957–58. Member Glencoe School Board 1980—, executive board American Jewish Committee (Chicago) 1978—, vice–president 1981–83, executive board Juvenile Diabetes Foundation (Chicago) 1981—. Member American Bar Association, Chicago Bar Association, Order of the Coif, Beta Gamma Sigma. Clubs: Law, Legal, Mid–Day, World Trade Center (New York). Principal areas of specialization: Communications, utility and litigation.

RICHARD T. PETERS
Associate 1973–77; partner 1977

Born September 24, 1946, La Mesa, California. B.A. 1968 University of Santa Clara, J.D. 1971 University of California, Los Angeles (managing editor law review 1971). Member board of governors Financial Lawyers' Conference 1976–80, State Bar of California (debtor–creditor relations and bankruptcy subcommittee, business law section 1979–81, chairman 1981–82, executive committee business law section 1982—), Order of the Coif. Publications in professional journals. Principal areas of specialization: Bankruptcy, insolvency, and corporate reorganization.

DONALD S. PETERSEN
Counsel 1978–80; partner 1980

Born May 14, 1929, Pontiac, Illinois. B.A. 1951 Augustana College (Illinois), J.D. 1956 Northwestern University. United States Army 1951–53. Practice Chicago 1957–78. Director Chicago Exhibitors Corporation 1967— (president 1972—), Mt. Olive Cemetery Association 1972—, Lutheran General Hospital 1968— (chairman 1979–81), Parkside Foundation, Inc. 1980— (chairman 1980–81), Danish Old People's Home 1976—. Member Illinois State Bar Association, Chicago Bar Association. Club: Union League. Principal areas of specialization: Probate, trust, and corporate.

WAYNE E. PETERSON
Associate 1972–78; partner 1978

Born October 28, 1947, Chicago, Illinois. A.B. 1968 University of Illinois, J.D. *magna cum laude* 1972 Northwestern University. Member American Bar Association, Illinois State Bar Association, State Bar of California, Los Angeles County Bar Association, Chicago Bar Association, Order of the Coif. Principal areas of specialization: Corporate, securities, commodity law and financial transactions.

GEORGE A. PLATZ III
        Associate 1964–71; partner 1972
        Born September 12, 1939, Safford, Arizona. B.S. 1960 Northwestern University, LL.B. 1963 Harvard University. Member American Bar Association, Chicago Bar Association. Clubs: Chikaming (Michigan), Monroe. Principal areas of specialization: Litigation and general.

HENRY A. PRESTON*
        Associate 1948–56; partner 1956
        Born October 5, 1919, Chicago, Illinois. A.B. 1941 Yale University, J.D. 1948 Harvard University. Trustee Shimer College 1968–76, Ragdale Foundation 1983—. Chairman Lake Forest Plan Commission 1974–80, co-chairman Chicago Lawyers Committee for Civil Rights Under Law 1976–78. Director Du-Kane Corporation, Profit Counselors, Incorporated. Member American Bar Association, Illinois State Bar Association, Chicago Bar Association, Lake County Bar Association, Phi Beta Kappa. Clubs: Harvard Law Society, Law, Legal, Mid-Day, Old Elm, Shoreacres (past president), Little (Gulfstream, Florida), Yale (Chicago). Principal areas of specialization: Litigation, trusts, and estates.

DAVID T. PRITIKIN
        Associate 1974–80; Partner 1981
        Born May 2, 1949, Freeport, Illinois. B.A. 1971 Cornell University, J.D. 1974 Harvard University. Principal area of specialization: Anti-trust and litigation.

ANDREW C. QUALE, JR.
        Partner 1982
        Born July 7, 1942, Boston, Massachusetts. A.B. *magna cum laude* 1963 and LL.B. *cum laude* 1966 Harvard University. Knox Fellow Queens' College, Cambridge 1966–67. Practice Boston, New York 1969–82. Fellow International Legal Center, Bogota, Colombia and advisor to Colombian Tax Reform Commission 1967–69. Lecturer international and domestic banking law University of Virginia School of Law 1976—. Consultant United Nations 1981. Director Hambro America, Incorporated 1975—, American Scandinavian Banking Corporation 1981—. Consultant Harvard Institute of International Development, Advisory Mission to Indonesian Ministry of Finance 1981—. Member American Bar Association (Latin-American law committee 1974—), Association of the Bar of the City of New York (chairman committee on Inter-American affairs 1981—), American Arbitration Association (committee on international law 1973—). Clubs: Harvard, Bronxville Field. Contributor articles on interna-

tional banking and fiscal reform to legal and economic publications. Principal areas of specialization: International banking, finance, and commercial law.

ERIC F. QUANDT
> Associate 1976–83; Partner 1983
>
> Born June 22, 1951, Beaver Dam, Wisconsin. B.S. 1973, LL.B. 1976 University of Wisconsin. Member American Bar Association, Illinois State Bar Association, Chicago Bar Association. Club: Union League. Principal areas of specialization: Products liability and medical malpractice.

MARY HUTCHINGS REED
> Associate 1976–83; partner 1983
>
> Born March 7, 1951. Chicago, Illinois. A.B. with honors 1973 and M.A. 1973 Brown University (Economics), J.D. 1976 Yale Law School. Member American Bar Association, Chicago Bar Association, Phi Beta Kappa, Chicago Lawyers Committee for Civil Rights Under Law, Lawyers for the Creative Arts, Freedom to Read Foundation. Principal areas of specialization: Advertising, copyright, trademark, and sports promotion.

DAVID A. RICHARDS
> Partner 1982
>
> Born September 21, 1945, Dayton, Ohio. B.A. *summa cum laude* 1967 and J.D. 1972 Yale University, B.A. first class honors 1969 and M.A. 1973 Cambridge University (Keasbey Fellow 1967–69). Member Association of the Bar of the City of New York (real property committee 1978–80), New York State Bar, American Bar Association (committee on foreign investment United States, vice–chairman 1978–80, chairman 1980–83, real property division council 1983), Anglo–American Real Property Institute (board of governors 1983—), American College of Real Estate Lawyers, Phi Beta Kappa. Speaker American Law Institute, Practicing Law Institute, World Trade Institute, Mortgage Bankers Association, Association of Offshore Trust Companies (Netherlands Antilles), State Bars of Florida, New York, Texas and Virginia. Author many articles in professional journals. Principal area of specialization: Real estate.

WILLIAM P. RICHMOND*
> Associate 1960–67; partner 1967
>
> Born April 5, 1932, Cicero, Illinois. A.B. 1954 Albion College, J.D. 1959 University of Chicago. United States Army 1954–56. Law clerk to Judge James Bryant 1959–60. Member American Bar Association, Illinois State Bar Association, Chicago Bar Association, Seventh Federal Circuit Bar Association,

Society of Trial Lawyers, American College of Trial Lawyers. Clubs: Legal, Ruth Lake Country (Hinsdale), Union League. Principal areas of specialization: Product liability, litigation, and labor.

ALBERT RITCHIE
Associate 1964–71; partner 1972

Born September 29, 1939, Charlottesville, Virginia. B.A. *summa cum laude* 1961 Yale University, LL.B. 1964 University of Virginia. Served to captain United States Army 1965–67. Director United Charities of Chicago 1979— (vice-president 1982—), Erie Neighborhood House 1972—, Legal Aid Bureau. Member American Bar Association, Illinois State Bar Association, Chicago Bar Association, Phi Beta Kappa, Order of the Coif. Clubs: Legal (director, secretary-treasurer 1982—), University (Chicago), Indian Hill (Winnetka). Principal area of specialization: Real estate.

MARTIN F. ROBINSON
Associate 1966–71; partner 1972

Born July 5, 1939, Trenton, New Jersey. A.B. 1961 Rutgers University, LL.B. 1964 University of Pennsylvania. Law clerk to Judge Joseph Halpern, Superior Court of New Jersey 1964–65. Counsel National Labor Relations Board Washington 1965–66. Member American Bar Association, Chicago Bar Association, National Association of Bond Lawyers. Club: Monroe. Principal area of specialization: Municipal securities.

TOMAS M. RUSSELL
Associate 1967–73; partner 1973

Born February 27, 1934, Kankakee, Illinois. B.S. 1963 and J.D. 1967 University of Wisconsin (co-founder, chairman Civil Rights Research Council 1965–66). Director and member executive committee Illinois Institute for Continuing Legal Education, Wisconsin Law Alumni Association 1976 (president 1978), Wisconsin Benchers Society. Member American Bar Association (chairman committee on product safety 1975—, member litigation section legislation committee 1981—), Illinois State Bar Association (chairman judicial administration section governing council 1982), Chicago Bar Association (chairman committees on food, drug and product safety 1975, continuing legal education 1979, peer review and trial bar rules 1982–83), joint CBA-ISBA standing committee on judicial salaries 1982–83, American Judicature Society 1967—, American Civil Liberties Union, Urban League, Chicago Council on Foreign Relations, Art Institute of Chicago. Clubs: Law, Offshore Racing Club of America, University (Chicago), United States Yacht Racing Union. Principal area of specialization: Litigation.

THOMAS F. RYAN

      Associate 1972–78; partner 1978

      Born November 4, 1943, Detroit, Michigan. B.S. 1965, Ferris State, J.D. *magna cum laude* 1972 Wayne State University. First lieutenant United States Army 1965–68. Member American Bar Association, Illinois State Bar Association, Chicago Bar Association, Seventh Judicial Circuit Bar Association (meetings chairman). Club: University (Chicago). Principal areas of specialization: Litigation and anti-trust.

JOHN J. SABL

      Associate 1976–83; partner 1983

      Born June 16, 1951, Los Angeles, California. A.B. with distinction 1973 Stanford University, J.D. 1976 Stanford Law School (associate managing editor law review 1975–76). Member American Bar Association, Chicago Bar Association (secretary securities law committee 1981–82), Phi Beta Kappa. Principal area of specialization: Corporate and securities.

GEORGE L. SAUNDERS, JR.*

      Associate 1962–66; partner 1967

      Born November 8, 1931, Mulga, Alabama. A.B. 1957 University of Alabama, J.D. 1959 University of Chicago. United States Air Force 1951–54. Law clerk to Chief Judge Richard T. Rives, Court of Appeals for Fifth Circuit 1959–60, United States Supreme Court Justice Hugo L. Black 1960–62. Member American Bar Association (chairman committee on freedom of speech and press 1971–73), Illinois State Bar Association, Chicago Bar Association, Chicago Council of Lawyers. Clubs: Chicago, Law, Legal Mid-America, Mid-Day, Monroe, Quadrangle, Saddle & Cycle, Union League. Principal areas of specialization: Litigation and utility.

WILLIAM G. SCHAEFER, JR.

      Associate 1966–73; partner 1973

      Born June 16, 1941, Kansas City, Missouri. B.A. 1963 University of Kansas, J.D. 1966 Harvard University. Vice–president, general counsel DEKALB AgResearch, Incorporated 1974–77. Director Chicago Neighborhood Law Office Program 1968–70, Geneva Community Chest 1974–77, Children's Hospital National Medical Center. Member American Bar Association, District of Columbia Bar, Chicago Bar Association, Washington Lawyers Committee for Civil Rights Under Law 1982 (executive committee). Principal areas of specialization: Anti–trust and administrative litigation.

A. BRUCE SCHIMBERG*

Partner 1966

Born August 26, 1927, Chicago, Illinois. Ph.B. 1949 and J.D. 1952 University of Chicago (managing editor law review 1952). Second lieutenant United States Army 1945–47. Practice Cincinnati, Chicago since 1952. Lecturer University of Chicago College 1961–62. Director University of Chicago Law School Alumni Association 1969–72, Visiting Committee University of Chicago Law School 1980–83. Member American Bar Association (chairman Uniform Commercial Code committee, subcommittee Article 9 1979–81), Illinois State Bar Association (chairman commercial law, banking and bankruptcy section 1972–73), Chicago Bar Association (chairman UCC committee 1966, member board of managers 1968–70, chairman judiciary committee 1971–72), Seventh Circuit Bar Association. Author articles in *The Business Lawyer, Commercial Law Journal, The Journal of Commercial Bank Lending.* Clubs: Lake Shore Country, Carlton, Mid-Day. Principal areas of specialization: Banking, commercial law and bankruptcy.

EDWIN G. SCHUCK, JR.

Partner 1983

Born September 6, 1944, New York City. B.S. 1967, M.B.A. 1970, and J.D. 1970 Columbia University. Practice New York, Los Angeles 1971-80. Member Association of the Bar of the City of New York, Los Angeles County Bar Association (chairman income tax sub-division of taxation division), New York State Bar Association, American Bar Association, International Bar Association, State Bar of California, Phi Beta Kappa. Director Arthritis Foundation of Southern California. Principal area of specialization: Taxes.

DONALD L. SCHWARTZ

Associate 1974–80; partner 1980

Born December 8, 1948, Milwaukee, Wisconsin. B.A. *magna cum laude* 1971 Macalester College, J.D. 1974 University of Chicago. First vice-chairman Wisconsin Federation of Young Republicans 1972–74. Director Illinois Conservative Union, Incorporated 1976—(president 1979–81). Member American Bar Association (committee on Uniform Commercial Code), Illinois State Bar Association (secretary commercial banking and bankruptcy section council 1982–83, editor commercial, banking and bankruptcy law newsletter 1975–79), Chicago Bar Association (chairman commercial law committee 1980–81, chairman financial institutions committee 1982–83), Phi Beta Kappa, Order of the Coif, Phi Sigma Alpha, Omicron Delta Epsilon. Clubs: Monroe, Thorngate Country. Principal area of specialization: Commercial law.

LEE J. SCHWARTZ
>Counsel 1980–83; partner 1983
>
>Born May 23, 1942, Chicago, Illinois. A.B. 1963 Columbia University, J.D. 1966 Harvard University. Practice Chicago 1970, 1975–80. Democratic staff counsel Illinois House of Representatives 1967–70. Law clerk to Illinois Supreme Court Justice Arthur McGloon 1970–71. Legislative counsel City of Chicago 1971–75. Principal research associate Chicago Home Rule Commission 1972. Special counsel to Speaker, Illinois House of Representatives 1975–80. Member Illinois State Bar Association, Chicago Bar Association. Co-author, co-editor *Chicago Home Rule Commission Report and Recommendations* 1972, chapter on "Finance and Tax" in Illinois Municipal Law 1974. Principal areas of specialization: Legislative law and finances.

BENJAMIN P. SHAPIRO
>Associate 1979–80; partner 1980
>
>Born May 3, 1943, Chicago, Illinois. B.S. 1965 University of Illinois, J.D. 1968 Northwestern University. Staff attorney Federal Reserve Bank of Chicago 1968–72, regional counsel Federal Deposit Insurance Corporation 1972–79. Lecturer banking law John Marshall Law School 1979. Illinois Bankers' Association School 1979, Bank Administration Institute 1977—. Trustee Congregation B'nai Jehoshua Beth Elohim, 1981–82. Member American Bar Association, Illinois State Bar Association, Chicago Bar Association (chairman financial institutions committee 1977–78). Principal area of specialization: Banking and consumer credit law.

DAVID SHAYNE
>Associate 1969–72; partner 1972
>
>Born November 6, 1934, Chicago, Illinois. B.A. 1956 Yale University, LL.B. 1959 Harvard University. Trustee Francis W. Parker School. Member American Bar Association, Illinois State Bar Association, Chicago Bar Association (trust law committee), Chicago Council of Lawyers, Chicago Estate Planning Council, Phi Beta Kappa, Chicago Council on Foreign Relations, Lyric Opera Guild, Chicago Symphony Society, American Civil Liberties Union, Art Institute of Chicago, Lakeview Citizens Council, Chicago Opera Theatre Society. Clubs: Law, Harvard Law Society. Principal areas of specialization: Estate and trust.

LANGLEY R. SHOOK
>Associate 1978–82; partner 1982
>
>Born December 22, 1947, Alexandria, Virginia. A.B. 1969 and J.D.

1974 University of Michigan. Practice Chicago, Washington 1974–78. Member American Bar Association, District of Columbia Bar Association, Order of the Coif, Sigma Chi. Principal areas of specialization: Litigation and labor law.

ROBERT H. SHUTAN*

Partner 1971

Born May 12, 1918, Chicago, Illinois. University of Chicago, B.S. 1939 University of California at Los Angeles, LL.B. 1942 University of California Boalt Hall (law review 1941–42). Lieutenant United States Navy 1942–46. Member American Bar Association, State Bar of California (chairman bankruptcy and debtor–creditor committee of business law section 1978–79), Los Angeles County Bar Association, Beverly Hills Bar Association. Director American Civil Liberties Union Foundation of Southern California. Lecturer–panelist California Continuing Education of Bar programs. Principal areas of specialization: Bankruptcy and corporate reorganizations.

MICHAEL S. SIGAL

Associate 1967–73; partner 1973

Born July 9, 1942, Chicago, Illinois. B.S. 1964 University of Wisconsin, J.D. 1967 University of Chicago (law review 1965). United States Army Reserve 1968–74. Director EMRE Diagnostic Services, Incorporated. Member American Bar Association, Illinois State Bar Association, Chicago Bar Association, Phi Beta Kappa, Phi Kappa Phi, Phi Eta Sigma (president 1962–63). Clubs: Law, Mill Creek Hunt, Monroe, Principal areas of specialization: Corporate and securities.

SAMUEL K. SKINNER

Partner 1977

Born June 10, 1938, Chicago, Illinois. B.S. 1960 University of Illinois, J.D. 1966 DePaul University. United States Army 1960–61. Sales representative International Business Machines 1960–68. Assistant United States Attorney Department of Justice (Chicago) 1968–75, United States Attorney (Chicago) 1975–77. Recipient Distinguished Service Award Justice Department 1972, 1974, Outstanding Alumni Award DePaul University 1976. Named one of 10 Outstanding Young Citizens of Chicago, Chicago Jaycees 1974. Member American Bar Association, Illinois State Bar Association, Chicago Bar Association, President's Commission on Organized Crime 1983. Clubs: Law, Legal, Shoreacres (Chicago). Principal areas of specialization: Civil and criminal litigation, anti-trust and insurance.

STANTON K. SMITH, JR.

Associate 1956–63; partner 1964

Born February 14, 1931, Rockford, Illinois. B.A. 1953 Yale University, J.D. 1956 University of Wisconsin. General counsel American Natural Resources Company 1975. Director American Natural Resources Company, Great Lakes Transmission Company, J.L. Clark Manufacturing Company, Self-Service Oil Company. Trustee Rockford College. Member American Bar Association, Illinois State Bar Association, Michigan Bar Association. Principal areas of specialization: Securities, finance, mergers, acquisitions, public utility, natural gas and joint ventures.

LISA SPRY–LEVERTON

Associate 1977–83; partner 1983

Born July 18, 1949, New York City. B.A. with honors 1971 Barnard College, Columbia University. Diploma Exam International Law 1973 Manchester University, England. College of Law, Trinity Bar Exam, Second Class Honors. Member Honourable Society of the Inner Temple. Senate of the Inns of Court and the Bar. Pupillage Essex Court, Temple, London 1974–75. Honorary director American Theatre Company, London. Part-time director various London theatres. Lecturer Drama Studio, London. Principal areas of specialization: Commercial and entertainment law.

RICHARD J. STONE

Counsel 1981; partner 1982

Born April 30, 1945, Chicago, Illinois. B.A. 1967 University of Chicago, J.D. 1970 University of California, Los Angeles (editor-in-chief *Law Review* 1970). Practice Los Angeles 1971–77. Deputy assistant general counsel United States Department of Defense 1978–79, assistant to Secretary United States Department of Defense 1979–80. Recipient special citation for outstanding performance Secretary Department of Energy 1981. Delegate California State Bar Conference of Delegates 1982—. Member United States delegation Micronesian Political Status Negotiations 1978–79. Member advisory panel Council Energy Resource Tribes 1981—. Recipient Amos Alonzo Stagg medal and Howell Murray alumni medal University of Chicago 1967. Honoree National Conference Black Mayors 1980. Elder Presbyterian Church. Member American Bar Association, California Bar Association, Los Angeles County Bar Association, Association of Business Trial Lawyers, Phi Gamma Delta. Principal areas of specialization: Federal and state civil litigation and anti-trust.

THOMAS E. SWANEY
Associate 1968–73; partner 1973

Born April 25, 1942, Detroit, Michigan. B.A. 1963 and J.D. 1967 University of Michigan, London School of Economics 1967–68. Member American Bar Association, Illinois State Bar Association, Chicago Bar Association. Club: Legal. Principal areas of specialization: Estates and trusts.

MICHAEL J. SWEENEY
Associate 1976–83; partner 1983

Born February 17, 1953, Chicago, Illinois. B.A. with high honors 1973 University of Illinois. J.D. with honors 1976 University of Chicago. Member Phi Beta Kappa, Order of Coif. Principal area of specialization: Commercial Litigation.

WILLIAM H. THIGPEN*
Associate 1958–66; partner 1966

Born January 6, 1928, Mascot, Tennessee. B.S. 1950 and M.A. 1951 Northwestern University, J.D. 1958 Harvard University. Administrative assistant to vice–president Northwestern University 1951–55, general counsel 1971—. Member American Bar Association, Illinois State Bar Association, Chicago Bar Association, Chicago Council of Lawyers, American Judicature Society, American Society of Hospital Attorneys, National Association of College and University Attorneys. Clubs: Harvard Law Society (president 1975–76), Harvard Law School Association (vice-president 1976–77). Economic, Law, University (Chicago). Principal areas of specialization: Estate and trust, charitable organizations, and health care.

CAREN D. THOMAS
Associate 1975–83; partner 1983

Born February 2, 1950, New Jersey. A.B., *magna cum laude* with honors in Urban Studies, 1972 Barnard College, J.D. 1975 Yale Law School. Law clerk United States Court of Appeals for Second Circuit 1975–76. Member International Bar Association (officer 1982—), American Bar Association, Illinois State Bar Association, Chicago Bar Association, Phi Beta Kappa, Ely Chapter, Lambda Alpha. Director Music of the Baroque. Trustee The Three Arts Club of Chicago. Principal areas of specialization: Regulatory, environmental and land use law.

DALE E. THOMAS
Associate 1974–80; partner 1981

Born January 25, 1947, New Rochelle, New York. A.B. 1969

Princeton University, M. Div. 1973 and J.D. 1974 Yale University (editor law journal 1974). Law clerk to Judge Robert P. Anderson, United States Court of Appeals, Second Circuit 1974–75. Member American Bar Association, Illinois State Bar Association, Chicago Bar Association, Phi Beta Kappa. Clubs: Princeton, University (Chicago). Principal areas of specialization: Anti-trust, utility regulation, and communications technology.

STEPHEN P. THOMAS
        Associate 1965–70; partner 1970
        Born July 30, 1938, Bloomington, Illinois. B.A. 1959 University of Illinois, LL.B. 1962 Harvard University. Lecturer Malawi Institute of Public Administration 1963–65. Member Chicago Bar Association, Chicago Council of Lawyers. Principal area of specialization: Corporate and securities.

JOSEPH B. TOMPKINS, JR.
        Associate 1975–79; partner 1982
        Born April 4, 1950, Roanoke, Virginia. B.A. *summa cum laude* 1971 Washington and Lee University, M.P.P. 1975 and J.D. 1975 Harvard University. Associate Director Office of Policy and Management Analysis, Criminal Division, United States Department of Justice, 1979–81, Deputy Chief Fraud Section, Criminal Division, 1981–82. Member American Bar Association (chairman computer crime task force, 1982—), Federal Bar Association, Virginia Bar Association, District of Columbia Bar Association. Author *National Priorities for the Investigation and Prosecution of White Collar Crime* 1980. Principal areas of specialization: Federal court and administrative agency litigation, transportation and energy law, and white collar crime.

HOWARD J. TRIENENS*
        Associate 1949–50, 1952–55; partner 1956
        Born September 13, 1923, Chicago, Illinois. B.S. 1945 and J.D. *magna cum laude* 1949 Northwestern University. United States Air Force, 1943–46, first lieutenant. Law clerk to United States Supreme Court Chief Justice Fred M. Vinson 1950–52. Director G.D. Searle 1968–78, R.R. Donnelley & Sons Company 1978–79. Trustee Northwestern University, 1967—. Vice-president and general counsel American Telephone and Telegraph Company 1980—. Member American Bar Association, Illinois State Bar Association, Chicago Bar Association, American College of Trial Lawyers (fellow), American Law Institute, American Judicature Society, Sigma Chi. Clubs: Casino, Chicago, Commercial, Commonwealth, Law, Legal, Mid-Day, Metropolitan (Washington), Old Elm, Glen View Country, Skokie Country. Principal areas of specialization: Regulatory and anti-trust appellate litigation.

J. RONALD TROST*

Partner 1971

Born November 17, 1932, Fresno, California. B.A. 1954 Rice University, LL.B. 1957 University of Texas. Department of Justice (Washington) 1957–59. Practice Washington 1959–62, Los Angeles 1963—. Adjunct professor University of California at Los Angeles Law School, instructor University of Southern California Law School. Consultant United States Commission on Bankruptcy Laws. Member American Bar Association, American Law Institute, National Bankruptcy Conference. Author articles on bankruptcy. Principal areas of specialization: Insolvency, bankruptcy, and corporate reorganization.

R. TODD VIEREGG*

Associate 1970–73; partner 1973

Born October 3, 1934, Woodstock, Illinois. B.A. 1955 Michigan State University, J.D. *cum laude* 1970 Northwestern University. Carrier Jet Fighter Pilot United States Navy 1956–59. Restaurateur 1960–65, stockbroker 1966–67. Member American Bar Association, Illinois State Bar Association, Chicago Bar Association. Clubs: Law, Glen View, Union League. Principal areas of specialization: Corporate and securities.

CHARLES S. VOGEL*

Partner 1981

Born August 26, 1932, Los Angeles, California. B.A. 1955 Pomona College, LL.B. 1959 University of California, Los Angeles. Practice Pomona 1959–69, Los Angeles 1977–81. Judge Municipal Court Pomona Judicial District 1969–70, Los Angeles Superior Court 1970–77. Fellow American Bar Foundation. Member Los Angeles County Bar Association (trustee 1980–82, vice-president 1982—), UCLA School of Law Alumni Association (president 1977). Principal areas of specialization: Commercial and environmental litigation.

ROGER A. VREE

Associate 1969–75; partner 1975

Born October 2, 1943, Chicago, Illinois. B.A. 1965 Wheaton College, M.A. 1966 and J.D. 1969 Stanford University. Member American Bar Association, Illinois State Bar Association, Chicago Bar Association. Clubs: Law, Legal, University (Chicago), Stanford Law Society-Midwest (past president). Principal area of specialization: Real estate.

D. WILLIAM WAGNER

Associate 1969–74; partner 1974

Born January 14, 1943, Dixon, Illinois. B.A. 1965 and J.D. 1968

Northwestern University. Member American Bar Association, Illinois State Bar Association, California Bar Association, Los Angeles County Bar Association. Club: Legal. Principal area of specialization: Real estate.

ROBERT R. WATSON
Associate 1974–78; partner 1978

Born March 10, 1944, Buffalo, New York. A.B. 1967 Wheaton College, J.D. 1972 University of Chicago. Law Clerk to United States District Judge Richard W. McLaren 1972–74. Member American Bar Association, Illinois State Bar Association, Chicago Bar Association, Chicago Council on Foreign Relations. Clubs: Chicago Yacht, Legal. Principal areas of specialization: Litigation and general.

H. BLAIR WHITE*
Associate 1951–61; partner 1962

Born August 2, 1927, Burlington, Iowa. B.A. 1950 and J.D. 1951 University of Iowa (comment editor law review 1951). Director DEKALB AgResearch, Incorporated 1967—, Kimberly-Clark Corporation 1971—, R.R. Donnelley & Sons Company 1979—. President board of directors Cook County School of Nursing 1966–71. Director Auxiliary Cook County Hospital 1971—. Member American Bar Association, Illinois State Bar Association, Bar Association Seventh Federal Circuit, American College of Trial Lawyers (Fellow), Order of the Coif, Children's Memorial Hospital. Clubs: Chicago, Commercial, Economic, Law, Legal, Skokie Country. Contributor articles to professional journals. Principal areas of specialization: Litigation and anti-trust.

QUINCY WHITE*
Associate 1960–67; partner 1967

Born January 16, 1933, Chicago, Illinois. B.A. 1954 Yale University, J.D. 1960 Harvard University. Served to lieutenant United States Army Air Force 1954–56. Honorary consul-general Pakistan for Illinois 1978—, recipient Sitari-i-Quaid-i-Azam Award 1982. Director, secretary McLaughlin & Company 1964–68. Secretary national governing board The Ripon Society. Director, vice-president Juvenile Protective Association 1965—. Director, counsel 1974 Off-the-Street Club. President, co-founder Conference on Chicago Government 1970–73. Executive Committee 43rd and 44th Wards Regular Republican organizations (chairman committee on local government 1965–68), Chicago Council of Lawyers, Council on Foreign and Domestic Affairs 1970–76. Principal area of specialization: Intellectual property and advertising.

395

JAMES S. WHITEHEAD

Associate 1975–80; partner 1981

Born December 22, 1948, Rockford, Illinois. B.A. 1970, Yale University, J.D. 1974 University of Chicago. Law clerk to United States Court of Appeals Judge John Paul Stevens 1974–75. Director Scholarship & Guidance Association 1979—, vice–president 1981–. Public Interest Law Internship 1981–82. Member American Bar Association, Chicago Bar Association, Order of the Coif, Phi Beta Kappa. Principal areas of specialization: Labor and employment law.

MARSHALL W. WILEY

Partner 1981

Born April 26, 1925, Rockford, Illinois Ph.B. 1943, J.D. 1948 and M.B.A. 1949. University of Chicago. Lieutenant United States Naval Reserve 1943–45. Staff assistant Ford Foundation 1951–52. Foreign service officer Department of State 1958. Economics officer Amman 1963–64. Detailed to Rand Corporation 1968–69. Deputy principal officer Cairo 1969–73. Director North African affairs (Washington) 1974. Principal officer Baghdad, Iraq 1975–77. Deputy Chief of Mission American embassy Jidda, Sauda Arabia 1977–78. Ambassador to Sultanate of Oman, Muscat 1978–81. Member American Bar Association, Bar Association of the District of Columbia. Club: Cosmos (Washington). Principal area of specialization: International commercial law, with emphasis on Middle East.

JEREMY N. WILLIAMS

Partner 1982

Born December 23, 1945, New York City. B.A. 1967 Amherst College, M.A. 1968 Yale University, J.D. 1974 Harvard University. Practice California 1974—. Lecturer University of Southern California Law School 1982—. Judge pro tem Beverly Hills Municipal Court 1980–81. Director Amherst Alumni Association of Southern California 1980—. Principal area of specialization: Entertainment law.

JOHN C. WILLIAMS*

Associate 1954–63; partner 1964

Born June 11, 1930, Chicago, Illinois. B.A. 1951 Wesleyan University, LL.B. 1954 Yale University. Village official Northbrook (trustee 1965–69, president 1969–73, plan commission and zoning board of appeals 1965–69), Glencoe (police pension fund board 1980–82, chairman public safety commission 1982—). Director North Suburban Association for Health Resources 1973 (president 1974–75, director blood center 1973–75). Fellow American College Probate Counsel. Member American Bar Association, Illinois State Bar Association (chairman legislative committee 1969–71), Chicago Bar Association (chairman legislative committee 1969–71, chairman probate practice committee 1972–73, co–chairman committee on independent administration of decedents' estates 1975–79). Clubs: Economic, Law, Legal, Skokie Country, University (Chicago). Principal areas of specialization: Estate and trust.

R. MERINDA WILSON
Associate 1979–83; partner 1983

Born February 24, 1952, Pittsburgh, Pennsylvania. B.A. *magna cum laude* 1973 University of Pennsylvania, J.D. 1976 Harvard University, Member American Bar Association, Georgia State Bar Association, Atlanta Bar Association, Bar Association of the District of Columbia, Mortar Board, Big Brothers/Big Sisters (1978–79), Atlanta Ministry With International Students (1978–79), United Way Agency Evaluation Task Force and Budget Panel (1977–79). Trustee Public Defender Service 1983—. Principal area of specialization: Litigation.

ELROY H. WOLFF
Associate 1969–70; partner 1970.

Born May 20, 1935, New York City. A.B. 1957 Columbia College, LL.B. 1963 Columbia University School of Law, (board of editors law review 1962–63). Lieutenant United States Air Force, 1957–60. Legal assistant to Commissioner Philip Elman, Federal Trade Commission, 1965–67. Senior trial attorney, Office of General Counsel United States Department of Transportation, 1967–79. Member Federal Trade Commission advisory committee on practice and procedure 1969–71. Chairman Civil Aeronautics Board advisory committee on procedural reform 1975. Member American Bar Association, Federal Bar Association, Bar Association of the District of Columbia, Association of the Bar of the City of New York. Principal areas of specialization: Anti-trust, trade regulation, and regulatory litigation.

JOHN C. WOULFE*
Associate 1978–80; partner 1980

Born October 2, 1929, St. Paul, Minnesota. B.A. 1956 Illinois College, J.D. 1959 University of Chicago. Member American Bar Association, Illinois State Bar Association. Club: Union League. Principal areas of specialization: Litigation and utility.

MICHAEL S. YAUCH
Associate 1971–75; partner 1975

Born September 2, 1943, Lafayette, Indiana. B.S. 1965 Case Institute of Technology, J.D. 1968 Case Western Reserve University. Club: Legal. Principal areas of specialization: Anti-trust and public utility regulation.

JOHN D. ZEGLIS

Associate 1973–78; partner 1978

Born May 2, 1947, DeKalb, Illinois. B.S. 1969 University of Illinois, J.D. *magna cum laude* 1972 Harvard University (law review 1970–72). Knox Memorial Fellowship 1972–73. Member American Bar Association, Illinois State Bar Association, Chicago Bar Association. Principal areas of specialization: Antitrust and utility litigation.

APPENDIX III

Counsel

JAMES E. S. BAKER

Born May 23, 1912, Evanston, Illinois. A.B. 1933 and J.D. 1936 Northwestern University. Associate 1936–47, partner 1948–81. Served to commander United States Naval Reserve 1941–46 USS *Pelias* (AS14) navigator, first lieutenant and additional duty as Judge Advocate, General Courts Martial, and recorder, United States Foreign Claims Commission, United States naval forces, Western Australia, USS *New Kent,* (APA 217) executive officer, commanding officer; in Pearl Harbor December 7, 1941. Lecturer Northwestern University Law School 1951–52. President Northwestern University Law Alumni Association 1952–54. President John Henry Wigmore Club 1968–69. Chairman John Evans Club (NU) 1983—. National chairman Stanford University Parents Committee 1970–75. Member visiting committees Stanford University Law School 1976–79, 1982—, DePaul University Law School 1982—, Northwestern University School of Law 1980—. Official American College of Trial Lawyers (fellow 1956—, regent 1974–81, secretary 1977–79, president 1979–80). Member American Bar Association, Bar Association of the Seventh Federal Circuit, Society of Trial Lawyers of Illinois, Illinois State Bar Association, Chicago Bar Association, Order of the Coif, Phi Lambda Upsilon, Sigma Nu. Clubs: Law (president 1983–84), Legal, Mid-Day, University (Chicago), Westmoreland Country. Principal areas of specialization: Litigation and general.

WILEY A. BRANTON

Born December 13, 1923, Pine Bluff, Arkansas. B.S. 1950 and J.D. 1953 University of Kansas. United States Army 1943–46. Practice in Pine Bluff 1952–62, Little Rock 1971–78. Director Southern Regional Council voter education project 1962–65. Special assistant United States Attorney General

399

1965–67. Executive director United Planning Organization 1967–69, Council United Civil Rights Leadership 1953–65. Director community and social action Alliance for Labor Action 1967–71. Dean Howard University School of Law 1978—. Member board of National Association for the Advancement of Colored People legal defense and education fund, Columbia Federal Savings and Loan Association, Consolidated Railway Corporation. Named one of 100 most important young men in United States, *Life* 1962, one of 100 most influential Negroes, *Ebony* 1963. Recipient numerous awards for participation in civil rights litigation, including Henry W. Edgerton award American Civil Liberties Union 1977. Member American Bar Association, National Bar Association (Charles Houston Hamilton medallion 1978), Federal Bar Association, National Association for the Advancement of Colored People, National Urban League, Omega Psi Phi, Sigma Pi Phi, Phi Alpha Delta. Principal areas of specialization: Civil rights and torts.

HERBERT GROSSMAN

Born May 10, 1912, Chicago, Illinois. A.B. 1934 University of Illinois, LL.B. 1938 Loyola University at (Los Angeles). United States Army 1942–46. Deputy district attorney Los Angeles County 1940–50. General counsel The Larwin Group, Ticor Title Insurers (Title Insurance and Trust Company, Pioneer National Title Insurance Company) retired. Lecturer Practicing Law Institute. Member State Bar of California (chairman subsection commercial–industrial properties real property section 1980–82). Principal area of specialization: Real estate.

NATHALIE HOFFMAN

Born December 29, 1946, Pittsburgh, Pennsylvania. B.S. with high honors 1968 University of Michigan, J.D. 1973 University of California at Los Angeles. Practice Los Angeles 1973–78, 1982. Private consultant entertainment companies in Brazil 1978–80. Director business affairs in telecommunications division Twentieth Century-Fox 1980–82. Current attache Brazilian Olympic delegation. Member American Bar Association (patents, copyrights, and trademarks section), Los Angeles County Bar Association, Beverly Hills Bar Association, Century City Bar Association, Brazil-California Trade Association, California State Board of Behavioral Science Examiners, Phi Beta Kappa, Order of the Coif. Principal area of specialization: Entertainment law.

FRANK R. KENNEDY

Born July 27, 1914, Stafford, Missouri. A.B. 1935 Southwestern Missouri State University, LL.B. 1939 Washington University, J.S.D. 1953 Yale University. Sterling Fellow 1939–40. Served from ensign to lieutenant-commander United States Naval Reserve 1943–46. Teacher, forensic coach Lebanon, Missouri high school 1935–36. Instructor to professor 1940–61 State University of Iowa Law School, professor University of Michigan Law School 1961–78, Thomas M. Cooley professor 1979—, visiting law professor University of Pennsylvania 1966. Executive director United States Commission on Bankruptcy Laws 1971–73. Acting chief counsel to industrial user unit, rationing division Office of Price Administration 1942–43. Reporter advisory committee on bankruptcy rules United States Judicial Conference 1960–76. Member American Bar Association, American Association of University Professors, National Bankruptcy Conference, American Law Institute, Order of the Coif, Delta Theta Phi, Omicron Delta Kapp, Pi Sigma Alpha. Co-author *Collier on Bankruptcy* several volumes 14th edition. Contributor articles to legal, technical journals. Principal areas of specialization: Bankruptcy and reorganization.

MELVILLE B. NIMMER

Born June 6, 1923, Los Angeles, California. B.A. 1947 University of California, Berkeley, LL.B. 1950 Harvard University. Vice-chairman National Commission on New Technological Uses of Copyrighted Works 1977–78, Consultant United International Bureau for Intellectual Property (Geneva, Switzerland) 1965–66, Ministry of Justice (Jerusalem, Israel) 1969–70, Ministry of Education (Ghana) 1972. Member Bar of the Supreme Court of the United States, State Bar of California. Author *Nimmer on Copyright* (2nd edition, four volumes) 1978 and *Cases and Materials on Copyright and Other Aspects of Law Pertaining to Literary, Musical and Artistic Works* 1979. Principal area of specialization: Copyright.

EDMUND N. WISE

Born March 27, 1931, Columbus, Ohio. B.A. 1953 Yale University, LL.B. 1956 Harvard University. Counsel Development Loan Fund 1959–61. Director Latin America housing guaranty program, Agency for International Development, United States Department of State 1962–63. Member District of Columbia Bar Association. Principal area of specialization: International, particularly Middle East.

APPENDIX IV

Thomas W. Albrecht, Chicago 1979
Mark A. Angelson, Rutgers 1975
Amy L. Applebaum, California 1980
Richard W. Astle, Georgetown 1980
Salvatore A. Barbatano, Wisconsin 1973
Larry A. Barden, Washington & Lee 1982
Rupert V. Barry, Howard 1979
Steven A. Baskin, Chicago 1982
William H. Baumgartner, Jr., Harvard 1979
Jack M. Beard, Michigan 1983
James F. Bendernagel, Columbia 1976
Steven N. Bersch, California 1980
Stephen V. Beyer, Wisconsin 1981
Steven M. Bierman, Georgetown 1976
Susan J. Blankenbaker, Indiana 1983
Michael R. Blankshain, Illinois 1981
Shell J. Bleiweiss, Northwestern 1982
Jeffrey S. Bork, Valparaiso 1976
Robin Bronzaft, Stanford 1983
John R. Box, California 1981
Thomas P. Brown, Northwestern 1983
Michelle Burke, Harvard 1983
Robert J. Burson, Yale 1980
Thomas F. Bush, Jr., Chicago 1979
Ann E. Bushmiller, Chicago 1982
Jay S. Bybee, Brigham Young 1980
Craig L. Caesar, Northwestern 1978

James N. Cahan, Washington 1976
Richard A. Campbell, Illinois 1983
Timothy J. Carey, Norte Dame 1980
Walter C. Carlson, Harvard 1978
Thomas K. Cauley, Illinois 1983
Eva Yulan Chan, California 1978
Shelley C. Chapman, Harvard 1981
Walid S. Chiniara, New York 1982
Linda J. Chiron, Iowa 1980
Daniel G. Clement, Georgetown 1975
Zack A. Clement, Virginia 1975
David Cohen, New York 1983
Patrick J. Coughlin, Golden Gate 1979
Garry B. Crowder, Northwestern 1982
Tom W. Davidson, Wisconsin 1977
Richard T. deBelder, Manchester Polytechnic 1976
James C. Dechene, Michigan 1980
Barbara M. DeCoster, Iowa 1978
William D. Delahoyde, Northwestern 1982
Leslie R. Desmond, Chicago 1982
Jean Dobrer, New York 1980
Margaret R. Dollbaum, California 1980
Nancy J. Engberg, California 1982
Sharon L. Fabian, Northwestern 1979
Yvonne O. Featherstone, Law Society's College of Law 1978
Ronald S. Flagg, Harvard 1978

403

Maripat Flood, DePaul 1982
Todd D. Freer, Loyola 1979
Joy D. Fulton, Northwestern 1982
Alan Gabbay, Harvard 1978
Clifford W. Garstang, Indiana 1981
Maryann E. Gashi, Harvard 1983
Alan C. Geolot, Virginia 1979
June K. Ghezzi, Loyola 1983
Debra G. Glazer, Yale 1980
Sara J. Gourley, Illinois 1980
David F. Graham, Chicago 1979
Kathleen A. Grosso, Georgetown 1982
Thomas A. Hale, Duke 1982
Thomas P. Hanrahan, Columbia 1975
Dennis R. Hansen, Columbia 1980
Scott A. Harbottle, William & Mary 1981
Lisa A. Hausten, Chicago 1983
Kevin M. Hawley, Duke 1983
David D. Hiller, Harvard 1978
Jonathan S. Hoak, Drake 1977
Gregg Homer, Loyola 1979
Paul Homsy, Dickinson 1975
Terence M. Hynes, Duke 1979
Mary M. Jacobs, Northwestern 1981
James W. Jandacek, Harvard 1974
David B. Johnson, Loyola 1983
Elaine L. Johnston, Virgina 1982
George W. Jones, Yale 1980
Linzey D. Jones, Illinois 1982
Timothy E. Kapshandy, Notre Dame 1981
Charles H. Kennedy, Chicago 1976
Gina B. Kennedy, Boston 1979
Ellen C. Kerrigan, George Mason 1981
Chaim T. Kiffel, Northwestern 1982
J. Timothy Kleespies, Oregon 1980
Delrose A. Koch, Iowa 1981
Kathryn E. Korn, Illinois 1976
Bryan Krakauer, Chicago 1981
Michael C. Lamb, Boston 1981
Perry L. Landsberg, Hastings 1982
Nicholas R. LaTerza, Toledo 1977
Deborah B. Leahy, Virginia 1983
Anthony R. Licata, Harvard 1979
Frederick C. Lowinger, Chicago 1980

Marc E. Manly, Michigan 1977
Barbara F. Markham, Boston 1979
Prentice H. Marshall, Jr., Iowa 1977
Gina Hubbell McCareins, Northwestern 1981
John H. McFadden, Fordham 1978
David M. McIntosh, Chicago 1983
John A. McLees, Chicago 1974
Idell S. Melamed, Marshall 1981
Scott T. Mendeloff, Georgetown 1983
Thomas W. Merrill, Chicago 1977
Richard J. Metzger, Chicago 1976
Sam A. Miley, Northwestern 1982
Robert W. Millen, Indiana 1982
Joshua J. Mintz, Miami 1981
Paul D. Monson, Illinois 1982
Ann E. Morea, California 1983
Deborah H. Morris, Chicago 1977
John Mussman, Michigan 1983
Patricia A. Needham, Loyola 1982
Julie D. Nelson, Iowa 1978
Robert L. Nelson, Columbia 1980
George A. Nicoud, Texas 1982
William J. Noble, Michigan 1980
Lawrence J. Nyhan, Loyola 1980
Richard J. O'Brien, Jr., Georgetown 1979
Mary Ann O'Connor, Notre Dame 1980
Robert M. Olian, Harvard 1977
Richard F. O'Malley, Illinois 1983
William P. O'Neill, Michigan 1976
John W. Ongman, Northwestern 1976
James G. Pachulski, Michigan 1982
Tim R. Palmer, Virginia 1983
Linda S. Peterson, Yale 1977
Theodore A. Pinako, Michigan 1975
Thomas R. Potter, Michigan 1982
John R. Power, Columbia 1982
Vincent F. Prada, Chicago 1981
Joan P. Protess, Northwestern 1980
Imad I. Qasim, Georgetown 1982
Grier C. Raclin, Northwestern 1978
William C. Ramsayer, California 1980
Thomas D. Rein, Harvard 1983
Bruce M. Resnikoff, California 1982

Clements Ripley, Michigan 1979

Thomas O. Roberts, Northwestern 1983

Terry Ann Ross, DePaul 1981

Jeffrey S. Rothstein, Chicago 1982

Priscilla E. Ryan, Loyola 1983

Lora K. Sanberg, Northwestern 1980

Naima Satti, Khartoum 1981

David R. Sawyier, Harvard 1977

David M. Schiffman, Harvard 1977

J. Andrew Schlickman, Chicago 1978

Eugene A. Schoon, Valparaiso 1980

Marilyn J. Schramm, Northwestern 1981

Monica A. Schwebs, Virginia 1982

Andrew H. Shaw, Cornell 1979

Jeffrey P. Silberman, California 1983

Joan M. Singer, Southern California 1981

L. Gilles Sion, Harvard 1981

Lorna J. Soroko, Harvard 1982

Sara A. Staebell, Iowa 1983

Pamela J. Steele, Queensland 1971

James R. Stinehart, Iowa 1980

Gary B. Stern, Northwestern 1982

James R. Stinson, Illinois 1977

Elaine H. Stangland, California 1978

Nurelle Subjally, Warwick 1978

Steven M. Sumberg, Washington 1977

Mary H. Swanson, William Mitchell 1980

Don A. Tarkington, Northwestern 1983

Paula S. Teske, Loyola 1979

Theodore J. Theophilos, Chicago 1979

Heather Gilchrist T'Kindt, Valparaiso 1983

Jeffrey R. Tone, Illinois 1978

Constantine L. Trela, Jr., Northwestern 1979

Sherry S. Treston, DePaul 1983

Gary L. Tygesson, Northwestern 1980

John C. Vryhof, Michigan 1983

Maureen F. Walsh, Northwestern 1980

James F. Warchall, DePaul 1981

Thomas W. Weaver, New York 1979

Susan R. Weinberg, Indiana 1983

Nancy L. White, Loyola 1981

Jeanne G. Whiting, Brigham Young 1980

Douglas H. Williams, Chicago 1977

Arthur Winter, California 1980

William J. Wippich, Stanford 1983

Susan I. Wiviott, Harvard 1982

Robert P. Wootton, Yale 1979

Thomas H. Yancey, Virginia 1980

Michael H. Yanowitch, Chicago 1977

Ted K. Yasuda, Indiana 1982

Bennett G. Young, Hastings 1982

Richard E. Young, Virginia 1978

Dean A. Ziehl, Loyola 1978

APPENDIX V

Law Schools

Law School	*Number of* Lawyers	Law School	*Number of* Lawyers
Boston (University)	3	Loyola (Chicago)	12
California (Boalt Hall)	15	Loyola (Los Angeles)	5
California (Davis)	2	Michigan	23
Chicago	48	New York	5
Columbia	8	Northwestern	44
DePaul	9	Notre Dame	4
Dickinson	2	Pennsylvania	2
Drake	2	Southern California	4
Duke	4	Stanford	4
Fordham	2	Texas	2
Georgetown	8	UCLA	13
Golden Gate	8	Valparaiso	3
Harvard	67	Virginia	10
Hastings	2	Washington	2
Howard	2	William Mitchell College	
Illinois	17	of Law	2
Indiana	5	Wisconsin	6
Iowa	9	Yale	15
John Marshall	3		

The following schools were attended by one lawyer: Boston (College), Brigham Young, Case-Western Reserve, Chicago-Kent, Cornell, Emory, George Mason, George Washington, Iowa State, Khartoum, Law Society's College of Law, Manchester Polytechnic, Miami, Ohio State, Oregon, Queensland, Rutgers, Toledo, Warwick, Washington & Lee, Wayne State, William & Mary (Marshall Wythe).

APPENDIX VI

Former Partners

WILLIAM D. BANGS

Born May 15, 1885, St. Louis, Missouri. Graduated Princeton University 1907, LL.B. 1910 Harvard University. Practice Chicago 1910–17. Partner Holt, Wheeler & Sidley 1917–30. Instructor Northwestern Law School. Secretary Municipal Voters League of Chicago. General counsel Illinois Bell Telephone Company 1922–30. Clubs: Attic, Chicago, Law, Harvard-Yale-Princeton, University (Chicago), Princeton (New York), Geneva Golf. Died November 9, 1930.

HARLOWE E. BOWES

Born January 8, 1905, Blue Earth, Minnesota. B.A. 1926 Hamline University, student Harvard Law School 1927–28, LL.B. 1931 University of Minnesota. Practice in New York 1931–42. Associate 1942–44, partner 1944–74. Director DuKane Corporation, Farmers Seed & Nursery Corporation. Trustee Village of Golf, Illinois Children's Home and Aid Society. Past president First Ward Non-Partisan Civic Association, Evanston. Member Order of the Coif. Clubs: Law, University (Chicago). Died January 31, 1981.

FREDERIC F. BRACE, JR.

Born January 24, 1934, Greenville, Michigan. B.A. 1956 and J.D. 1959 University of Michigan (editor law review 1958–59). Associate 1959–68, partner 1959–82. Member American Bar Association, Illinois State Bar association, Chicago Bar Association, Seventh Circuit Bar Association, advisory boards Salvation Army and Booth Memorial Hospital (past chairman), Order of the Coif. Director Ohio-Sealy Corporation 1976—. Contributor articles *Chicago Bar Record*. Clubs: Law, Legal.

MERRITT C. BRAGDON

Born November 19, 1892, Evanston, Illinois. B.A. 1913 Northwestern University, LL.B. 1916 Harvard University. Practice in Chicago 1916–17, 1919–20. First lieutenant United States Army World War I. Law clerk 1920–27, partner 1928–58. Member Chicago Bar Association (chairman judiciary, admissions committees, member legal aid, grievances, candidates committees, librarian 1949–52). Club: University (Chicago). Died January 30, 1958.

ALICE M. BRIGHT

Born September 18, 1917, Homewood, Illinois. A.B. 1939 and J.D. *cum laude* 1941 University of Chicago. Associate 1942–55, partner 1956–82. President Women's Bar Association. Member Chicago Bar Association (chairman probate practice committee). Co-author *Contested Estates*. Died October 25, 1982.

KENNETH F. BURGESS

Born October 16, 1887, Oshkosh, Wisconsin. Graduated 1910, LL.B. 1912 University of Wisconsin. Honorary LL.D. University of Wisconsin, 1959 Northwestern University. Practice Lancaster, Wisconsin 1912–15. Attorney, general attorney, general solicitor Chicago, Burlington & Quincy Railroad Company 1915–30. Regional commerce counsel United States Railroad Administration 1918–20. General counsel Illinois Bell Telephone Company 1931–52. Partner 1931–65. Trustee Northwestern University 1933–65 (board president 1937–59), Newberry Library, Museum of Science and Industry. Director Chicago, Burlington & Quincy Railroad Company, Colorado & Southern Railroad Company, State Bank and Trust Company of Evanston, Burton-Dixie Corporation, Chicago Association of Commerce and Industry, Transportation Association, American Judicature Society. Governing life member Art Institute of Chicago. Fellow American Bar Foundation. Member American Bar Association (chairman public utility section, member many other committees). Clubs: Chicago Commercial (president), Commonwealth (president), University (Chicago), Indian Hill. Law, Legal, Glen View Country, Old Elm. Author (with J.A. Lyons) *Commercial Law* 1915, (with Homer V. Vanderblue) *Railroads—Rates, Service, Management* 1923, and articles on railroad law. Died May 24, 1965.

EMERSON T. CHANDLER

Born March 24, 1921, Chicago, Illinois. B.A. 1942 Yale University, J.D. 1949 University of Michigan. Served to lieutenant commander United States Naval Reserve, commanding naval destroyer escort South Pacific World War II. Associate 1949–61, partner 1962–71. President Civic Federation. Director Central YMCA and YMCA Community College. Member Illinois State Bar Association (taxation committee), Chicago Bar Association (legal education com-

410

mittee), Chicago Association of Commerce and Industry, Illinois State Chamber of Commerce, Phi Beta Kappa, Order of the Coif. Clubs: University (Chicago), Onwentsia, Huron Mountain (Michigan). Died October 21, 1971.

GALE A. CHRISTOPHER

Born September 17, 1920, Winona, Minnesota. B.A. 1942 Wabash College, LL.B. 1948 Harvard University. Associate Leibman, Williams, Bennett and Baird 1948, partner 1956–77. Served to lieutenant commander United States Navy Submarine Service 1942–45. President Park Forest District 163 school board. Chairman Park Forest Zoning Board of Appeals, Human Relations Commission, Committee for Nonpartisanship in Local Government. Member American Bar Association, Illinois State Bar Association, Chicago Bar Association, Phi Beta Kappa. Clubs: Union League, Law, Legal. Died November 23, 1978.

GEORGE E. CRAPPLE

Born April 23, 1944, Chicago, Illinois. B.A. 1966 University of Wisconsin, J.D. *magna cum laude* 1969 Harvard University (law review 1968–69). Associate 1969–75, partner 1975–83. Member American Bar Association, Illinois State Bar Association, Phi Beta Kappa.

WALTER J. CUMMINGS, JR.

Born September 29, 1916, Chicago, Illinois. A.B. 1937 Yale University, J.D. 1940 Harvard University. Associate 1946–50, partner 1953–66. Member staff United States Solicitor General 1940–46. Solicitor General of United States 1952–53. Judge United States Court of Appeals for Seventh Circuit 1966—. Director American Cancer Society. Trustee Loyola University (Chicago). Advisory board St. Vincent's Infant Hospital. Knight of Malta. Knight of Holy Sepulchre. Member American Bar Association, (chairman various committees) Illinois State Bar Association, Chicago Bar Association, Seventh Federal Circuit Bar Association, American Law Institute. Clubs: Law, Legal, Metropolitan (Washington), Racquet, Saddle and Cycle, Shoreacres, Yale (New York).

CHARLES S. CUTTING

Born March 1, 1854, Highgate Springs, Vermont. Attended Willamette University, Salem, Oregon early 1870s, honorary A.B. 1916, honorary LL.D. 1907 University of Michigan. Newspaper editor Cedar Rapids, Iowa, school principal Palatine, Illinois 1870s. Practice Chicago firms 1880–1900. Master in chancery Cook County Circuit Court 1890–1900. Cook County Probate Judge 1900–13. Partner 1913–36. Member State Board of Law

Examiners, Illinois State Constitutional Convention 1920. Director Chicago Title and Trust Company, Austin State Bank. President Chicago Bar Association, Cook County Board of Education. Chairman Lewis Institute. Clubs: Chicago, Chicago Literary Society (president), City, Hinsdale Gold (president), Law (president), New England Society (president), Union League (President), Wayfarers (president), University (Chicago). Died April 17, 1936.

J. EDWARD DAY

Born October 11, 1914, Jacksonville, Illinois. A.B. 1935 University of Chicago, LL.B. *cum laude* 1938 Harvard University. Associate 1939–41, 1945–49, partner 1963–72. Served to lieutenant United States Naval Reserve 1940–45. Associate general solicitor, other positions Prudential Insurance Company of America 1953–60. Legal and legislative assistant Governor Adlai E. Stevenson 1949–50. Illinois Commissioner of Insurance 1950–53. United States Postmaster General 1961–63. Director, member executive committee four companies Zurich Insurance Group. Member advisory board United States Customs Bureau 1966–68, Vice-president National Capital council Boy Scouts of America 1959. Trustee Meridian House Foundation 1974—, Project Hope 1974—. Fellow American Bar Foundation. Member American Bar Association, Federal Bar Association, District of Columbia Bar Association, Chicago Bar Association, Maryland Farm Bureau, Phi Kappa Psi. Clubs: International, Legal, National Lawyers, National Press, Touchdown (Washington), Union (Cleveland). Author *Bartholf Street, Descendants of Christopher Day of Bucks County Pennsylvania, My Appointed Round, Humor in Public Speaking.*

JOHN DERN

Born July 27, 1903, Salt Lake City, Utah. B.S. 1924 and LL.B. 1927 University of Pennsylvania. Practice New York 1927–29. Law clerk 1929–34, partner 1935–58. General Counsel and director American Natural Gas Company, American Natural Gas Service Company. President 1949–50 United Light and Railways Company, Continental Gas and Electric Corporation. Director Carson Pirie Scott & Company, Burgess Battery Company, Burgess Cellulose Company, American Natural Gas Company subsidiaries, Chicago Hearing Society. Member American Bar Association (securities law committee 1947–48), American Law Institute. Trustee University of Pennsylvania. Member Orchestral Association. Clubs: Chicago, Cliff Dwellers, Executives, Law, Kansas City, Indian Hill (Winnetka), Old Elm. Died May 21, 1958.

J. DWIGHT DICKERSON

Born January 30, 1883, Chicago, Illinois. B.A. 1904 and LL.B. 1907 University of Chicago. Law clerk 1908–20, partner 1920–1934. Trustee Morgan

Park Military Academy, Francis Shimer Junior College, Baptist Theological Union of University of Chicago. Clubs: Quadrangle, Union League. Died October 20, 1934.

ROBERT DILLER

Born November 17, 1907, Diller, Nebraska. A.B. 1929 and M.A. 1933 University of Nebraska, J.D. *cum laude* 1937 and J.S.D. 1940 University of Chicago. Member Phi Beta Kappa. Associate 1942–50, partner 1951–78. Author *Farm Ownership, Tenancy and Land Use in a Nebraska Community*, 1941, manuscript history of Sidley & Austin, predecessor firms 1966. Died March 18, 1980.

ROBERT L. FOOTE

Born December 4, 1914, Evanston, Illinois. B.A. 1938 Yale University, LL.B. 1941 Harvard University. Associate 1941–45, 1946–50, partner 1951–81. Lieutenant United States Naval Reserve 1942–45. Director A.C. Nielsen Company, Brooks-Scanlon Company, Northwest Engineering Company, Erdco Engineering Company, Grant Publishing Company, Chicago Council Community Nursing. Member zoning board Glencoe (former trustee). Secretary Chicago Educational TV Association. Trustee American Library Association, Hoover Foundation. Member American Bar Association, Illinois State Bar Association, Chicago Bar Association (grievance committee), American Judicature Association, Phi Beta Kappa. Clubs: Chicago, Economic, Law, Legal, Skokie Country, Wausaukee (Wisconsin).

RAY GARRETT

Born September 17, 1889, Murphysboro, Illinois. University of Illinois 1906–08, LL.B. 1916 Illinois Wesleyan University. Lieutenant to major United States Army 1917–19. Official stenographer Illinois Supreme Court 1910–17. Practiced Springfield 1916–17, Chicago 1919–42. Associate 1942–44, partner 1944. Fellow American Bar Foundation. Member American Law Institute, American Bar Association (past-chairman corporation, banking and business law committees). Co-author Illinois Business Corporation Act, Model Business and Non-Profit Corporation Acts. Past president Midland Subsidiary Corporation, Chicago, South Shore & South Bend Railway Company, Indiana Railroad. Counsel to board and director Denver & Rio Grande Western Railroad Company. Clubs: Law, Mid-Day. University (Chicago), Michigan Shores, Newcomen Society. Died November 23, 1969.

JOHN E. HALEY

Born December 6, 1937, Beacon, New York. A.B. 1960 Fordham University, J.D. 1962 University of Michigan. Practice New York, Washington

413

1962–73. Partner 1973–83. Member American Bar Association, New York State Bar Association, District of Columbia Bar Association, Bar Association of the City of New York, American Arbitration Association (arbitrators' panel 1974).

PAUL V. HARPER

Born January 5, 1889, New Haven, Connecticut. B.A. 1908 and LL.B. 1913 University of Chicago. Captain United States Army World War I. Law clerk 1913–15, private practice 1916–17, law clerk 1925–27, partner 1928–49. Trustee University of Chicago, Baptist Theological Union of University of Chicago. President Chicago Council on Foreign Relations. Clubs: Attic, City, Quadrangle, Union League. Died September 16, 1949.

CHARLES S. HOLT

Born October 21, 1855, Chicago, Illinois. Graduated Williams College 1874. Studied law Williams & Thompson 1876–77. Studied law Harvard University 1877–78. Law clerk Williams & Thompson 1878–82, partner 1882–1918. Trustee Chicago Orphan Asylum, Williams College. Director McCormick Theological Seminary. Active Young Men's Christian Association, lay Presbyterian affairs. Clubs: Chicago, Chicago Literary, Law, Onwentsia, South Shore, Union League, University (Chicago). Died December 13, 1918.

MARK E. MacDONALD

Born January 21, 1943, Cincinnati, Ohio. B.A. 1964 and J.D. 1967 Northwestern University. Associate 1967–73, partner 1973–83. Lecturer Illinois Institute of Continuing Legal Education 1970—, Practicing Law Institute 1977—. Member American Bar Association, Seventh Circuit Bar Association, Illinois State Bar Association, Chicago Bar Association, Phi Beta Kappa, Order of the Coif. Clubs: Skokie Country, University (Chicago).

CLARENCE B. MANNING

Born November 5, 1945, Richmond, Virginia. B.A. 1968 Washington & Lee University, J.D. 1971 University of Virginia (notes editor law review) Associate 1971–78, partner 1978–83. Member American Bar Association, Chicago Bar Association, Phi Beta Kappa.

C. BOUTON McDOUGAL

Born June 17, 1907, Chicago, Illinois. B.A. 1929 Princeton University, J.D. 1932 University of Chicago. Associate 1932–48, partner 1948–49. Served to lieutenant commander United States Naval Reserve 1942–45. Vice-president, secretary, general counsel, director R.R. Donnelley & Sons Company 1949–79. President Winnetka Board of Education. Chairman Legal Aid Committee United Charities of Chicago. Director and vice-president Chicago Crime Commission. Member American Bar Association, Illinois State Bar Association, Chicago Bar Association. Clubs: Commonwealth, Indian Hill, Law, Legal, Old Elm, Princeton, University (Chicago).

EDWARD D. McDOUGAL, JR.

Born April 13, 1896, Peoria, Illinois. Graduated Princeton University 1918, LL.B. 1923 University of Chicago, Honorary LL.B. 1964 Lake Forest College. Associate 1922–30, partner 1931–47. General counsel and secretary (later vice-president) International Miners & Chemical Corporation 1949–59. Captain United States Army infantry World War I, captain United States Naval Reserve World War II (Navy Price Adjustment Board, vice-chairman War Contracts Price Adjustment Board). Practice Chicago 1959–70. President United Charities of Chicago, Chicago Council on Foreign Relations, Welfare Council Metropolitan Chicago. Vice-chairman Illinois Public Aid Commission. Member executive committee Chicago Community Trust. Trustee Chicago Symphony Orchestra, Presbyterian-St. Luke's Hospital, Ravinia Festival, Citizens' board University of Chicago. Member American Judicature Society, Order of the Coif. Clubs: Chicago, Commonwealth, Legal (president), University (Chicago), Princeton (president), Old Elm, Onwentsia, Cosmos (Washington). Died October 20, 1982.

DONALD F. McPHERSON

Born August 26, 1884, Buffalo, New York. Graduated Princeton University 1906, attended Harvard Law School 1907–08, LL.B. 1909 Northwestern University. Law clerk 1909–13, partner 1913–44. Served to captain United States Army First World War. Head of Foreign Commerce Corporation, J.P. Morgan & Company affiliate, 1920–21. Director Committee of Fifteen, Illinois Legislative Voters League. President Chicago Council on Foreign Relations. Member Chicago Bar Association (assorted committees), English Speaking Union, Art Institute of Chicago, Field Museum of Natural History, Chicago Historical Society. Clubs: Adventurers, Casino, Caxton, Chicago, Commercial, Harvard, Old Elm Country, Pittsfield (Massachusetts), Princeton, Wayfarers. Member vestry Christ Church (Winnetka). Died March 17, 1944.

NATHAN G. MOORE

Born January 23, 1853, Cherry Tree, Pennsylvania. Graduated Lafayette College 1873. Honorary LL.D. 1922 Wooster College. Practice Peoria

1878–85, Chicago 1885–1919. Partner 1919–46. Trustee Lafayette College. Director Presbyterian Theological Seminary. Vice-president Chicago Presbyterian Church extension board. Vice-moderator General Assembly Presbyterian Church in the U.S.A. Member Committee of Fifteen. Author *The Theory of Evolution— an Inquiry* and *Man and His Manor*. Clubs: Union League, University (Chicago). Died August 16, 1946.

HOWARD NEITZERT

Born September 23, 1905, Syracuse, Missouri. A.B. 1927 and J.D. 1929 University of Michigan. Associate 1929–41, partner 1942–81. Chief counsel Eastern, Western, Southeastern Carriers Conference Committee. Chief counsel National Railway Labor Conference. Life member Art Institute of Chicago, Missouri Historical Society. Member American Bar Association, Illinois State Bar Association, Chicago Bar Association, Phi Beta Kappa, Order of the Coif. Numerous articles in legal publications.

RICHARD A. NOFFKE

Born June 11, 1947, Appleton, Wisconsin. B.A. 1969 Northwestern University, J.D. 1973 University of Illinois. Associate 1973–1980, partner 1980–83. Director Chicago District Tennis Association 1981—. Member American Bar Association, Illinois State Bar Association, Chicago Bar Association, Order of the Coif, Delta Upsilon. Clubs: River, Tennaqua (Deerfield).

JAMES F. OATES, JR.

Born November 11, 1899, Evanston, Illinois. Graduated Princeton University 1921, LL.B. 1924 Northwestern University. Associate 1924–30, partner 1931–48. Second Lieutenant United States Army infantry World War I, legal advisor Chicago Ordnance District, chief purchase policy Office Chief of Ordnance World War II. Board chairman, chief executive officer Peoples Gas Light & Coke Company 1948–57. Board chairman and chief executive officer Equitable Life Assurance Society of the United States 1957–77. Director New York Telephone Company, Colgate-Palmolive Company, First National Bank of Chicago, Chase Manhattan Bank, other corporations. Trustee Princeton University, Young Men's Christian Association national board, Northwestern University, other organizations. Member New York Chamber of Commerce, Bankers of America. Honorary degrees Illinois College, Lake Forest College, George Williams College, Hampden-Sydney College, Nebraska Wesleyan University, Pace College. Clubs: Chicago, Commercial, Lotos, River, Onwentsia, Old Elm, University (Chicago), Century (New York), Connetquot River (Long Island), University Cottage (Princeton), Rolling Rock (Pennsylvania). Died October 27, 1982.

GEORGE RAGLAND, JR.

Born January 1, 1904, Waco, Texas. Graduated 1925, LL.B. 1928 University of Kentucky, S.J.C. 1930 University of Michigan. Law clerk 1931–44, partner 1944–61. Member United States Supreme Court advisory committee on bankruptcy rules, University of Illinois Board Examiners in accountancy, Chicago Bar Association (committees on public service, Saturday programs, restatement of law, bankruptcies and reorganizations, civil procedure). Board chairman Young Men's Christian Association hotel. Member Harbor Light Committee for Rehabilitation of Man, Glencoe Union Church, Prudential Committee, Author *Discovery Before Trial* 1932, professional articles. Clubs: Law, Legal. Died January 30, 1961.

GEORGE A. RANNEY

Born May 30, 1912, Chicago, Illinois. A.B. 1934 and LL.B. 1939 Yale University. Associate 1939–50 (except for military service), partner 1951–62. First lieutenant United States Army 1942–45. Vice-president Inland Steel Company 1962–71, vice-chairman 1971–77. Director Welfare Council of Metropolitan Chicago, Community Fund of Chicago. Trustee University of Chicago.

HOWARD P. ROBINSON

Born May 2, 1900, Franklin, Indiana. A.B. 1923 and LL.B. 1925 Indiana University. Associate 1942–47, partner 1948–73. United States Army 1918. Prosecuting attorney Eighth Judicial Circuit, Indiana 1930. Legal department Phillips Petroleum Company 1934–42. Fellow American College of Trial Lawyers. Member American Bar Association, Illinois State Bar Association, Chicago Bar Association. Club: University (Chicago). Died January 19, 1973.

JOHN H. ROCKWELL

Born November 2, 1911, Oak Park, Illinois. A.B. 1933 Dartmouth College, LL.B. 1936 University of Michigan. Practice Chicago 1936–42. Partner 1946–74. Ensign to lieutenant United States Naval Reserve 1942–46. Practice New Hampshire 1974–79. Research assistant Research and Information Service National Center for State Courts, Williamsburg, Virginia 1980—. Member Community Chest Budget Committee Oak Park, Oak Park Plan Commission, Oak Park Community Relations Commission, Planning Board Grantham, New Hampshire Regional Plan Commission, S.C.O.R.E., Hanover, New Hampshire, Council of Eastern Virginia Center for Mental Health Studies, Williamsburg, Virginia, President's Council The College of William and Mary, treasurer, executive committee member Lord Chamberlain Society, Virginia Shakespeare Festival.

EDWARD W. SAUNDERS

Born August 10, 1917, St. Louis, Missouri. A.B. 1939 Princeton University, J.D. 1942 University of Chicago. United States Navy 1942–45. Associate 1942–51, partner 1952–78. Director Baird & Warner, Incorporated, and Carson International, Incorporated, Fine Arts Music Foundation of Chicago. Trustee, vice-president Lake Forest Academy. Past president Music Center of the North Shore. Past vice-president Chicago Crime Commission. Member Chicago Bar Association (committee on post-admission education), American Judicature Society. Clubs: Chicago, University (Chicago), Mid–America, Indian Hill (Winnetka). Died August 26, 1978.

ARTHUR R. SEDER, JR.

Born April 20, 1920, Oak Park, Illinois. University of Minnesota 1938–39, B.S.L. 1941 and LL.B. 1947 Northwestern University. Major United States Army Air Force 1942–56, Distinguished Flying Cross, Air Medal with four clusters. Law clerk to United States Supreme Court Chief Justice Fred Vinson 1948–50. Associate 1950–55, partner 1956–72. President American Natural Resources Company 1973–76, chairman and chief executive officer 1976—. Director National Bank of Detroit, Burroughs Corporation, Detroit Symphony, Detroit Grand Opera. Trustee St. John Hospital (Detroit), Northwestern University. Member American Bar Association, Illinois State Bar Association, Michigan Bar Association, Order of the Coif. Clubs: Country of Detroit, Detroit, Detroit Athletic, Links (New York).

WILLIAM P. SIDLEY

Born January 30, 1868, Chicago, Illinois. Graduated Williams College 1889, student Williams, Holt & Wheeler 1889–91, graduated Union College of Law 1891, M.A. 1892 Harvard University. Law clerk 1892–96, partner 1897–1958. Vice–president 1908–33, general counsel 1908–27 Western Electric Company. Director Harris Trust and Savings Bank, Chicago Association of Commerce and Industry. Trustee Williams College, Newberry Library, Chicago Sunday Evening Club, Chicago Young Men's Christian Association. First chairman YMCA Hotel. Governing member Art Institute of Chicago. President Chicago Bar Association 1930–31. Clubs: Chicago, Commercial, Law (vice-president 1934–35), Legal (president 1897–98), Indian Hill, Mid-Day, Union League (president 1911–12), University (Chicago, New York). Died April 23, 1958.

DOUGLAS F. SMITH

Born March 2, 1893, Council Bluffs, Iowa. LL.B. 1917 University of Michigan. United States Army 1917–18. Law department Union Pacific Rail road Company, Omaha 1920–35. Partner 1935–73. Member American Bar Association, Chicago Bar Association, Order of the Coif. Club: University (Chicago). Died May 15, 1973.

ADLAI E. STEVENSON

Born February 5, 1900, Los Angeles, California. Graduated Princeton University 1922, LL.B. 1926 Northwestern University. Associate 1926–33, 1934–35, partner 1936–41. Special counsel Agricultural Adjustment Administration 1933–34. Assistant general counsel Federal Alcohol Control Administration 1934. Special assistant Secretary of Navy 1941–44. Special governmental missions to Europe 1943–44. Special assistant Secretary of State 1945. Advisor United States delegation United Nations Preparatory Commission, London 1945. Member United States delegation United Nations general assemblies 1946–47. Democratic candidate for President 1952, 1956. Governor Illinois 1949–53. Practice Chicago, New York 1955, 1957–61. United States representative United Nations 1961–65. Trustee, director numerous corporations, philanthropic and educational organizations. Author *Call to Greatness* 1954, *What I Think* 1956, *The New America* 1957, *Friends and Enemies* 1958, *Putting First Things First* 1960, other books, numerous articles. Clubs: Attic, Chicago, Law, Legal, Onwentsia, Century (New York), Metropolitan (Washington). Honorary degrees Northwestern University, Oxford, Cambridge, other American and foreign universities and colleges. Died July 14, 1965.

D. ROBERT THOMAS

Born August 25, 1911, Fairview, Oklahoma. A.B. 1932 University of Michigan, LL.B. *magna cum laude* 1935 Harvard University. Associate 1937–47, partner 1948–80. Served to lieutenant commander United States Naval Reserve 1942–45. Law clerk to United States District Court Judge Augustus N. Hand 1935–36. Practice New York 1936–37. Member American Judicature Society, Chicago Bar Association, Illinois Supreme Court Character and Fitness Commissioners. Director Burgess Vibrocrafters, Incorporated, Glencoe Caucus, Winnetka Caucus, United Charities of Chicago. Trustee Onward Neighborhood House. Clubs: Law, Legal. Harvard Law Society of Illinois, Skokie Country, University (Chicago).

JOHN LEVERETT THOMPSON

Born February 2, 1835, Plymouth, New Hampshire. Attended Dartmouth College 1852–54 (honorary A.M. 1867), Williams College (honorary A.M. 1875). Graduated Harvard Law School 1858. Studied civil law Universities of Berlin, Munich, Paris 1858–60. Practice Chicago 1860–61. Served to brigadier–general United States Army 1861–65, battles of Second Bull Run,

Fredericksburg, Chancellorsville, Gettysburg. Founding partner Williams & Thompson 1866–88. Alderman Chicago 1876–78. Director Chicago Telephone Company, Central Union Telephone Company. President Citizens' Association of Chicago 1983–85. Clubs: Chicago Literary, Union League (president 1888). Died January 31, 1888.

J. DEAN VAIL, JR.

Born April 28, 1911, Goshen, Indiana. A.B. *cum laude* 1932 Harvard University, J.D. 1936 Northwestern University. Associate 1942–46, partner 1948–70. President Gardner-Vail, Incorporated. Past trustee Village of Kenilworth. Member American Bar Association, Illinois State Bar Association, Chicago Bar Association, Phi Beta Kappa, Order of the Coif. Died April 23, 1970.

M. OGDEN WEST

Born November 11, 1899, Chicago, Illinois. Graduated Princeton University, LL.B. 1925 Northwestern University. Law clerk 1928–34, partner 1935–36. Clubs: Onwentsia, Mill Creek Hunt. Died January 17, 1936.

ARTHUR D. WHEELER

Born March 2, 1861, Kenosha, Wisconsin. Graduated Lake Forest College 1881. Union College of Law 1884. Law student, clerk Williams & Thompson 1882–86, partner 1887–1912. President 1903–08, chairman 1908–12 Chicago Telephone Company. Director Western Electric Company. Board of managers Presbyterian Hospital. Active Young Men's Christian Association, especially its Institute and Training School. Trustee Fourth Presbyterian Church. Clubs: Chicago, Chicago Literary, Commercial, Marquette, Press, Onwentsia, Union League, University (Chicago). Died August 29, 1912.

NORMAN WILLIAMS

Born February 1, 1835, Montreal, Canada (family home Woodstock, Vermont). Graduated University of Vermont 1855. Studied law Woodstock, Albany Law School 1855–58. Practice Chicago 1858–60, partner King, Kales & Williams 1860–66. Founding partner Williams & Thompson 1866–99. President American District Telegraph Company. Vice President and member executive committee Chicago Telephone Company 1881–99. Director Pullman Palace Car Company, Western Electric Company, Chicago Public Library, John Crerar Library (first president). United States Commissioner to International Exposition of Electricity, Paris 1881. Chairman board of trustees Second Presbyterian Church. Clubs: Calumet, Chicago (seventh president 1884–95), Chicago Literary Society (charter member), University (Chicago, New York). Died June 19, 1899.

APPENDIX VII

Barbara A. Anderson
Mary M. Atkinson
Charles Baker
Doris I. Balogi
Mary T. Bernat
Elizabeth Black
Christina Bookman
Elizabeth Bowen
Margery A. Breneman
Sara Brody
John Carr
Michael Caulfield
Adrienne Cook
Susan B. Cory
Edward P. Cuccias
Anita S. Cross
Kathleen A. Devens
Kevin DiLallo
Janice L. Dymitro
Kirk Edgar
Linda Ebert
Ellen Farraye
Janet M. Fasano
Deborah J. Greenwald
Mitchell Grossman

Curt Haensel
Suzanne Hall
Thomas Hall
Suzanne Helfrich
Eloise R. Henkel
Catherine Hodgson
Sara Hoehn
Natalie A. Holden
Marianne Holkeboer
Gary W. Jacob
Roma M. Jacura
Michael E. Jones
Diana J. Kaspic
Lani Kaye
Patricia J. Kinsella
Marilyn C. Kutzen
Linda Langhorst
Barbara Lawrence
Patricia Libby
Jeri Loeb
Bernadine A. Majeski
Bettina Mak
Lilly C. Martin
Marc A. Mattlin
Sandra McNaughton

Nancy Montroy
Virginia F. Mullen
Margaret Murphy
Jennifer Nolte
Nellie M. Olk
Andrea Pickard
Dominick Pilli
Jane W. Pluss
Betty E. Robinson
Peggy M. Rose
Michael P. Ruben
Jenifer Rubloff
Barbara S. Schmidt
Annette R. Siegel
Iris K. Sims
Joseph Stewart
Susan J. Tucker
Kathleen Victory
Janis Wacksman
Linda Walck
Marilyn J. Willard
Don Willenburg
Harold Yuille

Staff
As of August 1, 1983

Wendy Abbott
John Adkisson
Adrian Alexander
Jane Alexander
Jean Aldridge
Icyfeane Allen
Simoko Allen
Mary L. Almandarz
Mary Anne H. Amsbary
Jackie Anderson
Linda M. Anderson
Lorraine M. Anderson
Mary L. Arden
Marian Armbruster
Laurie H. Augustine
David Aungst
Kim Austin
Barbara J. Axell
Ronald Bacon
Audrey Baran
Elena Barbieri
Karen A. Barnes
Karen A. Barnes
Rebecca E. Batzek
Dorothy F. Bay
Myrna Beard
Eleanor Bednash
Connie Bell
Patricia A. Bell
Anthony P. Bellion

Bruce Berman
Debbie Bezold
Bennett Bigman
Karen Bjurstrom
Brenda Blackburn
Thomas L. Blackburn, Jr.
JoAnn Blellach
Elyce L. Block
Robert W. Boatman
Joyce Bochenski
Joan M. Bonnefoi
Linda Bost
Sandy D. Boyer
Myrtle Braunsdorf
Barbara Breen
Arthur Broadwin
Sharon Brookins
LaJuan Brooks
Robena Broussard
David Brown
Ruth J. Brown
Sandra L. Brown
Valerie Z. Brown
Helen L. Budorick
Patricia Bunn
Margaret M. Burger
Kathleen A. Burghgraef
Carole J. Butler
Tonya Cannon
Isabelle Butler

Dawn M. Capone
Sarita Carden
Camille Cardosa
Judith L. Carlile
Lucille Casteel
Rita L. Cerceo
Beatrice M. Chodera
Chiquita D. Clark
Erin Clarke
Barbara Clemens
Ellen Coates
Elizabeth K. Cohen
Gloria Colbert
Grace Cole
Charmaine Coleman
Dorothy Coleman
Jerome W. Collins
Mary A. Conway
Dale A. Coonrod
Debbie Corr
Anthony J. Corrado
Kathleen M. Corrigan
Dimitra A. Costas
Constance Coutee
Marjorie H. Cowman
Jessie L. Cox
Susie Cruz
Kathy Crystal
Mary Cummings
Wanda J. Dandridge

Joyce L. Davis
Saundra E. Dawson
Julie F. DeBoer
Sheila de Buren
Nancy A. DeFranco
Joanne de la Chappelle
Ruth R. Demikis
Kevin Densmore
Barbara A. Deutsch
Janice H. Deutschman
Geraldine M. Devlin
Christina Dexter
Betty DiPasquale
Diane M. Discher
Nikki Dixon
Joan M. Dolle
Una L. Dolley
Elizabeth Donegan
Tara Donahue
Carol J. Doose
Kathleen Dougherty
Thomas S. Doyle
Rosemary DuBois
Raimundo I. Duncan
Gloria Dunlap
Shirley D. Dyrda
Sharon Early
Alanna F. Eckert
Carolyn S. Edwards
Fred G. Engram
Susan Epler
Cathleen S. Ernest
Fran Escobar
Benny Estorga
Frances M. Evans
Rhonda A. Evett
Robert Feldman
Carolyn M. Fischer
Michael P. Flanagan
Leslie Fleishman
Patricia Fontaine
Kathleen Forster
Susan Franzblau
Sheri F. Friedman
Joy M. Fujishima
Cheryl Gabriel
Vella Gaines

Ann L. Gardner
Judith Garrels
Debra Gaylor
Carole A. Gebbia
Catherine Gebhard
Barbara A. Geittman
Phyllis J. Gibson
Phillip T. Gills
Alison Gold
Sharon Gold
Michelle Goldberg
Melissia Gordon
Diane M. Gorgosz
Kathleen P. Gould
JoAnne B. Grant
Annabel Gray
Dolores V. Greabe
Jennifer Green
Moria E. Green
Karen Gregg
Lee E. Gregory
Eugenia M. Griffin
Linda M. Guerrero
Marian Gulbransen
Sandra Haas
Mary Hamilton
Helen I. Hammond
Irene M. Hand
Helen M. Hanson
David W. Harleston
Kim E. Harrison
Karen Hay
Denise Hayes
Susan Hempel
Julie M. Henderson
Agnes Herbert
Patricia J. Herrick
Monica Hewitt
Kathleen A. Hickman
Dorothy Hicks
Joan Hill
Margaret Hindmarsh
Kimberly Hines
Christine Hinson
Christine Hodge
Mary-Therese C.
    Hoenselaar

Debra D. Holloway
Cheryl Holmes
Philomena Holmes
Doris Holtz
Chad Howlin
Lucille D. Hudson
Denise M. Hughes
Marie Hughes
Katherine Hunter
Nadine Jackson
Ronald James
Dolores M. Janusz
Jeanne L. Jeziorski
Belinda D. Johnson
Bobbette Johnson
Lee M. Johnson
Pamela A. Johnson
Tacia A. Johnson
Dayle Jones
Delores Jones
Deloris Jones
Susan P. Jordan
Veronica A. Kacena
Dorothy L. Kaehler
Jeffrey Kandel
Doreen J. Kaplan
Ilene Kapustin
Diana J. Kaspic
Sharon Kass
Kathryn I. Kaufmann
Veronica M. Kazmierczak
Margaret K. Keane
Teresa Kelly
Edward J. Kernan
Steve Kilian
Shirley King
Lynne J. Klein
Barbara J. Kloos
Lolita Knight
Lynne A. Koch
Ruth Ann Kokelaar
Lydia Kolch
Margaret Korn
E. J. Kotalik
Nancy L. Kovacic
Eva Kozenko
Janet M. Kral

424

Janet K. Kralovec
Tina Kramer
Genevieve F. Kresen
Eugenia Kribales
Janelle A. Krische
Victoria A. Krob
Teresa M. Kuzel
Laverne A. Lane
Daniel B. Laubhan
Elisha Lawrence
Penny J. Lewin
Goldie Levy
Kathryn Lindley
Sondra A. Link
Judith Littenberg
Yvonne Logan
Walter Lojuk
Mary A. Long
Jeanne A. Loosli
Phyllis J. Lowther
Mary D. Luchitz
Doris A. Lukas
Joan M. Lyons
Victoria A. Maack
William B. Mackin
Patricia A. Mackowski
Marilyn Madison
James R. Mahoney
Carol D. Manion
Arlette B. Mann
Lydia Mantel
Debra Mapperson
Jayne Marinelli
Elizabeth V. Markley
P. J. Marksbury
Gabrielle Martin
Virginia K. Martin
Gloria P. Martinez
Homer J. Mattingly
Judy McAlpine
Sarah McBride
Pamela McCants
Faith McCarthy
Monika McCarthy
Marianne S. McDonald
Rita M. McGrath
Wilma E. McIntosh

Mildred L. McKay
Maureen McLaughlin
Sheryl N. McLeod
Rosemarie McNally
Abron McSwain
Mary T. McVaddy
Christine E. Meczynski
Nanci Medina
Janet Mezzack
Doris Minas
Charlene M. Misek
Clay J. Mitchell
Michael D. Mitchell
Jonathan Mobley
Susan M. Moch
Donna Monson
Nicolina Mooney
Virginia Moore
Christina Moorehead
Oscar Moseley
Miriam M. Moss
Rebecca Murphy
Angela Nash
Barbara A. Nash
Betty Nathanson
Lisa Neiman
Barbara Newell
Leone Newell
Doris J. Newton
Hang N. Ngo
Mai Thi Nguyen
Barbara J. Nichols
Stacie Nichols
Cindy Nishihara
Patricia North
Phyllis A. Nowak
Marcia D. Occomy
Joan M. Ogden
Linda J. O'Hearn
Marjorie S. Olson
Kenneth W. Orr
Joyce Ortis
Kathleen M. O'Shea
Janet C. Paley
Eugene Palmer
Audrey Parker
Cynthia L. Patterson

Estelle Paul
Joan R. Pellettiere
Doris M. Perozzi
Lynn M. Perrone
Patricia Petroccione
Virginia Petrosoff
Gene Philley
Lisa J. Polk
Nancy Potrzeba
Rebecca Poynton
Linda A. Preuss
Edith Prusak
Mary M. Pryor
Thomas L. Ptasinski
Helen M. Purtell
Mary Putt
Joan R. Radak
Linda A. Rasimas
Susan J. Ratz
Janette Reardon
Carol Reed
Peggy A. Regan
Karen Reid
Jan Reinglass
Lynette Rembert
Terri Rhoades
Carol A. Ridley
Alice A. Riley
Steve Ring
Diane Roberts
Ethel R. Rochlin
Mamie L. Rodgers
Jacqueline A. Rogalski
Laverne M. Rohr
M. Kathleen Rose
Caren V. Rosenbloom
Michael Rubin
Mary L. Rux
Catherine A. Sadowski
Laurie A. Sakali
Jeanette Salzman
Dorothy J. Sandlin
Susan M. Sanocki
Lou Ann Saunders
Beata M. Schaefer
Kathy J. Schultz
Laura A. Segvich

Vararie Sellers
Donna Settles
Arla R. Shaevitz
Maureen A. Shannon
Patrice A. Shaugnessy
Kathy S. Shelonzek
Annette Siegel
Bernice Silvers
Lisa A. Simnick
Edna C. Sims
Christine Shintani
Regina T. Sloane
Jerome Smith
Kathleen Smith
Nancy Sohl
Elynore M. Sohmer
Robyn Sowers
Sylvia R. Spungin
Deborah L. Staley
Sandy M. Staley
Evelyn Stanczyk
Carolyn S. Steffel
Barbara Steltzner
Cecelia L. Stenzel
Michael A. Sternberg
Paula E. Stetler
Barbara Stevenson
Trudy V. Stevenson
Thomas S. Stoehr
Margaret A. Stoffel
Barbara Stone
Joanne Stone
Barbara A. Storey
Judith L. Strand

Gwendolyn L. Suggs
Susan Sullivan
Verna Supel
Patricia Svientek
Danna L. Swanson
Elaine Syrek
Anne M. Szeszol
Louise Tamburrino
Teresa E. Tancredi
Jeryl Taryle
Kimala Taylor
Keith H. Temby
Judy L. Thaden
Celeste D. Thomas
Corrine Thomas
Delphine T. Thomas
Vanita Tilden
Dorothy M. Tillman
Milton Townsend
Carol Tropea
Bonnie S. Turbeville
Mary A. Tymec
Michelle A. Vanek
Ann Vaughn
Barbara J. Vaughn
Mary Vaughn
Patricia Vaughn
Diane P. Vlahos
Antoinette L. Vlasak
Jeannette A. Voelker
Mary A. Vonesh
Jennifer Waldorf
Michelle Walker
John Wallace II

Robyn Wallin
Cartherine P. Walsh
Vanessa Ware
Helen Weatherell
Field Weber
Karen A. Weidenski
Celeste K. Weilandt
Diane Whitson
Lela Whitted
Connie G. Wichman
Debbie Wilder
Nancy Williams
Ruth Williams
Sylvia J. Wills
Earl R. Wilson
Kim S. Wiorski
Susan I. Wiviott
J. Suzanne Wolfe
Susan Wolff
Esther Wondergem
Linda Wood
Jacquelyn Wyatt
Leatrice Young
Lee Young
Pamela J. Zadenetz
Sandra K. Zaffer
Andrea R. Zahour
Evelyn M. Zajacque
Julie Zerg
Carol E. Zgama
Barbara L. Ziermann
Johanna Zoric
Genevieve S. Zwadlo

Acknowledgments

IN ADDITION to persons cited in the Preface, there were many others without whose help of varied sorts the writing of this book would have been unduly arduous, if not impossible.

Current and former members of Sidley & Austin provided detailed answers to written interrogatories and in interviews, and many who read pertinent portions of the manuscript supplied vital information, incidents and anecdotes, and offered valuable suggestions for revisions and essential emendations. Present and past non-legal personnel whose services in diverse ways were salutary were Helen M. Hanson, Carol A. Jansto, William Jensen, Dorothy L. Kaehler, Doris M. Minas, Donna Monson, Sylvia Nelsen, Rebecca Poynton, Elynore M. Sohmer, Carolyn Steffel, and Harley E. Stephenson.

Other lawyers knowledgeable about the firm and insightful about its reputation and standing in the legal community offered thoughtful and candid estimates. Among their number were Morris B. Abram, George Bogert, Robert E. English, Julian Frazin, Samuel Freifeld, Alexander Hehmeyer, Fred Hickman, Stanley A. Kaplan, Arnold B. Kanter, Harold A. Katz, Norman H. Nachman, Don Reuben, and Louis L. Spear. As ever, Judge Abraham Lincoln Marovitz of the United States District Court was a knowing, wise, and perceptive mentor. I am grateful to Barbara Foote for her careful reading of the final draft of the manuscript.

Valuable assistance was afforded by officials and staff members of various client companies and organizations with replies to letters and with records, historical documents and publications. Most responsive were Edward Block of American Telephone and Telegraph Company; Louise Lutz of the Art Institute of Chicago; Richard E. Briggs and Daniel L. Lang of the Association of American Railroads; Jim Crowell of Brooks-Scanlon, Incorporated; J. A. Hagle of Burlington Northern; Barbara Foote and Barbara L. Massey of The Chicago Community Trust; James F. Golden of Commerce Clearing House; Virginia Butts of Field Enterprises, Incorporated; John O'Toole and Robert Koretz of Foote, Cone & Belding; Ray C. Babcock of Graybar Electric Company; H. E. Buker of The Hoover Company; Kenneth Hildreth, Roger B. Johnston, and Joseph P. O'Brien of Illinois Bell Telephone Company; George McCann of Illinois Central Gulf Railroad; Larry Christmas of Metropolitan Housing and Planning Council; Jerry Beaman of A. C. Nielsen Company; L. M. Phelps of Norfolk and Western Railway Company; Richard Johnson of Pullman, Incorporated; James V. O'Connor of G. D. Searle & Company; David Wilkinson of Urban Investment and Development Company; Robert Jerich and Young Hi Quick of Western Electric Company; and Joanne Shade of the Young Men's Christian Association.

Thomas Mikula, headmaster of Kimball Union Academy, Meriden, New Hampshire, supplied data about the boyhood years there of Norman Williams and John Leverett Thompson. Virginia Christy and Marjorie Vail of The Norman Williams Public Library in Woodstock, Vermont, furnished sources for letters of Norman Williams. Leonard Machlis, executive director of the National Commercial Finance Conference, passed on historical information about the commercial financing and factoring industry. Aid in research came from Virgil E. Tipton, Jr., editor of the *Illinois Bar Journal*, and Dorothy Davies, Chicago bookseller specializing in railroad history. Kathleen C. Yannias, staff attorney of the Chicago Lawyers' Committee for Civil Rights Under Law, provided annual reports of that worthy organization. Dr. James Conway of Children's Memorial Hospital lent items from his Chicagoana collection. Other assorted aid, useful comment and suggestions came from Abra Prentice Anderson, Saul Bellow, Dominic Farina, Morton H. Kaplan, Marilew Kogan, Professor Liston Lyndecker of Colorado State University, Jack McBride of the Chicago Bar Association, Robert L. Nelson, research attorney for the American Bar Foundation, John O'Dowd, Fritz Plous, railroad buff without compare, Gardner H. Stern, James B. Stewart, Jr., executive editor of *The American Lawyer*, and Lois Weisberg of the Chicago Council of Lawyers.

In keeping with their traditions, these officials and aides at libraries furnished essential volumes and ancillary materials: Stephen Czike and his able staff, particularly Donna Wojcik, of the Chicago Bar Association; Ray Murphy of Kirkland & Ellis; Evelyn Nelson and Shirley Haas of the Chicago Public Library; E. W. Quinn of the John Crerar Library; James B. Wells, Peggy Tuck Sinko, and Callista Ward of Newberry Library; Patricia Watters of Loyola University Law School Library; and the staffs of the Chicago Municipal Reference Library, the Chicago Historical Society, the Michigan City, Indiana, Library, and the New Buffalo, Michigan, Library. The reference departments of Chicago's major metropolitan newspapers graciously allowed me to scour their files for thousands of clippings, and for this boon I am grateful to Barbara Newcombe of the *Chicago Tribune* and Ernest Perez of the *Chicago Sun-Times* and their staffs.

Colleagues in journalism who were, as usual, cooperative in a variety of ways included Marshall Field, chairman of Field Enterprises, Incorporated, and Shirlee De Santi, Henry Herr Gill, Rick Kogan, Virginia Martino, Arthur Petacque, Kay Rutherford, James Warren, and Lois Wille of the *Chicago Sun-Times*, Jack Fuller and Kenan Heise of the *Chicago Tribune*, Paul Greenfeder and Herbert Mitgang of the *New York Times*, Morry Roth of *Variety*, and George Harmon, assistant professor at Northwestern University's Medill School of Journalism. I owe a special debt of gratitude to the late Emmett Dedmon, author, senior consultant to Hill and Knowlton, Incorporated, and former editorial executive in the newspaper division of Field Enterprises, Incorporated. For advice and encouragement in fallow periods, I express ardent thanks to fellow-authors Harry Homewood, Harry Mark Petrakis, Studs Terkel, and Lloyd Wendt.

Bibliography

In four years of research for *Traditions and Challenges* I delved into a vast amount of bibliographical materials.

These included manuscripts of Edwin C. Austin's memoir, later published as *Reminiscences For My Family*, Robert Diller's *Jurisconsulti Per Centum Annos*, Nathan G. Moore's *The Story of a Simple Life,* and Harry J. Dunbaugh's *History of Isham, Lincoln & Beale 1872–1961;* texts of addresses by Austin, particularly "The Bar That Was" (1966) to the Legal Club of Chicago and "Three Worlds of the Law Club" (1973) to the Law Club of Chicago; various publications of American Telephone and Telegraph Company, especially *Events in Telecommunication History;* Brooks-Scanlon, Incorporated; Burlington Northern; Chicago Committee for Civil Rights Under Law; The Chicago Community Trust; Illinois Bell Telephone Company; A. C. Nielsen Company; Norfolk and Western Railway Company; United Charities of Chicago, and the Chicago Young Men's Christian Association. Other diversified sources were the *Chicago Bar Record* from 1910 to date, the *American Bar Association Journal*, the *American Bar Foundation Research Journal*, notably its Winter, 1981, issue devoted entirely to Robert L. Nelson's authoritative study, "Practice and Privilege: Social Change and the Structure of Large Law Firms;" *The Practical Lawyer*, for its article by Austin in the April, 1957 issue, "Some Comments on Large Law Firms;" the *Chicago Legal News* from 1874 to its final issues in 1925; *The Sidley & Austin Briefer;* selective issues of the *Chicago Daily Law Bulletin, Chicago Lawyer, Illinois Bar Journal, Legal Times, National Law Journal*, and *The American Lawyer;* and such other magazines as the *Atlantic, Business Week, Chicago, Chicago History, Dun's*

Review, Fortune, Harper's, Inquiry, Journal of the Illinois Historical Society, The Nation, The New Republic, Newsweek, The Progressive, Time, U. S. News and World Report, and *Washington Monthly* and newspapers as, in Chicago, the *American, Daily News, Daily Times, Evening Journal, Evening Post, Herald and Examiner, Sun, Sun-Times, Tribune,* and *Today* and elsewhere the *New York Times, Plattsburgh, N. Y. Press-Republican, The Wall Street Journal,* and *Washington Post.*

Following is a representative list of books used:

Adams, Russell B., Jr. *King C. Gillette.* Boston and Toronto: Little, Brown and Company, 1978.

Andreas, A. T. *History of Chicago.* Chicago: A. T. Andreas, Three volumes, 1884–86.

Angle, Paul M. *Philip K. Wrigley: A Memoir of a Modest Man.* Chicago, New York, and San Francisco: Rand McNally & Company, 1952.

Anonymous. *A Memorial to John Leverett Thompson.* Chicago: Craig Press, 1890.

Anonymous. *Chicago As It Is.* Chicago: Religious and Philosophical Publishers Association, 1866.

Anonymous. *Eastland Disaster Relief 1915–1918.* Chicago: American Red Cross, 1918.

Anonymous. *Sullivan & Crowmell: A Century at Law 1879–1979.* New York: Privately published, 1979.

Anonymous. *The John Crerar Library, 1895–1944.* Chicago: Privately published, 1945.

Arnold, Isaac N. *Recollections of Early Chicago and the Illinois Bar.* Chicago: Fergus Printing Company, 1882.

Austin, Edwin C. *Reminiscences For My Family.* Winnetka: Privately published, 1980.

Ball, Donald, Jr. and Whitaker, Rogers E. M. *Decade of the Trains.* New York: New York Graphic Society, 1977.

Ball, George W. *The Past Has Another Pattern.* New York: W. W. Norton & Company, 1982.

Barmash, Isadore. *Great Business Disasters.* Chicago: Playboy Press, 1972.

Bishop, Glenn A. and Gilbert, Paul T. *Chicago's Accomplishments and Leaders.* Chicago: Bishop Publishing Company, 1932.

Brooks, John. *Telephone: The First Hundred Years.* New York, San Francisco, and London: Harper & Row Publishers, Incorporated, 1976.

Bryant, Keith, Jr. *History of the Atchison, Topeka and Santa Fe Railway.* New York: Macmillan Company, 1974.

Busch, Francis X. *In and Out of Court.* Chicago: M. A. Donohue & Company, 1942.

Caton, John Dean. *Early Bench and Bar of Illinois*. Chicago: Fergus Printing Company, 1893.

Collier, Peter and Horowitz, David. *The Rockefellers*. New York: Holt, Rinehart & Winston, 1976.

Cook, Frederick Francis. *Bygone Days in Chicago*. Chicago: A. C. McClurg & Company, 1910.

Corliss, Carlton J. *Main Line of America: The Story of the Illinois Central*. New York: Creative Age Press, 1950.

Crossley, Frederic B. *Courts and Lawyers of Chicago*. Chicago: American Historical Society, 1916.

Danilov, Victor J. *The Future of Science and Technology*. Chicago: Museum of Science and Industry, 1975.

Darrow, Clarence. *The Story of My Life*. New York and London: Charles Scribner's Sons, 1932.

Dedmon, Emmett. *A History of the Chicago Club*. Chicago: The Lakeside Press, 1960.

_____. *Fabulous Chicago*. New York: Random House, 1953 and 1982 (revised).

_____. *Great Enterprises: One Hundred Years of the YMCA of Metropolitan Chicago*. Chicago, New York, and San Francisco: Rand McNally & Company, 1957.

Doty, Duane. *The Town of Pullman*. Pullman: T. P. Struhsacker, 1983.

Douglas, George H. *Rail City: Chicago U.S.A.* LaJolla: Howell-North Books, 1981.

Dunbaugh, Harry J. *The YMCA Hotel of Chicago*. Chicago: Privately published, 1940.

Farr, Finis. *Chicago*. New Rochelle: Arlington House, 1973.

Fergus, Robert. *John Dean Caton*. Chicago: Fergus Printing Company, 1882.

Fiedler, George. *The Illinois Law Courts in Three Centuries 1673–1973*. Berwyn, Illinois: Physicians' Record Company, 1973.

Friedman, Lawrence. *A History of American Law*. New York: Simon & Schuster, 1973.

Furnas, J. C. *The Americans*. New York: G. P. Putnam's Sons, 1969.

Gilmore, Grant. *The Ages of American Law*. New Haven and London: Yale University Press, 1977.

Goodspeed, Thomas W. *John Crerar and the Will of John Crerar*. Chicago: Privately published, 1939.

Goff, John S. *Robert Todd Lincoln*. Norman: University of Oklahoma Press, 1969.

Grant, Bruce. *Fight for a City*. Chicago, New York, and San Francisco: Rand McNally & Company, 1955.

Harrison, Gilbert A. *A Timeless Affair: The Life of Anita McCormick Blaine*. Chicago and London: The University of Chicago Press, 1979.

Hazard Jr., Geoffrey C. *Ethics in the Practice of Law*. New Haven and London: Yale University Press, 1978.

Hibbard, Angus. *Hello Goodbye*. Chicago: A. C. McClurg & Company, 1941.

Howard, Robert P. *Illinois*. Grand Rapids, Michigan: Wm. P. Eerdmans, 1972.

Hurwitz, Howard L. *An Encyclopedic Dictionary of American History*. New York: Washington Square Press, Incorporated, 1968.

Johnson, Claudius O. *Carter Henry Harrison*. Chicago and London: The University of Chicago Press, 1928.

Josephson, Matthew. *The Robber Barons*. New York: Harcourt, Brace and Company, 1931.

Kanter, Arnold B. *The Secret Memoranda of Stanley J. Fairweather*. Chicago: The Swallow Press, 1981.

Kilian, Michael and Fletcher, Connie and Ciccone, F. Richard. *Who Runs Chicago?* New York: St. Martin's Press Incorporated, 1979.

King, Willard L. *Melville Weston Fuller*. New York: The Macmillan Company, 1950.

Kirkland, Joseph. *The Story of Chicago*. Chicago: Dibble Publishing Company, Two volumes, 1892–94. Kleinfeld, Sonny. *The Biggest Company on Earth*. New York: Holt, Rinehart and Winston, 1981.

Kogan, Herman. *A Continuing Marvel*. New York: Doubleday & Company, Incorporated, 1973.

_____. *The First Century: The Chicago Bar Association 1874–1974*. Chicago, New York, and San Francisco: Rand McNally & Company, 1974.

_____ and Cromie, Robert. *The Great Fire: Chicago 1871*. New York: G. P. Putnam's Sons, 1971.

_____ and Kogan, Rick. *Yesterday's Chicago*. Miami: E. A. Seamann Publishing, Incorporated, 1976.

_____ and Wendt, Lloyd. *Chicago: A Pictorial History*. New York: E. P. Dutton & Company, Incorporated, 1958.

Lamar, Howard R. *The Readers' Encyclopaedia of the American West*. New York: Thomas Y. Crowell, 1977.

Lens, Sidney. *The Labor Wars*. New York: Doubleday & Company, Incorporated, 1973.

Lewis, Lloyd and Smith, Henry Justin. *Chicago: The History of its Reputation*. New York: Harcourt, Brace and Company, Incorporated, 1929.

Lieberman, Jethro K. *Crisis at the Bar*. New York; W. W. Norton & Company, Incorporated, 1978.

_____. *Milestones!* New York: Oxford University Press, 1976.

Linder, General Usher F. *Reminiscences of the Early Bench and Bar of Illinois*. Chicago: The Chicago Legal News Company, 1879.

Lindsey, Almont. *The Pullman Strike*. Chicago and London: The University of Chicago Press, 1942.

Link, Arthur S. *American Epoch*. New York: Alfred A. Knopf, Incorporated, 1955.

Lord, John S. *A History of The Law Club of The City of Chicago*. Chicago: The Law Club of Chicago, 1968.

Lowe, David. *Lost Chicago*. Boston: Houghton Mifflin Company, 1975.

McDonald, Forrest. *Insull*. Chicago and London: The University of Chicago Press, 1962.

Marshall, James. *Santa Fe*. New York: Random House, 1945.

Martin, John Bartlow. *Adlai Stevenson of Illinois*. New York: Doubleday & Company, Incorporated, 1976.

_____. *Adlai Stevenson and the World*. New York: Doubleday & Company, Incorporated, 1977.

Massey, Robert V. Jr. *Dechert Price & Rhoads: A Law Firm Centennial*. Lancaster, Pennsylvania: Intelligencer Printing Company, 1975.

Masters, Edgar Lee. *The Tale of Chicago*. New York: G. P. Putnam's Sons, 1933.

Mayer, Martin P. *The Lawyers*. New York, Evanston, and London: Harper & Row Publishers, Incorporated, 1967.

Miller, Marvin. *The American Dream*. Covina, California: Classic Publications, 1976.

Minow, Newton N. and Mitchell, Lee M., and Martin, John Bartlow. *Presidential Television*. New York: Basic Books, Incorporated, 1973.

Morison, Samuel Eliot. *The Oxford History of the American People*. New York: Oxford University Press, 1965.

Morris, Richard B. *Encyclopedia of American History*. New York, Evanston, San Francisco, London: Harper & Row Publishers, Incorporated, 1976.

Mosley, Leonard. *Blood Relations*. New York: Atheneum Publishers, 1980.

Nash, Jay Robert. *Hustlers and Con Men*. New York: M. Evans & Company, Incorporated, 1976.

Nock, O. S. *Railways of the USA*. New York: Hastings House, 1979.

O'Toole, John. *The Trouble with Advertising*. New York and London: Chelsea House, 1981.

Palmer, John M. *The Bench and Bar of Illinois*. Chicago: Lewis Publishing Company, 1899.

Pierce, Bessie Louise. *A History of Chicago*. New York and London: Alfred A. Knopf, Incorporated, Three volumes, 1937–57.

_____ and Norris, J. L. *As Others See Chicago: Impressions of Visitors, 1673–1933*. Chicago and London: The University of Chicago Press, 1933.

Randall, Frank A. *History of the Development of Building Construction in Chicago*. Urbana: University of Illinois Press, 1949.

Rembar, Charles. *The Law of the Land*. New York: Simon & Schuster, 1980.

Roth, George J. *Slaying the Law School Dragon*. New York: Dodd, Mead & Company, 1980.

Saunders, Richard. *The Railroad Mergers and the Coming of Conrail*. Westport and London: Greenwood Press, 1978.

Schlesinger, Arthur, Jr. *The Politics of Upheaval*. Boston: Houghton Mifflin Company, 1960.

Schwartz, Bernard. *The Law in America*. New York: McGraw-Hill Book Company, 1974.

Siegel, Arthur. *Chicago's Famous Buildings*. Chicago and London: The University of Chicago Press, 1965.

Sinclair, Andrew. *Corsair: The Life of J. Pierpont Morgan*. Boston and Toronto: Little, Brown and Company, 1981.

Smith, Henry Justin. *Chicago's Great Century 1833–1933*. Chicago: Consolidated Publishers, Incorporated, 1933.

Stokes, J. Tyson. *Morgan, Lewis and Bockius: Memoir of a Law Firm*. Philadelphia: Privately published, 1973.

Strick, Anne. *Injustice for All*. New York: G. P. Putnam's Sons, 1977.

Swaine, Robert T. *The Cravath Firm and its Predecessors (1819–1948)*. New York: Ad Press, Limited, Two volumes, 1946–48.

Weil, Gordon L. *Sears, Roebuck, U.S.A.* New York: Stein and Day, 1977.

Wellman, Francis. *The Art of Cross-Examination*. New York: Garden City Publishing Company, Incorporated.

Wendt, Lloyd. *Chicago Tribune: The Rise of a Great Newspaper*. Chicago, New York, and San Francisco: Rand McNally & Company, 1952.

——————— and Kogan, Herman. *Bet A Million!* Indianapolis and New York: Bobbs-Merrill Company, Incorporated, 1948.

———————. *Big Bill of Chicago*. Indianapolis and New York. Bobbs-Merrill Company, Incorporated, 1953.

———————. *Give the Lady What She Wants!* Chicago, New York and San Francisco: Rand McNally & Company, 1952.

———————. *Lords of the Levee*. Indianapolis and New York: Bobbs-Merrill Company, Incorporated, 1943.

Williamson, Harold F. and Wild, Payson S. *Northwestern University: A History 1850–1975*. Evanston: Northwestern University, 1976.

White, John H., Jr. *The American Railroad Passenger Car*. Baltimore: Johns Hopkins University Press, 1978.

Wilkie, Franc B. *Sketches and Notices of the Chicago Bar*. Chicago: Western News Company, 1872.

Wille, Lois. *Forever Open, Clear and Free*. Chicago: Henry Regnery Company, 1972.

Winsor, Edward. *Edwards & Angell: A Firm History*. Providence, R. I.: Privately published, 1978.

Woodard, Harold R. *A Firm Foundation*. Indianapolis: Privately published, 1979.

Index

ABA House of Delegates, 288, 289, 290, 325

Acheson, Dean, 130

Ackerson, Nels J., 285

A. C. Nielsen Company, 154–57, 166, 321

Adler, Dankmar, 39

Aetna Life Insurance Company, 310

Aga Khan, 235

Agnes Allerton Wing, 233

Agricultural Adjustment Act, 126

Agricultural Adjustment Administration, 98

Albany Law School, 5

Albert, Robert A., 276–77, 286

Alberto Balsam, 302

Alberto-Culver Company, 302

Ali, Muhammad, 276

Alien Property Custodian, 160

Allen, Steve, 199

Allen, Worth, 80

Allerton, Robert, 232–34

AMAX, Incorporated, 319

Ambassador Oil Company, 166

Ambrose, Gerald A., 334

America First Committee, 148

American Arbitration Association, 247

American Bar Association, 74, 120, 201, 287–90, 292, 325, 326, 331

American Bar Association Journal, 288–89

American Bar Foundation, 325

American Bell, 298

American Bell Telephone Company, 31, 36, 63

American Bicycle Company, 72

American Breeders Service, 168

American Civil Liberties Union, 333, 335

American College of Probate Counsel, 325

American College of Trial Lawyers, 325

American District Telegraph Company, 29, 30, 31, 32

American Expeditionary Force, 87

American Historical Association, 41

American Insurance Company, 317

American Judicature Society, 325

American Law Institute, 188

"American College of Large Law Firm Consultants," 189

American Library Association, 41

American Linseed Company, 72

American Medical Association, 290–92

American Natural Gas Company, 132, 177, 191

American Natural Resources Company, 192, 310

American Photocopy Equipment Corporation, 255–56

American Piano Company, 72

American Red Cross, 83

American Revolution, 334n

American Society of International
Law, 325
American Speaking Telephone
Company, 29
American Stock Exchange, 264
American Sugar Company, 321
American Telephone and Telegraph Company, 68, 100, 110, 120, 263, 267, 286, 293
Kingsbury Commitment, 71
MCI suit, 294–95, 298
1974 government suit, 292–94, 296–98
origins, 63
problems in 1912, 70–71
American Tobacco Company, 243–44
American Union Telegraph Company, 27
American War Claimants Association, 91
Anchor Hocking Glass Corporation, 256
Anchorage Daily News, 322
Anchorage Times, 322
Andreas, A. T., 6
Andrews, Clement Walker, 44–45
Angelson, Mark, 285
Archer, James G., 190, 231–32, 312
Arizona Bar Association, 64
Arizona Biltmore Hotel, 137
Arizona Supreme Court, 64
Armour, George, 43
Armour, J. Ogden, 138, 141
Army Air Corps, 143n
Army Counter-Intelligence Corps, 240
Army Information and Education Division, 235
Army Signal Corps, 260
Art Institute of Chicago, 107–09, 233
Arthur Andersen & Company, 195, 265, 269
Arthur Frommer Company, 316
A. S. Hansen Company, 321
Association of American Law Schools, 326
Association of American Railroads, 209ff
Association of the Bar of the City of New York, 325
Association of Third Class Mail Users, 195
Association of Western Railways, 209ff, 216
Astor, John Jacob, 27

Atchison, Topeka and Santa Fe Railroad, 38–39
Atlantic and Pacific Telegraph Company, 27
Atlantic Monthly, 3
"Audimeter," 155
Auditorium Hotel Company, 39
Auditorium Theater, 39
Austin, Barbara, 178
(See also Barbara Foote)
Austin, Charles, 78
Austin, Edwin C., 95, 96, 97, 99, 103, 114, 117, 120, 127, 130, 140–41, 144–46, 148–49, 151, 154, 155–57, 158–59, 160, 161–62, 166, 169, 178, 182–83, 188–90, 192, 198, 199, 202, 231–32, 234–35, 272, 320, 325, 327, 329, 338, 344, 346
death, 337
early life and education, 78–79
early service with firm, 80–86
Edith Rockefeller McCormick estate, 136
fiftieth anniversary, 195–97
junior partnership, 92
managerial role with Burgess, 173–75
multiple domicile case, 140–41
1972 merger, 268, 269, 271
on Sidley, 114
The Practical Lawyer article, 188–90
Union League Club, 144
United Light and Power, 130
William H. Miner, 110–11
World War I service, 86, 91
Wrigley family, 170ff
Austin, Luella, 78
Austin, Marion Roberts, 86
Avalon ballroom, 138
Averill, Edward M., 105–06
Avery, William H., 99–100, 109, 152, 164, 167, 170, 178, 192, 193, 194, 199, 202, 203, 205, 228, 230, 233–34, 237, 267, 268, 272, 287, 309, 326, 327, 329, 331, 337
Edith Rockefeller McCormick estate, 137
fiftieth anniversary, 283

Globe Varnish case, 184
IBT case, 185–87
1972 merger, 268–71, 279
Pressed Steel Car case, 184–85
real estate, 228ff
Ayer, Benjamin, 49
Ayer, Edward E., 61
Ayers, Thomas, 323

Baird, Russell M., 240, 241, 245, 246,
    252, 254, 258, 259–60, 262–3,
    268, 272, 302
Baker, George S., 36–37
Baker, James E. S., 127, 153, 157, 159,
    160, 161, 162, 171, 320, 325, 327
    summer associates program, 177–78
Ball, George W., 148, 152, 153–54,
    168, 198
Ball, Stuart, 198, 200, 208–09, 210–12,
    226, 227, 272, 337
Ballard, Ernest S., 120–21
Baltimore and Ohio Railroad, 317, 318
Bangs, William D., 74, 87, 95, 96, 100,
    101, 102, 110, 114, 120, 121, 292
Bär & Karrer, 205
Bar Association of the District of Colum-
    bia, 315
Bar Association of the Seventh Federal Cir-
    cuit, 325
Barker, W. Gardner, 250
Barnes, Ernest G., 291
Barnes, Judge John P., 104, 123, 209
Bart, Peter, 258
Bartlett, Robert C., 246–47
Barton, Enos, 25–26, 32, 111
Bates, Henry M., 64, 85, 99
Battle, Frank V., Jr., 313
Baumann, Harry T., 203, 229–30
Baumgartner, William H., Jr., 289
Baxter, William, 296–97
Beach, James S., 106
Beale, William G., 47
Beam, Robert T., 221, 272, 310,
    313ff, 338
    Burlington Northern, 221–25, 313–14
Beatrice Foods, 300, 321
Beckwith, Corydon, 10
Bedenfield, Judge Newell, 311

Beer-Wine Revenue Act, 126
Belding, Don, 242ff, 249
Bell, Alexander Graham, 28–29, 32
Bell Mabel, 29
Bell System, 63, 67ff, 100ff, 292ff
Bell Telephone Company of Illinois, 30
Bell Telephone Laboratories, 68, 229–30,
    292, 297–98
Belmont Dairy Company, 208ff
Beloit College, 321, 327
Beloit Dairy Company, 208ff
Beman, Solon, 132
Bennett, Russell O., 241, 242, 243, 252,
    256, 258, 262–63, 269, 272, 284
Berlin, Arnold, 167
Berlin, Maurice H., 167
Berner, Frederic G., Jr., 310–11
Berning, Larry D., 309, 330
Bernstein, H. Bruce, 265, 283, 316, 318
Bethlehem Steel, 312
B.F. Ferguson Memorial Building, 109
B.F. Ferguson Monument Fund, 109
Bickner, Bruce P., 228
Bierbower, James J., 275
Bierbower & Rockefeller, 275
Bierig, Jack R., 290
Bilandic, Michael, 306
Biro, Laszlo, 253
Bishop, Henry, 33
Bissell, M. C., 11
Bixby, Frank L., 233, 236
Black, Justice Hugo L., 217
Black, John D., 117
Blackmun, Justice Harry, 291
Blackstone Hotel, 85, 114
Blaine, Anita, 133
Blair, William McCormick, Jr.,
    169, 261
Blatchford, Eliphalet W., 17, 40, 42, 66
Blodgett, Judge Henry W., 49
Bloom, Edgar S., 111
Bonn University, 73
Borden Company, 208, 320
Borden's Condensed Milk Company, 72
Borden Dairy Company, 177
Borden, Mary, 94
Boston & Maine Railroad, 218
Boutwell, George S., 26

Bowes, Harlowe E., 160, 164, 165, 167, 178, 182, 198, 205, 227, 235–36, 268–71, 272
Bowman Dairy Company, 208
Bowman, Roy, 312
Bracelen, Charles M., 120, 121
Bradley, William H., 40
Bragdon, Merritt C., 95, 145, 160, 178, 191–92
Breeder Reactor Project, 323
Breitenbach, Eugene, 247
Brennan, James J., 195
Brennan, Justice William J., Jr., 293
Brevoort Hotel, 95
Bright, Alice M., 160–61, 162, 170, 334–35, 337n
Brooklyn Dodgers, 163, 170
Brooks, Edward, 154
Brooks-Scanlon Company, 154, 166
Brooks-Scanlon Lumber Company, 166
Brotherhood of Locomotive Engineers, 213ff
Brotherhood of Locomotive Firemen and Enginemen, 212ff
Brotherhood of Railroad Trainmen, 213ff
Brothers, Judge William V., 108, 185
Brown, Charles L., 295, 297, 298
Brown, John Paulding, 115–17
Brownell, Emory, 325–26
Bruckhaus, Kreifels, Winkhaus, Lieber-knecht, 205
Buckingham Corporation, 300
Budd, John, 219ff
Bureau of Contracts and Adjustments, 87
Bureau of the Budget, 266
Burger, Chief Justice Warren E., 224–25
Burgess' Commercial Law, 119
Burgess, Geraldine, 202
Burgess, Kenneth F., 123, 145, 147–48, 178, 184–85, 186–87, 192, 194, 196, 202, 209, 212, 292, 327, 338n
  as recruiter, 175–77
  Burlington Northern, 219–22
  early education and practice, 119–21
  Illinois Bell Telephone Company general counsel, 120ff, 127ff, 292
  illness and death, 197–98

  joins firm 1931, 119, 121, 145
  managerial role with Austin, 173–75
  Northwestern University trustee, 124–26
  railroad matters, 121, 219ff
  war reparations case, 180–81
  YMCA Hotel, 141–42
Burgess, Mary Louise, 178, 194
Burgess Plaza, 198
Burleson, Albert S., 101
Burlington Northern, Incorporated, 225, 313–14, 317
Burnham Building, 92, 117
Burnham, Daniel H., 63, 87
Burrus, Clark, 306
Busch, Francis X., 240
Busch, Kathryn, 240
Butcher, Paul, 140
Butler, Charles F., 22

Cacciatore, Frank, 230–31
California Supreme Court, 282
Camp Keewatin, 79, 80
Camp Pokegama, 79, 86
Campbell, Christian L., 318
Campbell Soup Company, 140
Campbell, Judge William J., 208ff
Canteen Corporation, 265
Carl Byoir and Associates, 209ff
Carlstrom, Oscar, 102
Carnegie, Andrew, 14
Carnegie Steel Company, 60
Carney, Crowell and Leibman, 241ff
  clients, 242–50
  early practice, 241ff
Carney, Robert F., 237ff, 248–49, 250, 258
Carpenter, David W. 293–94
Carriers' Conference Committees, 212
Carroll, James, 334
Carry, Champ, 182
Carson Pirie Scott & Company, 98, 228–29, 315, 316
Carter, Jimmy, 311
Cartier, Henri, 136–37
Casino Club, 283
Cassels, Potter & Bentley, 99
Castle, Latham, 185
Catherine the Great, 136

Catholic Archdiocese of Chicago, 305, 334

Catholic Charities, 334–35

Caton, Arthur, 23

Caton, John Dean, 14–15, 22, 23, 63

Caverly, Judge John R., 103–04

Cedar Rapids Times, 74

Central & Southwest Power, 310

Central Music Hall, 43

Central Public Service Corporation, 112ff, 145

Central Public Utility Company, 113

Central Telephone Company, 36, 166

Central Transportation Company, 14

Central Union Telephone Company, 36, 63, 67, 70, 100

Century City, 284

Century Park East, 284

Champion International, Incorporated, 315

Chandler, Emerson T., 180, 185

Chanen, Franklin A., 252, 322

Charles Luckman Associates, 248

Charterways Transportation, 317

Chase National Bank, 128

Chazy Central Rural School, 109–10

Chesapeake & Ohio Railroad, 218, 318

Chessie System, 318

Chicago, Alton and St. Louis Railroad, 10, 12, 13, 14

Chicago and Galena Union Railroad, 6

Chicago and North Western Railway, 2, 11, 88, 123, 163, 176, 213, 216, 221ff, 226, 256, 304

Chicago Arc Light and Power Company, 37–38

Chicago As It Is: A Stranger's Guide to the City of Chicago, 2–3

Chicago Auditorium Association, 39

Chicago Bar Association, 47, 52, 76, 85, 92, 117, 149, 169, 177–78, 252, 299, 324, 331

Chicago Bar Foundation, 325

Chicago Bar Record, 163

Chicago Bible Society, 43

Chicago Board of Education, 333

Chicago Board of Trade, 2, 37

Chicago, Burlington and Quincy Railroad, 34, 119, 220ff

Chicago Chamber of Commerce, 2

Chicago City Council, 36, 50, 60, 108, 186, 304, 305

Chicago City Hall, 93, 94

Chicago City Railway Company, 61

Chicago Club, 33, 114, 268, 269

Chicago Common Council, 3, 34

Chicago Community Trust, The, 149, 329–30

Chicago Council of Lawyers, 325

Chicago Council on Foreign Relations, 97, 148, 163, 169

Chicago Cubs, 138, 139, 163, 171–72, 308

Chicago Daily News, 60, 143, 213, 263, 322

Chicago Edison Company, 37–38

Chicago Evening Post, 65

Chicago Fire of 1871, 18–19, 23, 24, 26, 41, 98, 201

Chicago Historical Society, 17, 24

Chicago Journal, 3, 50

Chicago Latin School, 73

Chicago Law Institute, 22

Chicago Legal News, 15

Chicago Literary Club, 43

Chicago Medical Society, 176

Chicago Memorial Hospital, 138

Chicago Mercantile Exchange Center, 303

Chicago, Milwaukee, St. Paul and Pacific Railroad, 123, 184, 318 (see also Milwaukee Road)

Chicago Musical Instrument Company, 167

Chicago Natural History Museum, 63

Chicago, North Shore & Milwaukee Railroad, 123

Chicago Opera Company, 132

Chicago Orphan Asylum, 89

Chicago Park District, 313

Chicago Plan, 87

Chicago Plan Commission, 89, 305

Chicago Public Library, 44, 45

Chicago Republican, 10

Chicago River & Indiana Railroad Company, 214–15

Chicago, Rock Island & Pacific Railroad, 123, 226, 317, 318

Chicago Sun, 158

Chicago Sunday Evening Club, 198

Chicago Sun-Times, 158n, 183, 257, 263, 321–22

Chicago Telephone Company, 32–33, 37ff, 47, 63, 67ff, 80, 82, 84, 87, 100, 101ff, 292

Chicago Telephonic Exchange, 30

Chicago Times, 3, 33

Chicago Title and Trust Company, 135, 149, 230

Chicago Tribune, 3, 15, 38, 50, 60, 61, 88, 111, 135, 194n, 201, 226n, 271

Chicago 21 Plan, 304ff

Chicago Union Station, 2, 12, 257

Chicago Union Station Company, 257

Chicago Union Stockyards, 2, 65, 215

Chicago Urban League, 335

Chicago World's Fair of 1992, 301, 323

Chipman, George, 64

Christian Science Monitor, 322

Christiana Securities Company, 206ff

"Christmas Spirits," 117, 252

Christopher, Gale A., 249, 254, 272, 303, 332, 337n

Chrysler Corporation, 282–84

Citizens Association, 49

Citizens for a Better Environment, 299

Civil Aeronautics Board, 266

Civil Service Commission, 332–33

Civil War, 1, 3, 7, 15, 25

Civilian Conservation Corps Reforestation Relief, 126

Clark, Justice Tom, 207

Clark, William, 201

Clayton Act, 207

Claytor, Robert, 218

Clean Air Act, 300

Cleary, Gottlieb, Friendly & Ball (also Cleary, Gottlieb, Friendly & Cox), 168

Clemens, Richard G., 276, 312, 313

Cleveland, Grover, 39

Cleveland Telephone Company, 70

Clinchfield Line, 318

Coca-Cola of Los Angeles, 300

"Cocoa Hardwater Castile," 105–07

Cohan, George M., 202

Cohen, Benjamin, 129

Cohen, Judge Nathan M., 335

Cole, Kendall M., 249, 254

Cole, Thomas A., 300

Colgate-Palmolive-Peet Company, 239

College of St. Theresa, 321

Collier's, 65

Columbia Broadcasting System, 263

Columbia Gas System, Incorporated, 310, 311

Columbia University College of Pharmacy, 105

Columbia University Law School, 64, 146, 266, 276, 318, 328

Columbian Museum of Chicago (see also Field Columbian Museum), 61

Columbus, Christopher, 323

Colvin, Mayor Harvey Doolittle, 34

Commerce Clearing House, 245–47, 321

Commercial Club of Chicago, 39, 169, 198

Commercial Discount Corporation, 264, 265

Commission on Chicago Historical and Architectural Landmarks, 304

Committee to Defend America By Aiding the Allies, 148

Commonwealth and Southern Corporation, 128–29

Commonwealth Edison Company, 127, 166, 263, 309–10, 323

Computax Corporation, 247

Concoff, Gary O., 284

Cone, Fairfax M., 242–44, 245, 248–49, 258

Conley's Patch, 2

Connell, Gerald A., 296

Consolidated Electric and Gas Company, 113

Consolidated Rail Corporation ("Conrail"), 218n

Consumer Price Index, 293
Continental Illinois National Bank and Trust Company, 140, 313
Cook County Bar Association, 325
Cook County Board of Education, 149
Cook County Board of Review, 77
Cook County Circuit Court, 5, 15, 43, 49, 68, 77, 92, 107, 136, 142, 185, 186, 231, 334
Cook County Court of Common Pleas, 17
Cook County Courthouse, 2, 5
Cook County Probate Court, 74–75, 76, 97, 149, 236
Cook County Recorder's Court, 5
Cook County Superior Court, 5, 18, 92, 103, 133
Cook, Daniel Pope, 330
Cook Scholarships, 330
Corbin, Abel, 26
Corcoran, Thomas, 129
Cornell University Law School, 311
Corporate Fiduciaries Association, 309
Cottrell, Joseph, 265, 316–17
Coudert Brothers, 285
Coughlin, Alderman John "Bathhouse John," 60–61
Council on Legal Education in Professional Responsibility, 326
Cousins, Windsor, 180
Covelli, Judge Daniel A., 334
Covington & Burling, 176, 206n, 224
Cowan, Gary L., 192
Cox, Hugh B., 206, 224
Crane Company, 63
Crapple, George E., 315
Crawford, David A., 182
Crerar, Adams and Company, 13–14, 42
Crerar, Agnes, 42
Crerar, Donald, 43
Crerar, John, 13–14, 24, 32, 33, 42ff, 63
Crerar, John (father), 43
Crerar Library, John, 42–45, 48, 65, 66
Crocker National Bank, 282
Crosby, Uranus H., 2
Crowell and Leibman, 250–55
    clients, 250–55
Crowell, G. Kenneth, 239ff, 248, 249

CSX Corporation, 318
Cummings, Homer J., 130
Cummings, Walter J., 174–75, 201, 209, 215–16, 230
Curran, Mark C., 321
Curtis Publishing Company, 263
Cutting, Austin & Castle, 78
Cutting, Charles S., 76, 80, 85, 86, 92, 95, 96, 97, 103, 121, 191, 324, 329
    and Edith Rockefeller McCormick, 133–37
    as editor, 74
    joins firm, 76
    last years and death, 149–50
    Probate Court judge, 74–75
    Sears case, 77–78
Cutting, Moore & Sidley, 91–151
    "boom times" of 1920s, 93–94
    clients in 1920s, 100–13
    clients in 1930s, 120–44
    Great Depression, 122ff, 144ff
    internal developments, 146–47
    internal "hi-jinks," 115–18
    move to Roanoke Building, 92
    New Deal legislation, 126ff
    Northwestern University, 124–26
    progressive promotion policy, 92, 95
    Public Utility Holding Company Act, 129ff

Daily Pantagraph, 96, 97
Daily Princetonian, 96
Daley, Richard J., 306
Daly, Augustin, 24
Darby, Edwin, 257
Darrow, Clarence, 83–84, 133, 240
Dartmouth College, 6, 125, 143, 328
Dato, Edward A., 134ff
Davis, O. C., 311
Dawes, Charles G., 87, 158
Day, Doris, 282
Day, J. Edward, 151, 169, 178, 184, 194–95, 199n, 275
Dean, Arthur H., 98
Dean Milk Company, 208n
Dearborn Park, 305
Dearborn Park Corporation, 304ff

Dearborn Street Station, 38

Debevoise, Plimpton, Lyons & Gates, 283

DeButts, John, 294–95

Dechert Price & Rhoads, 204

Degnan, Suzanne, 336

DEKALB AgResearch, Incorporated, 227–28, 284

DeKalb County Soil Improvement Association, 227

Delaware & Hudson Railroad, 218

Delaware Realty and Investment Corporation, 206ff

Delta Queen, 312

Denver & Rio Grande Western Railroad, 123

DePaul University Law School, 240, 313, 327, 334

Dern, George H., 98

Dern, John, 98, 116, 151, 166, 176–78, 191–92, 228

  general counsel, American Natural Gas Company, 177

  general counsel, United Light and Railways, 131ff

  illness and death, 190–91

  United Light and Power, 130ff

Detroit, Toledo and Ironton Railroad, 317

Dewey, F. H., 6

Dickerson, J. Dwight, 73, 79, 91, 92, 93, 96, 228

Dighton, Judge Henry Timmons, 233

Diller, Robert, 160, 193, 200

Dillon, Read, 130

Discovery Before Trial, 123

Disraeli, Benjamin, 41n

District of Columbia Superior Court, 275

Dobbs Houses, Incorporated, 315–16

Donnelley and Sons Company, R. R., 166, 170, 278, 299–300

Donovan, Thomas, 306

Dooley, James A., 231, 234–35

Dorrance, Dr. John Thompson, 142

Douglas, Stephen A., 4

Douglas, Justice William O., 224–25

Dowd, Peter A., 31

Downing, Robert A., 307

Dr. Scholl Company, 301–02

Drake Hotel, 135

Drake, John B., 29

Drew, Daniel, 26

Duggan, John E., 48

Duke University Law School, 318

Duluth, South Shore & Atlantic Railroad, 123, 218

Dunne, Edward F., 69, 76

DuPage County Circuit Court, 307, 316

Dupee, Eugene, 161, 193

duPont de Nemours & Company, E. I., 206–08

Dutilh, vander Hoeven & Slager, 205

Duval Corporation, 319

Dyke, James W., Jr., 313

Eastern Railroads Presidents' Conference, 209ff

Eastland, 81–84, 103–05

Eastman Kodak Company, 255

Eastman, Judge Sidney C., 61

Ebbets Field, 170

Eckhart, Percy B., 108–09

Economic Club, 267–68

Economic Development Administration, 312

Economic Recovery Tax Act, 307

Edens Plaza, 229

Edison, Thomas, 29, 37, 38

Edith Rockefeller McCormick Trust, 133

Edithton, 134

Edna L. Dunning Medical Student Loan Program, 330

Edsel, 258

Edwards, Judge Claire E., 77–78

Edwards, Willard, 194n

Edwin C. Austin Scholarships, 327n

E. F. Hutton, 306

Ehrman, Joseph S., 315–16

Eimer, Nathan P., 319

Eisenhower, Dwight, 169, 213, 286

Elder, Robert F., 155

Eldred, Horace, 30

Ely, Edward, 11

Emergency Banking Relief Act, 126

Emmons, Lawrence E., 151

Encyclopaedia Britannica Films, 261

Encyclopaedia Britannica, Incorporated, 262, 263

English, Judge Robert E., 230–31
Enlund, E. Stanley, 306
Ennis, Alfred, 14
Enovid, 320
Environmental Protection Agency, 299ff, 302
Epstein, Edna Selan, 335
Equitable Life Assurance Society of the United States, 24, 170, 310
Equitable Trust Company, 24
Equity Funding Corporation of America, 316
Equity Funding Life Insurance Company, 316
Erickson, Donald, 269
Erickson, Joseph, 83ff
Erie Canal, 11
Erie Lackawanna Railroad, 218
Erie Railroad, 26, 27
Ettelson, Samuel, 102
Evans, Judge Evan A., 121, 149
Evans, John, 125
Evanston First National Bank, 333–34
Evanston Hospital, 191
Evanston Latin-American Association, 335
Evanston Review, 124
Eversharp, Incorporated, 254
Ewing, W. G., 49

Facts on File, Incorporated, 247
Family Lines, 318
Fanning, Katherine, 321–22
Fanning, Lawrence S., 322
Faricy, William T., 210
Farrell, Frank, 224
Farwell Hall, 24
Farwell, John V., 24
Fearons, George H., 37
Federal Alcohol Control Administration, 147
Federal Bankruptcy Act, 123
Federal Bar Association, 325
Federal Communications Commission, 261–62, 292, 293, 294, 295
Federal Defendant Panel Program, 335
Federal departments:
    agriculture, 221, 244
    energy, 211
    housing and urban development, 332
    justice, 174, 182, 221ff, 226, 287ff, 292ff, 318
    transportation, 266
Federal Emergency Relief Act, 126
Federal Energy Regulatory Commission, 310–11
Federal Housing Administration, 312
Federal Power Commission, 129
Federal Securities Act, 126ff
Federal Service Entrance Examination, 332–33
Federal Steel Company, 60
Federal Trade Commission, 105–06, 127, 227, 245, 266, 290–91
Federal Trade Commission Act, 106, 259, 291
Feiser, Louis, 180–81
Ferencz, Robert A., 315, 328
Ferguson, B. F., 108–09
Field, Barbara, 322
Field, Benjamin C., 12, 14
Field Columbian Museum, 62–63
Field, Delia, 72
Field Enterprises, Incorporated, 158n, 321, 322
Field, Frederick, 322
Field, Katherine, 322
Field, Marshall, 2, 14, 24, 33, 42, 44, 54, 62–63, 72, 321
Field, Marshall III, 158
Field, Marshall IV, 263, 322
Field, Marshall V, 322
Field Museum of Natural History, 62–63
Firman, Leroy B., 29
First Chicago Corporation, 312
First Federal Savings and Loan Association, 306
First Illinois Light Artillery, 7
First National Bank of Chicago, The, 91, 125, 157, 203, 265, 282, 303, 311, 313, 315
First New Hampshire Cavalry, 7
First Rhode Island Cavalry, 7
First Trust and Savings Bank, 69
Fisher, Judge Harry T., 186–87
Fisk, James, 26
Fitzpatrick, Peter, 235

Flair pens, 255
Flanagin, Neil, 252
Flint, Margaret A., 201
Florida Supreme Court, 140
Flynn, Richard J., 195, 210–12, 224, 272, 310–11, 318
Foote, Barbara, 329
    (See also Barbara Austin)
Foote, Cone & Belding, 242–44, 248–49, 255, 258
Foote, Emerson, 242ff, 248, 249n
Foote, Robert L., 156, 166–67, 178, 203, 268–71, 272, 279–80
Ford Foundation, 326, 331
Ford, Henry, 317
Ford Motor Company, 258
Foreign Commerce Corporation, 95
Foss, Martin H., 158
Franks, Bobby, 103
Frawley, Patrick J., Jr., 253–54
Fred Harvey restaurant chain, 168
Freeport Minerals Company, 319
Frei, Robert R., 183, 272, 276, 315–16, 328
French Purchasing Commission, 168
Fried, Frank, Harris, Shriver & Jacobson, 282
Friedlund, J. Arthur, 265
Fuerst Bismarck, 56
Fuller, Melville W., 49
Fuller, Samuel W., 6
Fullerton Hall, 108
Fuson, Douglas F., 301

Gaj, Gustav, 57ff
Galena and Chicago Union Railroad, 2, 17
Garcin, Thomas E., 281, 283
Garlinghouse, F. Mark, 295
Garrett, Ray, 160, 164, 166, 167, 178, 192, 199, 219, 314
    Burlington Northern, 221ff
Garrett, Ray, Jr., 179n
Garrett, Sylvester, 216–17
Gary, Joseph E., 5
Gateway Center, 257
Gemmill, Kenneth, 205
General Electric Company, 38, 70, 293, 323

General Electric Railway Company, 60–61
General Motors Corporation, 184–85, 206ff
Geo Space Corporation, 264
George Washington Law School, 310
George Williams College, 321, 327
Gibson Company, 167
Gide Loyrette Nouel, 205
Gifford, George, 31
Gilbert, Carl J., 245, 254
Gillette Company, The, 245, 253–54, 302
Gillette Safety Razor Company, 244ff
Gilliland Electric Company, 32
Globe Varnish Company, 184
Goldberg, Justice Arthur J., 214
Golden, William C., 328, 329, 330
Goldman, Sachs & Company, 309
Goldstein, Samuelson, Incorporated, 282
Goodman, Benny, 138
Goodrich, Judge Herbert, 189
Gould, Jay, 26–28, 31, 37
Graceland Cemetery, 18
Grady, Judge John F., 295
Gralen, Donald J., 203, 229
    real estate practice, 229ff, 302ff, 315
Grand Central Station, 257
Grand Opera House, 38
Grand Pacific Hotel, 42, 43
Grant Park, 42, 63, 108
Grant, Ulysses S., 26
Gray and Barton, 26, 111
Gray, Elisha, 25–26, 29, 111
Graybar Electric Company, 111
Great Northern Railroad Company, 219ff
Great Plains Coal Gasification Project, 310–11, 315
Great Plains Gasification Associates, 310
Green, Dwight, 169
Green, Hetty, 24
Green, Leon, 125
Greene, Judge Harold H., 296, 297–98
Greenwood Cemetery, 43
Gregg, John Wyatt, 233–34
Gregg, Jon M., 311, 315
Gregg, Thomas J., 221

Griswold, Erwin N., 290
Gunsaulus Hall, 108
Guthman, Jack, 304–06, 323

Hairtrigger Block, 3
Halic, Nick, 55ff
Hall, Henry C., 64
Hall Printing Company, W. F., 265
Hallicrafter Company, 167
Halsey, Stuart & Company, 127, 166
Hand, Judge Augustus N., 122
Hanley, Robert, 295
Hapgood, Norman, 64–65
Haralovic, Dane, 56ff
Haralovic, George, 56ff
Harding, Carroll R., 182
Hardscrabble Row, 2
Harlan, John (son), 64
Harlan, Justice John M. (father), 49,
    51, 64
Harlan, John M. (grandson), 206
Harper, Paul V., 73–74, 79, 87, 95, 115,
    123, 138–40, 145, 160, 162–63,
    166, 170, 176
Harper, William Rainey, 72, 73
Harper's Weekly, 65
Harrington, Judge Cornelius, 232
Harris, Albert W., 232, 329
Harris & Company, N. W., 232
Harris, Hayden, 231–32
Harris, Irving, 244–45
Harris, Norman Dwight, 232
Harris, Norman Wait, 232
Harris, R. Neison, 244–45, 254–55
Harris, Stanley G., 231–32
Harris Trust and Savings Bank, 232, 329
Harrison, Benjamin, 39
Harvard Business School, 323
Harvard Law Review, 87
Harvard Law School, 6, 10, 23, 55, 64,
    86, 87, 95, 96, 99, 110, 122, 146,
    151, 156, 176, 178, 183, 195, 231,
    241, 245, 249, 252, 260, 265, 271,
    285, 287, 289, 290, 298, 301, 310,
    311, 313, 315, 318, 323, 328, 332
Harvard School of Medicine, 105
Harvard University, 44, 180–81, 276
Harvey, Daggett, 168, 198, 327

Hastings, Laurens G., 240, 256
Havel, Richard W., 281
Havighurst, H. C., 176
Hawthorne Club, 81, 83, 84, 103
Hawthorne Works, 67, 81
Haynie, Howard, 307
Heads & Threads, 256
Hearst's International Magazine, 65
"Heart's Delight," 109
Heineckel, Arthur Herbert, 157
Heineman, Ben W., 216–17, 226,
    256, 301
Heirens, William, 335–36
Henry Crown & Company, 303
Hensley, Stuart K., 254
Herrick, John J., 76
Hershey, Loren, 296
Hibbard, Angus S., 69, 70
Hibbard, Spencer, Bartlett &
    Company, 63
Hill, George Washington, 243
Hill, James J., 220
Hill, Thomas W., 284–85
Himmelhoch, Ralph, 153
Hirsch, Samuel E., 136
Hoffman, Judge Julius, 183
Holabird, William, 53, 92
Holloway, Edwin G., 105–07
Holly, Judge William H., 144
Holmes, Justice Oliver Wendell, 220, 286
Holt, Charles S., 23, 24, 29, 37, 46, 48,
    51, 60, 63, 64, 65, 73, 86–87, 88,
    114, 141, 158, 326, 338n
  as firm head, 67ff, 75ff
  death, 89
Holt, Mrs. Charles, 73
Holt, Cutting & Sidley, 76–90
  clients, 77–78, 84
  fiftieth anniversary, 84–86
  World War I problems, 87
Holt, Ellen, 158
Holt, Wheeler & Sidley, 67
  and Bell System, 67ff
  Chicago Telephone Company, 67ff
  clients during early 1900s, 67–76
  internal changes, 73ff
Home Insurance Building, 53
Honolulu Academy of Art, 233

Hoover Company, 154
Hoover, Earl, 154
Hoover, Herbert, 122
Hope, Bob, 247
Horner, Judge Henry, 97
Hotchkiss, Willis L., 209
Hotel Pierre, 199
House Ways and Means Committee, 306
Howard University Law School, 313
Howell, Kenneth, 333
Hoyne, Maclay, 69
Hubbard, Gardiner G., 29–30
Hubbard, Mabel, 29
Hunt, George, 49
Hunter, Robert S., 291
Hutchins, Robert Maynard, 124–26
Hyatt Regency Hotel, 303
Hyde, Charles Cheney, 64
Hyde Park, 2
Hyman-Michaels Company, 104
Hynes, Terence M., 318

Ickes, Harold L., 97
Ideal Plastic Industries, Incorporated, 319
Illinois Adoption Act, 233
Illinois and Mississippi Telegraph Company, 15
Illinois Appellate Court, 79, 108, 109, 136, 230, 231, 232, 293, 299, 334, 335
Illinois Bar Journal, 250–52
Illinois Bell Telephone Company, 101ff, 120, 121ff, 127, 145, 148, 166, 176, 185–87, 217, 228, 231, 292, 293
Illinois Business Corporation Act, 160
Illinois Central Railroad, 34–35, 48–50, 326
Illinois Commerce Commission, 102, 121, 257
Illinois Courts Commission, 324
Illinois Department of Revenue, 184–85
Illinois Environmental Protection Agency, 299
Illinois General Assembly, 27, 77, 142, 233
Illinois Home for Crippled Children, 138

Illinois House of Representatives, 37
Illinois Institute of Technology, 45
Illinois Insurance Code, 316
Illinois Law Review, 78, 260
Illinois Legislative Voters League, 163
Illinois Life Insurance Company, 92
Illinois Manufacturers' Association, 68
Illinois State Bar Association, 150, 324–25
Illinois State Board of Law Examiners, 325
Illinois State Historical Library, 201
Illinois Steel Company, 55ff, 60, 63
Illinois Supreme Court, 6, 7, 15, 18, 40, 44, 69, 77, 89, 108, 142–43, 161, 185, 186–87, 231, 294, 299, 325, 327, 334, 336
Illinois Supreme Court Reports, 22, 90
Index to Periodical Literature, 41
Indiana Business Corporation Act, 160
Indiana Public Service, 310
Indiana University Law School, 309
Institute for Paralegal Training, 277
Insull, Samuel, 38, 104
Insurance Exchange Building, 230
Internal Revenue Code, 306
Internal Revenue Service, 183, 243, 276, 328
International Bar Association, 325
International Business Machines Corporation, 155–56, 235, 278, 297
International Cellucotton Products Company, 237ff, 250
International Harvester Company, 132, 134
International Law Chiefly As Interpreted by the United States, 64
International Minerals and Chemical Corporation, 169, 311–12, 315, 319
International Trade Administration, 312
Interstate Commerce Commission, 60, 71, 119, 123, 180, 181, 210, 217, 218, 219, 220, 222, 223, 225, 226n, 266, 317, 318
Interstate National Insurance Corporation, 316
Iowa-Illinois Gas and Electric Company, 166, 310
Isaacs, Theodore J., 325
Isham, Edward S., 21, 33, 40

Isham, Lincoln & Beale, 47, 201
Jackson, Huntington W., 43
Jacobs, J. L., 142
James, Harry, 138
James S. Kirk & Company, 87–89,
    105–07
Jeffreys, Ivor, 80
Jenner & Block, 295
Jenney, William Le Baron, 53
Jensen, William, 151–52, 153, 199,
    271, 278
Jewett, John N., 49
Jinkenson, Earl A., 208
John Crerar Library, 42–47, 48, 65, 66
John Marshall Law School, 159, 327
Johnson, E. Mead, 140–41
Johnson, James D., 315, 322
Johnson, Kirk, 318
Johnston, Joseph, 180
Joliet Steel Company, 55n
Jones & Laughlin Steel Corporation, 229
Jones, W. Clyde, 135
Juhl, Loren E., 231–32, 234–35,
    272, 329
J. Walter Thompson, 302

Kaiser Corporation, 322
Kales, Francis H., 6
Kamin, Chester, 295
Kansas City Power & Light, 310
Kansas Pacific Railroad, 27
Kapnick, Harvey, 269
Kassuba, Walter Judd, 306–07
Keith, Edson G., 55
Kekic, Peter, 57
Kellogg Company, 330–31
Kellogg Foundation, W. K., 330–31
Kellogg Foundation Trust, W. K.,
    330–31
Kellogg, Will Keith, 330–31
Kendall College, 321, 327
Kennedy, John F., 194, 214, 216,
    261, 331
Kennedy, Joseph, 127
Kennedy, Robert, 261
Kenneth Sawyer Goodman Memorial
    Theater, 108

Kent College of Law, 327
Kent, Sidney A., 72, 96
Kernan, Edward J., 278, 284
Kidder Peabody & Company, 309
Kimball Union Academy, 5, 6, 11
Kimberly-Clark Corporation, 177, 237,
    255, 315, 320
King, John, 229
King, Martin Luther, 331
King, William H., 6
Kingdom Oil Company, 166
Kingsbury Commitment, 71
Kingsbury, Nathan C., 71
Kinsley's, 2
Kipperman, Lawrence I., 321
Kirk, James, 88
Kirk, John, 88
Kirk, Milton, 88
Kirk, Wallace, 88
Kissel, James W., 159–60, 231, 299,
    320, 323, 324
Kleenex tissues, 237–38
Klehm, Carl G., 308
Klingbiel, Justice Ray I., 325
Klitenic, Nathan, 226
Klutznick, Philip M., 263, 303, 304–05
Knickerbocker, Judge Joshua C., 74
Knox, Frank, 148
Knox, Philander C., 72
Kohlsaat, Judge C. C., 75
Kohn, Shalom L., 323
Koller, Levin, 59
Kotex sanitary napkins, 237–38
Krenn, Edwin D., 134ff
Krenn & Dato, 134ff
Kresge Centennial Hall, 327
Kresge Foundation, 327
Ku Klux Klan, 65
Kuhn, Bowie, 171
Kutak, Robert, 306

LaBuy, Judge Walter J., 206ff
Lake County Circuit Court, 77–78
Lake Forest Academy, 48
Lake Forest College, 47
Lake Front Act, 34–35, 48–50, 51
Landis, Kenesaw Mountain, 158

Larmon Building, 4
Lasker, Albert D., 242
Lauai-Kai, 233
Law Club of Chicago, 117, 149,
    202–03, 325
Lawson, Victor F., 143
Lawson YMCA, 143
Lawyers' Committee for Civil Rights
    Under Law, 331–33
Lawyer's Encyclopedia, 190
Leadership Council for Metropolitan Open
    Occupancy, 335
"Le Club," 205, 276, 284, 308
Lee, Robert E., 7
Legal Aid Bureau of Chicago, 331
Legal Assistance Foundation of
    Chicago, 333
Legal Club of Chicago, 325
Legal Times, 345
Leibman, Morris I., 240–41, 243–44,
    245, 246, 247, 248, 249, 250–52,
    254, 256, 257, 262–63, 265,
    267–68, 272, 279, 283, 325
    clients, 240–66
    early career, 240–41
    head of firm, 248–66
    with Carney and Crowell, 240–48
Leibman, Williams, Bennett and Baird,
    255–60, 262–63
    clients, 255–60
    internal changes, 255–56, 259–60
Leibman, Williams, Bennett, Baird and
    Minow, 263–71, 272, 304, 312, 332
    clients, 263, 264–65
    internal changes, 263–64, 265–66
    1972 merger, 267–71
Leighty, George, 216
Leiter, Levi Z., 2, 54, 62
Leopold, Nathan, 103
Lever Brothers, 241, 247–48
Lever House, 248
Levinson, Marc A., 281–82
Lewis, David J., 293
Lewis Institute, 149
Liberty Broadcasting System, 171
Life, 201, 299–300
Lincoln, Abraham, 7, 13, 42, 43, 65

Lincoln Library Forum, 169
Lincoln, Mary Todd, 13, 24–5, 200
Lincoln, Robert Todd, 7, 21, 25, 32, 33,
    37, 40, 43
Lindheimer, Benjamin F., 121
Lines, Spooner & Quarles, 237
Linklater & Paines, 205
Lippmann, Walter, 128
List, David P. 256
Little Boar's Head, 65–66
"Little Kentucky," 11
Loeb, Richard, 103
Loesch, Frank J., 158
Loewy, Raymond, 241
Logan County Circuit Court, 234–35
Lomax, Charles E., 276
Lopp, W. James II, 306
Lord & Thomas, 242
Los Angeles Airways, 282
Los Angeles Angels, 170
Los Angeles Dodgers, 170–71
Los Angeles Superior Court, 284
Louisville & Nashville Railroad, 318
Louisville Courier-Journal, 265
Loyola University Law School, 175,
    203, 327
Lucente, Martin M., 212, 214, 216, 272
    Burlington Northern, 221–25
    railroad cases, 221, 318
Luckman, Charles, 239, 241,
    247–48, 266
Lucky Strike cigarettes, 243–44
Lumberman's Exchange Building (see also
    Roanoke Building), 92
Lyons, Richard J., 185

McBurney, George, 285
McCagg, Ezra B., 6, 7, 49
McCain, Charles H., 127, 129–30
McCann-Erickson agency, 248, 248n
McCartney, James, 40, 49
McChesney, Fred S., 289
McClatchy newspaper chain, 322
McCormick, Cyrus Hall, 1, 21, 62, 132,
    141, 201
McCormick, Edith Rockefeller,
    132–37, 149

452

McCormick, Harold F., 132ff

McCormick, John, 133

McCormick Theological Seminary, 89

McCurdy, Robert, 155

McCutcheon, John T., 88

McDonald, Judge Charles A., 133

MacDonald, Mark E., 307

McDonald, Michael Cassius, 34

McDonough, John, 271, 329

McDougal, C. Bouton, 148, 166, 170, 196, 331

McDougal, Edward D., Jr., 95, 96, 105–07, 121, 145, 157, 166, 169, 196, 198–99, 228

Macfarlane, Robert S., 219ff

McGillicudy, Judge Helen F., 327–28

McGoorty, Judge John P., 103

McGowan, Carl, 216

McGowan, William G., 294

McKinley, William, 72

McLaren, Judge Richard, 333

McLaughlin, James A., 86

McLaughlin, Kathleen, 135

MacLean, Pearl Harris, 232

McLean, Robert D., 287

MacLeish, Bruce, 98

MacLeish, Jean, 98

McLelland, Lloyd, 161

McLendon, Gordon, 171

MacLeod, Donald S., 249, 255

McMahon, Thomas M., 299ff, 303

McPherson, Donald F., 73, 86–87, 92, 95, 96, 98, 100, 114, 120, 144, 145, 147–48, 151, 329
   and Central Public Service Corporation, 112–13
   "Cocoa Hardwater Castile" case, 105–07
   illness and death, 163–64

McPherson, Frances, 98, 163

McReynolds, James, 71

McSwain, William, 109

MacKay, Clarence, 70–71

Mackie, David I., 210

Magna Carta, 334n

Magruder, Justice Benjamin D., 52

Manufacturers' Telephone Company, 68–69

Marine Bank Building, 7, 10, 18–20, 201

Marine Fruit Carriers, 312

Maritime Administration, 312

Marovitz, James L., 257, 304

Marriott Hotel, 303

Marsh & McLennan, 64

Marshall Field Building, 44

Marshall, Chief Justice John, 328

Marshall, Judge Prentice, 319, 345–46

Marshall, Justice Thurgood, 287

Martin, Freddy, 138

Martin, R. Eden, 217, 286, 318, 339

Martindale-Hubbell directory, 100

Mason, Henry L. III, 271, 293–94, 301, 323, 335

Mason, Lewis F., 104

Mason, Robert E., 252, 323

Massachusetts Institute of Technology, 44–45, 155

Mattingly, Homer, 278

Maxwell, W. Sterling, 170–72

Mayer, Meyer, Austrian & Platt, 125, 260

Mayo Clinic, 105

MCI Communications Corporation, 294–95, 298

Mead Johnson Company, 140

Mechem, John, 74, 87

Melcher, Martin, 282

Mercantile Building, 30

Mercantile Trust Company, 24

Merchant Marine Act, 312

Merrill Lynch, Pierce, Fenner & Smith, Incorporated-Merrill Lynch White Weld Capital Markets Group, 309

Mesabi Range, 313

Messer, Wilbur, 142

Metromedia, Incorporated, 322

Metropolitan Life Insurance Company, 310

Metropolitan Structures, 303

Meyer, Arnold, 256

Michigan Central Railroad, 34

Michigan Consolidated Gas Company, 192

Michigan Department of Natural Resources, 301

Michigan State Telephone Company, 70
Mid-America Club, 195, 199
Mid-Day Club, 76, 157, 267, 271
Midland Hotel, 254
Midland Telephone Company, 36
Midwest Council for Airborne Television Instruction, 261
Mill, John Stuart, 41n
Miller, Edith M., 151, 199
Miller, Glenn, 138
Miller, J. Roscoe, 198, 327
Miller, Maurice J., 283, 315, 322, 339
Miller, Middleton, 110–11, 151, 152, 183, 203, 271, 272, 276
Miller, Theodore N., 217, 333, 334
Milwaukee County Superior Court, 55
Milwaukee Road, 120, 221ff (see also Chicago, Milwaukee, St. Paul and Pacific Railroad)
Milwaukee Symphony Orchestra, 163
Miner Agricultural Research Institute, Wm., 110
Miner, William H., 109–11
Minneapolis & St. Louis Railway, 256
Minneapolis, St. Paul & Sault Ste. Marie ("Soo") Railroad, 123, 219
Minow, Newton N., 260ff, 267–68, 272, 283, 322, 323, 327, 334, 339, 345
  American Medical Association, 290–91
  and municipal financing, 312–13
  and 1972 merger, 267–68
  Dearborn Park, 305
  early career, 260–62
Mississippi Queen, 312
Missouri Pacific Railroad, 317
Mitchell, James P., 213
Mitchell, Lee M., 266, 322
Mitsubishi Bank, 283
Moates, G. Paul, 318
Montgomery Ward & Company, 198, 228, 265, 321
Moody, Dwight L., 141
Moore, Nathan G., 87, 88–89, 96, 125, 151, 228
  and Art Institute, 108–09
  joins firm, 90
  retirement and death, 150

Moran, Judge James B., 289
Morera & Minoli, 205
Morgan, J. Pierpont, 60–61, 70, 72, 95, 220
Morgan Stanley & Company, 309
Morita, Akio, 267
Morrill, Judge Donald, 103
Morsch, Thomas H., 252, 260, 263, 335
Morse, Samuel Finley Breese, 15
MSL Industries, 256
Muhammad, Elijah, 276
Muhammad, Herbert, 276
Muhammad, Wallace, 276
Munsell, Harry, 130–31
Murphy, Martin, 304
Murphy, Robert H., 221ff
Murris, Timothy J., 289
Mutual Security Company, 23–24
My Appointed Round: 929 Days as Postmaster General, 194n

Naguib, Gamal N., 285, 338
Nation of Islam, 276
National Association for the Advancement of Colored People, 334
National Association of Broadcasters, 261
National Bell Telephone Company, 31
National Broadcasting Company, 290
National Council of Legal Clinics, 326
National Industrial Recovery Act, 126
National Labor Board, 126
National Labor Relations Act, 126
National Labor Relations Board, 321
National Legal Aid and Defender Association, 326, 331
National Potash Company, 319
National Press Club, 297
National Railroad Adjustment Board, 215, 216
National Railroad Industry Group, 215n
National Railway Labor Conference, 215
National Recovery Administration, 126
National Student Marketing Corporation, 264–65, 316–17,
Natural Gas Pipeline Company of America, 170
Nave, Frederick S., 64

Navy Pier, 303

Neely, Sally S., 282

Neighborhood Legal Assistance Center, 335

Neitzert, Howard, 98–99, 152, 162, 166, 192, 196, 200, 206–07, 209, 269, 272, 275, 320
  Eastland case, 103–04
  railroad industry cases, 212–17

Nelsen, Sylvia, 199

Nelson Brothers, 250

Nelson, J. Robert, 282

Nemarnich, Joseph, 57

Nemeroff, Michael A., 318

Nettles, J. Edward, 56–57

Newberry, Julia, 11, 17, 40

Newberry, Julia Rosa, 17, 40

Newberry Library, 40–41, 44–45

Newberry, Mary Louisa, 17, 40

Newberry, Walter L., 16ff, 40–42

New Energy Company of Indiana, 311

Newspaper Preservation Act, 322

New York Central Railroad, 12, 26, 120, 218, 223

New York Society of Security Analysts, 258

New York State Bar Bulletin, 190

New York Supreme Court, 201

New York Times, 258

New York University, 221

New York World, 27

Nibbler's Restaurant, 281

Nielsen, Arthur C., 154–57, 196, 308

Nielsen, Arthur C., Jr., 156

Nielsen Drug Index, 155

Nielsen Food Index, 155

Nielsen, Gertrude, 157

Nielsen Retail Index Services, 155

Nielsen Television Index Service, 155–56

Nimmer, Melville B., 284

Nixon, Richard M., 210, 307, 312, 324

Noguchi, Isamu, 109

Norfolk and Western Railway, 218, 317, 318

Norfolk Southern Corporation, 317–18

Norris-LaGuardia Act, 216

North Advertising, Incorporated, 255

North American Rockwell Corporation, 256

North Chicago Rolling Mill Company, 1, 55n

Northern Illinois Utilities Company, 127

Northern Pacific Railway, 219, 224

Northern Securities Company, 72–73, 220

Northern Trust Company, The, 72, 109, 165

Northwest Industries, 295, 300–01

Northwest Tollway, 308

Northwestern University, 46, 86, 95, 119, 124–26, 157, 198, 260, 263, 321, 327, 328

Northwestern University Law School, 64, 73, 78, 96, 98, 125, 127, 146, 158, 161, 169, 175, 176, 195, 198, 221, 252, 257, 260, 299, 307, 310, 319, 320

Northwestern University Medical School, 124–25

Oates, James F., Jr., 96, 100, 102, 105–07, 116, 121, 135, 144, 145, 169, 196, 199n, 200, 324, 327

Oberlin College, 25

O'Boyle, Thomas, 249, 256

O'Connell, Judge Harold P., 230

O'Connell, Judge John F., 136–37, 139

O'Connor, James, 323

Offield, Mrs. James, 139

Ogden Corporation, 248

Ogden Development Corporation, 248

Ogden, Mahlon, 41, 98

Ogden, William B., 2, 6, 17, 21

O'Hare Airport, 308

O'Hare, John, 310, 315–16

Ohio Public Utilities Commission, 210

Ohio Transportation Department, 300

Olds, Irving, 151

Olander, Natalie, 145, 151

Olds and Son, F. E., 167

O'Leary, Patrick, 18

Olian, Robert M., 301

Olk, Nellie H., 277

O'Malley, Walter, 170

One First National Plaza, 203, 266, 269n, 272

Oral Roberts University Law School, 289–90
Order of Railroad Telegraphers, 216–17
Order of Railway Conductors and Brakemen, 213ff
Order of the Coif, 299, 327, 342
Orrington Hotel, 219
Orton, William C., 29
Osgood, Roy C., 91
Ottertail Power, 310

Pacific Lighting Corporation, 311
Packwood, Senator Bob, 296
Page, Eleanor, 201
Palace of Fine Arts, 62
Palmer, Bertha Honore, 132
Palmer House, 21, 291
Palmer, John M., 34
Palmer, Potter, 2
Pan-American Building, 224, 257
Paper Mate Pen Company, 254
Paris Electrical Exposition, 33
Park Forest, 263
Parker, Judge Barrington D., 275
Parton, James, 3
Passavant Hospital, 236
Patti, Adelina, 39
Paul, Weiss, Rifkind, Wharton & Garrison, 261
PBB, 301
Peabody Coal Company, 314
Pearce, Charles Sumner, 237–38
Pearl Harbor, 159, 240
Peck, Ferdinand Wythe, 39
Peck, George R., 39
Pedersen, Captain Harry, 81ff
Peirce, Albert E., 112
Penn Central Railroad, 218
Pennsylvania Railroad, 12, 180, 210, 218, 223, 257
Peoples Gas Light and Coke Company, 127, 169–70, 310, 311
Pepsodent Company, 239, 241, 242, 247
Pereira, William, 248
"Performance Surveys," 154–55
Perlberg, Jules M., 195, 293, 332–33
Perry, Judge Joseph Sam, 214
Peter the Great, 137

Peters, Richard T., 282
Phelps, Editha, 48
Phi Beta Kappa, 327, 342
Philadelphia Centennial Exposition, 28
Phillips Academy, 74
Phillips Petroleum Company, 160
Physicians Hospital, 110
Piatt County Court, 233
Pincus, William, 326
"Pioneer," 13
Pittsburgh, Fort Wayne & Chicago Railway, 257
Plattsburgh Press-Republican, 110
Polales, Linda, 334–35
Polales, Sean, 334–35
Political Action Committees, 318
Pond, Judge William L., 88
Poole, William Frederick, 41
Postal Telegraph Company, 71
Potash Company of America, 319
PreFinish Metals, 300
Prentice, Abbie Cantrell, 162
Prentice, Alta, 133
Prentice, E. Parmalee, 55ff, 133, 147, 168
Prentice, J. Rockefeller, 146ff, 157, 162, 168
Presbyterian Brotherhood of America, 89
Presbyterian Hospital, 149, 191
Presidential Emergency Board, 216
Presidential Medal of Freedom, 325
Pressed Steel Car Company, 184–85
Preston, Henry A., 332
Price, Waterhouse and Company, 278
Princeton University, 87, 96, 98, 99, 159
Printing House Row, 305
Pritikin, David T., 287
Procter & Gamble Company, 106, 166, 299
Prudential Insurance Company of America, 194
Prystalski, Judge John, 142–43
Public Service Company of Indiana, 166
Public Service Company of Northern Illinois, 127
Public Utility Holding Company Act, 128–30

Puget Sound Navy Yard, 86
Pullman Car Works, 14
Pullman, George M., 11–14, 33, 62
Pullman, Incorporated, 182–83
Pullman's Palace Car Company, 14
Pure Oil Company, 226–27

Quale, Andrew C., Jr., 285
Queen Emma, 233
Queen Victoria, 29, 41n

Racquet Club, 253
Ragland, George, Jr., 123, 125, 164, 178,
    180–81, 207
*Railroad Rates, Service and
    Management,* 119
Railroad Revitalization and Regulatory
    Reform Act, 317
Railway Exchange Building, 112
Railway Labor Act, 213, 214, 216
Railway Mail Service, 30
Randell, Cortes W., 264–65
Randhurst Shopping Center, 229
Ranger National Life Insurance
    Company, 316
Ranney, George A., 151–52, 153, 166,
    196, 314
Rayburn, Sam, 128
REA Express, 266
Reagan, Ronald, 325
Reaper Block, 21, 22, 53, 200
Reconstruction Finance Corporation, 122
Regional Rail Reorganization Act, 218n
Reynolds International Pen
    Company, 253
Rhodes, Governor James, 300
Rice, Daniel F., 229–30
Rice, John B., 4
Rice University, 280
Richards, David A., 285
Richey, Judge Charles E., 298–99
Richmond, William P., 320
Rickey, Branch, 163
Ridgeview Farms Dairy,
    Incorporated, 208ff
Riegle, Senator Donald, 282
Riggio, Vincent, 243–44

Riss & Company, 209–12
Ritchie, John III, 328
Roanoke Building, 92ff, 112, 193, 203
Roberts, Thomas, 227
Roberts, Thomas, Jr., 227–28
Robinson, Albert Alonzo, 38
Robinson, Howard P., 160, 183, 320–21
Robinson, Martin F., 312
Robson, John E., 252, 266, 268,
    272, 275
Roche, Martin, 53, 92
Rockefeller Foundation, 124
Rockefeller, John D., 132ff
Rockefeller, John D., Jr., 135
Roosevelt, Franklin Delano, 97, 98,
    122–23, 126, 128–29, 148, 165, 227
Roosevelt, Theodore, 72, 220
Roosevelt University, 39, 235
Roseburg Lumber Company, 315
Rosenthal, Julius, 54
Rosenthal, Lessing, 54, 158
Rosenwald, Julius, 141
Roser, Mildred, 199
Rossetti, Dante Gabriel, 41n
Royal College of Agriculture, 234
Rush Medical College, 80
Russell, Tomas M., 302

St. Gaudens, Augustus, 42
St. Joseph-Chicago Steamship Company,
    83ff, 104
St. Louis-San Francisco Railway Company,
    225, 317
Salomon Brothers, 263, 309
Salt, Albert L., 111
Salvation Army, 138
Sammons, Dr. James H., 291
Sanders, Thomas, 29
Sanitary District of Chicago, 84, 230
Santa Catalina Island Company, 138
Saunders, Edward W., 159–60, 199, 203,
    228, 268, 272, 307, 334
    real estate group, 228ff, 302
Saunders, George L., Jr., 217, 224, 271,
    294, 295, 333, 334
Sawyier, Calvin, 335–36
SCA Services, Incorporated, 301

Scammon, Jonathan Young, 6, 7, 10, 21, 34–35
Scammon, McCagg and Fuller, 7
Scandrett, Henry A., 120
Schaefer, Walter V., 161
Schimberg, Archie, 264
Schimberg, A. Bruce, 264–65, 272, 280, 283, 307, 316–17, 318
Schlichting, Justus L., 246
Schofield, Philip, 160, 228
Schwartz, Lee, 313
Schweiger, Bernice, 199, 202
Schwemm, John, 195, 221, 299–300
Science Research Associates, 235
Scopes, John T., 96
Scott Paper Company, 255
Scott, Walter Dill, 124–26
Scully, Isabel, 234
Scully, Michael, 234
Scully, Peter, 234
Scully, Thomas A., 234–35
Scully, Violet, 234
Scully, William, 234
Seaboard Coast Line, 318
Searle, Dr. Claude Howard, 80, 196
Searle, Frances, 308–09, 330
Searle, G. D. & Company, 80, 154, 166, 266n, 295, 320
Searle, Gideon D., 80
Searle, Howard, 80
Searle, John, 80, 159, 196, 308–09, 330
Searle Scholars Program, 330
Sears, Anna, 77–78
Sears, Richard W., 77–78
Sears, Roebuck & Company, 77, 161
Second Baptist Church of Evanston, 334
Second Bull Run, 7
Second Presbyterian Church, 24, 42, 43
Securities and Exchange Commission, 127ff, 178n, 258, 264
Seder, Arthur R., Jr., 176–77, 185, 191–92, 260, 292, 311, 327, 335–36
Sessions, Judge Charles, 83–84
Sexton, William, 321
Seymour, Whitney North, 290
Shapiro, Irving, 208
Shaw, Andrew H., 311

Shedd, John G., 141
Sheridan, Philip H., 7, 18
Sherman Anti-Trust Act, 71, 207, 211, 220
Sherman-Marquette agency, 239
Sherman, Stuart, 239
Shimer College, 327
Shriver, R. Sargent, 261
Shutan, Robert, 280ff
Shutan & Trost, 280–84, 339
    clients, 281–82
    1980 merger, 282–84
Siddall, Roger B., 188–89
Sidley & Austin, 202–348
    clients, 224–25, 289–325
    corporate and securities practice, 309–16
    estate matters, 307–09
    environmental law practice, 299–302
    foreign operations, 276–77, 284–85, 338
    internal developments, 201–05, 267–86
    legal assistants, 277
    Los Angeles office, 284, 338
    move to One First National Plaza, 203
    New York office, 285–86, 338
    1980 merger, 280, 282–84
    1972 merger and aftermath, 267–72, 279ff
    present recruiting system, 339, 342
    product liability practice, 320n
    professional responsibilities, 326–40
    railroad matters in 1970s, 317–18
    real estate group, 302–06
    Washington office, 273, 275, 286, 338
Sidley, Austin, Burgess & Harper, 164–70
    heightened corporate practice, 165–68
    internal changes, 168–70
Sidley, Austin, Burgess & Smith, 170–201, 206–23, 226–36
    anti-nepotism policy, 178–79
    clients, 170–72, 180–87, 206–36
Washington office, 194–95
internal developments, 172–73, 188–205
100th anniversary dinner, 199–201

summer associates program, 177–78

Sidley, McPherson, Austin & Burgess, 151–64
  A.C. Nielsen Company, 154–57
  seventy-fifth anniversary, 157–59
  internal spirit, 152–54
  World War II conditions, 159–62

Sidley, William (father), 54, 55

Sidley, William P., 65, 75, 87, 90, 92, 94, 95, 96, 99, 100, 104, 110, 120, 144–45, 147–48, 158, 161, 163, 168, 173, 191, 192, 201, 292, 324, 327, 338n
  "Croatian Episode," 55–59
  early life and education, 54–55
  first employment by firm, 55
  Graybar Electric Company, 111–12
  illness and death, 191–92
  morale-building, 113–18
  Western Electric general counsel, 67ff, 83, 91, 111
  Young Men's Christian Association, 87, 141–43

Sigal, Michael S., 315

Sigma Phi fraternity, 154, 155, 157n

Simoniz Company, 250

Sinclair, Upton, 65

Sirica, Judge John J., 210–11

Sketches and Notices of the Chicago Bar, 33

Skidmore, Owings and Merrill, 257, 323

Skinner, Mark S., 17, 40

Skinner, Samuel K., 344

Sky Club, 224

Smith, Alfred E., 65

Smith Barney & Company, 166, 167

Smith Barney, Harris Upham & Company, 309

Smith, Chesterfield, 287

Smith, Douglas F., 123, 136, 162, 176, 180, 192, 202, 212, 217, 292

Smith, Darwin E., 177

Smith, Stanton K., 192

Solfisburg, Chief Justice Roy F., Jr., 325

Sony Corporation, 265, 267

Soo Line Railroad Company, 219

South Division High School, 54, 158

South Loop New Town, 304

South Park Board, 107

South Shore & Atlantic Railroad, 219

Southern Pacific Communications Company, 298

Southern Pacific Railroad, 182, 317

Southern Railway System, 317

Spacek, Leonard, 269

Sparks, Judge William M., 149

Spencer, Catherine, 236

Spencer, Charles, 103

Spencer, F. F., 63

Spencer, Lyle M., 235–36

Spencer Foundation, 236

Spokane, Portland & Seattle Railroad, 225

Sprague, Albert A., 11

Sprague, Warner & Company, 11

Sprecher, Robert A., 161

Spry-Leverton, Lisa, 277

Squibb Corporation, 315–16

Stager, Anson, 15, 25–26, 29, 32, 37

Staley's, 254

Standard Oil, 133, 134

Standard Trust and Savings Bank Building, 92

Stanford University Law School, 282

State Bar of Arizona, 288

State University of Iowa, 285

Stateville Penitentiary, 335–36

Stettinius, Edward, 168

Stevens Hotel, 107ff

Stevens, Justice John Paul, 176, 321

Stevenson, Adlai E., 96–98, 105, 110, 116, 117, 147–49, 151, 162, 168–69, 194, 196, 198–99, 260–61, 262

Stevenson, Adlai III, 199

Stevenson, Ellen, 98

Stevenson-For-Senator Committee, 169

Stevenson, Lewis, 96

Stewart, James B., Jr., 343

Story & Clark Piano Company, 167

Strong, William Barstow, 38

Studio Legale Bisconti, 205

Sullivan & Cromwell, 98, 151

Sullivan, Arthur A., 232

Sullivan, Louis Henri, 39

Sultanate of Oman, 284

Summers, Charles, 29

Summers, Flora, 29

459

Summers, Maud, 29
Sunny, Bernard E., 70
Swaney, Thomas E., 309
Swift, George, 60
Swinehart, Gerry, 210
Swiren, Max, 256
Switchmen's Union of North
    America, 213ff
Swygert, Judge Luther, 217

Tacoma Building, 53, 92, 201
Taft, William Howard, 75, 95
Talley, George A., 23, 24
Tame, 302
Tate, S. Shepherd, 288
Tatel, David, 332
Tauchen, John W., 137
Tavern Club, 201
Tax Reform Act, 307
Taylor, Miller, Busch & Boyden,
    240–41, 256
Teamsters Union, 321
Telephone Protective Association, 68
Telex, 205
Telpak, 292–93
Tenneco, Incorporated, 310
Terrace Row, 2
The American Lawyer, 291, 342–43
The Changing Years, 65
"The Crib," 117
The Jungle, 65
The Practical Lawyer, 188
Thigpen, William, 328
Third National Bank, 12
Thomas, D. Robert, 122, 180–81, 203,
    216, 272, 327, 331, 333
  Burlington Northern, 221ff
Thomas, Stephen P., 265
Thompson, John Leverett, 85, 158, 201,
    228, 324, 326, 338n, 346 (See also
    Williams & Thompson)
  and Mrs. Newberry, 18, 39–43, 63
  Civil War service, 7
  death and tributes, 50–51
  early life and career, 5–6
  firm's early years, 7–20 (See also Wil-
    liams & Thompson)

"Lake Front Steal," 34–35, 48–50
Thompson, Laura, 51
Thompson, Leverett, 51, 64, 178
Thompson, Susan, 51
Thompson, Thomas, 6
Thompson, William, 6
Thompson, William Hale "Big Bill,"
    89, 94
Till, Joan, 271
Tishman Midwest Management Corpora-
    tion, 303–04
Tishman Realty and Construction Com-
    pany, 257ff
Title XI financing, 312, 315
TNS Associates, 304
Toni Company, 244–45, 254
Towne, Charles E., 10, 20, 22, 23
Tracy, Converse and Barrett, 6
Traffic Executives Association-Eastern
    Railroads, 209
Transco Corporation, 310
Trans-Union Corporation, 265
Travelers Insurance Company, 282
Traylor, Melvin A., 125
Tremont House, 11, 21
Tribune Company, 172
Trienens, Howard J., 175–76, 203,
    216–17, 260, 263, 267–68, 272,
    283, 293, 294, 318, 327, 338–39,
    343, 345
  AT&T suit, 294ff
  firm chairman, 279–347
  general counsel, AT&T, 296–98
  MCI suit, 295, 296
  Northwest Industries, 300–01
  1972 merger, 267–71
  Northwestern University matters, 328
  railroad cases, 216–19
Trost, J. Ronald, 280ff, 339
Trude, Judge Daniel P., 136
Truman, Harry, 129
Trumbull, Lyman, 49
"Tucumcari Line," 317
Tuley, Judge Murray F., 68
Tuthill, Richard S., 51
Tweed, William, 27
"Twin Cities 400," 213

460

Ullman, Representative Al, 306
Union College of Law, 46, 55, 158
Union Iron and Steel Company, 55n
Union League Club, 34, 51, 61, 93, 114, 144, 149, 202
Union Oil Company of California, 226–27
Union Pacific Railroad, 27, 226, 317
Union Party, 4
Union Tank Car Company, 256
Union Telephone Company of Illinois, 32
United Arab Emirates, 284
United Charities, 331
United Light and Power Company, 127ff, 166
United Light and Railways Company, 131ff
United Nations, 169, 198
United Nations Preparatory Commission, 168
United States Chamber of Commerce, 235
United States Congress, 60, 122ff, 126, 127, 129, 165, 214, 242, 245, 282, 291, 296, 306
United States Court of Appeals, 104, 106, 121, 122, 161, 174–75, 184, 189, 201, 209, 211, 214, 215, 216, 217, 225, 293, 295, 298, 310, 332
United States District Court, 5, 31, 40, 49, 102, 104, 113, 122, 123, 129–30, 140, 182, 184, 206, 208, 209, 214, 215, 223, 275, 287, 289, 292, 295, 302, 332, 333
United States Equal Employment Opportunity Commission, 332
United States Financial, 282
United States Naval Academy, 41
United States Postmaster General, 194
United States Railroad Administration, 119
United States Railway Association, 218n
United States Rubber Company, 206ff
United States Steel Corporation, 60n, 99
United States Supreme Court, 15, 31, 49, 50, 60, 63, 71, 73, 102, 104, 106, 121, 125, 126, 130, 140, 143, 176, 182, 184, 185, 206n, 207, 209, 211, 214, 215, 217, 219, 220, 223,

225, 275, 288–89, 291, 293, 298, 318
Universal Screw Company, 256
University of California at Los Angeles, 281, 282, 284, 327
University of California School of Jurisprudence (Boalt Hall), 280
Universities of Chicago, The, 124–26
University of Chicago, 45n, 46n, 72, 74, 99, 124–26, 142
University of Chicago Law School, 4, 73, 95, 146, 148, 159, 160, 175, 192, 217, 240, 264, 266, 301, 315, 318, 320, 321, 333, 335
University of Illinois, 233, 248
University of Illinois College of Law, 190, 221, 293, 321
University of Iowa Law School, 175, 177, 315
University of Miami, 289
University of Michigan, 98
University of Michigan Law School, 64, 99, 123, 170, 175, 180, 195, 203, 252, 315–16, 334
University of Michigan School of Business Administration, 195
University of Minnesota Law School, 175
University of Pennsylvania, 98
University of Pennsylvania Law School, 98, 146, 176, 313
University of Texas Law School, 280
University of Vermont, 5
University of Virginia Law School, 276
University of Wisconsin, 78, 119, 120, 154, 159, 233
University of Wisconsin Law School, 119, 175, 192, 212, 233, 283, 302, 307
Urban Intern Program, 332
Urban Investment and Development Company, 303
Urban Systems Laboratory of Massachusetts Institute of Technology, 333
U.S.S. *Eurana*, 91
U.S.S. *Pelias*, 159
U.S.S. *Wilmette*, 104–05

Vail, J. Dean, Jr., 160, 166, 276

Vail, Theodore N., 30, 32, 70–72
Vanderbilt, Cornelius, 26
Vanderbilt, William H., 27, 31
Vanderblue, Homer B., 119
Van Osdel, John, 21
Variety, 247
Velsicol Chemical Corporation,
    300–01, 320
Victor Palmieri Company, 315
Vieregg, R. Todd, 310–11
Villa Turicum, 132ff
Vinson & Elkins, 227
Vinson, Chief Justice Fred M., 176, 195,
    260, 267
Vogel, Charles S., 284
Voss, Jack D., 249, 256

Wabash Railway Company, 50–51
Wacker, Charles H., 89
Waddy, Judge Joseph C., 294, 296
Wakefield, Sir Charles, 94
Walker, Daniel, 260
Walker, Samuel, 11
Waller High School, 240
Wallace, Henry A., 227
Walsh, Lawrence E., 287–88
War Claimants Association, 111
War Risk Insurance Division, 87
Ward, A. Montgomery, 107
Ward, Eber R., 1
Wardman Park Hotel, 224
Ware, Lillian K., 333–34
Warfield, William S. III, 99–100
Warren, Chief Justice Earl, 195, 224
Washington, George, 65
Watergate, 210
Waterstreet, W. N., 208n
Watson, Thomas A., 28–29, 32
Waugh, Judge William F., 137
WBBM-TV, 263
Webster, Daniel, 6, 65
Weese, Harry, 323
West, Mahlon Ogden, 98, 116
Westec Corporation, 264
Western Edison Light Company, 37
Western Electric Company, 32, 36, 63,
    67, 70, 83, 84, 91, 103, 104, 110,
    111, 230, 292, 297–98
Western Electric Manufacturing Company,
    26, 29, 32
Western Equities, 264
Western Indiana Railroad Company, 61
Western Maryland Railroad, 318
Western Pacific Railroad, 317
Western Telephone Company, 36
Western Union Telegraph Company, 11,
    15–16, 21, 25, 27–28, 29, 30ff, 37,
    70, 71
Western United Gas & Electric
    Company, 127
WFLD, 322
WFYR, 321
Wheelabrator-Frye Company, 183n
Wheeler, Arthur D., 46, 48, 65, 74, 75,
    85, 141, 292, 326–27
    as Chicago Telephone Company chair-
        man, 70ff, 292
    as Chicago Telephone Company pres-
        ident, 67ff, 292
Wheeler, Burton K., 128–29
White & Case, 151
White, H. Blair, 177, 209, 227–28, 272,
    280, 282ff, 319, 330, 339, 345
    and American Bar Association, 287–90
    International Minerals and Chemical
        case, 319
    managing partner, 280–347
    and 1980 merger, 282–84
White, Quincy, 260, 271
White, Weld & Company, 166
Whitehead, James S., 321
Whitman, Russell, 47
Whitted, Lela, 278
Wickersham, George H., 71
Wieboldt Stores, 228, 229
Wigmore Award, 260
Wigmore, John Henry, 158
Wiley, Marshall W., 285
Wilkerson, Judge James H., 149
Wilkie, Franc Bangs, 33
Willamette University, 74
William & Mary College, 285
William H. Miner Foundation, 110
William J. Cook fund, 330

William Wrigley Company, 139
Williams & Thompson, 1–53
  and George Pullman 11–14
  Chicago Telephone Company, 32–33, 37ff, 47, 63
  clients in the 1880s, 36–52
  early years, 7–20
  first clients, 10–11
  internal matters in 1880s, 47–48
  John Dean Caton influence, 14–16
  Newberry case, 16–18, 39–43
  "telegraph wars," 26–28
  telephone industry, 28–32, 36–37
  Western Electric, 29, 32ff
  Western Union, 15–16, 31–32, 37
Williams, Caroline, 15
Williams, Jr., Charles A., 32
Williams College, 6, 23, 54, 89
Williams, D. Benjamin, 241, 248, 250, 252, 257, 269n
Williams, Dr. Edward H., 66
Williams, Erastus S., 5, 40
Williams, Holt & Wheeler, 53–76
  clients in the 1890s, 53–66
  Field Columbian Museum, 61–63
  Illinois Steel Company, 60–61, 63
  internal changes, 73ff
  personnel, 64–65
  telephone industry, 63
Williams, Jesse, 5
Williams, John C., 308, 309
Williams, Laura, 23
Williams, Norman (father), 5, 66
Williams, Norman, 33, 72, 85, 96, 141, 158, 200, 228, 292, 324, 338n, 346
  (See also Williams & Thompson)
  and J. Pierpont Morgan, 60–61
  and Mrs. Lincoln, 24–25
  Chicago Club, 33
  Chicago Telephone Company president, 32ff, 292
  Crerar Library, 42–45
  early life and career, 5–6
  final years and death, 65–66, 89
  firm's early years, 7–20 (See also Williams & Thompson)
Willkie, Wendell, 128–29

Wilmette Youth Resources, 335
Wilmington Trust Company, 206ff
Wilson, Eleanor, 199
Wilson, Eugene S., 100–01
Wilson, Chief Justice Francis S., 152
Wilson, Moore & McIlvaine, 88
Wilson, Woodrow, 65, 71
Windes, Judge Thomas, 103
Winnetka Congregational Church, 337
Winston & Strawn, 335
Winston, Strawn, Shaw & Black, 125
Wirth, Representative Timothy E., 296
Wirtz, Willard, 261
Wisconsin Central Railroad, 123
Wisconsin Telephone Company, 70
Wise, Edmund, 285
Witt, Edward J., 48
Wittmer, John H., Jr., 228
Wolfe, James E., 214
Wolff, Elroy H., 266
Wolfson, Erwin S., 257
Women's Bar Association, 325
Woodruff, Louis, 155
Woodruff, Theodore T., 12
Woodward, Judge Alfred, 316
Woolfolk, William G., 130ff
World War I, 74, 86, 101, 167, 181, 183
World War II, 39, 104–05, 143n, 148, 157, 159–67, 189, 194, 228, 235, 242, 253, 263, 266
World's Columbian Exposition of 1893, 61, 107, 323
Wright, Judge Donald R., 282
Wright, Frank Lloyd, 137
Wrigley, Ada, 139, 170
Wrigley Building, 138
Wrigley Company, 308
Wrigley, Helen, 170
Wrigley, Joan, 170
Wrigley, Philip K., 73–74, 139, 163, 170, 308
Wrigley, William, Jr., 73, 74, 137–40, 141, 170
Wrigley, William, Jr. (grandson), 170
Wurlitzer Company, 167

Yale University, 72, 74, 244, 269

Yale University Law School, 146, 147, 151, 217, 285, 287, 304, 308
YMCA Hotel, 141–43, 331n
Yorktown shopping center, 229
Young, David, 226n
Young Men's Christian Association, 23, 24, 42, 46, 87, 89, 96, 141–43, 327
Young Men's Library Association, 17

Young Presidents' Organization, 236
Young, Robert R., 182

Zeglis, John D., 298
Zeta Psi fraternity, 233
Zoline, Joseph T., 256
Zurich Insurance Company, 321

About the author

A native Chicagoan, Herman Kogan was born in 1914 and educated in the city's public schools. He was graduated Phi Beta Kappa from the University of Chicago in 1936. His journalistic career began as a high-school reporter for the *Chicago Daily News* and *Chicago Evening Post*. Except for service in the Marine Corps in the Second World War, as director of company relations for Encyclopaedia Britannica, Incorporated, and as assistant general manager for news and newspapers for WFLD-TV, he has been a newspaperman ever since in such varied capacities as reporter, feature writer, columnist, book and drama critic, editorial writer and arts-and-amusements supplement editor, and editorial executive. He has worked for the City News Bureau of Chicago, the *Chicago Tribune*, the *Chicago Sun* and *Sun-Times* and the *Chicago Daily News* and is currently corporate historian of Field Enterprises, Incorporated. The magazines for which he has written range from *Fortune* and the *Illinois Bar Journal* to *The New Republic* and *Esquire*. For a decade he has been the host of "Writing and Writers" on Chicago's premier FM station, WFMT, and has served as a television commentator, an instructor at the Medill School of Journalism and on Pulitzer Prize juries and as a panelist for the National Endowment for the Humanities. His fifteen books include histories of the Chicago Bar Association and the *Encyclopaedia Britannica*. A number of them and his other writings have won awards, and "Newscope," the news program he devised for WFLD with the use of *Sun-Times* and *Daily News* reporters in on-air appearances, won two Emmys and set an innovative pattern for other stations.

Other books by Herman Kogan

THE GREAT *EB*

THE LONG WHITE LINE

LENDING IS OUR BUSINESS

A CONTINUING MARVEL

THE FIRST CENTURY

LORDS OF THE LEVEE
    with Lloyd Wendt

BET A MILLION!
    with Lloyd Wendt

GIVE THE LADY WHAT SHE WANTS
    with Lloyd Wendt

BIG BILL OF CHICAGO
    with Lloyd Wendt

CHICAGO: A PICTORIAL HISTORY
    with Lloyd Wendt

THE GREAT FIRE: CHICAGO 1871
    with Robert Cromie

YESTERDAY'S CHICAGO
    with Rick Kogan

SEMPER FIDELIS (CONTRIBUTOR)

UNCOMMON VALOR (CONTRIBUTOR)

Buildings in which present offices of Sidley & Austin are located.

Los Angeles

London

Washington

Cairo

New York

Singapore

Dubai

Oman